AMERICAN INTERGOVERNMENTAL RELATIONS

FOUNDATIONS, PERSPECTIVES, AND ISSUES

Fourth Edition

Laurence J. O'Toole Jr., Editor
University of Georgia

CQ PRESS

A Division of Congressional Quarterly Inc.
Washington, D.C.

CQ Press
1255 22nd Street, NW, Suite 400
Washington, DC 20037

Phone: 202-729-1900; toll-free, 1-866-427-7737 (1-866-4CQ-PRESS)

Web: www.cqpress.com

Cover design: Vincent Hughes

∞ The paper used in this publication exceeds the requirements of the American National Standard for Information Sciences—Permanence of Paper for Printed Library Materials, ANSI Z39.48-1992.

Printed and bound in the United States of America

10 09 08 07 06   1 2 3 4 5

Library of Congress Cataloging-in-Publication Data

American intergovernmental relations : foundations, perspectives, and
   issues / Laurence J. O'Toole, Jr., editor.—4th ed.
       p.   cm.
   Includes bibliographical references and index.
   ISBN 0-87289-307-3 (alk. paper)
     1. Federal government—United States.   2. Intergovernmental fiscal
relations—United States.   I. O'Toole, Laurence J., 1948– II. Title.

   JK311.A48 2007
   320.473'049—dc22   2006017093

For Mary

Contents

Part III: Fiscal Aspects of Intergovernmental Relations   177

Part IV: Administrative Aspects of
Intergovernmental Relations   259

Preface

As at other junctures in the evolution of the American system of federalism, the past several years have brought changes, challenges, and opportunities in both the study and the practice of intergovernmental relations in the United States. Today, the American intergovernmental system is a focal point of controversy. Yet today's debates have not been unanticipated. In fact, part of the idea behind the experiment with a federal system that the Founders introduced more than two centuries ago was to establish an adaptable structure within which issue-specific disputes could occur and competing values be engaged. Since then the framework has indeed been dramatically altered under forces of political, economic, and social development. These pressures have resulted in tremendously increased interdependence and complexity for all participants, whose multiple interconnections have made bargaining a fact of life. The foundations of such a system, its operations and consequences, and the issues occupying the attention of today's intergovernmental analysts and practitioners are the subjects of attention here.

The basic structure of the earlier editions has been retained in this fourth edition, as have those readings that remain pertinent. These have been supplemented with a number of new articles that suggest promising ways to understand the dynamism of the intergovernmental network and to document some of the major developments in recent times. Among the themes and topics introduced in the fourth edition are the impacts of intergovernmental financing and regulation on the nation's large cities; the implications of the salient issue of homeland security for states, localities, and the United States; the key place of the states themselves at the center of the system and their interactions with each other; implications of recent Supreme Court decisions on the distribution of power across levels; cross-national comparison to identify some of the distinctive features of federalism, U.S.-style; an intergovernmental analysis of recent disasters like Hurricane Katrina in 2005; and the increasingly important penetration of the American intergovernmental setting by international agreements and developments.

The readings have been selected to blend classic expositions with contemporary findings and controversies. To provide a broad survey of the system's foundations, perspectives, and issues—and in so doing to document the themes of complexity and interdependence—this book contains selections from many of the most important, enduring, and often controversial documents on American intergovernmental relations, as well as provocative analyses of today's most interesting and pressing intergovernmental issues. Criteria for selection of the individual articles was their significance to the field, their fit with the book's scope and themes, their current relevance, and their contrasting perspectives.

Part I explores the roots of today's American intergovernmental system. Readings convey the ideas behind the original federal bargain, the classic interpretations of how the system has developed (with an emphasis on cooperation and conflict between governments), and some important theoretical perspectives on the modern system. Parts II through IV explore the operations of contemporary American intergovernmental relations along political, financial, and administrative lines. Each part highlights the themes of interdependence and complexity, and the predictable tensions within and across governmental units. Readings include both analyses of the system as a whole (for example, its fiscal aspects) and explorations of the perspectives and activities of specific participants. Part V contains readings on a selection of emerging issues and challenges.

Each part opens with an interpretive essay that provides background and unites the selections. Discussion and review questions conclude each part and are designed to help readers test their understanding of the basic information contained in the articles, to stimulate independent thought, and to expand their knowledge by encouraging integration of the various readings. The overall goal is to give readers the opportunity to grapple with the issues and to think coherently and independently about the subject of American intergovernmental relations.

The book is designed for use as either a main or a supplementary text in upper-division undergraduate and graduate courses on federalism and intergovernmental relations. Students of state and local government and politics also will find the collection useful.

I thank the authors and publishers of the works excerpted or reprinted here for granting permission to include the fruits of their labors. This fourth edition has benefited from suggestions and assistance from Charisse Kiino, Dwain Smith, Hans Manzke, and Anne Stewart at CQ Press. Charisse also facilitated the gathering of systematic feedback from a number of instructors nationwide who had used an earlier edition as a text. I am grateful to these colleagues for their suggestions and insights. My research assistant, Liz Jarry, provided valuable help substantively and also expedited production. Mary, Conor, and Katie O'Toole continue to contribute just the right balance of encouragement, humor, and support—this family is simply an awesome combo.

AMERICAN INTERGOVERNMENTAL RELATIONS: AN OVERVIEW

Who should determine the provisions of public policy regarding health care, including care for those unable to afford it? What about the rapidly escalating costs of health care for the nation's aging population? Which authorities are most appropriate as the front line of defense in protecting the nation's environment? What about threats from international terrorists—who should have which types of responsibility for this pressing issue? Who decides where the social "safety net" is placed, and on whom, and with what flexibility? Should state governments be able to force localities to initiate new activities without providing the cash to cover the related expenses? How about Washington doing the same to the states themselves? Should the national government be able to require that local school districts produce certain results on a certain schedule, in the interests of "no child left behind," or else forfeit federal aid? Or are educational standards best left to the governments closest to the action?

In what ways, if at all, should states and the national government be involved in encouraging or restricting the economic development efforts of U.S. cities? In creating or limiting the instruments available to their leaders to advance these urban areas—be these the use of development authorities or the issuance of municipal debt? Who handles these, and by what instruments of aid? When counties and states allow or encourage the construction of megamalls and superhighways that contribute to sprawl, congestion, and the degradation of air quality and natural resources, should national authorities have any influence? How much? Which levels of government should deal directly with the global competitiveness of the nation's economy and the nation's role in contributing to such global environmental challenges as climate change? What is the best way for the federal government to be strongly involved in the enforcement of such important policies as ensuring civil rights and encouraging equal employment opportunity for all citizens? And how can national borders best be protected?

How should the people handle problems that confront one part of the United States but surpass that region's ability to cope? When localities or regions suffer immense natural disasters, for instance—as with hurricanes in New Orleans and elsewhere on the Gulf Coast—who should respond immediately? How, and how much, should the many jurisdictions affected coordinate? And what of the costs of recovery over the long haul? When an oil spill devastates parts of the precious Alaskan wilderness, who should take action, and how? When a reform of national tax law creates unintendedly negative effects on the finances of the states, what should be done? When acid rain from industrial air pollution contributes to the deterioration of natural resources a thousand miles away, whose problem and responsibility should it be? Each of these topics, and many more, are aspects of intergovernmental relations.

Intergovernmental relations is the subject of how our many and varied governments in the United States deal with each other, and what their relative roles, responsibilities, and levels of influence are and should be. This subject is no flash-in-the-pan concern; it has generated longstanding interest, indeed constant and pervasive controversy, throughout U.S. political and administrative history.

In fact, the establishment of the United States was itself a sort of experiment in intergovernmental relations, since an effort to create a federal system like it had never before been attempted. Nearly every major matter of domestic policy debated and decided throughout the nation's existence has been imbued with important intergovernmental aspects. Intergovernmental issues have contributed to such significant events in American history as the Civil War, the establishment of the social-welfare state during the New Deal era, the attack on poverty in the 1960s, the enactment of "welfare reform" in the 1990s, and the massive effort to enhance homeland security in the twenty-first century.

But the subject is more than a collection of isolated issues. Indeed, it would be difficult to make systematic sense of policy disputes like those mentioned without first understanding the intergovernmental system per se—its historical development as well as its current structure. To prepare for an exploration of current issues and disputes and to provide a context for the readings that follow, this chapter offers an overview of the intergovernmental system in the

United States, with an emphasis on the federal government's role in the system's development.

Federalism, as the term is understood today, means a system of authority constitutionally apportioned between central and regional governments.[1] In the American system, the central, or national, government is often called the federal government; the regional governments are the states. The federal-state relationship is interdependent: neither can abolish the other and each must deal with the other. *Intergovernmental relations* is the more comprehensive term, including the full range of federal-state-local relations.

As the new century dawns, there are approximately 87,000 governments in the United States—one national, fifty state, and the rest at the local level. These consist of several distinct types. *Counties,* numbering some three thousand units, are general-purpose governments originally created throughout most of the country to administer state services at the local level. Today, counties are genuine local governments that provide an array of services to their citizens. Many—especially the larger, more urban ones—are increasingly involved in complex intergovernmental arrangements with other local jurisdictions, states, and the national government.

Municipalities, numbering about nineteen thousand, are local governments established to serve people within an area of concentrated population. The nation's largest cities and small villages alike are municipalities, although the types of powers they have and the services they offer vary considerably. Municipalities are created to serve explicitly the interests of the local community. Through much of the nation's history, municipalities have had extensive and often highly conflicting relationships with their "parent" states—relationships sometimes made all the more challenging from the point of view of the municipalities since they are not granted independent status by the states, as the states are under the U.S. Constitution. Since the New Deal era in the 1930s and the rapid expansion of the intergovernmental system in the 1960s, municipalities—especially large cities—have dealt with Washington, as well, on many matters. And as federal cutbacks to these local governments have taken hold in certain important policy sectors off and on since the 1980s, municipalities have often developed defensive and somewhat conflictual relations with both state and national authorities as they have sought to develop additional revenue sources and less one-sided dependence on the other levels.

Additional local governments include:

- *townships* (approximately 17,000), which are usually subdivisions of rural counties and are relatively unimportant except in some parts of New England and the mid-Atlantic states;
- *school districts* (approximately 13,500), which are separate governments established in many parts of the country to direct public school systems; and
- *special districts* (numbering more than 35,000 in a recent count), which are limited-purpose governments set up to handle one or perhaps a few public functions over a specially designated area.[2]

Special districts are currently responsible for managing public housing; building and maintaining bridges, tunnels, and roads; supplying water and sewage services to residents; assessing and regulating air quality; and caring for mass transit needs. The creation of many of these districts over the years has been directly or indirectly encouraged by other governments—such as the states and Washington—which sought "coordinated" local action on one or another policy problem.

If given a chance to view their handiwork today, it is likely that the founders of this nation would be greatly surprised by the operations of its politics and government, especially in the intergovernmental workings. Yet intergovernmental developments over the past couple of centuries have been affected greatly by some fundamental choices consciously made by those early Americans.

The Founding and the Framework

The framers of the U.S. Constitution sought a way to combine states into a structure that would minimize "instability, injustice, and confusion," in the words of James Madison.[3] The Founders were familiar with the arguments of earlier political thinkers who claimed that government protection of individual rights would have to be small-scale and cover a geographically limited jurisdiction. Yet their own experience suggested problems with such an arrangement. Under the Articles of Confederation, enacted after the Revolution, the thirteen American states had agreed on a formal arrangement that is now called a *confederation*.[4] The states were loosely joined for certain purposes, but their association fell far short of a real nation. The states retained almost all power, and the "united states" under the Articles found it virtually impossible to act with dispatch on matters of importance.

To solve this problem, the "federalists" of the period proposed the organization of a nation able to act in a unified and central fashion for certain purposes. They argued that large republics, not small ones, were more likely to be able to prevent internal tyranny. They also suggested, however, that the states themselves remain independent governments with correspondingly independent jurisdictions. As a matter of fact, state autonomy was a political necessity at the time if widespread support of a new constitutional order were to be elicited. In the absence of any such historical precedent, this new experiment in intergovernmental relations would have to develop out of the American experience.

The Founders' construction of the new system virtually ensured continuing controversy about the respective roles of the national and state governments by creating sufficient ambiguity to leave many of the most important questions unresolved. As a result, later years were to see major changes in American intergovernmental relations under the influence of various political, economic, and social forces. The basic framework, however, remained constant.[5]

What does that framework actually stipulate? The Constitution seems to divide responsibilities between the two levels of government according to subject. Certain functions (for example, interstate commerce and national defense) are assigned to the national authorities, whereas many others (such as selection of presidential electors) are left to the states. Furthermore, the Tenth Amendment in the Bill of Rights asserts that "the powers not delegated to the United States by the Constitution, nor prohibited by it to the States, are reserved to the States respectively, or to the people." The states appear to have been given an advantage.

Yet the explanation cannot end here, for the same Constitution provides conflicting cues, authorizing the national Congress to "provide for the ... general Welfare" and to "make all Laws which shall be necessary and proper" for executing this and the other powers given to the legislature. What constitutes the "general welfare" and which laws are necessary and proper are inherently political questions. Thus, it should be no surprise that the answers adopted by different people and at different times have not been consistent. The Founders established a framework in which governments would have separate but not completely independent spheres. The different levels would find it both useful and necessary to engage in conflict and cooperation; neither would be willing or able to ignore the other.

The Idea of Dual Federalism

Even in the earliest decades of the nation's existence, this tension was evident between the idea of *dual federalism* (that is, each of the two levels of government operating independently within its separate jurisdiction without relying on the other for assistance or authorization) on the one hand and ambiguous overlap of responsibilities on the other.

The notion of dual federalism influenced the decisions of the Supreme Court at least until the early decades of the twentieth century. Furthermore, during the 1800s various presidents vetoed legislation that would have created a federal presence in policy fields, such as public works construction, on the grounds that the Constitution simply did not permit such national involvement in arenas reserved for the states.[6] In a number of fields, like education and social policy, dual federalism was the predominant view of federal-state intergovernmental relations. It is worth noting how strongly held this point of view remains in some quarters even today.

Conflict and Cooperation in Earlier Times

Despite any wishes to the contrary, neither sphere was completely independent, even in the early years. Throughout the nineteenth century, the national government and the states often disagreed about the limits of their own authority. The Civil War is perhaps the prime example, but conflict occurred on other matters as well, such as policy on labor, social welfare, and economic regulation. To resolve jurisdictional disputes, therefore, the federal and state governments found it necessary to recognize their interdependence.

Conflict was not the only stimulus for interaction. As various policy problems captured the attention of the nation's officials and citizenry, federal and state governments were sometimes able to piece together intergovernmental mechanisms to address immediate concerns. For instance, if some early national and state leaders viewed direct federal aid for such internal improvements as road and canal construction as a violation of constitutional restrictions on intergovernmental arrangements, the governments *were* able to agree to cooperate in the formation of *joint stock companies,* part public and part private entities created to surmount the restrictions on direct participation by the national government. (Governments and private businesses could buy stock in a company and appoint members to its board of directors, thus indirectly supporting and influencing its operations.)[7]

Another mechanism for cooperation during the nineteenth and twentieth centuries, before the dramatically increased intergovernmental interdependence of recent years, was the *land grant*. Through this device, the federal government offered some of its land (it owned plenty) to the states for specified purposes. The recipient government would be obliged to abide by certain federal requirements, but direct involvement by the national government was minimal. Land grants were intended to help achieve goals in the fields of education (thus the origins of today's nationwide set of land-grant colleges and universities), economic development, and (on a very limited scale) social welfare.

Other forms of intergovernmental cooperation, such as technical assistance from federal to state governments and informal exchanges and loans of personnel during peak or crisis periods, were relatively common occurrences even during the nation's first century. Nevertheless, it was not until the twentieth century that the dual federalism perspective declined appreciably in significance and American intergovernmental relations developed into a system with sustained high levels of *interdependence* and consequent *complexity*. Several political, economic, and social events and trends fueled these developments.

Developments in the Early Twentieth Century

From early in the last century until recent years, federal involvement, especially financial involvement, in intergovernmental relations escalated. The Progressive Era at the turn of the 1900s brought an expanded role for government in general, as reformers argued that society and the economy could not tolerate laissez-faire governance. The concentration of power in large corporations, the reluctance of some state governments to enact regulatory and other social welfare legislation (although other states were leaders in enacting farsighted and sometimes tough policy on such subjects), and the dawning recognition that the nation's natural resources were limited and would have to be conserved encouraged an expanded domestic policy role for Washington. This shift was often also encouraged by the newly developing and professionalizing state bureaucracies, which saw in federal involvement opportunities for upgrading and for expanded funding, and by some

interest groups that had been pushing at the state level for public attention to one problem or another. (Then, as now, organized interests—
whether concerned with expanded highway construction or social services, whether favoring workers' interests or the goals of big business—
have recognized that it is usually easier and more effective to deal with
one central government on such matters than with scores of divergent
ones throughout the states.)

The growing national will to attempt action in new arenas was
followed by the central government's acquisition of the practical
wherewithal for action. The resources needed were money and clear
authority; by the 1920s both had been generated.

Federal Financial Aid

In 1913 the U.S. Constitution was amended to permit the enactment of a federal income tax. The passage of the Sixteenth Amendment
enabled the national government to raise revenue more easily than the
subnational governments. The income tax, which was "elastic" (that is,
its receipts increased faster than the economy during periods of growth),
was a more politically palatable revenue source than other sources typically emphasized by the states and local governments. With the implementation of the income tax the federal government created a source of
money that could be tapped repeatedly to fill needs that had not yet
received the states' wholehearted attention. Previously, the national government had provided some limited financial support to the states, but
these intergovernmental fiscal ties were few and far between.

This situation has changed in recent decades. First, the income tax
increased its bite in individuals' paychecks during the period of rapid
inflation in the 1970s, resulting in a decline in its popularity and the
enactment of an indexing provision to control the effects of inflation.
Second, federal legislative changes during the 1980s reduced the pro-
gressiveness of the tax, that is, the extent to which it can draw revenue
from the affluent. Additional cuts in the 1990s created more tax breaks
for the middle class and above. Other federal taxes, especially Social
Security, began to assume a larger portion of the collected revenue. Still
further policy changes beginning in 2001 trimmed the tax burdens
especially sharply for those earning the most income. Third, most states
and even some local governments enacted income taxes of their own,
with formulas tied in complicated ways to various provisions of the federal tax code. The development of intergovernmental finances in recent

decades therefore documents one way in which the system has been linked via complexity.

The obvious mechanism of intergovernmental cooperation in many such cases was the *grant-in-aid.* By 1920 there were eleven grants-in-aid operating in the United States. Land grants and other varieties of intergovernmental assistance were never again to outstrip cash grants in importance. Because of the significance of grants-in-aid since the early twentieth century, it would be useful to explain at this point some of the basic implications of this kind of program.

A grant-in-aid is a transfer of funds from one government to another for a specified purpose. Typically, the recipient government is asked by the donor to abide by certain terms as conditions of the assistance.[8] These usually include a requirement that the recipient unit match the donor's financial contribution with one of its own, as well as a series of "strings," or stipulations, as to how the funds will be utilized, how the program will be managed, and how the recipient government will report to the donor.

Starting on a small scale in the twentieth century, and then expanding rapidly during certain periods—especially the New Deal and Great Society eras—grants-in-aid from the federal government to the states, and eventually to local governments, became extremely important features of the intergovernmental system in the United States. States too have provided financial support to their local governments. (In 2002–2003, total state aid to other governments amounted to $223 billion.[9]) But federal aid, because of its size, relative newness, and capacity to produce large-scale alterations in the intergovernmental system, may be considered an especially significant feature of fiscal federalism in the United States (see Table I-1).

Validation of Grants-in-Aid

As the national government began to exercise influence through the use of grants-in-aid in the early 1900s, some observers wondered if the grant mechanism was an unconstitutional federal intrusion into the affairs of the states. Armed with the doctrine of dual federalism, critics of federal grants argued that Washington's offers were actually coercive inducements that violated the notion of separate spheres for these two levels of government.

This debate was laid to rest in 1923 by a pair of landmark decisions by the Supreme Court. These decisions paved the way for major

Table I-1   Federal Aid to State and Local Governments, Selected
             Years

Year	Amount ($billions)[a]	Amount in Constant 2000 Dollars (Billions)	Number of Grants
1902	0.028		5
1912	—		7
1913	0.039		—
1920	—		11
1922	0.242		—
1932	0.593		12
1934	2.4		—
1937	—		26
1940	0.87	11.4	—
1946	0.82	8.2	28
1952	2.4	16.4	38
1960	7.0	39.0	132
1964	10.2	53.9	—
1967	15.2	78.1	379
1975	49.8	157.7	442
1978	77.9	199.3	—
1981	94.7	179.4	539
1982	88.1	154.7	441
1984	97.6	155.9	405
1987	108.4	155.4	435
1990	135.3	172.1	—
1992	178.1	211.4	—
1995	225.0	247.9	—
1998	246.1	257.3	—
2001	317.2	309.4	—
2004	406.3	371.9	—
2007 (est.)	444.7	375.2	—

[a] 1961 dollars through 1937; otherwise, current dollars.

Sources: U.S. Advisory Commission on Intergovernmental Relations, *The Federal Role in the Federal System: The Dynamics of Growth—A Crisis of Confidence and Competence* (Washington, D.C.: ACIR, July 1980), 120–121; *Significant Features of Fiscal Federalism 1990*, vol. 2, *Revenues and Expenditures* (Washington, D.C.: ACIR, August 1990), 42; American Council on Intergovernmental Relations, *Significant Features of Fiscal Federalism 1995*, vol. 2, *Revenues and Expenditures* (Albany, N.Y.: Nelson A. Rockefeller Institute of Government, February 1998), 38; and *Historical Tables, Budget of the United States Government, Fiscal Year 2006* (Washington, D.C.: Government Printing Office, 2005), Table 12.1, 220–221.

expansions in the grant system—and for tremendously increased interdependence and complexity among levels of government—in succeeding years. The Court asserted that grants were voluntary arrangements and that the federal government was therefore not violating the constitutionally established separation of functions in the federal system.[10]

As the years elapsed, the grant framework became a dominant feature of the American intergovernmental network; it tied thousands of governments intricately together, whatever the direction preferred or perturbations experienced from any point in the system.

Basic Types of Assistance

Grants have offered the opportunity for substantially expanded federal influence over state and local governments, and a number of important political and administrative consequences flow from this fact. Yet it is essential to recognize that while grants create chances for national involvement, they do not vitiate the pluralism of the intergovernmental system—at least not necessarily. Grants have developed as the prime instruments used to promote bargaining and jockeying for advantage among governments; they frequently stimulate both cooperation and conflict among such governments. It should therefore surprise no one that the system of aid employed in this country has elicited ambivalent evaluations from participants and citizens alike.

Grants come in many shapes and sizes. The donor government may structure the purpose quite narrowly, offering aid for the construction of only certain kinds of highways within a state, for example. Such *categorical grants* were typical in the early part of the twentieth century. The donor may also design an intergovernmental program for a variety of purposes within a broad field, such as education, community development, or social services. This type of aid, called a *block grant*, gained some prominence in more recent decades. In the early 1970s a new form of aid, *revenue sharing*, was created to enable one government to offer financial aid to another with virtually no restrictions as to its use.[11]

When enacted, all of these types of intergovernmental assistance require rules and regulations regarding the method of distributing the aid. For instance, how is a unit selected to receive assistance and how much is it entitled to? Some grants, including all federal block grants, specify a precise formula for these factors in the legislation creating the program. Such *formula grants* include quantifiable elements, such as size of population, amount of tax effort, proportion of population unemployed or below poverty level, density of housing, or rate of infant mortality. The specified formula is a rule that tells potential recipient governments precisely how they can calculate the quantity of aid to which they are entitled under the provisions of the law, so long as the recipient qualifies for such assistance under the other stipulations of the program. Usually, the elements in a formula are chosen to reflect characteristics related to the purpose of the aid (number of school-age children for an education grant, age and/or density of residential housing for housing assistance). Some factors in the formula are also likely to have political significance since there is no such thing as a "neutral" formula—all formulas reward some states or localities more than others, depending on their relative standing given the formula specified.

However, another method of distributing aid is possible. *Project grants* allocate funding on a competitive basis, and potential recipients have no advance knowledge about the size of the grant. Instead, the authorizing legislation typically indicates the sorts of jurisdictions that are eligible to apply for aid and the criteria that will be employed to judge the merit of a government's application. Whether or not a government then receives funding depends on how strong a case it can make in its own behalf. Bureaucrats in the federal departments that supply aid determine the relative worthiness of different proposals and different jurisdictions, often by means of a detailed decision-making and evaluation system.

Why bother to make these distinctions among types of aid? The answer is that different types of grants have tended to produce different types of relationships between and among the participating governments. Much of the intergovernmental system during the twentieth century (and into the twenty-first) can be rendered intelligible by analyzing the consequences of different types of aid, one of the subjects treated in the remainder of this chapter.[12]

The Legacy of the New Deal

Most of the grant-in-aid programs developed by the national government in the early decades of the 1900s were relatively limited. They provided assistance primarily in fields that commanded strong political support, such as agriculture and road construction. Federal assistance, and thus national influence, was directed almost entirely toward the states rather than local governments. During this period, and until the 1960s, the system of intergovernmental aid was dominated by categorical formula grants. For the first part of the century, these were accompanied by relatively few strings, but required considerable matching on the part of the recipients, and were rare enough that they did not seem to impose much of an administrative or political burden on the states.

With the New Deal in the 1930s, the federal government, under the leadership of President Franklin D. Roosevelt, tackled the challenging economic and social problems of the Depression era. Although it technically would have been possible to establish new national-level programs to cope with the difficulties of the period, the more politically palatable method of the grant-in-aid was repeatedly used instead. Thus, while the national government's role expanded, the states and local governments retained significant leverage. Within a two-year period, categorical grants were established in such a variety of fields—free school lunches, aid to dependent children, emergency work relief, and so on—that they became the foundation for the social-welfare state in America. The first real forms of assistance to some of the nation's local governments, the cities, were initiated during this period as well. For the states and some local governments, then, national authorities were no longer distant or sporadically communicating entities. Instead, in many areas of domestic policy, two or three levels of government were tied together in intricate patterns of intergovernmental relations—much like a "marble cake," rather than the "layer cake" of dual federalism.[13]

The New Deal period, therefore, witnessed a permanent increase in the density and importance of intergovernmental relationships in the United States, and during the next couple of decades—even during the administration of Republican president Dwight D. Eisenhower—the number of federal programs and quantity of federal aid continued to grow. But Eisenhower was nevertheless uncomfortable with the apparently prominent role of the national government in domestic policy matters, and he established the Commission on Intergovernmental Relations with the explicit charge of identifying areas of federal involvement that could feasibly be "returned" to the states. Even the very modest suggestions of this commission went unimplemented, however. During the 1950s it seemed, as it often has since then, that the idea of separating functions by level of government was supported (and possible) in the abstract, but was exceedingly difficult to execute. Concerted efforts to reduce the levels of interdependence and complexity in the intergovernmental system have been, for the most part, singularly unsuccessful. In later decades, occasional efforts to simplify had limited impact and, perversely, often only succeeded in introducing further complications, such as increased intergovernmental mandating in place of the grant mechanism in some policy sectors.

The difficulty experienced by governments in the United States when they try to reduce their reliance on one another is not surprising.

Since the New Deal citizens and public officials have tried to harness the national government's tremendous resources in order to attack pressing problems and redress inequities. At the same time, they have attempted to retain diversity and innovation through vital state and local governments wherever possible. Shifting to some form of dual federalism, with a much less intense pattern of relationships and dependencies, could affect federal commitments in a multitude of important policy areas, like environmental protection, civil rights, income security, and education. Furthermore, such a change might entail radical shifts in the nation's tax system. The policy debates on such issues during the presidential administration of George W. Bush reflect recent struggles with these complications, but these debates and tradeoffs are constants in this area. Even the most carefully considered plans developed in the future will face bewildering dilemmas about how to reduce intergovernmental interdependence without inflicting serious inequities on some states and localities.

These days, when, as in the 1950s, one hears proposals to limit the federal role in the intergovernmental system and simplify the pattern of American governments, such caveats are useful to keep in mind. While many states are assuming newly resurgent roles in numerous policy sectors in the new century, Washington is certain to play a crucial part for the foreseeable future. It may even be asserted that creating a radically simplified intergovernmental arrangement by moving the national government out of a direct rule in important policy arenas is not a practical or responsible option, especially given the increasingly *international* ramifications and commitments entailed by such an effort, as the article by O'Toole and Hanf in this book demonstrates.

Why, then, the clamorous call for reform? Why have so many policymakers and intergovernmental experts complained about the "overloaded" pattern?[14] Later in this book, the considerable validity of a number of the criticisms will become clear. Focusing on the major developments affecting the intergovernmental system during the past fifty years will be useful in understanding this controversy.

The Emergence of a Full-Scale Pattern of Intergovernmental Relations

With Lyndon Johnson's presidency and the election of a heavily Democratic and activist Congress in 1964, a several-year period of tremendously expanded intergovernmental activities and initiatives began. Johnson proposed a "creative federalism" that would signify multiple new national commitments to assist states, localities, and private individuals and organizations in their efforts to solve many of the domestic difficulties afflicting American society. These efforts of the Johnson era were directed primarily at problems of racial discrimination, poverty, and urban and rural development. The president and Congress responded not just with rhetoric but also with hundreds of intergovernmental programs.

Indeed, the number of federal programs of grant-in-aid tripled from the beginning of the 1960s to 1975 (Table I-1). Almost all of the new programs from Washington were categorical grants, and—unlike earlier times—most of them were project grants. By the late 1960s most of the grants available were project grants, although many of these were relatively small and in total constituted a minority of the aid dollars.

In addition, the amount of support aimed directly at local governments rose sharply. Many localities (especially the nation's older, larger, more fiscally strapped cities) came to consider the federal government more of an ally than their own state governments and became increasingly reliant on federal largesse. The results of these and other massive changes in the intergovernmental system enacted in such a compressed period were, as might be expected, mixed.

Intergovernmental Activism

In many respects the consequences of this major increase in intergovernmental activity were impressive. Although hampered by fiscal constraints, the nation made measurable progress on a number of troubling problems.[15] The dramatic increase in federal support was especially welcome to many state and local governments, which had difficulty obtaining the resources to fund programs demanded by their citizenry.

The explosion in the grants system had the further effect of encouraging or mandating the professionalization of personnel and the use of up-to-date financial procedures in the administrative agencies handling the programs in the recipient units. Intergovernmental programs became increasingly influenced by functional policy-sector specialists at all levels of government. The requirements attached to many of the new grants also forced states and localities to devote renewed attention to public problems they may have overlooked in the past.

Another trend fueled by creative federalism was the growth of interest groups in the nation's capital, especially intergovernmental groups. Those concerned with specific intergovernmental programs, whether on environmental pollution or juvenile delinquency, increasingly looked to Washington as they tried to influence legislation and the implementation of regulations, to monitor the actions of the federal agency involved, and to maintain contact with other interested parties. The tremendous expansion of the grants system in the 1960s and 1970s was both a result of and a stimulus for a burgeoning number of interest groups operating at the national level in intergovernmental politics. These changes, too, contributed to the growing complexity of intergovernmental policy making and have served, since then, as a brake on any substantial efforts to disentangle the system.

As the grants process became more important and the system increasingly more complex, state and local officials found it crucial to acquire information about and influence on the process in Washington and the decisions being made. Several groups of such officials organized for the first time, moved their operations to Washington, or expanded their activities. These groups, including such entities as the National Governors Association, the Council of State Governments, the National Association of Counties, and the U.S. Conference of Mayors, refer to themselves as public interest groups, or *PIGs*—believe it or not. By the 1960s they had become increasingly recognized as leaders in the representation of state and local interests in national policy making. In addition, other more functionally specialized groups of state and local officials, such as highway officials, budget officers, and social workers, have organized into national groups and participate in the policy process. Nowadays, even in the midst of the financial constraints influencing intergovernmental decisions quite directly, any discussion of an intergovernmental issue in Congress or an administrative agency is likely to elicit concern, participation, lobbying, and debate involving many such organizations.

Emergent Frustrations and Tensions

The almost limitless choices made available to state and local officials because of the tremendous increase in intergovernmental programs also meant that the potential recipients could afford to shop around among programs and federal agencies to bargain for the most favorable deal. As a result of the interagency competition for clients, federal policy in a program would sometimes be loosely enforced.

Recipients were more and more able to evade federal intent while absorbing federal dollars.

Conversely, the system, which now had huge numbers of partially overlapping grants, created vexing difficulties for officials at state and local levels. Grants established ostensibly for the same purpose might be housed in different federal agencies, require entirely different application and approval processes, stipulate very different matching requirements, and be implemented with conflicting schedules. The winners amid this complexity were not necessarily the most competent or the most needy jurisdictions. Instead, those who packaged proposals in the most salable fashion (exercising "grantsmanship") were often rewarded.

The systemic changes generated another set of tensions for state and local governments. With the multitude of programs, many of which were now funded by grants constructed with high matching ratios (that is, Washington would pay for most of the total expenses incurred under the program), state and local governments were finding it increasingly difficult either to abstain from commitments to federal aid or to make such commitments wholeheartedly. Instead of spending its locally generated revenue on the public services judged most important by its own officials and citizens, a city could be encouraged to utilize a substantial portion as matching funds for programs that were, in essence, national priorities. The expansion of the aid system prompted complaints from uneasy mayors, governors, and others concerned about their apparently declining ability to maintain some independence. Renewed versions of these criticisms have been heard at various times over the past few decades.

Such general-purpose officials had other concerns as well. Many of them believed the expanded system of categorical grants was composed of unduly narrow programs not easily adaptable to the needs in their own jurisdictions. Furthermore, numerous important, detailed decisions made as part of an intergovernmental grant bargain—for instance, determining the eligibility of clients for programs or establishing goals—were made far from the presence of the general-purpose officials. Increasingly important in the intergovernmental policy process were a great number of specialists across governmental levels—especially in administrative agencies charged with executing the program, legislative committees with responsibility for the substantive area, and pressure groups with a strong interest in the program. Intergovernmental experts dubbed these policy networks *vertical functional autocracies*.

In these chains of influence, it became ever more difficult for anyone, even major officials like governors or mayors, to decipher just *who* was causing *what* to happen intergovernmentally. When responsibility is so diffused, the mechanisms of democratic government cannot readily ensure that policy reflects the will of the people or their representatives. In other words, another possible cost of such an arrangement is a decline in political responsiveness.

Despite many differences in emphasis, approach, and impact, intergovernmental actors during the most recent period have grappled with a structure that exhibits common characteristics and daunting demands. The following pages first characterize the modern intergovernmental pattern in general terms and then explore important events and efforts during the last few decades.

Interdependence, Complexity, and Intergovernmental Bargaining

In the pattern that emerged from the explosive growth of creative federalism it became difficult for actors in the system to make rational decisions to benefit the individuals or activities for which they held responsibility. It was also difficult to design any coherent change in the system itself. These problems stemmed directly from the dominant characteristics of the intergovernmental system: its interdependence and related complexity.

Interdependence means that power is shared among branches and layers of government, even within policy sectors. Instead of one level consistently controlling decisions about policy, nearly any change requires mutual accommodation among several levels of government. No one is in control of the system itself, and unanticipated consequences are a fact of life. *Complexity* accompanies such interdependence. Complexity means that the intergovernmental network is large and differentiated; no one participant can possibly possess enough information about its components and dynamics to consistently make rational decisions on its own or to operate in isolation from the rest.

Especially since the era of creative federalism, but also as a consequence of the framework established by the Founders, many participants in the intergovernmental system have plenty of opportunities to exercise influence—particularly to delay or frustrate action to which they are opposed. It is much more difficult, however, to generate and systematically execute *positive* action in a straightforwardly rational manner.

An important result of the system's grounding in interdependence and complexity is that the typical style of decision making in the American intergovernmental system is one of bargaining under conditions of partial conflict among the participants. The actors in the system, including the various governments involved, have different interests to serve and objectives to seek; yet they cannot succeed by acting unilaterally. They may join together into one or more loose coalitions aimed at achieving some intergovernmental objective.[16] But they must negotiate as a nearly ceaseless activity if they are to have any chance of defending themselves or achieving even some of their goals.

Of course, bargaining under conditions of partial conflict is a very abstract notion and encompasses many different types of situations. The bargaining between governments in a project-grant structure differs in predictable and important ways from the bargaining activity likely to occur for a formula grant: the former setting typically provides more influence to bureaucratic actors associated with the donor government, those who write the rules and evaluate the competitive applications from potential recipients. The fact of bargaining and its pervasiveness throughout the system, however, is important to keep in mind. Bargaining is typical even today, a time when many grant programs have not grown at nearly the pace of earlier periods (and some have actually diminished) and when other—regulatory—ties have become prominent between levels. As readings in this book document, recent years have brought unfunded mandates that have become increasingly used as mechanisms of coordination across governments.

Yet these shifts do not unambiguously indicate a new centralization. In some ways, also documented later in this volume, the states are now able to initiate, or resist, more action than in earlier periods. And federal officials may have fewer levers to enforce their own efforts at intergovernmental influence when the grant mechanism is absent from, or less prominent in, the bargaining arena. It may be concluded, therefore, that the shifts of the last few decades have altered the *types* of bargaining and the issues subject to negotiation. The fact of bargaining nevertheless remains crucial to an understanding of American intergovernmental dynamics.

Some of the tensions inherent in such a system became visible decades ago and have escalated since. Red tape, which is the continuation of intergovernmental negotiation and conflict by other means, is one manifestation. The federal government has usually viewed the requirements it imposes on its grants as essential to ensure a program's integrity. Yet recipient units claim that the burdens have become excessive. (Localities also blame the states in part for their red-tape burden.) Federally created intergovernmental mandates have escalated sharply since 1975 and in the 1990s and later became the bête noire of state and local officials.

Two general points emerge. First, the problems and tensions in the modern system are not primarily the product of ill will or ignorance, nor can they be traced primarily to one level of government. Rather, the American intergovernmental system was founded on ambivalent principles and built to establish arenas for conflict and controversy. A second and related point is that changing the particular pattern of intergovernmental relationships or reforming certain aspects of the system—for example, through the enactment of spending and policy shifts such as the Republican Congress and president sought during the first decade of the twenty-first century—would have important consequences but could hardly resolve the value conflicts of a complex and interdependent system. At this point, accordingly, we should examine some of the most recent developments within the system. Many are made comprehensible by an awareness of the difficulties just surveyed, and many, in turn, presage some of the topics of current interest and controversy.

Initiatives to Reshape the System

Richard Nixon reacted to the tensions in the changing system by proposing reforms ostensibly aimed at increasing the influence of general-purpose (especially elected) officials at all levels, shifting power away from Washington and toward federal field offices and state and local governments, reducing the control exercised by functional specialists, and trimming intergovernmental red tape. (This direction was maintained, although with somewhat diminished effort and effectiveness, by his successor, Gerald Ford.)

This "new federalism" was comprised of series of initiatives:

1. *Revenue sharing.* One of Nixon's most ambitious suggestions was the establishment of a program of revenue sharing from the federal level to state and local governments. Revenue sharing (also called "general revenue sharing") seemed to meet the demands of state and local governments for more discretion, was attractive to the most financially hard-pressed jurisdictions, and could shift some influence to the general-purpose elected officials. In 1972 the State and Local Fiscal Assistance

Act was passed with the support of much of the Democratic leadership in Congress and of the major PIGs of state and local officials. This law established a revenue-sharing program of approximately $6 billion per year for five years. All state governments and general-purpose local governments were eligible for aid, which was to be allocated on the basis of complicated formulas. The program was extended, with modifications, in 1976, and again in 1980. In 1984, as the federal budget tightened, revenue sharing was reenacted for localities alone. The program ultimately ended in 1986 when Congress found itself facing an increasingly severe national deficit. During its tenure, revenue sharing helped many governments. But even at its peak, it constituted only a small fraction of total federal assistance for the larger recipient governments.

2. *Block grants.* These began during the Johnson administration, but the idea is most closely identified with Nixon, who proposed a set of enactments in six policy sectors along with the elimination of a series of closely related categorical grants. Defenders of these latter programs, including members of the vertical functional autocracies, resisted; their concerns would have no statutory protection once a block grant was put into place. Further, the proposals would have reduced the overall level of intergovernmental funding. Ultimately, only three of the additional block grants—in employment, social services, and community development—emerged from this period. Yet some of these programs have had a major impact on intergovernmental affairs, and they were followed by additional block grants enacted during the Reagan years.

3. *Administrative initiatives.* Nixon encouraged the implementation of administrative reforms by supporting a series of efforts to simplify and expedite the grant application and review process.

Despite all these changes, the intergovernmental system was not radically altered. The more traditional categorical grant was by no means decommissioned. Indeed, such programs and the amount of aid going to support them increased even through the Nixon years. And administrative and regulatory difficulties in the system proved to be more tenacious than many had anticipated. Impressively complex and interdependent, the system continued to face criticism from virtually all directions.

President Jimmy Carter was not the activist in intergovernmental matters that Nixon was—or, for that matter, that his successor was. The first part of Ronald Reagan's time as president saw perhaps the most systematic, if not the most sustained, effort to remake the nation's intergovernmental system since the New Deal. Reagan ardently believed that the United States had been created as a system in which national powers and jurisdiction were severely limited, and in which the states had the strongest, most vital governments, with the broadest jurisdiction over domestic matters. Accordingly, he sought to reshape the intergovernmental pattern in a manner consistent with this understanding. Since his other priorities included tax reductions and significant defense spending increases, a related consequence was a renewed vulnerability of intergovernmental aid to sizable cuts. Pressures by citizens and interest groups to address a whole set of policy issues at state and local levels did not abate either, so the stage was set for higher levels of tension and conflict in the system.

Reagan's major proposals, for which he adopted Nixon's term, the "new federalism," were as follows:

1. *An additional series of block grants.* Reagan proposed that more than one hundred categoricals be combined into a handful of broadly based block grants with very few regulations. Congress complied with several of these initiatives.

2. *A dramatic simplification of the system of intergovernmental aid.* Program responsibilities were to be shifted to single levels of government and away from the marble cake configurations. Congress made no move to approve this plan, and Reagan's attention was diverted from this contentious issue.

3. *A devolution of responsibilities for many policies from the national level to the states.* Reagan suggested that scores of programs involving federal participation, including most of the remaining expensive ones, be turned over to the states in their entirety and that an appropriate quantity of revenue be shifted to the states as well. No action was taken on this proposal. Yet several years after Reagan left office, some of the intent behind this idea was fulfilled. By the 1990s and the first decade of the twenty-first century, policy initiatives involving substantial new expenditures from Washington had become nearly impossible under the then-current political and budgetary climate, and particularly after federal tax cuts and budget increases directed toward Washington's antiterrorism measures and the war in Iraq. Meanwhile, many states, pressed by interest groups and the citizenry to address daunting problems like health care, infrastructure financing, education, and economic development, became centers of more policy activism than had been seen in years outside of the nation's capital.

4. *Administrative simplification.* The president worked to trim red tape and lighten the putative burden of federal mandates. In this regard, Reagan scored his "successes," as did his predecessors. Yet many complained about the abdication of federal responsibility for important national goals, and others felt the reforms did not go nearly far enough. Several years after Reagan's departure from the White House, the evidence accumulated that, overall, mandates from Washington had actually increased.

Reagan's efforts to restructure the intergovernmental system were often challenged. By the second half of his first term, the most ambitious proposals had been set aside in favor of further grouping of categorical programs into block grants. Even these suggestions encountered hostility or indifference in Congress.

Nevertheless, the Reagan administration's efforts, and the complicated responses they stimulated, presaged a series of changes in the intergovernmental system as the new century began. None of the next few presidents sought systematic changes in the intergovernmental pattern overall, but the system itself was buffeted by a series of challenges that ramified through the complex and interdependent structure.

Crosscurrents at the Dawn of the Twenty-first Century: Struggles for Reform, Pressures toward Globalization

The administration of President George H. W. Bush did not signal a major departure from the intergovernmental trends of Reagan's second term, nor did President Bill Clinton seek to grab center stage with dramatic attempts to recraft the nature of the system. Well into his second term, President George W. Bush spoke of ceding jurisdiction and authority to subnational governments, but the policy and political issues that often occupied center stage trumped any effort to devolve or reform systematically. By the first years of the new century, events and influences from elsewhere had combined to place the American intergovernmental network in the midst of a variety of consequential forces. Most of the issues receiving attention during the Reagan years remained on the agenda, and some had grown in salience, but shifts in political fortunes, international developments, economic conditions, and federalism jurisprudence combined to amplify the turbulence in the system. The resolution of these influences is still uncertain, with vectors pushing actively in quite different directions. What is clear is that a number of these recent developments will continue to be felt for a considerable period to come. It is equally clear that the prime characteristics of the system, complexity and interdependence, will continue to shape the details of intergovernmental bargaining and frustrate the efforts of reformers to impose or craft a clear and coherent design.

For instance, since the mid-1990s, Republicans have been in control of Congress. Early in this period, congressional leadership had touted a "Contract with America" that offered a governmental future in which Washington would march in marked retreat away from policy activism and leadership, and subnational governments would be freed from the shackles of irksome and expensive unfunded mandates imposed by the center. Real steps were taken to convert the "Contract" into reality. The Republican Congress sought to impose tight budgetary discipline, even to cut many programs dramatically, and passed an Unfunded Mandates Reform Act (UMRA) during their first year in power. But with resistance from President Clinton, a Democrat, as well as the growing unpopularity of some of the political maneuvering associated with the actions of Congress and the Oval Office, it became clear to the leadership in each branch that some accommodation with their counterpart institution would be necessary.

One result was a continuation, indeed increase, in intergovernmental assistance (see Table I-1), even as politicians like Clinton announced that the "era of big government is over." Leaders of both parties found agreement on such aid useful as a means of acquiescing to the continuing realities of interdependence while still energizing and devolving some real discretion to other governments. The continuing appeal of block grants in this regard was obvious, with political leaders of both parties supporting these in principle even as they disagreed on the details. It is significant to note that, for the longer term, an important block grant, the Temporary Assistance to Needy Families (TANF) program, was enacted in 1996. This initiative ended the nationally supported Aid to Families with Dependent Children (AFDC) program, which had been the intergovernmental assistance effort at the core of the nation's social welfare protection for many of its poorest people.

AFDC as a categorical grant program had come to symbolize "welfare," a program much maligned even if much less expensive than widely supposed. While Clinton and the Republican congressional leadership sought political advantage from the situation, they did agree to enact this major change in the nation's welfare policy—and major shift in responsibility—"downward" to the states. TANF put an end to long-term welfare assistance, a frequent occurrence under the older program, and was designed to encourage welfare recipients to move permanently into the workforce. The initiative also greatly increased the flexibility states would have to shape their own approach to social welfare and the financial responsibility they would have in order to fund the choices they made. TANF symbolized, in a sense, one of the major currents in the turbulent intergovernmental maelstrom of the time: increased state discretion and innovation amid continuing intergovernmental ties.

The TANF initiative has been important, but in monetary terms the stakes have been significantly larger in other intergovernmental policy arenas, particularly during the administration of President George W. Bush. Fiscal pressures have mounted in very expensive policy sectors like health, and Republican policymakers in Washington have sought to limit national support for covering the spiraling costs of such costly intergovernmental programs as Medicaid. Here the politics, the stakes, and the concern on the part of PIGs that they not be buried under huge and escalating costs have made radical action much more difficult, even as unprecedented pressures have been placed on state budgets.

More generally, the close of one century and beginning of the next produced evidence aplenty, amidst the partisanship and turbulence in Washington, that simple and dramatic shifts in the intergovernmental system would be unlikely—even as substantial efforts were mounted to make things happen in a big way. The complexity and interdependence of the system—and the fact of the public's mixed and ambivalent attitudes toward such major changes—continued to produce nuanced and complicated results, even for all the attempts at systematization and "revolution."

Several examples can be cited. The first is the quixotic effort at mandate reform. No one approves of unfunded mandates in principle, and yet their appearance escalated during the 1980s and 1990s. Republican leadership called for their elimination, and in the 1990s the Democratic White House initiated an administrative overhaul called the "National Performance Review" (NPR) that called for a rationalizing of the nation's approach to intergovernmental relations and indicated a need to end unfunded mandates imposed on the states and localities. The UMRA was enacted quickly, and yet years later it became clear that, while not completely ineffective, the act has been unsuccessful in legislating an end to the kinds of nationally initiated regulatory ties that stimulated its passage. As Paul Posner shows (see the excerpt included in this book), *both* political parties find reasons to support mandating, even if the mandates and sectors vary. And using legislation as a way of trying to prevent intergovernmental regulation and the associated (often acrimonious) bargaining does not address the more fundamental causes of these ties in the first place.

Note, for instance, three relevant actions taken during the administration of George W. Bush. By early 2002 the White House had succeeded in passing one of its top priorities, the No Child Left Behind Act. While indicating that public education is primarily a state and local responsibility, the new national policy called for strict accountability to Washington for the performance results of local schools and school systems, with mandates for those systems unable to deliver certain outcomes. National policymakers touted the initiative as one that would enhance opportunities for young Americans, even as many states and school districts complained bitterly about intrusive and poorly funded demands from the nation's capital.

The Bush administration then began to actively intervene in traditionally subnational responsibilities—when such action provided opportunities to tout the administration's social agenda. Perhaps the most striking, albeit heavily symbolic, instance of this pattern occurred in 2005, in a widely publicized "right-to-die" case in Florida. The feeding tube of a brain-damaged woman, Terry Schiavo, was removed under court sanction and amid a painful family dispute. The president and congressional leaders involved themselves in the case, sought reversal through the courts, and thus signaled the willingness of national leaders to put aside their qualms about extraordinary policy activism when certain social issues are on the line. The broad preferences for an intact system of federalism have not infrequently given way to the policy needs or preferences of the moment—and not just during the administration of George W. Bush but under the political leadership of both parties.

Lastly, serious national threats and disasters early in the twenty-first century have driven major initiatives from Washington, some of which will inevitably involve increased national involvement in, and increased costs for, state and local governments. The terrorist attacks in New York City and the Washington, D.C. area during 2001 catalyzed a massive upsurge in federal activities related to "homeland security," with major reverberations among the state and local agencies responsible for delivering the bulk of first-responder and public health support. Hurricane disasters, and especially the experiences of those along the Gulf Coast following Hurricane Katrina in August 2005, have highlighted the weaknesses of a rather loose intergovernmental system for dealing successfully with emergencies and have placed considerable pressure on Washington to develop a more muscular coordinative role.

The tension between a coherent and balanced overall system design on the one hand, and the strong political pressures for the nation to respond and deliver results effectively on an issue-by-issue basis on the other hand, plays out on a continual basis. Whoever is in power in Washington, the tendency over time has been to respond to policy demands by gradual centralization of functions,[17] even if almost no one intends such a result and even if the consequences for subnational jurisdictions are complex and sometimes unattractive.

The death in the 1990s of the widely respected U.S. Advisory Commission on Intergovernmental Relations (ACIR), a governmentally established forum for analysis and improvement of the system, stands as a prime example of the perils of modern American intergovernmental relations. The ACIR was caught in a political crossfire about which federal mandates to loosen, and by how much, in the interest of adding vibrancy to the overall intergovernmental system. While virtually everyone favors "reform" and "simplification," at least as general principles, the reality is that the complexity and interdependence endemic in the system are no accidents. They have emerged as products of a long series of function-specific demands and political supports for cost sharing, standard setting, and cross-governmental bargaining. Remaking the system on behalf of goals like allocating functions to "appropriate" levels of government, clarifying the often obscure mechanisms of intergovernmental influence and administration, and reducing fiscal pressures imposed from Washington can be expected to run afoul of intense support for problem solving and bargaining in adaptation to the crosscurrents of policy change. The general desire for "reform," coupled with the considerable difficulty in building a coalition supportive of concrete and significant steps in that direction, is not confined to one political party or another, nor is the tendency unique to the environment of Washington, D.C. The states, for instance, are themselves heavy imposers of mandates on their own local governments. Rather, the tension between pragmatic problem solving for concrete and pressing issues, on one side, and worthy but rather abstract desires for systemwide reform, on the other, has been a hallmark of intergovernmental relations throughout the past several decades. This uncomfortable tension is likely to continue.

Meanwhile, two additional forces besides mandate reform are also shaping the evolution of the system, although their impacts on that system thus far have been complicated and somewhat uncertain. One of these forces emanates from the federal judiciary, especially the U.S. Supreme Court, which can play a major role—particularly via the jurisprudence of federalism. The Court has stirred the waters with potentially important decisions aimed, in part, at protecting or reclaiming some distinctive policy space for subnational authorities. Perhaps most notably, in 1995 it voided a national law in *United States v. Lopez* on the grounds that Washington had enacted a policy with no connection to interstate commerce. This limitation on national authority was the first decided on these grounds since the 1930s, and some observers have become hopeful—or fearful—that the federal judiciary might begin to establish national-state boundaries limiting reach and interdependence in the system.

There has indeed been renewed attention by the Court to the importance of treating the federal principle seriously, and a series of decisions over a recent several-year period indicate that this perspective has begun to constitute a judicial brake on national activism on some policy efforts. Recent new appointments to the Court have added weight and importance to the issue, and observers of all persuasions are paying close attention to the signals about possible directions the Court will take in the future. The pattern nonetheless remains uncertain, with other precedents during the last two decades suggesting support for national authority[18]—and, as always, with issue-specific advocates caring more about policy rulings than intergovernmental design; note the intense attention to judicial candidates' positions on the regulation of abortion, for instance. Evidence on recent tendencies is examined in some of the readings in this book.

The second force vector has to do with what has become an ever increasing, more tightly wound pattern of intergovernmental interdependence on the economic dimension—a sort of "hyperinterdependence." Record budget deficits in Washington have resulted in remarkably tight pursestrings for some key grant programs at state and local levels. Yet escalating national demands reverberate across levels, as the expensive priorities of homeland security and health care demonstrate. Local governments now must scramble to replace national funding for some of their programs with state aid and other alternative sources. The PIGs, which in earlier decades had organized into nationally important forces with the onset of large-scale federal assistance, struggle to define new roles of comparable influence in this lingering era of budgetary constraint. The federal government, meanwhile, continues to seek day-to-day influence through the channels of the hundreds of existing programs and the scattering of new ones enacted in recent years. All these participants continue to jockey for influence in the interdependent, complex, and fiscally strained system.

As if this intricate pattern were not complex enough, increasing economic (and other) pressures toward "globalization" have now added another set of actors and considerations to the constraints and opportunities in the intergovernmental system. Economic developments in heavily populated and rapidly developing nations like China and India raise the theme of interdependence—and, often, competition—to new levels. Dramatic changes in information technology and other realms have lowered transaction costs across borders and woven new social and economic ties. Business and market connections around the world, and—importantly—national governmental commitments to international agreements in a multitude of policy sectors—have pulled city managers, state economic development experts, local and state education specialists, and national environmental policy makers, among many others, into the matrix of forces and constraints emanating from abroad.

In these crosscurrents of (primarily economic and national-security) influence, the bargaining has begun to include more parties and more options, for at least some of the decision makers. The overall system is, furthermore, even less transparent to citizens—with potential implications for responsiveness and the quality of democratic life. Potent pressures to extend and concentrate national influence to deal effectively with global forces have begun to penetrate domestic intergovernmental decision making. City managers and state legislators find themselves linked to institutions and actors much further away than Washington, but without the functional equivalent of the Constitution's explicit federal principle to sort out responsibilities and negotiate understandings. Hyperinterdependence has its benefits, of course, but also entails risks and complexities that would make the intergovernmental grant pale by comparison.

The dizzying transformations at the end of the twentieth century, then, have resulted in an intergovernmental arrangement buffeted by a variety of shifts and shocks. Certainly, the system differs in key respects from the one in place a generation ago, for instance. And yet any vision of radical simplification—like that articulated by Reagan or, for that matter, by congressional leadership during the 1990s—can be seen as chimerical. The notion of a dual federalism that could meet the challenges of the new century, of the nation's needs and aspirations in an increasingly interdependent world, seems increasingly remote—for all the apparent agreement on the attractiveness of reform and rationality. Despite the crosscurrents, [and] regardless of the multiple developments of the last several years, the most fundamental aspects of American intergovernmental relations, including the strengths, weaknesses, frustrations, and dilemmas of the pattern, have remained prominent.

There is no denying that the form of the system has changed considerably since the nation's founding. Political, economic, and social forces have stimulated major changes in the overall scope of governmental activity, in the mix of values that intergovernmental arrangements are meant to serve, in the relative influence of the different governments, and in their degree of reliance on one another. Far from preserving a simple, stratified pattern, the choices made centuries ago created opportunities for dramatic shifts toward new forms of interdependence and complexity in the intergovernmental network. Those new patterns are emergent but in flux. Citizens and public officials will contribute to their evolution, and analysts will pay close attention to how the dynamics shape the overall system. The results are not yet obvious but are likely to be exceedingly important. We live in interesting times.

Notes

1. Thus the term federal has two meanings in contemporary usage. One refers to a system of governance that employs a constitutional partitioning of authority between central and regional units. The other is as a synonym for the national government. Both notions are employed in this chapter and in various readings throughout the book. The meaning should be clear from the context.
2. U.S. Bureau of the Census, Economics and Statistics Administration, *2002 Census of Governments*, vol. 1, no. 1, *Governmental Organization* (Washington, D.C.: U.S. Government Printing Office, 2002), v.
3. *Federalist* No. 10, *The Federalist Papers*, ed. Clinton Rossiter (New York: New American Library, 1961), 77.
4. At the time, the term federation had a meaning close to that of confederation today. See Martin Diamond's essay in this volume. The meaning changed after the initiation of the American experiment in federated government.

5. The concepts of federalism (in the first sense mentioned in n. 1) and intergovernmental relations are linked but not identical. The former refers to certain aspects of the dealings between national and regional governments, while the latter is meant to encompass relations among all governments within a nation. Intergovernmental relations are considerably affected but not completely determined by federalism. This book examines federalism but focuses broadly on intergovernmental relations. Nevertheless, interstate and interlocal relations receive relatively less attention because of space limitations.

6. One example is Madison's veto of a bill to authorize construction of roads and canals in the states. See Daniel J. Elazar, *The American Partnership: Intergovernmental Co-operation in the Nineteenth Century* (Chicago: University of Chicago Press, 1962), 15.

7. Elazar, *The American Partnership*.

8. The terms recipient and donor are borrowed from Jeffrey L. Pressman, *Federal Programs and City Politics* (Berkeley and Los Angeles: University of California Press, 1975).

9. Organization for Economic Co-operation and Development, *Economic Surveys: United States* (Paris: OECD, 2005), 70.

10. The cases were *Massachusetts v. Mellon* and *Frothingham v. Mellon* 262 U.S. 447 (1923).

11. As explained later in this chapter, this experiment proved temporary. Federal financial constraints during the Carter and Reagan administrations persuaded Congress to follow presidential recommendations; the program was ended for state and then local governments, respectively.

12. Other forms of intergovernmental influence are possible via a channel of financial inducement entirely apart from grants-in-aid. Choices imbedded in the tax code at one level of government can induce decisions made at other levels. Individuals' responses to tax policy can also shape the fiscal circumstances of other governments. For example, federal policy allowing for the income tax-deductibility of home mortgages has shaped over the decades the locational decisions of households, and thus the suburbanization of the country, and thus the associated patterns of infrastructural and human service needs experienced in many local jurisdictions. These sorts of subsidies in the tax code are commonly referred to as tax expenditures. In scale and importance, they can even surpass intergovernmental grants in affecting the intricate patterns of complexity and interdependence in the overall system. See, for instance, Lester M. Salamon, ed., *The Tools of Government: A Guide to the New Governance* (New York: Oxford University Press, 2002).

13. See Morton Grodzins's classic essay in Part I of this volume.

14. For example, David B. Walker, *Toward a Functioning Federalism* (Cambridge, Mass.: Winthrop, 1981); and see Deil S. Wright, *Understanding Intergovernmental Relations*, 3d ed. (Pacific Grove, Calif.: Brooks/Cole, 1988), 94.

15. See Norman Furniss and Timothy Tilton, *The Case for the Welfare State: From Social Security to Social Equality* (Bloomington: Indiana University Press, 1977); and John

E. Schwarz, *America's Hidden Success: A Reassessment of Twenty Years of Public Policy* (New York: Norton, 1988).

16. Thomas Anton, *American Federalism and Public Policy: How the System Works* (Philadelphia: Temple University Press, 1989).

17. For evidence on this point, see Ann O'M. Bowman and George A. Krause, "Power Shift: Measuring Policy Centralization in U.S. Intergovernmental Relations, 1947–1998," *American Politics Quarterly* 31, no. 3 (2003): 301–325.

18. See, for instance, *Tennessee v. Lane* 541 U.S. 509 (2004) in which the Supreme Court upheld disabled persons' use of Title II of the Americans with Disabilities Act to sue the states over inadequate accommodations in courthouses. Another instance is *Gonzales v. Raich* 125 S.Ct. 2195 (2005), in which the Court upheld Congress' power to prohibit local cultivation and use of marijuana in compliance with California's Compassionate Use Act of 1996.

Part I

HISTORICAL AND THEORETICAL PERSPECTIVES

American governments exhibit an impressive variety and complexity. This rich intergovernmental world is best understood by learning something of American history. We would also benefit from learning more about the theoretical perspectives that experts have used to analyze, explain, and predict intergovernmental events.

In the field of intergovernmental relations, history and theory have typically been closely linked. To clarify this point, let us first define what is meant by *theory*. A theory is a coherent set of statements that describes and explains the relationships and underlying principles of some aspect of the world. A useful (although somewhat oversimplified) distinction may be made between two kinds of theory: normative theory seeks to explain and justify how the world *ought* to be; empirical theory offers explanations and predictions for how some part of the world actually *is* or *will be*.

These two types of theory are directed at quite different goals. In the field of intergovernmental relations, however (and, typically, in analyses of the related topic of American federalism), efforts to explain intergovernmental systems are often bound up with attempts to persuade others that certain forms of intergovernmental relations are preferable. One obvious and understandable example was the Founders' attempt to design a basic framework and then persuade the public to accept it. Madison, Hamilton, and the others constructed powerful normative arguments in support of certain goals (such as the preservation of freedom), yet they also had to use empirical theories to help determine which governmental—and intergovernmental—structures were likely to result in the preferred outcomes. In other words, many intergovernmental theories have been both normative and empirical.

As was noted in the introductory chapter, dramatic changes have taken place in intergovernmental relations (despite stability in the overall framework) during this nation's history. A clear understanding of these developments is essential because, first, knowing the nature and significance of such changes can alert one to some of the most important features of the current system; second, history can explain some of today's apparently haphazard or irrational intergovernmental patterns; and third, many discussions about intergovernmental relations are highly normative, since modern debates and proposals often use history to justify certain courses of action. Lyndon Johnson and his advisers evoked history to bolster some of their innovative notions of intergovernmental cooperation. Similarly, the administration of Ronald Reagan used historical events to explain and defend its contrasting efforts to move the nation closer to a dual federal structure. In its reform efforts as a part of the National Performance Review, the Clinton administration invoked enduring problems as it called for bold new action. And during the years of the George W. Bush presidency, the White House justified its nominations to the U.S. Supreme Court in terms of the need to respect the intentions and constitutional perspective of the original Founders and avoid giving power to "activist judges."

The selections in Part I describe the historical evolution of intergovernmental relations and further explain its twofold theoretical aspects. Several articles in later parts of this book also contain useful theoretical perspectives and historical interpretations, although these are typically directed at a limited aspect of the system or a more truncated historical period. The readings in the present part include a number of classic expositions with which any serious student of the subject should be familiar. As the reader will see, however, the experts are hardly in complete agreement on either history or theory. Also, it may be useful as one examines later readings in this book to consider the extent to which the evidence from the current operations of the American intergovernmental system supports or undermines the arguments developed in this set of initial readings.

The first selection in this part is the *Federalist* No. 39. The *Federalist* was actually a series of political tracts published as newspaper letters at about the time the Constitution was being considered for adoption. The papers, signed "Publius," were written by James Madison, Alexander Hamilton, and John Jay, three well-known supporters of the new Constitution, and were intended to persuade citizens to support the proposal. In the paper included here, Madison characterizes the American structure as one that combines national *and* federal characteristics. Although more than two hundred years have passed since the essay was first penned, it remains one of the most explicit discussions of what the

Founders intended. Pay particular attention to Madison's use of key terms, the complexity of the political structure he describes, and his argument in defense of the new American experiment in intergovernmental relations.

In the second selection, Martin Diamond explains what the Founders were attempting to build and how they sought to justify the governmental structure. He emphasizes the link between the founding of the United States and certain important values, such as liberty and the preservation of representative government.

Whereas the first two readings concentrate on the period of the founding and on the basic structure within which American intergovernmental relations would have to develop, the next two cover some important aspects of historical and modern intergovernmental relations in practice.

The essay by Morton Grodzins excerpted here is perhaps the most widely quoted argument in intergovernmental relations. Employing the now famous images of layer cakes and marble cakes, Grodzins aptly describes the intergovernmental interdependence and complexity that were beginning to attract attention in the mid-1960s. Grodzins's essay is worth reading for a number of other reasons as well. For instance, he explains the ties so often developed on intergovernmental matters among administrators, legislators, and interest groups, and he analyzes the link between intergovernmental relations and the structure of American political parties, at least as they developed prior to today's emphasis on television campaigns, direct mail, the Internet, and political action committees. Grodzins's overall goal, as he explains in a part of the essay not included here, is to describe the American system as one of "decentralization by mild chaos," which he labels "an important goal for the American federal system."

By way of contrast, Harry N. Scheiber critiques and rejects Grodzins's historically based claims, as well as those of his student Daniel Elazar, which state that sharing and cooperation, not conflict, have been more prevalent in American intergovernmental relations. He also explains why such interpretations of intergovernmental history may have an important effect on the course of contemporary intergovernmental policy making.

Deil S. Wright is one of the most prominent experts on intergovernmental matters in the United States today. His interest is specifically American intergovernmental relations and management, rather than federalism, because he regards intergovernmental themes as more accurate and inclusive in the contemporary context. For him, the "hallmarks of this system" of "increased complexity and interdependency" are "(1) the number and variety of governmental units; (2) the number and variety of public officials involved; (3) the intensity and regularity of contacts among the officials; (4) the importance of the officials' actions and attitudes; and (5) the preoccupation with financial policy issues."[1] In the reading taken from his major text, Wright sketches three models of intergovernmental relations, surveys the evidence available to support each, and chooses one model as particularly appropriate to explain and describe contemporary intergovernmental activity.

The last two readings implicitly raise questions about the coherence or contemporary soundness of crafting the intergovernmental system around the kind of federal design analyzed and often extolled by observers. Martha Derthick, a distinguished scholar of the subject, points to the somewhat ambiguous status of the states in the system. She indicates that these days they are "both reviving and falling under the federal yoke at the same time" and seeks to explain their primacy-*cum*-subsidiarity today with a historically based analysis. Edward L. Rubin, a professor of law, concludes that the national government has acquired preeminence but views this finding with equanimity. Indeed, he indicates, the United States exhibits a level of "political unity" now that makes the federal framework itself somewhat anachronistic. Our nostalgia for the venerable design drives a sort of affectionate view held by most Americans, he says, whereas present-day realities have changed the actual pattern into a softer, nation-centered "puppy federalism." These selections should stimulate reflection about the appropriateness of the classic framework for addressing the imperatives of twenty-first-century governance.

Note

1. Deil S. Wright, *Understanding Intergovernmental Relations*, 3d ed. (Pacific Grove, Calif.: Brooks/Cole, 1988), 14.

1

Federalist No. 39

James Madison

The last paper having concluded the observations which were meant to introduce a candid survey of the plan of government reported by the convention, we now proceed to the execution of that part of the undertaking.

The first question that offers itself is whether the general form and aspect of the government be strictly republican. It is evident that no other form would be reconcilable with the genius of the people of America; with the fundamental principles of the Revolution; or with that honorable determination which animates every votary of freedom to rest all our political experiments on the capacity of mankind for self-government. If the plan of the convention, therefore, be found to depart from the republican character, its advocates must abandon it as no longer defensible.

What, then, are the distinctive characters of the republican form? Were an answer to this question to be sought, not by recurring to principles but in the application of the term by political writers to the constitutions of different States, no satisfactory one would ever be found. Holland, in which no particle of the supreme authority is derived from the people, has passed almost universally under the denomination of a republic. The same title has been bestowed on Venice, where absolute power over the great body of the people is exercised in the most absolute manner by a small body of hereditary nobles. Poland, which is a mixture of aristocracy and of monarchy in their worst forms, has been dignified with the same appellation. The government of England, which has one republican branch only, combined with an hereditary aristocracy and monarchy, has with equal impropriety been frequently placed on the list of republics. These examples, which are nearly as dissimilar to each other as to a genuine republic, show the

From *The Federalist Papers*, ed. Clinton Rossiter (New York: New American Library, 1961), 240–246.

extreme inaccuracy with which the term has been used in political disquisitions.

If we resort for a criterion to the different principles on which different forms of government are established, we may define a republic to be, or at least may bestow that name on, a government which derives all its powers directly or indirectly from the great body of the people, and is administered by persons holding their offices during pleasure for a limited period, or during good behavior. It is *essential* to such a government that it be derived from the great body of the society, not from an inconsiderable proportion or a favored class of it; otherwise a handful of tyrannical nobles, exercising their oppressions by a delegation of their powers, might aspire to the rank of republicans and claim for their government the honorable title of republic. It is *sufficient* for such a government that the persons administering it be appointed, either directly or indirectly, by the people; and that they hold their appointments by either of the tenures just specified; otherwise every government in the United States, as well as every other popular government that has been or can be well organized or well executed, would be degraded from the republican character. According to the constitution of every State in the Union, some or other of the officers of government are appointed indirectly only by the people. According to most of them, the chief magistrate himself is so appointed. And according to one, this mode of appointment is extended to one of the coordinate branches of the legislature. According to all the constitutions, also, the tenure of the highest offices is extended to a definite period, and in many instances, both within the legislative and executive departments, to a period of years. According to the provisions of most of the constitutions, again, as well as according to the most respectable and received opinions on the subject, the members of the judiciary department are to retain their offices by the firm tenure of good behavior.

On comparing the Constitution planned by the convention with the standard here fixed, we perceived at once that it is, in the most rigid sense, conformable to it. The House of Representatives, like that of one branch at least of all the State legislatures, is elected immediately by the great body of the people. The Senate, like the present Congress and the Senate of Maryland, derives its appointment indirectly from the people. The President is indirectly derived from the choice of the people, according to the example in most of the States. Even the judges, with all other officers of the Union, will, as in the several States, be the choice, though a remote choice, of the people themselves. The duration of the appointments is equally conformable to the republican standard and to the model of State constitutions. The House of Representatives is periodically elective, as in all the States; and for the period of two years, as in the State of South Carolina. The Senate is elective for the period of six years, which is but one year more than the period of the Senate of Maryland, and but two more than that of the Senates of New York and Virginia. The President is to continue in office for the period of four years; as in New York and Delaware the chief magistrate is elected for three years, and in South Carolina for two years. In the other States the election is annual. In several of the States, however, no explicit provision is made for the impeachment of the chief magistrate. And in Delaware and Virginia he is not impeachable till out of office. The President of the United States is impeachable at any time during his continuance in office. The tenure by which the judges are to hold their places is, as it unquestionably ought to be, that of good behavior. The tenure of the ministerial offices generally will be a subject of legal regulation, conformably to the reason of the case and the example of the State constitutions.

Could any further proof be required of the republican complexion of this system, the most decisive one might be found in its absolute prohibition of titles of nobility, both under the federal and the State governments; and in its express guaranty of the republican form to each of the latter.

"But it was not sufficient," say the adversaries of the proposed Constitution, "for the convention to adhere to the republican form. They ought with equal care to have preserved the *federal* form, which regards the Union as a *Confederacy* of sovereign states; instead of which they have framed a *national* government, which regards the Union as a *consolidation* of the States." And it is asked by what authority this bold and radical innovation was undertaken? The handle which has been made of this objection requires that it should be examined with some precision.

Without inquiring into the accuracy of the distinction on which the objection is rounded, it will be necessary to a just estimate of its force, first, to ascertain the real character of the government in question; secondly, to inquire how far the convention were authorized to propose such a government; and thirdly, how far the duty they owed to their country could supply any defect of regular authority.

First.—In order to ascertain the real character of the government, it may be considered in relation to the foundation on which it is to be established; to the sources from which its ordinary powers are to be drawn; to the operation of those powers; to the extent of them; and to the authority by which future changes in the government are to be introduced.

On examining the first relation, it appears, on one hand, that the Constitution is to be rounded on the assent and ratification of the people of America, given by deputies elected for the special purpose; but, on the other, that this assent and ratification is to be given by the people, not as individuals composing one entire nation, but as composing the distinct and independent States to which they respectively belong. It is to be the assent and ratification of the several States, derived from the supreme authority in each State—the authority of the people themselves. The act, therefore, establishing the Constitution will not be a *national* but a *federal* act.

That it will be a federal and not a national act, as these terms are understood by the objectors—the act of the people, as forming so many independent States, not as forming one aggregate nation—is obvious from this single consideration: that it is to result neither from the decision of a *majority* of the people of the Union, nor from that of a *majority* of the States. It must result from the *unanimous* assent of the several States that are parties to it, differing no otherwise from their ordinary assent than in its being expressed, not by the legislative authority, but by that of the people themselves. Were the people regarded in this transaction as forming one nation, the will of the majority of the whole people of the United States would bind the minority, in the same manner as the majority in each State must bind the minority; and the will of the majority must be determined either by a comparison of the individual votes, or by considering the will of the majority of the States as evidence of the will of a majority of the people of the United States. Neither of these rules has been adopted. Each State, in ratifying the Constitution, is considered as a sovereign body independent of all others, and only to be bound by its own voluntary act. In this relation, then, the new Constitution will, if established, be a *federal* and not a *national* constitution.

The next relation is to the sources from which the ordinary powers of government are to be derived. The House of Representatives will derive its powers from the people of America; and the people will be represented in the same proportion and on the same principle as they are in the legislature of a particular State. So far the government is *national,* not *federal.* The Senate, on the other hand, will derive its powers from the States as political and coequal societies; and these will be represented on the principle of equality in the Senate, as they now are in the existing Congress. So far the government is *federal,* not *national.* The executive power will be derived from a very compound source. The immediate election of the President is to be made by the States in their political characters. The votes allotted to them are in a compound ratio, which considers them partly as distinct and coequal societies, partly as unequal members of the same society. The eventual election, again, is to be made by that branch of the legislature which consists of the national representatives; but in this particular act they are to be thrown into the form of individual delegations from so many distinct and coequal bodies politic. From this aspect of the government it appears to be of a mixed character, presenting at least as many *federal* as *national* features.

The difference between a federal and national government, as it relates to the *operation of the government,* is by the adversaries of the plan of the convention supposed to consist in this, that in the former the powers operate on the political bodies composing the Confederacy in their political capacities; in the latter, on the individual citizens composing the nation in their individual capacities. On trying the Constitution by this criterion, it falls under the *national* not the *federal* character; though perhaps not so completely as has been understood. In several cases, and particularly in the trial of controversies to which States may be parties, they must be viewed and proceeded against in their collective and political capacities only. But the operation of the government on the people in their individual capacities, in its ordinary and most essential proceedings, will, in the sense of its opponents, on the whole, designate it, in this relation, a *national* government.

But if the government be national with regard to the *operation* of its powers, it changes its aspect again when we contemplate it in relation to the extent of its powers. The idea of a national government involves in it not only an authority over the individual citizens, but an indefinite supremacy over all persons and things, so far as they are objects of lawful government. Among a people consolidated into one nation, this supremacy is completely vested in the national legislature. Among communities united for particular purposes, it is vested partly in the general and partly in the municipal legislatures. In the former case, all local authorities are subordinate to the supreme; and may be controlled, directed, or abolished by it at pleasure. In the latter, the local or municipal authorities form distinct and independent portions of the supremacy, no more subject, within their respective spheres, to the general authority than the general authority is subject to them, within its own sphere. In this relation, then, the proposed government cannot be deemed a *national* one; since its jurisdiction extends to certain enumerated objects only, and leaves to the several States a residuary and inviolable sovereignty over all other objects. It is true that in controversies relating to the boundary between the two jurisdictions, the tribunal which is ultimately to decide is to be established under the general government. But this does not change the principle of the case. The decision is to be impartially made, according to the rules of the Constitution; and all the usual and most effectual precautions are taken to secure this impartiality. Some such tribunal is clearly essential to prevent an appeal to the sword and a dissolution of the compact; and that it ought to be established under the general rather than under the local governments, or, to speak more properly, that it could be safely established under the first alone, is a position not likely to be combated.

If we try the Constitution by its last relation to the authority by which amendments are to be made, we find it neither wholly *national* nor wholly *federal*. Were it wholly national, the supreme and ultimate authority would reside in the *majority* of the people of the Union; and this authority would be competent at all times, like that of a majority of every national society to alter or abolish its established government. Were it wholly federal, on the other hand, the concurrence of each State in the Union would be essential to every alteration that would be binding on all. The mode provided by the plan of the convention is not rounded on either of these principles. In requiring more than a majority, and particularly in computing the proportion by *States,* not by *citizens,* it departs from the national and advances toward the *federal* character; in rendering the concurrence of less than the whole number of States sufficient, it loses again the *federal* and partakes of the *national* character.

The proposed Constitution, therefore, even when tested by the rules laid down by its antagonists, is, in strictness, neither a national nor a federal Constitution, but a composition of both. In its foundation it is federal, not national; in the sources from which the ordinary powers of government are drawn, it is partly federal and partly national; in the operation of these powers, it is national, not federal; in the extent of them, again, it is federal, not national; and, finally in the authoritative mode of introducing amendments, it is neither wholly federal nor wholly national.

PUBLIUS

2

What the Framers Meant by Federalism

Martin Diamond

. . . Relatively little serious attention has been given to the Framers' own view of federalism, because something confidently called "modern federalism" has been understood to have superseded the original version. It is the contention of this essay that the recovery of the Framers' view of federalism is necessary to the understanding of American federalism. In what follows, an attempt is made to indicate what the Framers meant by federalism, as that is revealed in the proceedings of the Federal Convention.

I

The American Republic has been regarded by nearly all modern observers as *the* example of a federal government. Indeed the various modern definitions of federalism are little more than slightly generalized descriptions of the American way of governing. . . .

According to these typical definitions, the essential federal characteristic is the "division of political power," a division of supremacy (sovereignty, as used to be said) between member states and a central government, each having the final say regarding matters belonging to its sphere. There is a corollary to this sort of definition which has also come to be generally accepted. All college students are now taught that, in this respect, there are three kinds of government—confederal, federal, and unitary (national)—and that the United States exemplifies the middle term. This familiar distinction illuminates the definitions of federalism. In this view, a confederacy and a nation are seen as the extremes. The defining characteristic of a confederacy is that the associated states retain all the sovereign power, with the central body entire-

Author's note: This paper was written while the author was enjoying a fellowship year at the Center for Advanced Study in the Behavioral Sciences.

From Robert A. Goldwin, ed., *A Nation of States* (Chicago: Rand McNally, 1974), 25–41. Reprinted by permission, Kenyon College.

ly dependent legally upon their will; the defining characteristic of a nation is that the central body has all the sovereign power, with the localities entirely dependent legally upon the will of the nation. In this view, then, federalism is truly the middle term, for its defining characteristic is that it modifies and then combines the best characteristics of the other two forms. A *federal* system combines states which *confederally* retain sovereignty within a certain sphere, with a central body that *nationally* possesses sovereignty within another sphere; the combination is thought to create a new and better thing to which is given the name federalism.

Now what is strange is this. The leading Framers viewed their handiwork in an entirely different light. For example, *The Federalist*, the great contemporary exposition of the Constitution, emphatically does not regard the Constitution as establishing a typically federal, perhaps not even a primarily federal system of government. *The Federalist* regards the new American Union as departing significantly from the essentially federal character. The decisive statement is: "The proposed Constitution, therefore, is, in strictness, neither a national nor a federal Constitution, but a composition of both."[1] As will become clear, our now familiar tripartite distinction was completely unknown to the men who made the Constitution. They had a very different understanding than we do of what federalism is. For them, there were but two possible modes: confederal or federal as opposed to unitary or national. They had, therefore, in strictness, to regard their Constitution as a composition of federal and national features. We now give the single word federal to the systems the Framers regarded as possessing both federal and national features. This means we now regard as a unique principle what they considered as a mere compound.

Consider Tocqueville's opinion: "Evidently this is no longer a federal government, but an incomplete national government, which is neither exactly national nor exactly federal; but the new word which ought to express this novel thing does not yet exist."[2] For good or ill, the word that came to express the novel thing turned out to be the old word federal. It is no fussy antiquarianism to assert the necessity to understand the Constitution the way its creators did, as possessing both federal and national features. In order to understand the system they created for us and how they expected it to work, we must be able to distinguish the parts that make up the whole, and see the peculiar place of each in the working of the whole. Now they regarded certain parts as federal and certain parts as national, and had different expectations regarding each.

To use the word federal, as we do now, to describe both the "federal" and "national" features of their plan is to lump under one obscuring term things they regarded as radically different. It becomes thus difficult if not impossible to understand their precise intentions. This is a sufficient reason to do the job of recovering precisely what they meant by federalism.

Federalism meant then exactly what we mean now by confederalism: "a sort of association or league of sovereign states." . . . A brief consideration of the Articles of Confederation will further reveal what men meant then by a federal arrangement, especially when comparison is made to the Constitution.

In recent years we have come to think of the Articles as having created too weak a central government. This is not precise enough. Strictly speaking, neither the friends nor the enemies of the Confederation regarded the Articles as having created any kind of *government* at all, weak or otherwise. Article III declared that "the said states hereby enter into a firm *league of friendship* with each other." . . . Men referred then to the Articles as a kind of treaty, and, no more than any other treaty organization is thought to create a government, was it thought that the Articles had created one. The language of the Articles makes this clear. The word government never appears in that document, whereas the Constitution speaks repeatedly of the Government, the Treasury, the Authority, the Offices, the Laws of the United States. There are no such terms in the Articles; there could be none because it was fatally a federal arrangement, a league not a government.

Article I declared that "the stile of this confederacy shall be 'The United States of America.'" Twice more at the outset that capitalized expression occurs. But on every subsequent occasion (about forty times) the term is given in lower-case letters as the "united states." That is, as a mere league, the Confederacy was not a governmental being to which a proper name could be strictly applied. In the Constitution, on the contrary, the term United States is invariably capitalized. Indeed, the formal language of the Articles makes clear that the Confederacy had no real existence save when the states were formally assembled. When speaking of its duties or functions, the Articles invariably refer to the Confederacy as "the united states *in Congress assembled.*" All men seem to have referred to the Confederacy in this exact phrase. It must be remembered also that the word "Congress" did not then mean an institution of government. As an ordinary word it meant then simply a "meeting," especially "an assembly of envoys, commissioners, deputies, etc. from different courts, meeting to agree on terms of political accommodation."[3] Under the Articles the United States had no being; its existence consisted solely in the congregation of envoys from the separate states for the accommodation of certain specified matters under terms prescribed by the federal treaty. The slightest glance at the Constitution, of course, shows that it refers to the duties and powers of the government of a country.

The Founding Fathers, like all other men at the time and perhaps all other men up to that time, regarded federalism, not as a kind of government, but as a voluntary association of states who sought certain advantages from that association. For example, at the very outset of the Convention, it became necessary for the delegates to state openly their understanding of the nature of the federal form. Gouverneur Morris "explained the distinction between a *federal* and *national, supreme* government; the former being a mere compact resting on the good faith of the parties; the latter having a complete and *compulsive* operation."[4] The entire Convention, with the single exception of Hamilton, in one remark, concurred in this view of the nature of federalism.[5]

From this view it followed that any federal arrangement would be characterized by certain ways of doing things. As one delegate put it, "a confederacy supposes sovereignty in the members composing it and sovereignty supposes equality."[6] That is, when forming a league, the member states retain their political character, i.e., sovereignty; and, each being equally a political entity, each state participates in the league as an equal member. That is, each state has one equal vote in making the league's decisions; moreover, because the league is a voluntary association of sovereign states and rests upon the "good faith" of the members, extraordinary or even unanimous majorities are to be preferred. Compare the Articles which called for at least a majority of nine of the thirteen states in all important cases. From this view of federalism it further followed that a league had no business with the individual citizens of the member states, the governing of them remaining the business of the states. In its limited activities, the central body was to deal only with *its* "citizens," i.e., the sovereign states.

According to the Framers, then, a federal system was federal in three main ways. First, the member states were equals in the making of the central decisions. Second, these central agreements were to be carried out by the member states themselves. Third, the confederal body was not to deal with the vast bulk of political matters; governing, for all practical purposes, remained with the member states. Given this view of the meaning of federalism, we can readily see why the Framers could not possibly regard the new Constitution as merely a federal system, but rather regarded it as a "composition" of both federal and national elements.

II

The Federal Convention began its work by considering the detailed plan carefully prepared in advance and presented to it by the Virginia delegation. The Virginia plan proposed the creation of a powerful government which it throughout described by the shocking term *national.* It clearly went far beyond the common understanding that the Convention was only to propose amendments to the existing Confederacy. The great issue so abruptly placed before the Convention was made perfectly explicit when Governor Randolph, at the suggestion of Gouverneur Morris, proposed a substitution for the initial clause of the Virginia Plan. The original formulation was: "Resolved that the articles of Confederation ought to be so corrected and enlarged, as to accomplish the objects proposed by their institution; namely, common defense, security of liberty and general welfare."[7] The substitute formulation left no possible doubt about how far the Virginia Plan went. Resolved "that a Union of the States merely federal will not accomplish the objects proposed by the articles of Confederation, namely common defense, security of liberty and general welfare"; and resolved further "that a *national* Government ought to be established consisting of a *supreme* Legislative, Executive and Judiciary."[8]

Randolph said, in short: by the Articles we meant to insure our defense, liberty and general welfare; they failed; no system of the merely federal kind will secure these things for us; we must create a supreme, that is, national government.

Discussion centered on the resolution proposing a national and supreme government. Oddly enough, the resolution was almost immediately adopted, six states to one. At this moment the Convention was pointed to a simply national government, and not the "composition" which finally resulted. But the matter was not to be so easily settled, not least because several small state delegations, which happened to be federally minded, subsequently arrived. Despite the favorable vote on the Randolph resolution, the Convention had not yet truly made up their mind. Too many delegates remained convinced federalists. They would have to be persuaded to change their minds or the final plan would have to be compromised so as to accommodate the wishes of those who would not go so far as a straightforwardly national plan. Therefore, as specific portions of the Virginia Plan were discussed in the ensuing weeks, the fundamental issue—a federal versus a national plan—came up again and again.

The most important feature of the discussions is the following. The Convention had originally squared off on the issue of federalism *versus* nationalism, the true federalists regarding nationalism as fatal to liberty, the nationalists regarding confederalism as "imbecilically" incompetent. Compromise would have been impossible across the gulf of two such opposed views. One or the other of the two original views had to be modified so that the distance between the two could be bridged by compromise. And that is precisely what happened. After three weeks of discussion, the issue had subtly changed. The opponents of a purely national government found themselves unable to defend the pure federal principle. The simple nationalists remained such in principle, while the pure federalists implicitly found themselves forced to acknowledge the inadequacy of the federal principle. Now the question was between those still advocating a purely national plan and those who, having abandoned a purely federal scheme, were determined only to work some federal features into the final outcome. Thus the famous compromise, the "composition" which finally resulted, was a compromise between the simple nationalists and half-hearted federalists, i.e., federalists who were themselves moving toward the national principle. Only because of this underlying victory of the simple nationalists was the issue finally made capable of compromise.

This does not mean that the pure federalists yielded easily or completely. The ideas which led them to their federalist position had a powerful hold over their minds. A fundamental theoretical issue, as we shall see, had to be raised before they could be made substantially to retreat from their federalist position. And, even then, important concessions had finally to be made to the unconvinced and only partially convinced. Moreover, the ideas supporting that federalist position have long retained their vitality in American politics; and the federal elements which finally found their way into the Constitution have always supplied historical and legal support to recurring expressions of the traditional federalist view. It is necessary to acknowledge the survival of this view and the grounds for its survival. But it is impossible to understand the work of the Convention without seeing that the view survived only after having first been shaken to its very root, and hence that it survived only in a permanently weakened condition.

How this happened is perfectly revealed in a notable exchange between Madison, straightforwardly for the national plan at that point, and Sherman of Connecticut, one of the intelligent defenders of the federal principle.

> The objects of Union [Sherman] thought were *few*. 1. defence against foreign danger. 2. against internal disputes & a resort to force. 3. Treaties with foreign nations. 4. regulating foreign commerce, & drawing revenue from it. These & perhaps a few lesser objects *alone rendered a confederation of the States necessary*. All other matters civil & criminal would be much better in the hands of the States. *The people are more happy in small than in large States.*[9]

Whereas Madison

> differed from the member from Connecticut in thinking the objects mentioned to be all the principal ones that required a National Government. Those were certainly important and necessary objects; but he combined with them the necessity of providing more effectually for the security of private rights, and the steady dispensation of Justice. Interferences with these were evils which had more perhaps than anything else, produced this convention. Was it to be supposed that republican liberty could long exist under the abuses of it practised in some of the States?[10]

Madison was skillfully pressing a sensitive nerve. Not only were the delegates concerned with the inadequacy of the Confederacy for "general" purposes, but nearly all were also unhappy with the way things had been going in the states themselves since the Revolution. Above all, the delegates agreed in fearing the tendency in many of the states to agrarian and debtors' measures that seemed to threaten the security of property. The Shays' Rebellion, for example, had terrified many of the delegates. Sherman had himself, after the passage quoted above, adverted to this dangerous tendency, and had, moreover, admitted that "too small" states were by virtue of their smallness peculiarly "subject to faction." Madison seized upon this.

> The gentleman had admitted that in a very small State, faction & oppression would prevail. It was to be inferred then that wherever these prevailed the State was too small. Had they not prevailed in the largest as well as the smallest tho' less than in the smallest; and

were we not thence admonished to enlarge the sphere as far as the nature of the Government would admit. This was the only defence against the inconveniencies of democracy consistent with the democratic form of Government.[11]

Sherman, the defender of the federal principle, considered the ends of union to be few. Madison, the defender of the national principle, considered the ends of union to be many. Sherman would leave the most important matters of government to the individual states. Madison would place the most important matters—e.g., "security of private rights, and the steady dispensation of justice"—under a national government. Sherman believed that the people would be happiest when governed by their individual states, these being the natural dwelling place of republicanism. Madison believed that republican liberty would perish under the states and that therefore the people would be happiest when under a national government; only such a government made possible the very large republic which in turn supplied the democratic remedy for the inconveniences of democracy.

Madison, then, argued with Sherman and the other defenders of the federal principle in two ways. First, he appealed to the delegates to acknowledge that they really wanted very much more from union than Sherman admitted. . . . the Convention's decisive action turned on just this issue. The fact that nearly all the delegates, themselves included, wanted a very great deal from union became *the* stumbling block to the defenders of a federal plan. . . . the explicit endorsement of a national plan dramatically followed the most powerful showing of how much was wanted from union and how little could be supplied by the federal principle. But it would not have sufficed merely to demonstrate the incompatibility of federalism and a union from which much was desired. The delegates could still have done what any man can do who has two equal and contradictory desires. They could have abandoned their preference for the federal principle in favor of firm union, as Madison wished, or they could have abandoned a firm union in favor of the federal principle, as Madison emphatically did not wish. Madison therefore had also to give the delegates a reason to choose only one of the two incompatible alternatives, namely, a firm union under a national government. This meant persuading the delegates to renounce their attachment to federalism. And that is precisely what Madison attempted. He sought to undermine that attachment by supplying a new solution to the problem for which federalism had been the traditional answer.

The best men, like Sherman, who defended the federal principle at the Convention, and those, like R. H. Lee, who subsequently opposed adoption of the Constitution, did not defend federalism for its own sake. Who could? They defended the federal principle against the plan of a national or primarily national government because they thought they were thereby defending a precious thing, namely, republican liberty. They saw a connection between republicanism and federalism. They regarded federalism as the sole way in which some of the advantages of great size could be obtained by those who wanted to enjoy the blessings of republicanism. . . .

The true federalists rested their case on the proposition that only the state governments, and not some huge national government, could be made or kept truly free and republican. In this they were following the very old belief, popularized anew in the way men understood Montesquieu, that only small countries could enjoy republican government. The reasoning that supported the belief ran something as follows. Large countries necessarily turn to despotic rule. For one thing, large countries need despotic rule; political authority breaks down if the central government does not govern more forcefully than the republican form admits. Further, large countries, usually wealthy and populous, are warlike by nature or are made warlike by envious neighbors; such belligerency nurtures despotic rule. Moreover, not even the best intentions suffice to preserve the republicanism of a large country. To preserve their rule, the people must be patriotic, vigilant, and informed. This requires that the people give loving attention to public things, and that the affairs of the country be on a scale commensurate with the people's understanding. But in large countries the people, baffled and rendered apathetic by the complexity of public affairs, at last become absorbed in their own pursuits. Finally, even were the citizens of a large republic able to remain alert, they must allow a few men actually to conduct the public business. Far removed from the localities and possessed of the instruments of coercion, the necessarily trusted representatives would inevitably subvert the republican rule to their own passions and interests. Such was the traditional and strongly held view of the necessity that republics be small. . . .

It is clear, then, that Madison had to persuade the delegates, as it were, that they could have their cake and eat it, too. That is, they could have the firm union that would supply the blessings they wanted, *without* sacrificing the republicanism for which they had hitherto thought federalism was indispensable. Federalism was indispensable only so long as men held to the small-republic theory. And that is the theory Madison tried to demolish. Nothing is more important to an understanding of both the theoretical and practical issues in the rounding of the American Republic than a full appreciation of Madison's stand on behalf of the very large republic. . . .

Madison turned the small-republic argument upside down. On the contrary, he argued, *smallness* was fatal to republicanism. The small republics of antiquity were wretched nurseries of internal warfare, and the Convention itself had been "produced" by the fear for liberty in the "small" American states. "Was it to be supposed that republican liberty could long exist under the abuses of it practised in some of the States. . . . Were we not then admonished to enlarge the sphere as far as the nature of the Government would admit." Smallness is fatal to republican liberty. Only a country as large as the whole thirteen states and more could provide a safe dwelling-place for republican liberty. Republicanism not only permits but requires taking away from the states responsibility for "the security of private rights, and the steady dispensation of Justice," else rights and justice will perish under the state governments.

This was the great and novel idea which came from the Convention: a large, powerful republic with a competent national government regulated under a wise Constitution. . . .

Notes

1. *Federalist* 39, p. 250. All references are to the edition of Henry Cabot Lodge, introduction by Edward Mead Earle (New York: Modern Library, 1941).
2. *Democracy in America,* ed. Phillips Bradley (New York: Alfred A. Knopf, 1945), I, 159.
3. Samuel Johnson, *Dictionary of the English Language* (2 vols.; Heidelberg: Joseph Englemann, 1828).
4. *Documents Illustrative of the Formation of the Union of the American States,* ed. C. C. Tansill (Washington, D.C.: U.S. Government Printing Office, 1927), p. 121. Italics supplied.
5. Ibid., p. 216.
6. Ibid., p. 182.
7. Ibid., p. 116.
8. Ibid., p. 120.
9. Ibid., pp. 160–61. Italics supplied.
10. Ibid., pp. 161–62.
11. Ibid., p. 162.

3

The Federal System

Morton Grodzins

Federalism is a device for dividing decisions and functions of government. As the constitutional fathers well understood, the federal structure is a means, not an end. The pages that follow are therefore not concerned with an exposition of American federalism as a formal, legal set of relationships. The focus, rather, is on the purpose of federalism, that is to say, on the distribution of power between central and peripheral units of government.

I. The Sharing of Functions

The American form of government is often, but erroneously, symbolized by a three-layer cake. A far more accurate image is the rainbow or marble cake, characterized by an inseparable mingling of differently colored ingredients, the colors appearing in vertical and diagonal strands and unexpected whirls. As colors are mixed in the marble cake, so functions are mixed in the American federal system. Consider the health officer, styled "sanitarian," of a rural county in a border state. He embodies the whole idea of the marble cake of government.

The sanitarian is appointed by the state under merit standards established by the federal government. His base salary comes jointly from state and federal funds, the county provides him with an office and office amenities and pays a portion of his expenses, and the largest city in the county also contributes to his salary and office by virtue of his appointment as a city plumbing inspector. It is impossible from

Author's note: This paper is the product of research carried out in the Federalism Workshop of the University of Chicago. I am indebted to the workshop participants, particularly Daniel J. Elazar, Dennis Palumbo, and Kenneth E. Gray, for data they collected. . . .

From The Report of the President's Commission on National Goals, The American Assembly, *Goals for Americans* (Englewood Cliffs, N.J.: Prentice-Hall, 1960), 265–282.

moment to moment to tell under which governmental hat the sanitarian operates. His work of inspecting the purity of food is carried out under federal standards; but he is enforcing state laws when inspecting commodities that have not been in interstate commerce; and somewhat perversely he also acts under state authority when inspecting milk coming into the county from producing areas across the state border. He is a federal officer when impounding impure drugs shipped from a neighboring state; a federal-state officer when distributing typhoid immunization serum; a state officer when enforcing standards of industrial hygiene; a state-local officer when inspecting the city's water supply; and (to complete the circle) a local officer when insisting that the city butchers adopt more-hygienic methods of handling their garbage. But he cannot and does not think of himself as acting in these separate capacities. All business in the county that concerns public health and sanitation he considers his business. Paid largely from federal funds, he does not find it strange to attend meetings of the city council to give expert advice on matters ranging from rotten apples to rabies control. He is even deputized as a member of both the city and the county police forces.

The sanitarian is an extreme case, but he accurately represents an important aspect of the whole range of governmental activities in the United States. Functions are not neatly parceled out among the many governments. They are shared functions. It is difficult to find any governmental activity which does not involve all three of the so-called "levels" of the federal system. In the most local of local functions—law enforcement or education, for example—the federal and state governments play important roles. In what, *a priori,* may be considered the purest central government activities—the conduct of foreign affairs, for example—the state and local governments have considerable responsibilities, directly and indirectly.

The federal grant programs are only the most obvious example of shared functions. They also most clearly exhibit how sharing serves to disperse governmental powers. The grants utilize the greater wealth gathering abilities of the central government and establish nationwide standards, yet they are "in aid" of functions carried out under state law, with considerable state and local discretion. The national supervision of such programs is largely a process of mutual accommodation. Leading state and local officials, acting through their professional organizations, are in considerable part responsible for the very standards that national officers try to persuade all state and local officers to accept.

Even in the absence of joint financing, federal-state-local collaboration is the characteristic mode of action. Federal expertise is available to aid in the building of a local jail (which may later be used to house federal prisoners), to improve a local water purification system, to step up building inspections, to provide standards for state and local personnel in protecting [people] against dishonest butchers' scales, to prevent gas explosions, or to produce a local land use plan. States and localities, on the other hand, take important formal responsibilities in the development of national programs for atomic energy, civil defense, the regulation of commerce, and the protection of purity in foods and drugs; local political weight is always a factor in the operation of even a post office or a military establishment. From abattoirs and accounting through zoning and zoo administration, any governmental activity is almost certain to involve the influence, if not the formal administration, of all three planes of the federal system.

II. Attempts to Unwind the Federal System

[During the 1940s to the 1960s] there [were] four major attempts to reform or reorganize the federal system: the first (1947–49) and second (1953–55) Hoover Commissions on Executive Organization; the Kestnbaum Commission on Intergovernmental Relations (1953–55); and the Joint Federal-State Action Committee (1957–59). All four of these groups . . . aimed to minimize federal activities. None of them . . . recognized the sharing of functions as the characteristic way American governments do things. Even when making recommendations for joint action, these official commissions [took] the view (as expressed in the Kestnbaum report) that "the main tradition of American federalism is the tradition of separateness." All four . . . , in varying degrees, worked to separate functions and tax sources.

The history of the Joint Federal-State Action Committee is especially instructive. The committee was established at the suggestion of President Eisenhower, who charged it, first of all, "to designate functions which the States are ready and willing to assume and finance that are now performed or financed wholly or in part by the Federal Government." He also gave the committee the task of recommending "Federal and State revenue adjustments required to enable the States to assume such functions."[1]

The committee subsequently established seemed most favorably situated to accomplish the task of functional separation. It was composed of distinguished and able men, including among its personnel three leading members of the President's cabinet, the director of the Bureau of the Budget [now the Office of Management and Budget—Ed.], and ten state governors. It had the full support of the President at every point, and it worked hard and conscientiously. Excellent staff studies were supplied by the Bureau of the Budget, the White House, the Treasury Department, and from the state side, the Council of State Governments. It had available to it a large mass of research data, including the sixteen recently completed volumes of the Kestnbaum Commission. There existed no disagreements on party lines within the committee and, of course, no constitutional impediments to its mission. The President, his cabinet members, and all the governors (with one possible exception) on the committee completely agreed on the desirability of decentralization-via-separation-of-functions-and-taxes. They were unanimous in wanting to justify the committee's name and to produce action, not just another report.

The committee worked for more than two years. It found exactly two programs to recommend for transfer from federal to state hands. One was the federal grant program for vocational education (including practical-nurse training and aid to fishery trades); the other was federal grants for municipal waste treatment plants. The programs together cost the federal government less than $80 million in 1957, slightly more than two per cent of the total federal grants for that year. To allow the states to pay for these programs, the committee recommended that they be allowed a credit against the federal tax on local telephone calls. Calculations showed that this offset device, plus an equalizing factor, would give every state at least 40 per cent more from the tax than it received from the federal government in vocational education and sewage disposal grants. Some states were "equalized" to receive twice as much.

The recommendations were modest enough, and the generous financing feature seemed calculated to gain state support. The President recommended to Congress that all points of the program be legislated. None of them was, none has been since, and none is likely to be.

[In a section omitted here, Grodzins surveys some of the history of intergovernmental cooperation in the United States.—Ed.]

IV. Dynamics of Sharing: The Politics of the Federal System

Many causes contribute to dispersed power in the federal system. One is the simple historical fact that the states existed before the nation. A second is in the form of creed, the traditional opinion of Americans that expresses distrust of centralized power and places great value in the strength and vitality of local units of government. Another is pride in locality and state, nurtured by the nation's size and by variations of regional and state history. Still a fourth cause of decentralization is the sheer wealth of the nation. It allows all groups, including state and local governments, to partake of the central government's largesse, supplies room for experimentation and even waste, and makes unnecessary the tight organization of political power that must follow when the support of one program necessarily means the deprivation of another.

In one important respect, the Constitution no longer operates to impede centralized government. The Supreme Court since 1937 has given Congress a relatively free hand. [In more recent decades, this generalization would require qualification. The reading by Donald L. Doernberg in Part II of this book updates the subject.—Ed.] The federal government can build substantive programs in many areas on the taxation and commerce powers. Limitations of such central programs based on the argument, "it's unconstitutional," are no longer possible as long as Congress (in the Court's view) acts reasonably in the interest of the whole nation. The Court is unlikely to reverse this permissive view in the foreseeable future.

Nevertheless, some constitutional restraints on centralization continue to operate. The strong constitutional position of the states— for example, the assignment of two senators to each state, the role given the states in administering even national elections, and the relatively few limitations on their law-making powers—establish the geographical units as natural centers of administrative and political strength. Many clauses of the Constitution are not subject to the same latitude of interpretation as the commerce and tax clauses. The simple, clearly stated, unambiguous phrases—for example, the President "shall hold his office during the term of four years"—are subject to change only through the formal amendment process. Similar provisions exist with respect to the terms of senators and congressmen and the amendment process. All of them have the effect of retarding or restraining centralizing action of the federal government. The fixed terms of the President and the members of Congress, for example, greatly impede the development of nationwide, disciplined political parties that almost certainly would have to precede continuous large-scale expansion of federal functions.

The constitutional restraints on the expansion of national authority are less important and less direct today than they were in 1879 or in 1936. But to say that they are less important is not to say that they are unimportant.

The nation's politics reflect these decentralizing causes and add some of their own. The political parties of the United States are unique. They seldom perform the function that parties traditionally perform in other countries, the function of gathering together diverse strands of power and welding them into one. Except during the period of nominating and electing a president and for the essential but nonsubstantive business of organizing the houses of Congress, the American parties rarely coalesce power at all. Characteristically they do the reverse, serving as a canopy under which special and local interests are represented with little regard for anything that can be called a party program. National leaders are elected on a party ticket, but in Congress they must seek cross-party support if their leadership is to be effective. It is a rare president during rare periods who can produce legislation without facing the defection of substantial numbers of his own party. (Wilson could do this in the first session of the sixty-third Congress; but Franklin D. Roosevelt could not, even during the famous hundred days of 1933.) Presidents whose parties form the majority of the congressional houses must still count heavily on support from the other party.

The parties provide the pivot on which the entire governmental system swings. Party operations, first of all, produce in legislation the basic division of functions between the federal government, on the one hand, and state and local governments, on the other. The Supreme Court's permissiveness with respect to the expansion of national powers has not in fact produced any considerable extension of exclusive federal functions. The body of federal law in all fields has remained, in the words of Henry M. Hart, Jr., and Herbert Wechsler, "interstitial in its nature," limited in objective and resting upon the principal body of legal relationships defined by state law. It is difficult to find any area of federal legislation that is not significantly affected by state law.

In areas of new or enlarged federal activity, legislation characteristically provides important roles for state and local governments. This is as true of Democratic as of Republican administrations and true even of functions for which arguments of efficiency would produce exclusive federal responsibility. . . . A large fraction of the Senate is usually made up of ex-governors, and the membership of both houses is composed of [people] who know that their re-election depends less upon national leaders or national party organization than upon support from their home constituencies. State and local officials are key members of these constituencies, often central figures in selecting candidates and in turning out the vote. Under such circumstances, national legislation taking state and local views heavily into account is inevitable.

Second, the undisciplined parties affect the character of the federal system as a result of senatorial and congressional interference in federal administrative programs on behalf of local interests. Many aspects of the legislative involvement in administrative affairs are formalized. The Legislative Reorganization Act of 1946, to take only one example, provided that each of the standing committees "shall exercise continuous watchfulness" over administration of laws within its jurisdiction. But the formal system of controls, extensive as it is, does not compare in importance with the informal and extralegal network of relationships in producing continuous legislative involvement in administrative affairs.

Senators and congressmen spend a major fraction of their time representing problems of their constituents before administrative agencies. An even larger fraction of congressional staff time is devoted to the same task. The total magnitude of such "case work" operations is great. . . . Special congressional liaison staffs have been created to service this mass of business, though all higher officials meet it in one form or another. . . .

The widespread, consistent, and in many ways unpredictable character of legislative interference in administrative affairs has many consequences for the tone and character of American administrative behavior. From the perspective of this paper, the important consequence is the comprehensive, day-to-day, even hour-by-hour, impact of local views on national programs. No point of substance or procedure is immune from congressional scrutiny. A substantial portion of the entire weight of this impact is on behalf of the state and local governments. It is a weight that can alter procedures for screening immigration applications, divert the course of a national highway, change the tone of an international negotiation, and amend a social security law to accommodate local practices or fulfill local desires.

The party system compels administrators to take a political role. This is a third way in which the parties function to decentralize the American system. The administrator must play politics for the same reason that the politician is able to play in administration: the parties are without program and without discipline.

In response to the unprotected position in which the party situation places him, the administrator is forced to nurse the Congress of the United States, that crucial constituency which ultimately controls his agency's budget and program. From the administrator's view, a sympathetic consideration of congressional requests (if not downright submission to them) is the surest way to build the political support without which the administrative job could not continue. Even the completely task-oriented administrator must be sensitive to the need for congressional support and to the relationship between case work requests, on one side, and budgetary and legislative support, on the other. "You do a good job handling the personal problems and requests of a Congressman," a White House officer said, "and you have an easier time convincing him to back your program." Thus there is an important link between the nursing of congressional requests, requests that largely concern local matters, and the most comprehensive national programs. The administrator must accommodate to the former as a price of gaining support for the latter.

One result of administrative politics is that the administrative agency may become the captive of the nationwide interest group it serves or presumably regulates. In such cases no government may come out with effective authority: the winners are the interest groups themselves. But in a very large number of cases, states and localities also win influence. The politics of administration is a process of making peace with legislators who for the most part consider themselves the guardians of local interests. The political role of administrators therefore contributes to the power of states and localities in national programs.

Finally, the way the party system operates gives American politics their over-all distinctive tone. The lack of party discipline produces an openness in the system that allows individuals, groups, and institutions (including state and local governments) to attempt to influence national policy at every step of the legislative-administrative process. This is the "multiple-crack" attribute of the American government. "Crack" has two meanings. It means not only many fissures or access points; it also means, less statically, opportunities for wallops or smacks at government.

If the parties were more disciplined, the result would not be a cessation of the process by which individuals and groups impinge themselves upon the central government. But the present state of the parties clearly allows for a far greater operation of the multiple cracks than would be possible under the conditions of centralized party control. American interest groups exploit literally uncountable access points in the legislative-administrative process. If legislative lobbying, from committee stages to the conference committee, does not produce results, a cabinet secretary is called. His immediate associates are petitioned. Bureau chiefs and their aides are hit. Field officers are put under pressure. Campaigns are instituted by which friends of the agency apply a secondary influence on behalf of the interested party. A conference with the President may be urged.

To these multiple points for bringing influence must be added the multiple voices of the influencers. Consider, for example, those in a small town who wish to have a federal action taken. The easy merging of public and private interest at the local level means that the influence attempt is made in the name of the whole community, thus removing it from political partisanship. The Rotary Club as well as the City Council, the Chamber of Commerce and the mayor, eminent citizens and political bosses—all are readily enlisted. If a conference in [a] senator's office will expedite matters, someone on the local scene can be found [to] make such a conference possible and effective. If technical information is needed, technicians will supply it. State or national professional organizations of local officials, individual congressmen and senators, and not infrequently whole state delegations will make the local cause their own. Federal field officers, who service localities, often assume local views. So may elected and appointed state officers. Friendships are exploited, and political mortgages called due. Under these circumstances, national policies are molded by local action.

In summary, then, the party system functions to devolve power. The American parties, unlike any other, are highly responsive when directives move from the bottom to the top, highly unresponsive from top to bottom. Congressmen and senators can rarely ignore concerted demands from their home constituencies; but no party leader can expect the same kind of response from those below, whether he be a President asking for congressional support or a congressman seeking aid from local or state leaders.

Any tightening of the party apparatus would have the effect of strengthening the central government. The four characteristics of the system, discussed above, would become less important. If control from the top were strictly applied, these hallmarks of American decentralization might entirely disappear. To be specific, if disciplined and program-oriented parties were achieved: (1) It would make far less likely legislation that takes heavily into account the desires and prejudices of the highly decentralized power groups and institutions of the country, including the state and local governments. (2) It would to a large extent prevent legislators, individually and collectively, from intruding themselves on behalf of non-national interests in national administrative programs. (3) It would put an end to the administrator's search for his own political support, a search that often results in fostering state, local, and other non-national powers. (4) It would dampen the process by which individuals and groups, including state and local political leaders, take advantage of multiple cracks to steer national legislation and administration in ways congenial to them and the institutions they represent.

Alterations of this sort could only accompany basic changes in the organization and style of politics which, in turn, presuppose fundamental changes at the parties' social base. The sharing of functions is, in fact, the sharing of power. To end this sharing process would mean the destruction of whatever measure of decentralization exists in the United States today. . . .

Note

1. The President's third suggestion was that the committee "identify functions and responsibilities likely to require state or federal attention in the future and . . . recommend the level of state effort, or federal effort, or both, that will be needed to assure effective action." The committee initially devoted little attention to this problem. Upon discovering the difficulty of making separatist recommendations, i.e., for turning over federal functions and taxes to the states, it developed a series of proposals looking to greater effectiveness in intergovernmental collaboration. The committee was succeeded by a legislatively based, 26-member Advisory Commission on Intergovernmental Relations, established September 29, 1959.

4

The Condition of American Federalism:
An Historian's View

Harry N. Scheiber

... Debate has been colored lately by differences of opinion concerning the actual historic tradition of American federalism. The long-standing view was that throughout the 19th century, and in most respects until the New Deal, "dual federalism"—in which the functions of the three levels of government were well delineated and in which their administrative activities were kept separate and autonomous—was the prevailing system. Only in the 20th century did there emerge a new order, termed "cooperative federalism," in which all the levels of government became "mutually complementary parts of a *single* governmental mechanism all of whose powers are intended to realize the current purposes of government according to the applicability of the problem at hand."[1]

Now there has become popular a new historical view, associated mainly with the late Morton Grodzins, that dual federalism never characterized the American political system. From the beginning, it is asserted, there was a high degree of intergovernmental activity, involving shared functions and responsibilities; indeed, there was "as much sharing" in the period 1790–1860 as there is today.[2] Surprising as it may seem, this historical construct has gained wide currency among political scientists and bids fair to become the new conventional wisdom about American federalism.[3] ...

The Fallacy of Continuity

The model of "cooperative federalism" portrays the present-day federal system as one in which most of the important functions of

From a study submitted by the Subcommittee on Intergovernmental Relations Pursuant to S. Res. 205, 89th Congress, to the Committee on Government Operations, U.S. Senate, October 15, 1966 (Washington, D.C.: U.S. Government Printing Office). Reprinted with permission of the author, Harry N. Scheiber. All rights reserved.

government are shared. Professor Grodzins argued that the system does not resemble a layer cake "of three distinct and separate planes" so much as a marble cake: "there is no neat horizontal stratification," for both policy-making and administrative functions are shared by Federal, State, and local governments. Grodzins went further, declaring that the marble-cake analogy was applicable no less to American federalism in the 19th century than it is today. "There has in fact never been a time," he wrote, "when Federal, State, and local functions were separate and distinct. Government does more things in 1963 than it did in 1790 or 1861; but in terms of what government did, there was as much sharing then as today."[4]

This historical construct has enormous potential in terms of its political impact. For it lends the weight of historical authority and precedent to the *status quo,* or indeed to any centralization of power that is accompanied by arrangements for the sharing of administrative functions. It has the further advantage of discrediting those who might fear centralization because they attribute the historic strength of representative government in America to the tradition of dual federalism. "One cannot hark back to the good old days of State and local independence," Grodzins declared, "because those days never existed." This refrain was echoed, with good political effect, by Lyndon Johnson during his 1964 Presidential campaign. . . .

Grodzins himself provided little evidence on which to judge his version of historic federalism. He asserted, *ex cathedra,* that "whatever was at the focus of State attention in the 19th century became the recipient of national grants" in the form of cash aid, land grants, or loans of technical personnel. To support such contentions, Grodzins relied heavily on the historical research of his student Daniel Elazar. Elazar in turn has asserted (1) that when government assumed responsibility in specific functional fields, government at all levels "acted in concert"; and (2) that "Federal funds provided the stimulus for new programs throughout the nineteenth century." In his research, he has found that "virtually every domestic governmental program involved intergovernmental cooperation in some form."[5]

There are three main flaws in the Grodzins-Elazar construct. First, it does not cover systematically the whole spectrum of State policy concerns and administrative activities to prove the contention that "whatever was at the focus of State attention" received Federal aid. The Grodzins-Elazar argument can be upheld, in short, only if one accepts a tautological definition of "the focus of State attention";

those programs which *did* receive Federal aid must be viewed as at "the focus."[6]

Second, Grodzins and Elazar do not establish plausible criteria as to what was trivial and what important in the field of "intergovernmental cooperation." Thus they treat the most superficial administrative contacts (for example, State libraries' exchange of legal volumes with Federal agencies, or loan of surveying instruments to the States by the U.S. Coast Survey) as evidence of viable cooperation.[7]

Finally, and most centrally, they do not consider the basic issue of power as it was distributed relatively among levels of government. Indeed, they do not even consider power as it was exercised at different levels in the few State programs that *were* aided with Federal grants of cash, personnel, or land.

The question of Federal cash grants in the 19th century can be disposed of readily: they were of negligible importance by any quantitative measure.[8] The first cash-grant program on a continuing basis, aside from cash aid for maintaining pensioned Civil War veterans in State homes, came in 1887, when the Hatch Act provided $15,000 per year to the States in aid of agricultural research. As late as 1902, less than one per cent of all State and local revenues came from the central government, by contrast with perhaps 20 per cent in 1934 and 14 per cent in 1963. Obviously there was *not* "as much sharing then as today," measured either by the relative magnitude of Federal grants in total State-local financing or by the proportion of State-local policy concerns affected by Federal cash aid. Loans of Federal technical personnel were even less important, comprising mainly the services of the Army Engineers for the brief period 1824 to 1838.[9]

The Federal land grants to the States comprise the only substantial evidence for the Grodzins-Elazar historical construct. These grants were mainly for two purposes: education and transportation.[10] In the field of education, there were two land-grant programs of importance, the cession of portions of the Federal land in public land States of the West for support of common schools; and the Morrill-Act cessions of 1862, granting scrip receivable for public lands to the States in proportion to their population, for support of agricultural and mechanical colleges.

Neither program, however, comprised genuine sharing comparable to that which characterizes the modern grant-in-aid programs—for neither significantly narrowed the range of policy-making discretion enjoyed by the States. In common education, the States continued to have exclusive control over professional and certification standards, over determination of levels of total support, over curriculum structure and content, and the like. There was no matching formula operative; there were no administrative contacts with agencies of the Federal government charged with policy or administrative functions (the U.S. Office of Education was not even established until 1867); and there was no auditing nor inspection by Federal officials.[11]

Federal grants for transportation offer somewhat more persuasive evidence of genuine "sharing" of 19th century policy-making functions. The grants to the States and to private railroad companies did affect vitally the pace and location of new transport construction. However, supportive and subsidy activity was only one aspect of policy-making in this field. Equally important was regulation of rates and operating practices on the lines of transport. One cannot find government at all levels "acting in concert" (Elazar's phrase) in this policy area. It was the States alone that established basic corporation, property, taxation, and eminent-domain law under which transportation facilities were built, financed, and operated. From the 1830's on, the States had control over railroad charges; and the Granger laws of the 1870's had ample precedent in State regulatory legislation of the preceding decades.[12] Not until 1887, when it established the Interstate Commerce Commission, did Congress first assert its power in the regulatory field. The relative distribution of power over transport costs in the national economy cannot, moreover, be judged alone by reference to statutes and court decisions. For in their administrative operations, the States exercised real control over the ostensibly free internal-transport market. As owners and operators of basic lines of internal transport in the canal era, 1825–1850, the States blatantly evaded Constitutional limitations on their power to regulate interstate commerce. In every major canal State, the public authorities levied discriminatory tolls that favored their own producers at the expense of those located out of State. As a result, the State canal tolls until 1850 constituted a web of effective barriers to free internal trade.[13]

In sum, even if one takes into account the cash value of Federal land ceded to the States, the 19th-century Federal grants did not involve pervasive sharing of policy-making powers. Intergovernmental administrative contracts were casual at best: even in the major land-grant programs, the Federal administrative role was limited mainly to the bookkeeping operations of the General Land Office. It requires tortured semantics and neglect of the critical issue—relative power—to argue basic continuity in the history of the 19th- and 20th-century federalism on evidence such as Grodzins and Elazar have adduced. If this historical construct of cooperative federalism is fallacious, what, then, is the record?

The federal system may be rather understood as having gone through four major stages of power distribution. The basic pattern of intergovernmental relations has been redefined and reformulated in each of these stages—and the "creative federalism" advocated by President Johnson must be comprehended in a context of successive transformations rather than as a mere variant of a timeless theme.

[The author continues, offering a detailed summary of these historical developments. Scheiber's views on the stages of American federalism are most clearly stated in another article, from which the next seven paragraphs are excerpted.—Ed.]*

The first stage, the era of dual federalism and rivalistic state mercantilism, runs from 1789 to 1861. This is a period when the behavior of the federal system conformed closely to the juridical model of dual federalism. The Supreme Court generally supported dualism in the responsibilities of the central and state governments, and Congress refrained from making innovative policy in many areas formally opened to it by the Court. Moreover, the relatively decentralized character of the economy meant that the states' geographic jurisdiction was congruent with decentralized promotional and regulatory powers.

The second stage, 1861–1890, was one of transitional centralization. Amendment of the Constitution, together with vast expansion of the policy responsibilities of the national government and an increase in the jurisdiction of the federal courts, meant significant centralization of real power. In 1887 Congress undertook national regulation of the railroads, and three years later the Sherman Act marked the beginning of general business regulation. Meanwhile, the Supreme Court's activism was itself a centralizing force, albeit along lines that served to attenuate state initiatives or federal civil rights laws.[14]

The years 1890–1933 constitute the third stage, accelerating centralization. Successive federal laws advanced national regulation; World War I brought intensive, if temporary, centralization; and the Supreme Court continued to "censor" state legislation with a heavy hand. Modern grants-in-aid originated in this period, although on only a small scale.

---

*From "Federalism and Legal Process: Historical and Contemporary Analysis of the American System," *Law & Society Review* 14 (Spring 1980): 679–681. Reprinted by permission of the Law and Society Association.

A residue of dual federalism from the antebellum era was evident in the area of civil rights, as Southern blacks were left virtually helpless against private coercion, state action, and often terrifying violence; the states continued to have almost exclusive control over labor policy, and they have also retained control over such traditional areas as education, family law, and criminal law.

The New Deal inaugurated the fourth stage, which brought the well-known "Constitutional Revolution" and the transformation of the American political economy. Increases in both the extent and intensity of federal regulation, the establishment of regional planning in the Tennessee Valley, federalization of labor policy, the reorganization of agriculture as a managed sector, and expansion of welfare programs all combined with the adoption of Keynesian fiscal policy and contemporary income and estate taxation policy. It was in this broad context of quick and intensive centralization that Cooperative Federalism emerged as a style or technique of intergovernmental relations.

The fifth phase is the post–World War II era, in which modern centralized government spawned the Creative Federalism of Johnson and the New Federalism of Nixon and Ford while the Warren Court validated enormous extensions of national power in the fields of race relations, criminal justice, and structural reform. Many areas of policy for which state and local government were responsible before 1933 have now become strongly centralized.

Again recognition must be given to vestiges of dual federalism, both in the law and in the dynamics of politics. Thus there is continuing rivalry among the states in the competition for industrial development; there is regional division on some major issues; and the Supreme Court has made some cracks even in the monolithic powers derived from the Commerce Clause (*National League of Cities v. Usery* 426 U.S. 833, 1976). As Lowi has written, however, the system is now a "modern, positive national state," if also "the youngest consolidated national government," among the large modern nation-states.[15]

[Here Scheiber's Senate subcommittee study resumes.—Ed.]

... This retrospective view suggests, first, a warning that behind us is no homogeneous history of cooperative federalism. . . . It may be comforting to assume that cooperative federalism dates from 1790, just as it is comforting to assume that the real power of State-local government has recently grown more rapidly than the Federal Government's, or that issues of relative power are now irrelevant. But such assumptions will foreclose meaningful discussion of how shifts in power distribution (which are not automatically negated by mere administrative sharing) will in the future affect the federal system and the welfare of the Nation. . . .

James Madison wrote in 1787:

> Conceiving that an individual independence of the States is utterly irreconcilable with their aggregate sovereignty, and that a consolidation of the whole into one simple republic would be as inexpedient as it is unattainable, I have sought for a middle ground which may at once support a due supremacy of the national authority, and not exclude the local authorities wherever they can be subordinately useful.[16]

We might do well to recall that purpose. . . .

Notes

The author acknowledges with thanks the support of the Public Affairs Center of Dartmouth College during [the] course of research for this study. Prof. Frank Smallwood contributed invaluable criticism and generously shared his own ideas with the author during each stage of the work. Prof. Gene M. Lyons, director of the Public Affairs Center, offered suggestions and criticism, and also a forum: for the paper was first read at the Orvil E. Dryfoos Conference on Public Affairs, Dartmouth College, Hanover, New Hampshire, May 21, 1966. Professors James A. Maxwell of Clark University, Roger H. Brown of American University, and Henry W. Ehrmann of Dartmouth also provided helpful suggestions and criticism.

1. Edward S. Corwin, "The Passing of Dual Federalism," in R. G. McCloskey, ed., *Essays in Constitutional Law* (New York, 1957), p. 205.
2. Morton Grodzins, "Centralization and Decentralization," in R. A. Goldwin, ed., *A Nation of States* (Chicago, 1963), p. 7.
3. For example, in a recent symposium on "Intergovernmental Relations in the U.S.," *Annals*, Vol. 359 (May 1965), many of the contributors quote Grodzins approvingly on the alleged historical continuity of American federalism.
4. Grodzins in *Nation of States*, pp. 3–4, 7.
5. Grodzins, "The Federal System," *Goals for Americans* (President's Commission on National Goals, New York, 1960), p. 270; Elazar in *Annals*, Vol. 359, p. 11; Elazar, *The American Partnership* (Chicago, 1962), p. 338.
6. For a decisive argument supporting the alternative view that power distribution in the American federal system changed markedly over the 19th century, cf. William H. Riker, *Federalism* (Boston, 1964), esp. p. 83.
7. Elazar, *Amer. Part.*, passim.
8. Up to 1860, only $42 million in cash was granted by the Federal Government to the States and localities, of which two-thirds comprised the 1837 distribution of the Treasury surplus, a one-time, unique effort. (This was in addition to Federal

assumption of State debts in 1790.) Paul B. Trescott, "The U.S. Government and National Income, 1790–1860," in National Bureau of Economic Research, *Trends in the American Economy in the 19th Century* (Princeton, 1960), pp. 337–61. Elazar's own analysis of Minnesota State finance, 1860–1900, supports my contentions. Federal cash payments constituted one-third total State receipts in 1863, a unique instance; all other years computed show Federal payments as 1 to 2 per cent of receipts at most (*Amer. Part.*, p. 280).

9. Forest Hill, *Roads, Rails, and Waterways: The Army Engineers and Early Transportation* (Norman, Okla., 1957).

10. Minor programs of aid—measured in terms of personnel and/or funds involved— many of them dating only from the 1890's, are given in Elazar, *Amer. Part.*, pp. 302–303n. Both Grodzins and Elazar treat "19th century origins" of intergovernmental programs in a loose temporal framework, often emphasizing the significance of Federal grants that originated only in the nineties. This, together with their emphases on trivial data (measured in terms of policy-making powers actually shared or in terms of cash magnitudes involved), is distortive, I think, of the actual evolution of techniques and principles at issue.

11. Harry Kursh, *The Office & Education* (Phila., 1965). Elazar views post 1900 changes as mere "routinization of sharing procedures" (*Amer. Part.*, p. 337). As will become evident, I consider the changes so designated as far more substantive and important in terms of power relationships than Elazar suggests.

12. On early regulation, see Robert S. Hunt, *Law and Locomotives* (Madison, 1958), a study of Wisconsin, and similar studies for other states; also, Frederick Merk, "Eastern Antecedents of the Grangers," *Agric. Hist.*, 23:1–8 (1949).

13. H. Scheiber, "Rate-Making Power of the State in the Canal Era," *Political Sci. Quar.*, 77:597–413 (1962).

14. Laurence Tribe, *American Constitutional Law* (Mineola, N.Y., 1978), p. 5; Harry N. Scheiber, "Federalism and the American Economic Order, 1789–1910," *Law and Society Review*, 10:100–118 (1975).

15. Theodore Lowi and Alan Stone (eds.), *Nationalizing Government: Public Policies in America* (Beverly Hills, Calif., 1978), p. 25.

16. James Madison, *The Forging of American Federalism*, ed. S. K. Padover (Torchbook edn., N.Y., 1965), p. 184 (letter to Geo. Washington, April 16, 1787).

5

Models of National, State, and Local Relationships

Deil S. Wright

...We can now formulate some simplified models of IGR [intergovernmental relations]. Figure 5-1 represents visually three models of authority relationships among national, state, and local jurisdictions in the United States. These models, like most simple models, fall far short of displaying the complexities and realities of governance in several respects, for example, numbers and types of entities, numbers and variations in personnel, different types of programs and functions, varying fiscal resources, and so on. The models depict three generic types of authority: coordinate authority (autonomy), dominant or inclusive authority (hierarchy), and equal or overlapping authority (bargaining). Despite its simplicity, each model, by concentrating on the essential features of a possible IGR arrangement, guides us in formulating hypotheses. (No two models, of course, generate identical sets of hypotheses.) By testing these hypotheses, we can discover which model best fits the U.S. political system as it operates today.[1]

Coordinate-Authority Model

In the coordinate-authority model of IGR sharp, distinct boundaries separate the national government and state governments. Local units, however, are included within and are dependent on state governments. The most classic expression of state-local relations is Dillon's Rule, named after the Iowa judge who asserted it in the 1860s, which summarizes the power relationships between the states and their localities:

From *Understanding Intergovernmental Relations,* 3rd edition, by Wright. Copyright © 1988. Reprinted with permission of Wadsworth, a division of Thomson Learning: www.thomsonrights.com. Fax 800 730-2215.

FIGURE 5-1   Three Models of Intergovernmental Relations in the United States

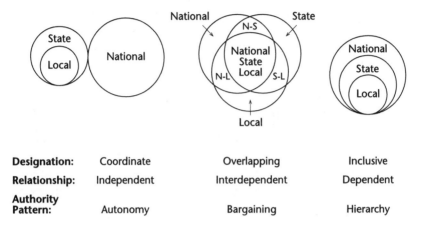

Designation:	Coordinate	Overlapping	Inclusive
Relationship:	Independent	Interdependent	Dependent
Authority Pattern:	Autonomy	Bargaining	Hierarchy

1. There is no common-law right of self-government.
2. Local entities are creatures of the state, subject to creation and abolition at the unfettered discretion of the state (barring constitutional limitations).
3. Localities may exercise only those powers expressly granted.
4. Localities are "mere tenants at the will of the legislature." [2]

For more than a century Dillon's Rule has been a nationwide guidepost in legal and constitutional relations between the states and their local governments. Hidden behind its seeming simplicity is a central issue in IGR and in the models of figure 5-1: Who should govern? This fundamental philosophical question clearly cannot be answered by the model, nor has Dillon's Rule succeeded in resolving it. But the model has helped frame a significant question, and that is one positive result from constructing models.

What does the coordinate-authority model imply concerning national-state power relationships? It implies, again, that the two types of entities are independent and autonomous; they are linked only tangentially. This model received implicit endorsement in the 1880s from Lord Bryce, an eminent Briton who visited the United States and observed its political system.... Bryce's analogy was drawn from observation and experience, but he could have cited an 1871 U.S. Supreme Court decision for a stamp of approval. In *Tarbel's Case* the Court stated:

There are within the territorial limits of each state two governments, restricted in their sphere of action, but independent of each
other, and supreme within their respective spheres. Each has its separate departments, each has its distinct laws, and each has its own
tribunals for their enforcement. Neither government can intrude
within the jurisdiction of the other or authorize any interference
therein by its judicial offices with the action of the other.[3]

Both an impartial foreign observer and the institution charged with
interpreting the Constitution agreed, then, that *each* of the two units—the
national and the state—governs within its respective sphere of authority.

What happened when the respective spheres of authority put the
national government and a state in conflict, when they ceased to be tan-
gential and clashed directly? The result is well known to students of
U.S. federalism. The Supreme Court became the arbiter of national-
state relations.[4] For several decades the Supreme Court, operating on
the premise of the coordinate-authority model, attempted to set distinct, insulated spheres of national and state powers. But Court decisions in the 1930s necessitated substantial rethinking of how this model
did (or did not) describe the operation of the U.S. political system.

Two scholars, Morton Grodzins and Daniel Elazar, extensively
explored the coordinate-authority model and found it woefully wanting,
not simply for the present and recent past but for the nineteenth century as well.[5] ... Indeed, many students of constitutional law and history
look back at Supreme Court decisions from the 1860s to the 1930s and
loudly applaud the discrediting of the so-called dual federalism (or what
we are calling the coordinate-authority) model. Many U.S. and state
courts seemed determined to impose that model on a growing industrial society of increasingly complex and interdependent units.

IGR model builders are probably in near-unanimous agreement
that the coordinate-authority model is obsolete, addressed as it is to
nonexistent social and political conditions. Before dispatching the
model to oblivion, however, consider the Supreme Court decision of
June 24, 1976. In *National League of Cities v. Usery* the Court, in sweeping language, ruled that Congress did not have the authority to require
that either the states or their local governments observe minimum-
wage and maximum-hour laws. In a 5–4 decision declaring unconstitutional a 1974 federal law extending wage-and-hour requirements to
state and city employees, the Court said the legislation violated the
"attributes of sovereignty attaching to every state government which
may not be impaired by Congress." [6] The Court concluded:

Congress has sought to wield its power in a fashion that would impair the States' ability to function effectively in a federal system.... We hold that insofar as the challenged amendments operate to directly displace the States' freedom to structure integral operations in areas of traditional governmental functions, they are not within the authority granted Congress [by the commerce clause].[7]

The decision in the *Usery* case was widely hailed as a significant revival of state-local prerogatives and protection based on three elements of judicial reasoning in the majority opinion by Justice [William] Rehnquist. First, it reasserted the relevance of the Tenth Amendment in guarding state (and local) interests from the otherwise unrestrained exercise of national (congressional) power, in some respects like the First Amendment guarantees to protect individual rights. Second, it defined those Tenth Amendment limitations based on state and local governments' "integral operations" in activities that involved "traditional functions." Third, the Court looked carefully at the 1974 amendments to the Fair Labor Standards Act involving minimum wages and extra payment for overtime hours worked by municipal employees, for example, police officers, firefighters. The majority found these "integral" and "traditional" activities were impaired by the congressional statute based on the commerce clause. The legislation, according to the Court, resulted in an unconstitutional infringement on state-local legislative options to control and direct governmental operations.

The legal legacy of the *Usery* case...cannot and need not be reviewed. Suffice it to say that hopes for a continued and even expanded judicial endorsement of the coordinate-authority model failed to materialize. Indeed, the trend in case law went in the opposite direction, culminating in 1985 in an explicit overruling of the *Usery* opinion in *Garcia v. San Antonio Metropolitan Transportation Authority*. In this 5–4 decision, delivered by Justice Harry Blackmun, the Court majority rejected "as unsound in principle and unworkable in practice, a rule of state immunity from federal regulation that turns on a judicial appraisal of whether a particular governmental function is 'integral' or 'traditional'."[8]

One effect of the *Garcia* determination, according to the language of the opinion, is a withdrawal of the Court from a role in defining the authority of, or jurisdictional boundaries between, the national and state governments—as the coordinate-authority model implies. On this point the Court majority was explicit about how state (or local) interests may be protected. "State sovereign interests...are more properly protected by procedural safeguards inherent in the structure of the federal system than by judicially created limitations on federal power." [9] In other words, the Court said in *Garcia* that effective restraints on Congress's use of the commerce power could and should be achieved through political rather than judicial processes.

The *Garcia* decision set alarm bells ringing in state and local personnel offices and in legislative chambers across the nation. Compliance costs, particularly for overtime pay (above forty hours) involving public-safety personnel, were variously estimated at $2–4 billion. Congress, under pressure from state and local officials, enacted legislation in 1985 that clarified and eased implementation of the Court decision. Passage of the legislation, some argued, confirmed that the Court majority assessment that federalism hinges on the political process was an astute conclusion. Others, particularly dissenting Justices Lewis Powell and Sandra Day O'Connor, challenged the majority's view.

> JUSTICE POWELL: The State's role in our system of government is a matter of constitutional law, not of legislative grace.
>
> Despite some genuflecting in the Court's opinion to the concept of federalism, today's decision effectively reduces the Tenth Amendment to meaningless rhetoric when Congress acts pursuant to the Commerce Clause. [10]
>
> JUSTICE O'CONNOR: In my view, federalism cannot be reduced to the weak "essence" distilled by the majority today. [11]

Commentary on *Garcia*, pro and con, has been extensive, even voluminous, but the complexity and the merits of the views expressed are not directly pertinent to the main point we are discussing: the nature of the coordinate-authority model. The *Usery* case suggested that this model of national-state-local relationships persisted in the attitudes and actions of IGR participants until very recently. Furthermore, the model was rejected by the Supreme Court with only the slimmest majority. Changes in Court composition or in legal philosophy could renew the relevance of this model.

Inclusive-Authority Model

The inclusive-authority model is represented in figure 5-1 by concentric circles diminishing in size from national to state to local. Let us suppose that the area covered by each circle represents the proportion of power exercised by that jurisdiction with respect to the others. Suppose also that the national government wants to expand its proportion of power in relation to states and localities. Two strategies are possible. One reduces the various powers of either the states or localities or both; the other enlarges the national government's circle with or without enlarging the state and/or local circles. For obvious reasons this second strategy is often called "enlarging the pie."

Both strategies can be understood by means of game theory: a systematic way of studying behavior in decision-making situations. The theory assumes that all participants strive to optimize their behavior, each trying to maximize gains and minimize losses within the limits of allowed behavior (hence the analogy with games). The outcomes depend not only on the behavior of any one participant but on the responses of other participants as well.

The first strategy above, Type I, is the classic case of a three-person, zero-sum game, like poker. The sum of the players' winnings equals the sum of their losses. An illustration of this in the IGR context occurs in the *Usery* and *Garcia* cases on the legislation requiring state and local units to meet minimum-wage and maximum-hour requirements. The national government exercised (expanded) its power at the expense of state and local powers. The gain in national power equaled the power lost by state and local units. The Supreme Court validation of the law required states and local governments to pay increased labor costs. Thus, national gains equaled state and local losses.

In game theory the second strategy above, Type II, or "enlarging the pie," is called a non-constant-sum game. All participants in this type of game can "win" or make gains. Perhaps the best IGR illustration of the Type II non-constant-sum strategy is fiscal: the conditional grant-in-aid. The national sector can expand by raising more money to offer as grants to states and localities. The funds can be offered with conditions ("losses") imposed on the recipients, but the benefits ("winnings") are so attractive that they appear to outweigh the attached constraints. From these examples of the two strategies we would expect national IGR policies to lean far more toward Type II strategies (such as grants-in-aid) than toward Type I.

Type II strategies assume, however, that the total resources ("winnings") *can* be expanded. That assumption is less likely in a period of fiscal and other resource constraints similar to that experienced since 1978 and predicted for the late 1980s and 1990s. Indeed, the phrases "cutback management" and "doing more with less" have become common partially as a result of Proposition 13 "fever," federal aid cutbacks, and the size of the federal deficit. It would not be surprising, then, to see more movement from Type II to Type I strategies in national-state-local relationships. Examples of zero-sum or polarized IGR relationships seem likely to persist and perhaps increase in fields such as energy, environment, and social regulatory arenas. More specific illustrations include nuclear waste storage, hazardous waste siting, abortion, drinking age, and school prayer issues.

The inclusive-authority model serves uses other than allowing predictions of IGR policies. It also conveys the essential hierarchical nature of authority. The dependency relationships imply power patterns that are similar to Dillon's Rule for state-local relations, that is, states and localities would be mere minions of the national government with insignificant or incidental impact on U.S. politics and public policy. To the question of who governs, this model provides an unequivocal answer: the national government.

How well (and in what areas) does the inclusive-authority model describe the realities of present-day U.S. politics, policy, and administration? Curiously enough, conservative and liberal observers alike see this model dominant in many aspects of our public life. Barry Goldwater, Reagan, and other conservatives [saw] a powerful federal engine rolling over weakened and supine states and localities.

On the liberal side Senator Joseph Clark, as early as 1960, saw with approval the inception of a "national federalism": the national government not only was in charge (according to Clark) but *should* be in charge.[12] A more extensive and thoughtful elaboration of the same idea appeared in practitioner-scholar James Sundquist's *Making Federalism Work*.[13] Writing in 1969, in the wake of the Great Society programs, Sundquist highlighted the following:

1. "The nation for decades has been steadily coalescing into a national society" (p. 10).
2. "The Great Society was, by definition, one society; the phrase was singular, not plural" (p. 12).
3. There was "centralization of objective-setting" (p. 13).
4. "Somewhere in the Executive Office must be centered a concern for the structure of federalism—a responsibility for guiding the evolution of the whole system of federal-state-local relations, viewed for the first time as a *single* system" (p. 246).

Sundquist left little doubt that the national government should be in charge, but he was not convinced that it controlled a single, hierarchical system.

Other observers, especially those who have focused on the capabilities or incapacities of the states, have also concluded that the states and their localities are governing entities in name only; hence, the choice of the term *nominal* or *centralized federalism*. This conclusion has been reached by four approaches.

One approach, the power-elite perspective, sees the ship of state guided by a select and cohesive corps of national leaders at the helm. State and local governments and their political leaders are carried along like barnacles on a hull.[14] They are insignificant and powerless to affect important political or societal choices. The most recent (fourth) edition of *Who's Running America* completely omits any state or local officials as part of an elite 6,000–7,000 persons who guide the nation.[15]

A second approach, the technocratic-pluralist position, identifies the dispersal of decision-making power into quasi-public or even private economic fiefdoms that are national in scope. The states or other entities, singularly or collectively, cannot counteract these powerful private-interest groups. This approach argues, for example, that organized medicine and the health industry control the health of the nation despite the "policy power" of the states to control the health, welfare, morals, and safety of their citizens.[16]

A third approach, which might be called economic federalism, has some views in common with the power-elite and technocratic-pluralist points of view. This facet of the inclusive model can be summarized by excerpts from an extensive 1958 essay on the subject by Arthur S. Miller.

> I do not mean to focus upon the administrative agency, but upon the recipient of economic power—the large corporate enterprise or factory community—probably the most important of the groups in American society. These are the functional units of economic federalism and the basic units of a system of private governments. ... It takes no fanciful mental gymnastics to say that the factory community operates as the recipient of delegated power to carry out important societal functions. It is the economic counterpart—and superior, be it said—of the unit of political federalism, the forty-eight state governments. It is the basic unit of functional federalism. It is a private governmental system, performing some of the jobs of government.[17]

A fourth approach to the conclusion that states and localities enjoy only a nominal existence is the administrative orientation. The states, it is argued, are little more than administrative districts of the national government, making state governors, in effect, "chief federal systems officers." . . . In the early 1950s L. D. White, in "The March of Power to Washington," wrote that the states were then well on the way to becoming hollow shells.[18] By the late 1950s Miller reported the district concept as an established fact.

> So far as the traditional federal system is concerned, the implications of this change are clear. Chief among them is that, to a large extent, states today operate not as practically autonomous units, but as administrative districts for centrally established policies. It is doubtless inaccurate to think of them as hollow political shells, but it does seem to be true that the once-powerful state governments have been bypassed by the movement of history. Save for "housekeeping" duties, they have little concern with the main flow of important decisions. When new problems arise, eyes swivel to Washington, not to the state capitol—where eyes also turn to the banks of the Potomac.[19]

The administrative district charge was vigorously challenged by William Anderson on the basis of his and his associates' empirical investigations in the 1940s and 1950s. Specifically addressing the grant-in-aid issue, Anderson contended that the states gained as much as the national government from the fund transfer.

> In short, as administrators of federal programs under grants-in-aid the state governments have acquired something in the nature of an added check upon the national administration. Political power, like electricity, does not all run in one direction.[20]

Whatever the past state of affairs in IGR, another writer, Ferdinand Lundberg, predicts a fully fused and centralized system in the twenty-first century. He contends that all state and local governments will be operated from a U.S. version of the United Kingdom's Home Office, such as a department of internal affairs. More specifically, he foresees:

> City managers and state executives will probably be appointed or declared eligible from civil service lists by the national government, although there may still be vestigial elections of purely symbolic governors, mayors, and town councilmen.
>
> Each of the present American states, it seems evident, is destined to become pretty much of an administrative department of the central government, just as counties and cities will be subdepartments.[21]

The hallmarks of the inclusive-authority model should now be clear. One is the premise that state and local governments depend totally on decisions that are nationwide in scope and arrived at by the national government, or by powerful economic interests, or by some combination of the two. A second premise is that non-national political institutions such as governors, state legislators, and mayors have approached a condition of nearly total atrophy. A third premise is that the functions formerly performed by these now-vestigial organs have been fused into a centralized, hierarchical system.

To what degree or extent is the hierarchical, inclusive-authority model present in the United States today? We cannot say with certainty because our measures of power relationships are poorly calibrated, and the immense body of data required to arrive at such a global conclusion is simply not available. There has been movement toward this model through court decisions, congressional statutes, and administrative regulations. . . .

[Wright then presents three cases. The first shows how the national government can acquire leverage via the "strings" on grants-in-aid. The second describes how the U.S. Department of Justice and federal courts intervened to regulate whether San Antonio, Texas, could annex some adjoining territory, the national concern being the effect the annexation decision had on political representation of Hispanics. The third case suggests that the U.S. Supreme Court has upheld the use of national legislation to require that states use certain criteria and procedures in setting rates for electricity generation and distribution.—Ed.]

Do these three examples confirm that the inclusive-authority model best summarizes the contemporary state of IGR in the United States? Despite their close approximation of the hierarchical model, we think that these examples are not fully representative of the broad spectrum and dominant pattern of IGR in the United States. Instead, we look to a third model.

Overlapping-Authority Model

The inclusive-authority and coordinate-authority models of IGR are at opposite ends of a spectrum. In the first, hierarchy prevails; in the second, the national and state governments are equal and autonomous. The past, present, or future applicability of either model for IGR in the United States has been sharply challenged. Although there are occasional instances of such hierarchical and autonomous IGR patterns, the weight of academic research suggests that these two models inadequately and inaccurately describe how the bulk of governmental operations are conducted in the United States.

The third and most representative model of IGR practice is the overlapping-authority model (see figure 5-1). The overlay among the circles conveys three characteristic features of the model:

1. Substantial areas of governmental operations involve national, state, and local units (or officials) simultaneously.
2. The areas of autonomy or single-jurisdiction independence and full discretion are comparatively small.
3. The power and influence available to any one jurisdiction (or official) is significantly limited. The limits produce an authority pattern best described as bargaining.

Bargaining is used in the common dictionary sense of "negotiating the terms of a sale, exchange, or agreement." Wide areas of IGR involve exchanges or agreements. For example, the national government offers scores of assistance programs to states and localities in *exchange* for their *agreement* to implement a program, carry out a project, or pursue any one of a wide variety of activities. Of course, as part of the bargain the recipient of assistance must usually agree to conditions such as the providing of matching funds and the satisfaction of accounting, reporting, auditing, and performance requirements.

[Wright then presents several illustrations of bargaining and exchange in intergovernmental relations. These are "aimed at illustrating several of the combinations and permutations of interjurisdictional connections": city annexation of county territory in Virginia, an example of local-local mediation; the use of the negotiated investment strategy to allocate more than $30 million in Social Service Block Grant funds in Connecticut, a case of state-local interaction; the Annual Arrangements and the Urban Development Action Grants processes used by the U.S. Department of Housing and Urban Development in the early 1970s and the mid 1980s, respectively, instances of local-national bargaining; and the first-term Reagan administration's unsuccessful effort to achieve "decongestion," or a sorting out of functional responsibilities by level of government, a case of national-state relations.—Ed.]

The prospects as well as the problems involving intergovernmental change seem sharply and clearly exposed when looked at from a bargaining-negotiation standpoint. It is as if we are looking at fundamental cell structures, like the DNA double helix, under a microscope when we look at IGR from the perspective of this model. A recent book, *Successful Negotiating in Local Government*, captured the essence of this approach to IGR.

> Past efforts to reform the intergovernmental system have been repeatedly hampered by the reformer's inability to appreciate the fact that while there is cooperation within the system, there is also competition, conflict, and even coercion among the various governmental levels. And while negotiations among government agencies are not uncommon, parties often come to and leave the negotiations with very different objectives. Thus, there is an obvious need for a process that facilitates recognition of the complex nature of intergovernmental relations and allows for developing a core of common objectives.[22]

It is appropriate in drawing this discussion to a close to highlight the chief characteristics of the overlapping-authority model. These are:

- limited and dispersed power
- modest and uncertain areas of autonomy
- high degree of potential or actual interdependence
- simultaneous competition and cooperation
- bargaining-exchange relationships
- negotiation as a strategy for reaching agreement

The analysis and interpretation of the overlapping-authority model, as approached here, have a clear bias in the direction of cooperation and negotiated settlement. An alternative overlapping authority model could also be applied from a competitive, quasi-market, public-choice approach. That is, the presence of multiple entities (and actors) operating as providers (and consumers) of public services could function more like an economic market as the basis for exchange relationships.

Numerous examples of market-type models could be cited. Only a generalized description of one approach is provided. An early (1961) formulation of this line of analysis was by Ostrom, Tiebout, and Warren; they argued that metropolitan areas, such as Los Angeles, were polycentric political systems.[23] The production and provision of public goods could be viewed as public service industries in which different cities, counties, and special districts (as well as the state and national governments) offered different "packages" of service levels to citizen-consumers. This public-choice view of the overlapping model was further elaborated by Bish and Ostrom.[24] One paragraph from their analysis captures the themes of this alternative interpretation of the overlapping model.

Intergovernmental relationships are especially important in a public economy composed of a multiplicity of overlapping governmental jurisdictions. Tax competition and coordination, fiscal transfers, and service contracts can facilitate mutually productive intergovernmental cooperation. Courts, legislatures, and informal arrangements are also available for the resolution of intergovernmental conflicts. Multiple agencies serving the same people with different bundles of public goods and services can be viewed as multiple firms in *public service industries*. Constrained competition between multiple "firms" operating in different public service industries can create relatively efficient and responsive systems of government in metropolitan areas.[25]

There is a major difference between the negotiated-agreement approach to the overlapping model and this latter, public-choice approach. The difference centers on the degree to which there is, can be, and should be a common interest served in spite of the conflicting and even chaotic character of IGR conditions. The public-choice approach is much less inclined to see, expect, and promote a basic aim or shared aims in an IGR situation.

Notes

1. The models discussed in this section have been used in two sharply contrasting investigations. One deals with the perceptions of state legislators about responsibilities for various functions: Robert D. Thomas, "Florida Legislator Attitudes toward Inter-Jurisdictional Policy Responsibilities," *Publius: The Journal of Federalism* 9 (Summer 1979): 119–33. The second uses the models to examine the changing nature of authority patterns within the Democratic and Republican parties: Gary D. Wekkin, "Political Parties and Intergovernmental Relations in 1984: The Consequences of Party Renewal for Territorial Constituencies," *Publius: The Journal of Federalism* 15 (Summer 1985): 19–38. For a contrasting urban focused policy approach to intergovernmental policy implementation, see Paul E. Peterson, *City Limits* (Chicago: University of Chicago Press, 1981), 268 pp.

2. *City of Clinton v. Cedar Rapids and Missouri River Railroad,* 24 Iowa 455 (1868). For a recent analysis of Dillon's Rule from a policy orientation, see John G. Grumm and Russell D. Murphy, "Dillon's Rule Reconsidered," *The Annals* 416 (November 1974): 120–32.

3. *Tarbel's Case,* 13 Wall. 397 (1872).

4. John R. Schmidhauser, *The Supreme Court as Final Arbiter in Federal-State Relations, 1789–1957* (Chapel Hill: University of North Carolina Press, 1958).

5. [Morton] Grodzins, *The American System: A New View of Governments in the United States,* Daniel J. Elazar, ed. (Chicago: Rand McNally, 1966); Elazar, *The American Partnership: Intergovernmental Cooperation in the Nineteenth-Century United States* (Chicago: University of Chicago Press, 1962).

6. *National League of Cities v. Usery,* 426 U.S. 833 (1976), at 845. See also *Wall Street Journal,* 25 June 1976, p. 1.

7. 426 U.S. 852.

8. 469 U.S. 546 (1985).

9. Ibid., at 552.

10. Ibid., at 560, 567.

11. Ibid., at 580.

12. Joseph Clark, "Toward National Federalism," in *The Federal Government and the Cities: A Symposium* (Washington, D.C.: George Washington University, 1961), pp. 39–49.

13. James L. Sundquist, with David W. Davis, *Making Federalism Work* (Washington, D.C.: Brookings Institution, 1969).

14. C. Wright Mills, *The Power Elite* (New York: Oxford University Press, 1956); G. William Domhoff, *Who Rules America?* (Englewood Cliffs, N.J.: Prentice-Hall, 1967); G. William Domhoff, *The Higher Circles: The Governing Class in America* (New York: Random House, Vintage, 1970).

15. Thomas R. Dye, *Who's Running America? The Conservative Years,* 4th ed. (Englewood Cliffs, N.J.: Prentice-Hall, 1986).

16. Grant McConnell, *Private Power and American Democracy* (New York: Knopf, 1966), especially pp. 166–95; Theodore J. Lowi, *The End of Liberalism: Ideology, Policy, and the Crisis of Public Authority* (New York: Norton, 1969).

17. Arthur S. Miller, "The Constitutional Law of the 'Security State'," *Stanford Law Review* 10 (July 1958): 620, 629, 634, 637 (footnotes omitted). Copyright 1958 by the Board of Trustees of the Leland Stanford Junior University.

18. Leonard D. White, *The States and the Nation* (Baton Rouge: Louisiana State University Press, 1963), p. 3.

19. Miller, "The Constitutional Law of the 'Security State'," p. 629.

20. William Anderson, *The Nation and the States, Rivals or Partners?* (Minneapolis: University of Minnesota Press, 1955), p. 204.

21. Ferdinand Lundberg, *The Coming World Transformation* (Garden City, N.Y.: Doubleday, 1963), p. 18.

22. Christine Carlson, "Negotiated Investment Strategy: Mediating Intergovernmental Conflict," in *Successful Negotiating in Local Government, National Forum: The Phi Kappa Phi Journal* 63, no. 4 (Fall 1983), 2829.

23. Vincent Ostrom, Charles M. Tiebout, and Robert Warren, "The Organization of Government in Metropolitan Areas: A Theoretical Inquiry," *American Political Science Review* 55 (December 1961): 831–42. See also Robert Warren, "A Municipal Services Model of Metropolitan Organization," *American Institute of Planners Journal* 30 (August 1964): 193–204.

24. Robert L. Bish and Vincent Ostrom, *Understanding Urban Government: Metropolitan Reform Reconsidered* (Washington, D.C.: American Enterprise Institute, 1973), 111 pp.

25. Ibid., pp. 1–2.

6

The Paradox of the Middle Tier

Martha Derthick

State administrators—particularly good state administrators and good governors and people who want to do things well—feel that they are on the receiving end of a very, very long pipeline that has no feedback loops whatever; that there is no way in which Washington understands what they need; that there is no way in which Washington is systematically learning from them and from the serendipitous way . . . things happen.

This comment comes from a veteran student of federalism and social welfare policy, Forrest Chisman.[1] I will assume that the Washington of which he speaks—the Washington that is so oblivious to the states—is primarily Congress, or at least Congress in the first instance. Federal administrators would probably not be indifferent to the states if Congress instructed them not to be.

For Congress to be obtuse or indifferent to state governments is genuinely baffling. The Senate, after all, was constituted initially to represent the states as such, a fact still signified by their being represented in it equally, with two members each. The authors of *The Federalist* fully expected members of the national legislature to be highly localistic.

Madison wrote in *Federalist* No. 46—a paper devoted to explaining why the advantage in federal-state relations would lie with the states—that "the prepossessions, which the members themselves will carry into the federal government, will generally be favorable to the States. . . . A local spirit will infallibly prevail much more in the members of Congress, than a national spirit will prevail in the legislatures of the particular States."[2] At least when I was growing up, textbooks in American government routinely portrayed Congress as being highly

From *Keeping the Compound Republic*, by Martha Derthick, pp. 43–55. Copyright © 2001 by the Brookings Institution. Reprinted with permission of the Brookings Institution Press, Washington, DC.

sensitive to the interests of state and local governments. What has happened to change this?

The answer is not to be found simply in the attitudes or behavior of incumbent members of Congress or of the small army of ideologically charged, fresh-faced congressional staff who are innocent of the history of American federalism. More fundamentally, it lies in the place of the states in our complicated and ambiguous constitutional system.

Two facts are pertinent. First, within the federal system, the states have had a formal and chronological primacy. They were the first governments, and the mediums, therefore, for creating the national and local governments. This primacy was embedded in the original constitutional theory: the national government possessed only those limited powers granted by the people. All else remained with the states and the people. This is what the Tenth Amendment says. For a long time, Americans took it very seriously. Second, the states are inferior governments. That is what the supremacy clause says, and it is reinforced by an implicit constitutional principle of surpassing importance: the United States Supreme Court, a national institution, determines what the Constitution means.

Juxtaposed, these two facts appear somewhat paradoxical, and in this paradox lies the explanation for the states' predicament. On one hand, they are governments "on the rise," as much journalistic and academic punditry over the past decade would have it. Their responsibilities are large and, arguably, growing. On the other hand, they receive a stream of orders from Washington, as Chisman says, and as the state governments themselves constantly complain. How can they be reviving and falling under the federal yoke at the same time? I hope to provide a plausible, if partial, answer with an excursion into constitutional history.

The States in Constitutional History

State governments, emerging out of the colonial ones, were, as I have said, the first fully constituted governments on the American scene. Except for Connecticut and Rhode Island, which clung to colonial charters that had provided for an exceptional measure of self-government, all of them prepared constitutions after the Declaration of Independence and before the framing of the United States Constitution. As the first governments, they were at least the mediums and, arguably, the agents for creating other governments, national and local, that would soon surpass them in functional importance.

The national government fought wars, including a civil war, to secure its own existence, promoted economic development with tariffs, and represented the hope for fulfilling America's destiny as a great republic, exemplar to the world. Local governments, which were well established in the colonial period and given a great deal of freedom by state constitutional conventions, legislatures, and courts in the mid-nineteenth century, built and maintained roads, maintained public decency and order, provided relief to the poor, taught children, and raised taxes. In short, they did the things that connected people to the polity on a daily basis. The bedrock of American domestic government for a very long time was local. At the opening of the twentieth century, American local governments were raising more revenue and doing more spending than the federal and state governments combined. "As compared either with the federal government or with local authorities, the central governments of the states lack vitality," Woodrow Wilson wrote in his textbook, *The State*, in the late nineteenth century. "[They] do not seem to be holding their own in point of importance. They count for much in legislation, but, so far, for very little in administration." [3]

Historically, then, the states did not actually do very much. Having created a framework of law within which local governments functioned, they did not closely supervise its application. At the same time, with respect to what they and their local subdivisions did, the states enjoyed a great deal of autonomy. There prevailed the concept of separate and equal sovereigns, to which the late Edward S. Corwin, a distinguished constitutional scholar, gave the name "dual federalism." Corwin identified four operative constitutional postulates as the components of dual federalism: (1) the national government is one of enumerated powers only; (2) the purposes which it may constitutionally promote are few; (3) within their respective spheres, the two centers of government are "sovereign" and hence "equal"; and (4) the relation of the two centers to each other is one of tension rather than collaboration. [4]

The doctrine may be found in stark form in such decisions as *Collector v. Day*, in which the Supreme Court ruled in 1871 that the federal government could not tax the salary of a county judge because he was a state officer; the *Civil Rights Cases* in 1883, which struck down congressional enactments regulating private conduct because they invaded the domain of local jurisprudence; and *Hammer v. Dagenhart*, which ruled in 1918 that Congress could not forbid the shipment in interstate commerce of the products of child labor because to do so invaded state authority. Justice Day wrote in *Hammer v. Dagenhart* that "if Congress can thus regulate matters entrusted to local authority by prohibition of the movement of commodities in interstate commerce, all freedom of commerce will be at an end, and the power of the States over local matters may be eliminated, and thus our system of government be practically destroyed."[5] To put it mildly, such rulings have an antiquarian ring today.

Equally antiquated is the constitutional doctrine, associated with the Civil War–era case of *Kentucky v. Dennison,* that the federal government may not give commands to officers of the states. Consider the following observations of Henry M. Hart, late professor of constitutional law at Harvard, written in 1954:

> Federal law often says to the states, "Don't do any of these things," leaving outside the scope of its prohibition a wide range of alternative courses of action. But it is illuminating to observe how rarely it says, "Do this thing," leaving no choice but to go ahead and do it.

Hart goes on to elaborate his point and to cite Justice Taney in *Kentucky v. Dennison:*

> "And we think it clear," said Chief Justice Taney, ". . . that the Federal Government, under the Constitution, has no power to impose on a State officer, as such, any duty whatever, and compel him to perform it." Taney's statement can stand today, if we except from it certain primary duties of state judges and occasional remedial duties of other state officers.[6]

Taney's statement does not stand today. It is in ruins. Formally overruled by the Supreme Court in 1987, it had been rendered obsolete by congressional practice long before.[7]

The Transformation of American Federalism

Clearly, something drastic happened to American federalism. Several things, actually.

First, beginning in the late nineteenth century, the states slowly asserted themselves vis-à-vis local governments, taking over at first more supervision, and then more actual performance, of the bedrock domestic functions: road construction, relief for the poor, schooling, public safety, and tax collection.

The process was uneven and, not accidentally, was given impetus by federal grants-in-aid whose conditions fostered state-level centralization. By 1950, state spending surpassed local spending for highways and welfare, functions that, unlike schools and the police, received heavy federal funding. Local spending continues even now to exceed state spending for schools, but states nonetheless play a much expanded role through bigger, more active education agencies and judicial and legislative action addressed to finance. Overall, state-raised revenue began to exceed locally raised revenue in 1965—a critical date for American federalism—and the gap has steadily widened. Although local employment still far surpasses state employment, the gap between the two has sharply narrowed. In 1929, state governments had only 318,000 employees, compared with 2 million for localities. As of 1987, the states had 4 million compared with the localities' 10 million.

Second, great nationalizing surges destroyed the old constitutional doctrines. The milestones are well known: the Civil War and two world wars, the New Deal, the Great Society. Dual federalism fell, as did the precept that state officers were not subject to federal commands. The warfare and welfare states rose on a national scale to consume the bulk of public resources. The civil rights and environmental revolutions, also national, produced a mass of tangled, nuanced regulation that is one of the numerous battlegrounds fought over in the federal judiciary. Constitutional commands emanating from the courts, statutory commands emanating from Congress and reinforced by judicial interpretation, and regulations emanating from federal agencies flood the land, constraining virtually every state and local act.

Finally—and this concludes my excursion into history and returns to Chisman's point—in recent years the national government has seemed to approach the limits of its power and political will. This development is too recent to know whether it is temporary or enduring. To understand why it has happened, for a start one may speculate commonsensically that bigness and its by-products have brought their own costs.

The war power, which historically was very advantageous to the national government, eliciting vast amounts of revenue and popular support, ceased to be so with Vietnam. When war turned unpopular, it impaired the legitimacy of both the government and its chief executive, who was seduced by his exalted place in the warfare state into deeply damaging abuses of power. Americans generally have embraced the welfare state: they have proved to have an undisciplinable appetite for entitlements. Costs of the major welfare state programs, income support and health care, have proved very hard to contain or predict.

As the national government's debt grew in the late twentieth century and its capacity for direct action waned, federal officeholders began looking habitually to get help with governing, and to get it on the cheap. They did not lose the urge or political incentive to act, only the capacity to do so effectively, with adequate political, financial, and administrative foundations. Under these circumstances, they turned increasingly to the state governments because of the states' peculiar combination of strength and vulnerability, which is a legacy of our federalism. This reliance on intergovernmental techniques is not new—far from it—but it is more pervasive, intrusive, routinized, and burdensome for the states than ever before.

Because the states are governments, yet subordinate, Congress can—or can try to—put much of the burden of governing on them. Because they are governments, they have the capacity to raise revenues and execute laws. Of themselves, even leaving local subdivisions aside, they have more employees than the federal government, although it is worth noting that this is a relatively recent development. State employment, at a mere 318,000 in 1929, was barely more than half of federal civilian employment. It surpassed federal employment between 1970 and 1975, and the gap has continued to widen. As governments, states are headed by elected officials who have to take heat from the public when hard choices are to be made. On the other hand, because they are subordinate governments, they have also to take orders from Washington.

President Clinton's health security plan, proposed in the fall of 1993 but never enacted, suggested the extremes to which federal intrusiveness might go. When the foundations of national health insurance were laid in 1965 with passage of Medicare, a national program financed with a payroll tax, most students of American social policy would probably have predicted that Medicare would grow incrementally until it covered the whole of the population. How many would have predicted what President Clinton laid before the country: a measure designed to achieve universal coverage, but with only marginal and obscure increases in federal taxation? Rather than a payroll tax, the president proposed to secure his objective with a pervasive and highly coercive increase in national regulation of individual consumers of health care, providers of care, employers, and state governments.

Must state governments submit to the national government as it commands them to perform administration and finance on its behalf? How have they responded historically to their paradoxical situation? Broadly, state governments can try to cling to their status and prerogatives as such, or they can accept subordination.

The States' Response

Madison devoted two numbers of *The Federalist*, 45 and 46, to explaining why the advantage in federal-state relations would lie with the states. Among the several reasons he adduced was that a state could more easily defeat unwarranted encroachments than could the national government. And the states collectively would be still more effective:

> Ambitious encroachments of the federal government on the authority of the State governments would not excite the opposition of a single State, or of a few States only. Every government would espouse the common cause. A correspondence would be opened. Plans of resistance would be concerted. One spirit would animate and conduct the whole.[8]

On the whole, that has not been true. Historically, state governments as such have not been able to concert action in defense of prerogatives within the federal system. States as polities have been divided within and among themselves in ways that have impeded their ability to collaborate as governments. And even when they have banded together in the name of states' rights, the cause has been patently disingenuous. Not states' rights, but the interests of various minorities—New England's Federalists in the War of 1812, southern slaveholders in the nineteenth century, and their descendants into the twentieth—were crucially at stake. As a doctrine espoused by minorities, states' rights has suffered devastating defeats. Even if southern state governments succeeded in fighting a war together, they did not win it. Moreover, their having waged a war elicited a use of national power so great as to transform the Constitution.

To organize cooperation among independent state governments in pursuit of a common goal is difficult, but the states have also failed historical tests far less exacting. Even when the Constitution offers formal mechanisms of protection—namely, in the amending process—state governments as a class have not used them to secure governmental prerogatives. The Fourteenth Amendment is perhaps a poor example because southern states were coerced into accepting it, but no such coercion obtained in regard to the Seventeenth Amendment. By providing for popular election of senators, it formally removed from the structure of American government one of the principal protections of state governments' interests. To be sure, the Seventeenth Amendment merely confirmed a change that had already taken place, but that change itself was rooted in the early nineteenth-century failure of state governments to enforce instructions upon their delegates to the United States Senate.[9]

In modern times, following development of the welfare state and very high levels of governmental interdependence, the state governments have succeeded in organizing to voice their interests vis-à-vis the national government. Government action often stimulates the formation of interest groups, and the involvement of the national government in state government affairs through regulation and grants-in-aid has either stimulated the formation, or heightened the activity, of such groups as the National Governors Association, the National Conference of State Legislatures, the National Association of Attorneys General, the State and Local Legal Center, and other, more specialized organizations of state officials. These organizations purport to articulate the interests of state governments before Congress and the courts.

Even thus organized, state governments continue to find it difficult to concert their interests beyond a relatively narrow range of issues. Threats to financial prerogatives unite them. When revenue sources are jeopardized, as in issues over national taxation of the interest income from state and municipal bonds, they find it easy to collaborate. Clearly, governmental prerogatives are crucially at stake also in regard to abortion, yet the states are unable to come together in opposition to *Roe v. Wade* in order to retain their prerogative to legislate on the subject. As in the past, the differences within and among them as political societies override what unites them as governments with prerogatives to defend in a federal system.

If the states have a very limited ability to cooperate in asserting themselves as independent governments with shared interests, do they accept a role as subordinate governments, in which they become agents of nationally defined purposes? On the whole, they do. When Congress sets standards for clean air and provides that states shall prepare implementation plans to achieve them, the states do it. When Congress authorizes grants-in-aid for highway construction and maintenance but attaches to them all kinds of conditions, some of which are onerous and extraneous, the states accept the money and the conditions. It is almost unheard of for state governments to decline to participate in a nationally prescribed regulatory regime or grant-in-aid program, even though the option of not participating is technically available.[10]

When President Clinton's health care plan was drafted calling for the states to "assume primary responsibility for ensuring that all eligible individuals have access to a health plan that delivers the nationally guaranteed comprehensive benefit package," states did not protest. Among the functions prescribed for them in the administration's proposal were administration of subsidies for low-income individuals, families, and employers; certification and financial regulation of health plans; establishment and governance of health alliances; data collection; and quality management and improvement programs. In short, the states were to do everything but make the rules, which would have been up to Congress and a presidentially appointed National Health Board.[11] A reasonable response to this incredibly difficult assignment might well have been: "Are you kidding? You do it." Publicly and collectively, at least, the states said no such thing.

The failure of state governments to be more assertive probably is to be accounted for by combined considerations of politics and organizational maintenance. Much of what Congress prescribes has strong popular or organized interest group support, or Congress would not prescribe it. (In the end, it is worth repeating, Congress did not prescribe the Clinton health plan.) Theoretically and practically, perhaps Madison's most telling point in *Federalist* Nos. 45 and 46 was that "the federal and State governments are in fact but different agents and trustees of the people . . . substantially dependent on the great body of the citizens of the United States." As elected politicians themselves, governors and members of state legislatures are not very likely to defy a Congress that is legislating on behalf of causes and constituencies as deserving as clean air, the disabled, or pregnant women. Nor are they very likely to surrender functions affected by federal commands when those functions include most of what their governments do.[12]

In theory, states might try to take refuge in constitutional tradition. They could claim that mandates are unconstitutional because they violate the prerogatives of coordinate governments in a federal system. Seven states did bring suit unsuccessfully against enforcement of the National Voter Registration (Motor Voter) Act of 1993, which required states to provide all eligible citizens the opportunity to register to vote when they applied for or renewed a driver's license. More modestly, in 1995 they succeeded in getting Congress to enact the Unfunded Mandates Reform Act, which requires the Congressional Budget Office to report to Congress concerning the effects of any intergovernmental mandate estimated to impose annual costs on state and local governments of $50 million or more.[13] Yet for the most part, state officials merely grumble that mandates come without money.

Their typical posture vis-à-vis the national government is that of financial supplicant. They want more money. Typical newspaper stories on the states' reaction to the Clinton health proposals were headlined "Health-Care Reform May Seem Like a Bitter Pill to Localities Sick of Unfunded Federal Mandates," and "States Trying to Ferret Fiscal Impact Data Out of Clinton Health Plan."[14]

The high priority that state governments individually and collectively attach to maximizing receipt of national government funds perhaps accounts for the fact that they are often treated in Congress not as governments at all, subordinate or otherwise, but as one more lobby—a mere interest group to be given no more recognition and access to decision processes than any other interest group.

Should this decline be a source of dismay? Has anything important been lost to American government generally as a result of the state governments' degeneration into something less than governments?

The Mismatches in Modern Federalism

At least three undesirable consequences are evident. I will call them "mismatches": between prescription and practicality; between the locus of responsibility for generating public benefits and for paying costs; and between the locus of responsibility for defining public goals and for making trade-offs among them.

National law and regulation often fail to come to grips with practicalities. They tend to be abstract and utopian, or, if concrete and particular, as when environmental laws set detailed, explicit standards, they turn out to be irrational when applied to particular places. State governments, converted into national administrative agents, are often called upon to enforce laws that do not suit the circumstances of their societies, be they the value preferences of their publics, the technology of their industries, or their geography or demography. When these mismatches result from differences of prevailing values—for example, if the national polity is pursuing egalitarian goals and the smaller-scale polity is defending hierarchical ones—the resolution one prefers will depend on value preferences or views of which political community ought to be superior. But often no very important value preferences are at stake; "mere" practicalities are. Mismatches between national prescription and on-the-ground practicalities turn up with such frequency in journalistic accounts and tales told by state and local officials that I am inclined to think the problem is real and serious, though I know of no attempt to document it rigorously.[15]

Accountability and fiscal responsibility are undermined when elected politicians in one government can create new benefits while elected politicians in many other governments are obliged to finance them. There is more involved here than Congress's being unfair to other governments because it gives them "mandates without money." To the extent that Congress is freed from the obligation to fund what it enacts, it is also free to act irresponsibly, without facing true tests of the public's preferences or being accountable for results.

Having been liberated by today's federalism from an obligation to fund what it enacts, Congress is more able to avoid weighing the relative urgency of, or demand for, different activities. It defines goals of public policy for one policy area at a time. The national government mandates innumerable environmental protections and educational programs and health programs without making the trade-offs among them that rational policy must entail. States and their local subdivisions receive commands for each policy area separately and are obliged to pay the costs of all, without having the freedom to weigh independently either the total cost or the allocation among those functions to which mandates apply. Did the public really want local governments to spend an additional $110.6 billion for sewage handling facilities by February 19, 1995, as federal environmental laws and regulations required?[16] Given the way in which intergovernmental relations have evolved, the American political system cannot yield answers to such a question.

It might be argued that while this critique of Congress may be valid, federalism does not fundamentally determine Congress's behavior. Mandates without money are not confined to state governments; Congress treats agencies of the national government the same way, obligating them to perform tasks for which it fails to provide enough, or sometimes any, appropriations. Nor has Congress ever been good at making trade-offs among competing programs, even when those programs are purely national. Perhaps the appropriate question to ask of contemporary American federalism is whether government in general is better by reason of Congress's relying so heavily on administrative agents that, though no longer fully governments, nevertheless have government-like properties. How do regimes of intergovernmental cooperation compare with direct federal administration?

One of the original justifications for federalism was that the task of governing a great nation would be too much for one government alone. If that was true in 1787, it remains so today. One may think of governmental tasks in conventional terms, such as taxation, education, defense, income support, public safety, public health, and development and administration of a system of private law (family relations, real property, corporations, contracts, torts). Or one may think of such tasks in the terms that social scientists have come to use, such as management of conflict, mobilization of consent, and policymaking and implementation.

Whatever concepts one employs, there is more to be done than a single set of representative institutions operating in the national capital is likely to do well. The United States is a sprawling, populous nation in which citizens have very high expectations of access to public power and responsiveness on the part of public officials. It is appropriate in this society that there should be many dispersed sets of representative and accountable institutions with powers of lawmaking, adjudication, and taxation. That is, there should be many governments, and the subnational governments should exist as creatures of the people rather than as creatures of the national government (that is what makes the system "federal" rather than "unitary"). The ultimate justification for the existence of all those governments is that it makes the system as a whole more truly republican, more truly "of the people," which is the touchstone for government in the United States.

When the national legislature enacts mandates without money and without ordering priorities, the resulting dilemmas are dealt with elsewhere in the governmental system, and it is arguable that they are more properly dealt with by subnational governments, which have representative properties, than by national administrative agencies, which do not. Subnational governments have more potential for considered response, resistance, and a legitimate (that is, popularly and deliberatively based) ordering of priorities. Whether such a response now occurs is debatable. There has been relatively little scholarly analysis of how states in fact respond to the various federal mandates: to what extent they actually implement them despite strains, or ignore them, or selectively adapt and revise them to fit particular circumstances, and through what processes.

For state governments to respond to the federal government assertively, entering into dialogue over policy ends and administrative means, puts a very heavy burden on them. It presumes that, in addition to reflexively asking Washington for more money, they will exert themselves to influence national policymaking so as to inject more realism and pragmatism into it. It also presumes that they will assert claims to governmental prerogatives, as indeed they have been seeking to do through the State and Local Legal Center. It requires them to be as inventive in their own defense as Congress has been inventive in devising new techniques of influence over them.

The customs of intergovernmental relations change constantly. One thinks, for example, of the post-Civil War decline of the practice of state legislatures formally addressing their representatives in Congress. In the nineteenth century, it was quite common for state legislatures to speak to Congress as follows: "Be it resolved that our senators in Congress are hereby instructed, and our representatives are hereby requested, to vote for . . . ." The practice of instruction, never having been successfully institutionalized even in the nineteenth century, is not likely to be revived today, but this old custom may help remind states that they are constitutionally entitled to at least a voice.

They need to keep developing their voices and to use them vigorously and responsibly on behalf of policy objectives they articulate, if they are to retain a credible claim to governmental status.

Notes

1. Transcript of First Planning Meeting, "Furthering Public Understanding of Social Insurance in a Federal System," National Academy of Social Insurance, January 29, 1993, p. 12.
2. *The Federalist Papers* (New York: New American Library, Mentor ed., 1961), p. 296.
3. Woodrow Wilson, *The State*, rev. ed. (D. C. Heath, 1898), p. 523.
4. Edward S. Corwin, "The Passing of Dual Federalism," in Alpheus T. Mason and Gerald Garvey, eds., *American Constitutional History: Essays by Edward S. Corwin* (Harper and Row, 1964), pp. 145–64.
5. 247 U. S. 251 (1918), in Alpheus T. Mason and William M. Beaney, eds., *American Constitutional Law* (Prentice-Hall, 1959), p. 280.
6. Henry M. Hart Jr., "The Relations between State and Federal Law," in Arthur W. Macmahon, ed., *Federalism: Mature and Emergent* (Doubleday, 1955), p. 194.
7. *Puerto Rico v. Branstad*, 483 U. S. 219 (1987).
8. *Federalist Papers*, p. 298.
9. William H. Riker, "The Senate and American Federalism," *American Political Science Review*, vol. 49 (June 1955), pp. 452–69.
10. Late in 1993, Indiana was flirting with an attempt to surrender to the federal government authority to regulate landfills and control water pollution. See *Governing*, vol. 7 (November 1993), p. 70.

11. *The President's Health Security Plan: The Complete Draft and Final Reports of the White House Domestic Policy Council*, pp. 52–59, in *The President's Health Security Plan* (Times Books, 1993).

12. For an extended analysis of the rise of mandates and the failure of state governments to resist them, see Paul Posner, *The Politics of Unfunded Mandates: Whither Federalism?* (Georgetown University Press, 1998).

13. For a review and analysis of the various measures that state governments employ in trying to protect their interests vis-à-vis the federal government, see John J. Dinan, "State Government Influence in the National Policy Process: Lessons from the 104th Congress," *Publius: The Journal of Federalism*, vol. 27 (Spring 1997), pp. 129–42. On passage of mandate reform, see David R. Beam and Timothy J. Conlan, "The 1995 Unfunded Mandates Reform Act: The Politics of Federal Mandating Meets the Politics of Reform," *Public Budgeting and Financial Management*, vol. 7 (Fall 1995), pp. 355–85.

14. *Wall Street Journal*, December 21, 1993, p. A14; and *Washington Post*, January 29, 1994, p. A8.

15. For a suggestive academic analysis of the federal-state difference from the field of criminal justice, see Robert M. Cover and T. Alexander Aleinikoff, "Dialectical Federalism: Habeas Corpus and the Court," *Yale Law Journal*, vol. 86 (1976–77), p. 1035. Cover and Aleinikoff identify two opposing tendencies in constitutional interpretation: the "utopian," which they associate with federal courts, and the "pragmatic," which they identify with state courts.

16. For a catalog of environmental mandates, see *Governing*, vol. 7 (March 1994), pp. 73–86.

7

Puppy Federalism and the Blessings of America

Edward L. Rubin

The United States is a nation that enjoys many blessings. We have vast reserves of petroleum (although we are using them up), magnificent forests (although we are cutting them down), spacious skies, amber waves of grain, lots of coal, and the world's leading supply of molybdenum. We also have wonderful political resources: the English tradition of liberty, well-established representative institutions, a willingness to channel political commitments into two major parties, a deep understanding of law, and a long-standing ability to solve civil conflicts through adjudication.

Perhaps the most valuable of these political resources, however, is our sense of national unity, our belief that we constitute a single people and a single polity. One of the reasons why this is such a great blessing is that it allows us to dispense with federalism. A subsidiary blessing is that it allows us to ignore the political questions that underlie federalism, issues that we would like to ignore because they point to the autocratic origins of all governments, and the impossibility of using democratic principles to constitute a polity.

This fortunate situation did not obtain at the beginning of our history, and we feel a bit guilty about basking in its glow today. Consequently, we have fashioned something for ourselves that can be described as puppy federalism; like puppy love, it looks somewhat authentic but does not reflect the intense desires that give the real thing its inherent meaning. The main purpose of puppy federalism is to convince ourselves that we have not altered the conception of the government that the Framers maintained, when, of course, we have; that we are not a bureaucratized administrative state, when, of course, we are;

From Edward L. Rubin, *Annals of the American Academy of Political and Social Science* (571/March 2001) pp. 37–51, Copyright © 2001 by Sage Publications. Reprinted by permission of Sage Publications, Inc.

and that we are a geographically diverse nation, whose regions exhibit interesting differences, when, of course, we are a highly homogenized, commercial, media-driven culture smeared across the width of an entire continent.

. . . The reason nations opt for federalism is that it is an alternative to dissolution, civil war, or other manifestations of a basic unwillingness of the people in some geographic area to live under the central government (Buchanan 1991; Sunstein 1991). Conversely, the reason groups of nations or other polities that want to combine opt to create a federal system, as opposed to a unified one, is that the people in the separate polities are unwilling to submit to unified, central control (Bartkus 1999). In either case, the motivation is a basic lack of national unity, an unwillingness of some groups to submit themselves to centralized control, to regard themselves as members of a single polity that must, for better or worse, reach collective decisions. They may feel that they will be discriminated against in the larger unit; that resources within the geographic region they inhabit will not be used for their benefit; that policies will be imposed on them that they find intolerable; or simply that they want to retain their own identity (Dikshit 1975; Duchacek 1970; Hannum 1990). Federalism is a solution to this problem, a compromise between unity and independence.

Decentralization is not sufficient in a situation where one or several groups are unwilling to submit to central control. The compromise that these groups want is federalism; they want the autonomy of their subunit's government to be protected as a right, not merely recognized as a desirable policy (Friedrich 1968, 188–227). By virtue of this recognition, the autonomy they have secured is placed outside the realm of ordinary politics. The king cannot eliminate it by an ordinary royal order; the voters, or their representatives, cannot do so by a simple majority. In our system, this means that the courts, acting in response to a claim of right, will invalidate normal legislation that trenches on the agreed-upon autonomy of the subunits (Choper 1980). That autonomy can be altered only by a constitutional amendment. . . .

The Blessings of National Unity

From the national perspective, a sense of unity among its citizens, a willingness to act as part of a single polity, is a political resource of enormous value, more valuable than petroleum, molybdenum, or rutabaga. It means that sectional disagreements or rivalries will be resolved within the context of the nation's political process and that a decision, having been reached, will be obeyed. Other disagreements will, of course, remain; there may be conflicts between social classes, ethnic groups, religious groups, or purely ideological alliances, and these conflicts may lead to violence. But the disagreements between groups of people who live in different geographic regions of the nation will not rise to this intensity; people will value their membership in the nation over their sectionally specific views and will compromise those views, or even abandon them, in conflictual situations.

Not only does a sense of national unity remove one major source of political conflict, but it removes the most dangerous source of such conflict. While it is possible for two contending groups that are geographically intermixed to rip a nation and themselves apart, as has occurred in Lebanon, Rwanda, and (at a regional level) Northern Ireland, most intense conflicts tend to be sectional, as Kosovo, Chechnya, Nagorno-Karabakh (Armenia-Azerbaijan), Kurdistan, Eritrea, the Ogaden (Ethiopia-Somalia), Western Sahara, Sudan, Kurdistan, Sri Lanka, and East Timor attest in recent history alone (Buchanan 1991; Cassese 1995). In part, this may be because a geographically defined group lacks the cross-cutting ties with others that racially or religiously defined groups often possess (Hannum 1990). In part, it may be that secession is a viable option only for geographically defined groups and that this extreme solution is an inducement to political extremism (Buchanan 1991; Dikshit 1975). Whatever the reason, a nation is not only fortunate—it is blessed—if it does not have any such groups, if the people in every region feel a greater loyalty to the nation as a whole than they do to their particular region.

In a democracy, national unity, and the resulting lack of sectional divisions, confers a further, if somewhat more abstract advantage. It conceals from the nation's citizens, and perhaps even from its political theorists, the awkward fact that democratic mechanisms cannot be used to constitute the nation. Creating a nation requires some form of autocracy. The reason is that the defining feature of democracy, in either its direct or representative varieties, is that major decisions are reached by the people themselves or by their elected representatives (Birch 1993, 45–68; Held 1996, 70–120). In practical terms, this means that the decisions are reached by having the people vote, either for the policy itself or for the representatives who in turn select the policy. Before a vote is taken, however, someone must decide who is eligible to vote and what the rules for conducting that vote will be.

That decision obviously cannot be determined by a vote; it requires an autocrat of some sort, an individual or an elite, who can establish the initial rules. Thus the principle of democracy, although it may be a perfectly good way to run the ordinary business of government, cannot stand on its own. If we start, either in reality or as a thought experiment, with people in a pregovernmental condition, no government can be established by purely democratic means.

. . . This is not an abstract matter; it is a crucial feature of national politics that implicates the precise issues to which federalism is addressed. From a national perspective, a proponent of representative democracy believes that a constitution should be established, and leaders should be chosen, by a majority of the electorate. But those whose primary loyalty is to a geographic region of this nation will object. "We do not want to be governed by strangers," they will say, "and the fact that those strangers are more numerous than us only makes the situation worse. We too believe in democracy, and we want a majority of the people—our people—to decide whether we want to join your nation, and on what terms. If a majority of our people want to have an independent nation, rather than being part of a larger one, that majority should not be overridden by outsiders." A sense of national unity that is shared by every region of a nation conceals this awkward difficulty in the theory and practice of democracy by making it essentially irrelevant.

Federalism in American History

For most of its history, the United States was a nation that needed federalism. The sense of national unity that would have led the voting populace to choose a unified, national regime did not prevail among the 13 American states at the time the Constitution was ratified and the United States was formed (Rakove 1979). People's loyalty to their own state was stronger than their loyalty to the nascent national regime, and thus they opted for a federal system, where the constituent states retained large areas of autonomy as a matter of right (Lutz 1988; Rakove 1996, 161–202). Nor was there sufficient unanimity about the federalist solution to mask the authoritarian origins of the government. While a majority of the people, when considered as a totality, probably favored a federal union, a majority of each state's population did not. In at least two states, North Carolina and Rhode Island, the majority was opposed, so that the autocratic manner in which the ratification process was established made a difference (Main 1961, 249; Van Doren 1948). In fact, these two states joined the Union only because they were compelled by further autocratic means. The same autocratic compulsion was applied to those regions within and beyond the established states with a Native American majority. It may also be assumed that, in any state, or section of a state, where the majority of the people were slaves, that majority would have preferred to establish an independent regime where they were free, rather than joining a nation that continued to enslave them.

During the first half of the nineteenth century, the new, federally organized nation was subject to two conflicting trends. On the one hand, the success of the central government, its general respect for white people's rights, its acquisition of vast territories, and the dramatic increase in national wealth that it seemed to engender all contributed to a growing sense of national unity. People began to think of themselves as Americans, rather than Georgians or New Yorkers (Ackerman 1991, 3–33; Beer 1993, 360–77). At the same time, however, the rejection of slavery in the North (Hildreth 1854; Olmstead 1953) and its enthusiastic continuation in the South (Fitzhugh 1854 [1965]) created an ever widening division. To the people of the North, slavery was a violation of the nation's true norms, and the people of the southern states were disruptive members of the polity who were violating those norms. But the white people of the southern states, the only people in those states with a political voice, were more committed to the institution of slavery than they were to the Union; despite their growing commitment to the nation in other areas, enough of their identification with their states remained that this identification could be reasserted, and become primary, when they found themselves unwilling to abide by the decisions of the majority regarding slavery. Consequently, they decided to secede (Stampp 1959).

At this point, of course, the democratic process and every other process of ordinary government broke down. The people of the North could no longer use voting, persuasion, or an appeal to national unity to convince the white people of the South to rejoin the Union because the southerners no longer regarded themselves as part of the same polity. The only remaining approach was to start killing them and devastating their lands until they decided that the amount of misery that was being inflicted on them exceeded their commitment to slavery. At that point, they rejoined the Union on the central government's terms.

Despite this unpromising beginning, the nation was restored and a sense of national unity gradually developed. Slavery was the principal thing that had distinguished the South from the North; the other characteristic features of southern culture had been products of that basic difference. With the military defeat of the South, and the subsequent recognition that slavery was beyond restoration, white southerners began to see themselves once more as members of the United States. Within that general framework, however, they still wanted to retain their familiar social hierarchy and so proceeded, through the Ku Klux Klan, the crop lien system, the Jim Crow laws, and a variety of other mechanisms, to deprive the freed slaves of their newly won rights and the opportunity to improve their political, economic, or social status (Gillette 1979; Litwack 1979; Woodward 1951). As the North's centralizing impulse, fueled by moral outrage at the southern treatment of the slaves, gradually waned, the southern states were allowed to maintain the distinctive institutions that continued African American subjugation. In every other major area—language, religion, culture, race, ethnicity, and political ideology—white southerners and northerners were largely identical, and federalism served no function. Its only purpose, in the period that followed the Civil War, was to allow the southern states to maintain their system of apartheid.

This system, and thus the role of federalism in the United States, lasted for about a century. Beginning in the 1950s, white people in the parts of the United States outside the South began to perceive the southern treatment of African Americans as morally unacceptable. The result was a series of actions by national institutions, which were dominated by these white nonsoutherners, to abolish southern apartheid; they included *Brown v. Board of Education*[1] and other Supreme Court decisions, the Civil Rights Act of 1964, and the executive policies of the Kennedy, Johnson, and Nixon administrations (Harvey 1971; Martin 1979). These actions were perceived, quite correctly, as an abrogation of America's remaining federalist commitment to allow distinctly different normative systems to prevail in different states. The success of the effort eliminated the major difference between the South and the rest of the United States. It contributed, moreover, to the elimination of the more subtle, incremental differences such as the South's lower levels of wealth, industrial development, and education. The New South that emerged during the 1970s and 1980s shared the highly uniform, homogenized commercial culture of the United States as a whole. Any further need for federalism was thus eliminated.

Puppy Federalism in Modern America

At present, the United States is a socially homogenized and politically centralized nation. Regional differences between different parts of the nation are minimal, and those that exist are based on inevitable economic variations, rather than any historical or cultural distinctions. . . . There are also variations in the concentration of various religious and ethnic groups throughout the country. The low salience of religious differences in the United States, however, makes these differences virtually irrelevant. Ethnic divisions are, of course, more salient, and the concentration of African Americans in the South prior to the 1950s was one of the bases of the South's distinctive culture and the continued relevance of federalism. The massive migration of African Americans to other sections of the nation has largely eliminated this regional distinction; race relations remain a major problem in America, but it is a problem that now exists in virtually every region, where it is played out in similar terms. Hispanic and Asian ethnicity is also salient, but these groups have also become widely diffused during the postwar era.

With the minor exceptions of Utah and Hawaii, there is no American state with a truly distinctive social profile. Those differences that do exist may loom large to us, but that is because of our insularity; once we compare our differences with the linguistic, religious, cultural, and historical differences that exist in large nations such as India, Indonesia, and Nigeria, or even smaller ones such as Spain, Cameroon, and itsy-bitsy Belgium, ours shrink to insignificance.

Our political culture is more uniform still. The overwhelming majority of Americans identify with one of two major political parties, whose differences, while again salient to us, are minuscule by international standards. Our states, supposedly free to establish their own regimes, have opted for highly similar structures with minor variations (Gardner 1992). No state has instituted a parliamentary system, for example, although that is the dominant pattern for democratic regimes in the world today; only one state, Nebraska, dispenses with the peculiarly American feature of a bicameral legislature; no state denies its courts the power of judicial review. Certainly, no American state has even attempted to establish a theocratic or autocratic regime; thus, under the current reading of the guarantee clause that restricts it to such matters (but see Merritt 1988), there has been no felt need to invoke the clause, or otherwise intervene in the political process of any state, during the entire course of the twentieth century (Bonfield 1962;

Chemerinsky 1994; Choper 1994). Most important, the primary political loyalty of the vast majority of Americans is to the nation. . . .

Despite this high level of national unity, there remains a certain nostalgia for our bygone federalist system. This nostalgia arises from at least three sources, and probably more. The first is that the Framers are correctly perceived as having established a federalist regime, for reasons described above, and we incorrectly fear that some horrible consequences will ensue if we admit that we no longer abide by their intentions. Second, the yearning of many Americans for the simplicity of the premodern era, and the more sinister yearning of some Americans for the moonlight, magnolia, and mint-julep era of the antebellum South, slides over to the federalism that prevailed at that time. Third, we dislike the centralized administrative state and see federalism as a welcome antidote to the government that we have created and that we need but do not like.

The result of all this yearning is that we continue to insist that we have a federalist system, even though we neither have it nor need it. The dangerous, debilitating problems that federalism is designed to resolve—the lack of national unity, the persistence of separatism, the underlying social and political differences that are cemented in place by centuries of history and hatred—are mercifully absent in the modern United States. Consequently, we no longer recognize federalism as an unfortunate expedient. . . . Thus we can enjoy the idea of federalism because we have forgotten the grave problems associated with its actuality. What we have instead is puppy federalism, a thin patina of rights talk draped across the areas where we have opted for decentralization as an administrative strategy.

The actions of the Republican-dominated Congress of the last six years illustrates the superficiality of American federalism. In general, the Republicans have declared a stronger commitment to federalism than the Democrats, yet recent Republican Congresses have continued the policies of their Democratic predecessors, enacting statutes that federalize areas previously reserved to state law and contradict the federalism decisions of a Supreme Court with which they supposedly agree. For example, the 104th Congress enacted the Church Arson Prevention Act of 1996, making destructive acts against religious institutions a federal crime. The act's basis of federal jurisdiction is the one that proponents of federalism often dismiss as a pretext and that was used in the statute struck down by *United States v. Lopez*[2]—interstate commerce. That same Republican Congress also enacted Megan's Law, requiring certain offenders to register with state law enforcement officers—apparently a case of the outrageous, Framer-ignoring, states'-rights-crushing commandeering of state officers that was struck down in *United States v. Printz*.[3] The 104th Congress also enacted the Drug-Induced Rape Prevention and Punishment Act of 1996, which makes the use of "date rape" drugs a federal offense. In spirit, this act is an extension of the Violence Against Women Act, which was passed just before the Republicans took control of Congress and was struck down in *United States v. Morrison*[4] on an interpretation of the interstate commerce clause. Technically, the act extends the Controlled Substances Act and will probably be invulnerable to judicial attack, but this only leads one to wonder why the Republican Congress feels comfortable endorsing and extending a statute drafted in 1970 by one of the most Democratic, nationalizing Congresses in history and taking away the states' police power authority to decide which substances they will forbid their own citizens to ingest. This is, incidentally, a live issue, as indicated by the various states that have tried to modify their prohibitions against marijuana, only to run afoul of federal authorities.

The reason a Republican Congress would enact statutes of this sort is that our federalism is puppy federalism. When state policies correspond to national norms in a given area, or when there is no national norm, that area can be left to state authority. As soon as a national norm emerges, and some states diverge from that norm, federal authorities will act, as they did against the southern states once racial equality became a general goal. In the last two decades, crime has become a matter of grave concern, and the result has been a steady federalization of the criminal law that continues regardless of the party in control of Congress. When the crunch comes, the crunch being a political demand for action, federalism counts for nothing.

The 104th Congress's most significant legislative action, the Personal Responsibility and Work Opportunity Reconciliation Act, might appear to reflect a commitment to genuine federalism, but it does not; rather, it only underscores the absence of any such commitment. It is true that this act changes prior law in providing block grants of federal funds to the states, rather than channeling federal grants to individuals through state administrators as had been the case under the prior Aid to Families with Dependent Children (AFDC) program. But the main reason for this, despite the federalist rhetoric that accompanied its enactment, was that the federal purpose and federal methodology had changed. The purpose is now to discourage the creation of out-of-wedlock children, not to provide these children with support; as the very first sentence of the act declares, "Marriage is the foundation of a successful society." The methodology is to compel the states to achieve specified results in accordance with the stated purposes, rather than compelling them to follow specified procedures. Thus the statute gives block grants and does not specify procedures. This undoubtedly gives the states more latitude in the procedural area, but it imposes much greater demands regarding the results. It defines criteria for an "eligible state" (two different sets of criteria, actually), a "qualifying state," a "high performing state," and a "needy state" (42 U.S.C. §403(a)). In accordance with these various criteria, it demands that each state submit a plan to show how it will achieve the statutory purpose, sets specific guidelines for rates of out-of-wedlock births and work participation, places numerous prohibitions and limitations on the use of the block grants, provides bonuses to high-performing states, imposes penalties on states that fail to abide by the limits on fund use or fail to achieve specified levels of results, and requires frequent and detailed reports (id. §§404–11).

Is this really federalism; is it really the way one sovereign treats another sovereign? It seems to bear a closer resemblance to the way a superior treats a subordinate administrator, and not a very trusted subordinate at that. There is a tone in all these provisions, and particularly in the bonuses and penalties, that is much more demeaning to the states than the AFDC idea that they should administer federal funds in a specified manner. The reason for this apparent breach of federalist etiquette by a Republican Congress is not difficult to discern. Because we have only puppy federalism, the national government will give states control over policy only in areas that are not of national concern. It will retain control over any policy that it regards as truly important. When AFDC was enacted, child poverty was the predominant concern, and the political subtext was that southern states could not be relied upon to treat their African American citizens fairly. With the rise of the New South, and the decline in Congress's commitment to racial justice, this concern no longer predominates. Instead, we have the new moralism, with public policy directed to preventing out-of-wedlock births and ensuring that no one but the severely disabled receive welfare payments without working. The new law reflects those concerns. It does not represent a decrease in federal control but a new methodology for control, a new public policy that the methodology is intended to achieve, and a new political subtext that seeks to discipline licentious New York and indulgent California, rather than racist Georgia and Louisiana.

Conclusion

There is no major law reform conclusion to be derived from this discussion. The United States possesses the blessing of national unity, and thus its national government will continue to legislate on any issue that it and the nation in general deem important. One possible conclusion is that the Supreme Court's recent federalism decisions are incorrect—which they are—but as long as the ideology of the justices is not overly divergent from that of the nation as a whole, they are not likely to hand down any decisions with significant impact. The real message of this discussion is for scholars. It is time to stop being fooled by political rhetoric and mistaking puppy federalism for the real thing. Real federalism is gone; America is a centralized administrative state. Rather than mourning its demise, we should feel grateful that our nation no longer needs this unfortunate expedient, and we should focus our attention on complex and important issues, such as decentralization. Instead of a theory of federalism, we need a theory about what policies should be centralized, what policies should be decentralized, and, in both cases, the optimal way for a national government to supervise the regional subordinates that we continue to describe as states.

References

Ackerman, Bruce. 1991. *We the People*. Vol. 1, *Foundations*. Cambridge, Mass: Belknap Press.

Bartkus, Viva. 1999. *The Dynamic of Secession*. New York: Cambridge University Press.

Beer, Samuel. 1993. *To Make a Nation*. Cambridge, MA: Belknap Press.

Birch, Anthony. 1993. *The Concepts and Theories of Modern Democracy*. London: Routledge.

Bonfield, Arthur. 1962. The Guarantee Clause of Article IV, Section 4: A Study in Constitutional Desuetude. *Minnesota Law Review* 46:513–72.

Buchanan, Allen. 1991. *Secession: The Morality of Political Divorce from Fort Sumpter to Lithuania and Quebec*. Boulder, CO: Westview Press.

Cassese, Antonio. 1995. *Self-Determination of Peoples*. New York: Cambridge University Press.

Chemerinsky, Erwin. 1994. Cases Under the Guarantee Clause Should Be Justiciable. *University of Colorado Law Review* 65:849–80.

Choper, Jesse. 1994. Observations on the Guarantee Clause. *University of Colorado Law Review* 65:741–47.

Dikshit, Ramesh. 1975. *The Political Geography of Federalism*. Delhi: Macmillan Co. of India.

Duchacek, Ivo. 1970. *Comparative Federalism: The Territorial Dimension of Politics*. New York: Holt, Rinehart & Winston.

Fitzhugh, George. 1854 [1965]. *Sociology for the South: Or, The Failure of a Free Society.* New York: B. Franklin.

Friedrich, Carl. 1968. *Constitutional Government and Democracy.* 4th ed. Waltham, MA: Blaisdell.

Gardner, James. 1992. The Failed Discourse of State Constitutionalism. *Michigan Law Review* 90:761–837.

Gillette, William. 1979. *Retreat from Reconstruction, 1869–1879.* Baton Rouge: Louisiana State University Press.

Hannum, Hurst. 1990. *Autonomy, Sovereignty, and Self-Determination.* Philadelphia: University of Pennsylvania Press.

Harvey, James. 1971. *Black Civil Rights During the Johnson Administration.* Jackson, MS: University & College Press of Mississippi.

Held, David. 1996. *Models of Democracy.* 2d ed. Stanford, CA: Stanford University Press.

Hildreth, Richard. 1854. *Despotism in America.* New York: Negro University Press.

Litwack, Leon. 1979. *Been in the Storm So Long: The Aftermath of Slavery.* New York: Knopf.

Lutz, David. 1988. *The Origins of American Constitutionalism.* Baton Rouge: Louisiana State University Press.

Main, Jackson Turner. 1961. *The Antifederalists: Critics of the Constitution 1781–1788.* Chapel Hill: University of North Carolina Press.

Martin, John. 1979. *Civil Rights and the Crisis of Liberalism: The Democratic Party, 1945–76.* Boulder, CO: Westview Press.

Merritt, Deborah. 1988. The Guarantee Clause and State Autonomy: Federalism for a Third Century. *Columbia Law Review* 88:1–78.

Olmstead, Frederick Law. 1953. *The Cotton Kingdom,* ed. Arthur Schlesinger. New York: Knopf.

Rakove, Jack. 1979. *The Beginnings of National Politics: An Interpretive History of the Constitutional Congress.* New York: Knopf.

——— 1996. *Original Meanings: Politics and Ideas in the Making of the Constitution.* New York: Knopf.

Stampp, Kenneth. 1959. *The Causes of the Civil War.* Englewood Cliffs, NJ: Prentice-Hall.

Sunstein, Cass. 1991. Constitutionalism and Secession. *University of Chicago Law Review* 58:633–70.

Van Doren, Carl. 1948. *The Great Rehearsal.* New York: Times Reading.

Woodward, C. Van. 1951. *The Origins of the New South, 1877–1913.* Baton Rouge: Louisiana State University Press.

Notes

1. 347 U.S. 483 (1954).
2. 514 U.S. 549 (1995).
3. 521 U.S. 898 (1997).
4. 120 S. Ct. 1740 (2000).

Part I

Review Questions

1. What did the Founders of the American system mean by such key concepts as republican government, federalism, and nation? How did they link these ideas? How has the meaning of federalism altered over time in the United States?

2. Discussions of American intergovernmental relations frequently include a discussion of federalism. Compare and contrast the two notions of intergovernmental relations and federalism.

3. For the Founders, the office of the presidency represented an arrangement meant to ensure vitality for both national and state governments. Explain how this could be the case. Identify other institutions in the structure of the national government designed by the Founders to perform similar functions. Do they do so today? Why or why not? (Take note of the discussions by Diamond, Derthick, and Rubin in this regard.)

4. Basic decisions made in the early years of the nation created substantial ambiguity and opportunities for increased intergovernmental interdependence in later years. Bearing this in mind, explain how Madison's position in his argument with Sherman (summarized in Diamond's essay) could be used to justify substantial expansion of national authority on such policy matters as civil rights.

5. Imagine a debate between Grodzins and Scheiber on American intergovernmental cooperation and conflict. What would be the major points of agreement and disagreement? Which arguments would be more convincing to you?

6. Your friend asserts that history is irrelevant to contemporary events, that it doesn't matter what the Founders thought or planned, and that it is a waste of time to try to determine what forms of intergovernmental arrangements were most prominent in the past. Can you rebut

these claims? (Take special note of Scheiber's discussion here.) What do you think Rubin would have to say about this matter?

7. Grodzins's essay is properly treated as a classic, but even in 1960 some of its assertions were controversial. It is clear, for instance, that he is far from neutral toward the system he examines. Is his positive evaluation warranted? What problems can you see with the "easy merging of public and private interests at the local level"?

8. When Grodzins wrote more than forty-five years ago, a dissenting footnote was appended to his essay by two other intergovernmental analysts, John A. Perkins and Emmette S. Redford. They argued, in part, that

> the present system of shared responsibility confuses rather than fixes responsibility. Ascertainable responsibility for policy, administrative performance, and financing is an essential feature of effective self-government. The possibility of achieving it needs to be explored. . . . The chaos of party processes itself impairs leadership for national functions and national aims. Mr. Grodzins's conclusion that the costs of this chaos are tolerable may be drawn too easily.[1]

Looking back on developments in the intergovernmental system during the last four decades (the introductory chapter in this volume may give you some ideas), have these criticisms been substantiated? Why or why not? (Review this question again after you have completed readings in later sections of this book.)

9. Consider Grodzins's essay in the light of modern political realities. Do today's increasingly *nationally* based party institutions, organized around such activities as fundraising and widespread use of the electronic media, weaken the political hold of federalism? Do parties today seem to encourage or discourage "leadership for national functions and national aims," a goal desired by Perkins and Redford (see the quotation excerpted in question 8)?

10. Which model does Wright identify as the most useful for explaining today's intergovernmental relations? Is his case persuasive? In what ways is this model consistent with the historical descriptions of Grodzins? Of Scheiber or Derthick? Of Rubin? Of the introductory chapter of this book?

11. Given the cutbacks in federal aid that have occurred at various times in recent decades, has there been a corresponding shift in the most appropriate model (from Wright's analysis) for describing the intergovernmental system? In some policy fields?

12. Is the role of the states in today's intergovernmental system clear? Are states "on the rise," are they under the thumb of Washington, or is there truth in both generalizations? Draw from Derthick's analysis in your response.

13. Could or should the United States consider abolishing the system of federalism? What, if any, would be the costs of doing so? Would such a change affect the practice of intergovernmental relations in this country? Why or why not? Consider the perspectives of both Derthick and Rubin.

Note

1. *Goals for Americans* (Englewood Cliffs, N.J.: Prentice-Hall, Inc., 1960), 282.

Part II

POLITICAL ASPECTS OF
INTERGOVERNMENTAL RELATIONS

The American intergovernmental network is fundamentally a *political* system, or a complex of such systems. As the readings in Part I suggested, this structure was designed to establish opportunities for different government units representing different interests to stake out positions and exercise influence while also seeking accommodation with one another. Part II focuses on the question of how that influence is distributed and exercised. The readings in the following pages examine political aspects of intergovernmental relations; however, as some of the essays in this and later parts of the book make clear, any attempt to analyze separately the political, fiscal, and administrative aspects of the system must be somewhat artificial. Politics and administration are inextricably linked, and financial resources are cause and effect of events in both spheres. Nonetheless, these three categories do help to organize some of the basic perspectives and issues of importance for the system.

A comprehensive study of the political aspects of American intergovernmental relations must analyze the roles, behavior, and interconnections of a long list of actors who can substantially influence intergovernmental decisions. This complexity, after all, is one of the hallmarks of the intergovernmental pattern—and it has political consequences.

Among those likely to be politically important in the system are, of course, the major national governmental institutions: the presidency, Congress, and the federal courts. In addition, as the opening chapter of this volume indicated, the national bureaucracy is often an especially significant participant. Also important are public interest groups (PIGs), whether centered on policy function or representing state and local governments or general-purpose public officials. Political parties can exert their effects on intergovernmental decisions and directions, as can more specialized bodies. A once-influential specialized body, the U.S. Advisory Commission on Intergovernmental Relations (ACIR), is now defunct following heated conflicts about intergovernmental issues in the mid-1990s; but nongovernmental think tanks of many types and state-level "little ACIRs" are among the institutions offering perspectives, analyses, and options for consideration. In fact, the national executive, legislature, courts, bureaucracy, interest groups, and parties all have their counterparts at the state level. Countless institutions and political organizations operate among the various kinds of local governments. City and county executives and other locally powerful interests are very active in intergovernmental politics. Quasi-independent economic development bodies seek to leverage the authority of government on behalf of local and regional political economies. A dizzying variety of special districts operate within the matrix to effect any number of other public purposes. And an array of coordinating bodies— councils of government, regional planning bodies, and functionally specific interlocal units (for example, those assisting in transportation planning)—exchange information and sometimes affect policy directly.

Because the participants in intergovernmental politics are too numerous and their relationships too complex to be covered in depth here, Part II offers an overview, organized primarily around a sampling of the actors, their links, and the kinds of political moves and consequences spawned in the dense and evolving pattern of interdependence.

The first reading (no. 8) concentrates not on specific intergovernmental actors and their political relations per se but on important features of the context within which politics develop: the diversity of governmental structures in the system and the implications stemming from the involvement of so many different kinds of units. This article by Robert Reischauer, who has had a distinguished career in research and public service, presents an interesting and somewhat disturbing analysis of the effects of diversity in the network. Reischauer documents specific policy consequences and demonstrates that the formal structure *does* make a difference. He asserts that it is impossible to achieve any coherent goal via an intergovernmental grant without encountering considerable problems as well. Although some of the data used by Reischauer in this classic piece would be different now, all of his basic points remain valid.

The next several articles examine some of the specific actors in intergovernmental politics. One (no. 9) considers in particular the efforts and impact of the PIGs in recent times. Anne Marie Cammisa conducted an empirical study of the PIGs during the 1990s, in a design intended to explore themes and findings originally developed in an important study previously conducted by Donald Haider. Cammisa's investigation centered on the main organizations that represent state and local general-purpose officials, as these organizations sought to influence important recent federal decisions in Washington. She generalizes, on the basis of several cases and survey research, the operations and the political strengths and weaknesses of the PIGs. The study is particularly useful in sketching some of the ways that these groups differ from more typical interest groups, the fashion in which their environments have become more challenging in the current era of more constrained federal intergovernmental grant support, and the issue of coalition building among the PIGs.

The essay by Ann Bowman (no. 10) focuses on the states, and this study reminds us that intergovernmental ties have a horizontal as well as vertical dimension. Whereas Martha Derthick's essay in the first part of this book analyzed the states as the middle link in the national-state-local scheme, Bowman explores the way that states interact with each other as well as with governments elsewhere in the system. She finds evidence of both competition and cooperation as states deal with each other, and her attention is directed in particular at the forms of interstate cooperative effort: interstate compacts, multistate legal action, and uniform state laws. The states vary considerably in the extent to which they join with their counterparts to effect policies and projects, and the politics of such efforts entail subtleties of various sorts, but it is clear that such interstate arrangements can be both important and also regularly used as governments seek to expand their influence and address their needs.

Over the last few decades, many observers of the U.S. Supreme Court have seen evidence of a shift toward more deference to the states vis-à-vis the national government. The trend is not unambiguous, nor is it unequivocal. Furthermore, recent changes in the composition of the Court require analysts to continue to examine the evolution of judicial thinking about issues of federalism and intergovernmental relations. Some actions by the Court carry direct implications for the ebb and flow of power across governmental levels. For instance, in 1995 the U.S. Supreme Court in *U.S. v. Lopez* invalidated a national law on the grounds that there was no interstate commerce–based constitutional justification for federal involvement on behalf of gun control in public schools. This and other decisions of a similar nature cause legal scholar Donald L. Doernberg to argue that the Court has displayed a "new federalism" in recent years, even as Congress pushes toward increased national authority. In an excerpt from his study (no. 11), Doernberg covers several aspects of the recent evolution in Supreme Court decisions. The reading included here focuses especially on shifts in the treatment of the Constitution's commerce clause, although other changes have also been significant. As Doernberg points out, the Court's thinking has become rather complex, and political actors at all levels need to take into account the judiciary's role in shifting the balance of the system.

The last two readings in this part move from individual and paired actors in intergovernmental politics to systemic features. One essay (no. 12), by Daniel Halberstam and Roderick M. Hills Jr., reminds us that the combination of many diverse political roles occupied by governmental actors, along with the subtleties of constitutional doctrine and pragmatic public decision making, must be taken into account in any serious effort to understand how power operates in an intergovernmental system. Their essay is unusual in that they analyze the operations of the U.S. system by comparing it directly with another federal system—that established by Germany. Halberstam and Hills argue that the constitutional rules of the game in these two systems differ considerably, and the differences carry practical implications for day-to-day intergovernmental politics. In particular, the German system provides more autonomy and protection for its "states," the *Länder*, but the operations of the U.S. system encourage more flexibility and efficiency of operations. Readers can more easily understand something of the variety possible even between Western, developed, federal regimes as regards intergovernmental politics.

The final excerpt (no. 13) is drawn from Martha Derthick's seminal book-length case study of one grant program as it was implemented in one state. Far more than a case study, Derthick's investigation contains profound theoretical insights and thus can be considered in connection with the issues raised in Part I as well. Her research on public assistance in Massachusetts covers decades of the program's operation in great detail. The analysis touches on the strategies and tactics of many participants in the intergovernmental system. In this selection she sketches the patterns of influence that exist primarily between the federal government and the state and, secondarily, between state and local—and federal and local—governments. Derthick covers the dynamics of intergovernmental influence, including the key roles of the bureaucracies, the limitations on state legislatures, and the possibilities of and limitations on national control as these are exhibited in the modern system. She also raises some intriguing questions about accountability and democratic government. Her analysis is especially valuable since grants continue to be the central mode of intergovernmental ties, despite the recent prominence of such alternative forms of intergovernmental influence as federal jurisprudence and mandating (on this last point, see Part IV of this book). Understanding how grants serve to persuade actors in the system, therefore, remains of the utmost importance.

In general, then, the essays in Part II discuss intergovernmental politics in the interactions of principal actors and their coalitions, and through the institutional arrangements of the overall system. In these excerpts several features of American intergovernmental relations are illuminated: important details of interdependence and complexity, sources of conflict, the scope of intergovernmental bargaining processes, some broadly systemic tendencies, possible directions of change, and at least a few normative implications of today's intergovernmental politics.

8

Governmental Diversity: Bane of the Grants Strategy in the United States

Robert D. Reischauer

... The tremendous diversity of governmental arrangements in the United States ... is inherent in the structure of American federalism and makes virtually impossible designing, generating support for, and implementing effective domestic grant programs.

Significant Aspects of Government Diversity

In a nation as physically large and populous as the United States, it is not surprising that subnational units of government are faced with very different sorts of problems, public service demands, and costs. It is surprising—but certainly not unique in federal systems—that the institutional arrangements that have evolved for providing public services are so diverse. Six basic types of government are found in the United States: states, counties, municipalities, townships, school districts, and special districts. From the perspective of the federal government, which is forced by Constitutional constraints to operate through existing governmental institutions rather than revise these structures, a number of characteristics of this diversity are important.

First, none of these governmental types is found everywhere in the nation. Residents of the District of Columbia are not served by a state government. County governments do not exist in two states (Rhode Island and Connecticut) and in 102 separate geographic areas in 21 other states. Municipal governments, which typically provide most local public services in closely settled areas, are nonexistent in rural areas as well as in some urban territories where strong county governments prevail. Townships—a type of local government that, like counties

---

From *The Political Economy of Fiscal Federalism*, ed. Wallace E. Oates (Lexington, Mass.: D. C. Heath, 1977), 115–127.

but unlike municipalities, exists to serve residents of geographic areas without regard to population concentration—are found throughout only one state (Indiana) and in parts of only 20 others. Separate independent school districts are the exclusive providers of elementary and secondary education in 30 states, do not exist in 5 others, and provide education in only parts of the remaining 15. Finally, special district governments, which generally have been created to perform a single governmental function, such as the conservation of natural resources or the provision of fire-protection services, are not found at all in one state (Alaska) and are lacking in parts of all others.

The second aspect of the structure of subnational government that has implications for a federal grants policy is the vast numbers of governments, their difference in scale, and their overlapping nature. . . .

A third, and by far the most important, aspect of this diversity is that the service and fiscal responsibilities imposed on various types of governments differ tremendously both among and within states. The most important state and local public service, elementary and secondary education, illustrates the variation in governments charged with providing a single service. In Hawaii, the state government alone provides elementary and secondary education, while in Maine schooling is provided in some areas by the state and in others by municipalities, townships, or separate school districts. A wide variety of other patterns exists elsewhere. . . . Education is by no means an isolated case. Welfare-related programs are provided in some areas by state governments and in others by counties or by counties and municipalities; within different areas of some states police services are provided by the state, county, municipal, or township government.

The diversity in the provision of services is matched by the diversity of responsibilities for supplying financial support. The existence of large amounts of intergovernmental grants means that often the jurisdiction responsible for providing a particular service is not the one responsible for its fiscal support. For example, elementary and secondary education in both New Hampshire and Alabama is provided exclusively by local governments, but in Alabama less than one-fifth of the costs are borne by local governments, while in New Hampshire nine-tenths of the support is provided by localities. Similarly, welfare . . . checks are written by local governments in both New York and Iowa, yet local governments in New York must provide over one-fourth of the funds needed to cover these checks, while local governments in Iowa must supply less than one-tenth of the funds.

Differences in service and fiscal responsibility translate into differences in the relative importance of the various types of governments. For example, state government is very important in Hawaii, where it is responsible for 89 percent of the state's direct service expenditures and 77 percent of its revenues; in Nebraska, where the similar percentages are 29 and 36, the state is not anywhere near as important a factor. Among local governments, counties are extremely important in North Carolina, where they are responsible for 70 percent of local government spending, but not so in Massachusetts, where 3 percent of such spending is in their hands. Municipalities and townships are responsible for 94 percent of local-government spending in Connecticut, but only 22 percent in Nebraska, for example.

A final critical aspect of the diversity of subnational government structure in the United States is the variation with respect to both the scope of government activity and the instruments used to raise revenues to support public services. No simple accepted view exists of the proper domain of state and local governments. Most, if not all, services provided by these governments are also available privately. In some areas, private vendors are the primary providers of such services as hospitals, fire protection, sanitation, housing, libraries, public transportation, higher education, and utilities (water, gas, and electricity) that elsewhere are supplied exclusively by the government sector. In general, a mixed situation prevails, but the level of services provided publicly varies tremendously. To take some simple examples: welfare payments per recipient vary by over 6 to 1 among the states; California's system of public higher education provides twice as many slots per high school graduate as that of New Jersey; levels of elementary and secondary public-school services—as measured by per pupil spending—vary by a factor of 10 to 1 within nine states and by over 2 to 1 within all but seven.

The revenue sources relied upon by similar types of governments also vary widely. . . .

The Implications of Governmental Diversity

For a nation that has emphasized grants-in-aid as a mechanism for solving domestic problems, the diversity of governmental structure and policy makers' lack of understanding of this diversity have a number of important implications.

First, the federal government is faced with a dilemma in choosing the appropriate governments with which it should interact when it wishes to act on a particular domestic problem area. One option is to deal exclusively with one type of government: states, counties, municipalities, etc. However, this results in certain areas of the nation not being served by the grant program, because the type of government chosen does not exist there.

More serious is the possibility that in some parts of the country the chosen type of government may lack the experience, ability, or even the legal authority to carry out the intent of the grant program. This situation has occurred to some extent in the . . . manpower . . . and community-development block-grant programs that explicitly designate urban county governments as the recipient governments—all urban areas except within the largest cities. In some regions, these counties have had little or no previous experience with manpower or community-development programs. When faced with the new grant, they tend to create a new, and sometimes duplicative, service structure rather than turn the resources over to another type of government that previously was responsible for providing such programs within that particular geographic area.

Another option for the federal government is to deal with whatever government is responsible for the particular service. This approach also has a number of problems. First, a decision must be made as to whether responsibility is to be judged in terms of providing or of financially supporting the service. In many areas, a focus on service delivery would require interaction between the federal government and local governments; an emphasis on financial support would call for the federal government to interact with state authorities. The former might appear to be more logical if the federal government is concerned with augmenting services directed at a certain problem, but it is of course possible for the states to change their own local grant strategy to blunt, if not negate, the impact intended by the federal government. This approach may also have the drawback of requiring the federal government to deal with an extremely diverse group of governments with different legal powers, constraints, and capacities. In many service areas, it may be impossible to design a grant program that would fit the needs and limits of all, or even a majority, of the governments responsible for providing the particular service in each part of the nation. In fact, in some geographic areas duplicate services are provided by overlapping jurisdictions.

Such considerations partially explain the prevalence of "project grants," which require that the governments interested in a program and capable of providing the specified service apply for part of the resources of federal grant programs. This method allows the federal government

to deal with the limited number of governments that have the appropriate responsibility, and it avoids the need to know which governments
have this authority. Furthermore, the project method allows the grant to
be tailored individually to the resources, legal authority, and experience
of the applicant government, whether it is a county, municipality, special
district, or whatever. While the "project grants" approach may circumvent some problems posed by the diversity of governmental structure, it
has been severely criticized in recent years for several reasons: subjective
elements can enter into the distribution of resources; a great deal of red
tape is necessarily generated; small and unsophisticated jurisdictions
have difficulty competing for projects; and the process leaves considerable control in the hands of federal administrators.

A final option for the federal government is to deal only with the
states, relying on them to handle any necessary distribution to lower
levels of governments. Until recently, this was the strategy followed by
most federal grant programs. . . .

This option may circumvent the problems of diversity and be more
constitutionally correct, since local governments are creations of the
states and not of the national government. But some suspect it is an
option that guarantees that the objectives of a grant program will not be
achieved. Many domestic problems brought to the Congress for action
. . . revolve around the distribution of income and the provision of public services to persons who have low incomes and/or who live in declining core cities. Generally, the affected local governments are too poor to
tackle the problems alone or cannot deal with them because of the open
nature of local economies. In many cases, state governments could deal
with the problems but are unwilling to do so. In such instances, providing federal aid to the state for distribution to the appropriate local governments may be like asking the fox to guard the chicken coop. . . .

Dissatisfaction with the "project grant" approach and with the
option of leaving federal grants in the hands of state governments has
led recently to an increased effort to design mechanisms for dealing
directly with the local governments that deliver services in the problem area. These efforts have met several obstacles caused by the diversity of governmental structure. First, the sheer numbers of governments involved make even the most simple programs difficult to
administer. . . . Grants for a specific purpose—such as education or
police protection—to a vast number of governments would probably
swamp the bureaucracy with problems, questions, and demands from
the recipient governments. A related issue involves program design. If

thousands of small, unsophisticated jurisdictions are included as recipients, complex demands cannot be placed on them. Nor, given the diversity of governmental arrangements, can the program be too specific in what it requires recipients to do, because they may not have the power to conform. . . .

A second obstacle to dealing directly with local governments is the difficulty in developing reasonable methods for allocating grant funds among their large numbers. The kinds of data needed to develop a sensible distribution formula are often unavailable. Considerable costs would have to be incurred to generate data that would allow the federal government to allocate grant funds to local governments in a way that followed the objectives of most programs. Faced with this situation, the federal government has taken a number of approaches. In some cases, clearly inadequate, but available, data have been used to distribute federal grants. This partially explains the use of population to allocate grants for such purposes as law-enforcement assistance, drug-abuse treatment, and other areas where the "need" or magnitude of the problem is correlated only weakly with population size. In other instances, hopelessly out-of-date information is used. . . . A more recent approach has been to reduce the number of eligible jurisdictions to a manageable number for which data are available or can be generated at a reasonable cost. . . . While this solution is reasonable, it threatens to undermine the political coalition supporting some grant programs. Governments cut out of direct participation are less willing to fight for larger appropriations or even continuation of the program because the benefits are uncertain from their perspective.

. . . [I]ncreasing concern has been expressed about interjurisdictional fiscal disparities. Many think that these disparities, as they are manifested in the "urban fiscal crisis," will be one of the major domestic problems of the next decade. Preliminary attempts to resolve this problem have been stymied not only by political forces but also by the difficulties posed by the diversity of government structures. While a general consensus can be reached that the amount of aid received by each government under an equalization program should relate positively to the jurisdiction's needs and inversely to its fiscal capacity, there is little agreement on the operational meaning of these terms in a nation where service responsibilities and revenue instruments vary tremendously from jurisdiction to jurisdiction. If all governments relied on similar sources of revenue, a relatively noncontroversial "fiscal capacity index" could be constructed based on a weighted average of the various revenue bases. However, methods of raising revenue are diverse, so such an index necessarily would include revenue sources not used by some jurisdictions either by choice or by lack of legal authority. As a result, federal grant programs have fallen back on the use of per capita income as a crude measure of the relative fiscal capacity of different jurisdictions. In a nation where a relatively small fraction of state and local government revenue is derived directly from income taxes and where states and localities understandably try to export as much of their tax burden as possible, this solution is clearly unsatisfactory. In some local areas, there is no correlation between income and fiscal capacity as measured by revenue sources utilized by the jurisdictions. . . .

The same situation exists with respect to service requirements. Lacking a uniform set of services that are provided by all governments, "needs" have generally been measured by some gross proxy such as population. However, it is clear that the services provided by state and local governments and those which are supported by most grant programs are directed at very specific subgroups of the population—and these are not distributed among jurisdictions in proportion to the general population. . . .

Conclusion

In concluding this discussion, two corollaries of the thesis that the diversity of American governmental structure dooms the grants strategy to failure should be pointed out. The first corollary is that intergovernmental frustration levels tend to rise rather than fall as grant levels increase. From the federal perspective, more is being done to solve a problem when grant levels increase; but, from the standpoint of the recipient jurisdiction and the public at large, the constraints imposed by the government structure may render the programs ineffective. The response of the federal government to the criticism that "things aren't working" is to tighten up the administrative control of the program, then blame the states for mismanagement. This, in turn, increases hostility at the state and local levels. The second corollary is that the federal government will increasingly tend to rely on what is called the *incomes strategy*. Faced with its inability to use grants to solve domestic problems and a reluctance to demand structural changes, national policy makers will tend to design programs in which the federal government deals directly with citizens rather than dealing through intermediary state and local governments. This will reinforce the tendencies toward centralization already apparent in American federalism.

9

Governments as Interest Groups
Anne Marie Cammisa

State and local government associations form a unique type of interest group. First, state and local associations mirror the constituency of Congress. State organizations of governors and legislatures represent the same constituents as senators; local organizations of mayors, cities and counties in some cases overlap with the constituents of representatives. Second, we most often think of interest groups as associations of private individuals that appeal to the government for their own private interest or for their perception of the public interest. In contrast, state and local interest groups are associations of public officials. They appeal to the national government for the interests of the subnational governments. They are lobbyists who themselves have been lobbied. Finally, the state and local groups are more concerned with the administration and funding of policies than with the substance of policies. These groups have an interest in maintaining or increasing their authority over federally funded programs. . . .

State and local groups . . . do not represent private interests, and they consist of public officials, so it has been assumed that they are public interest groups. Insofar as these groups "seek a collective good" then they should be classified as public interest groups. Whether this is the proper classification rests on whether their interests materially benefit a broader group than the members or activists. . . .

In fact, state and local interest groups differ from other public interest groups in that they are lobbying for the interests of their respective governments, not those of the governments' constituents. . . .

. . . Government lobbies have a spatial interest (maintaining authority over their own geographic sphere) as well as a functional (policy) interest. While government lobbies are interested in particular policies, they, unlike other groups (or at least to a greater extent than other groups), are also interested in the spatial dimension of any policy, that is, who will have the authority in implementation and control over the funds. While other public interest groups are generally formed around one particular policy area (housing, child care, environment, welfare rights), governmental interest groups form around a functional area (state or local government) that encompasses several policy areas. In one way, state and local interests are broader than those of other public interest groups: they are interested in a wide variety of domestic policies that are implemented at the state and local level. In another way, their policy interests are narrower. Subnational governments are interested in the process of policy (that is, who implements it) to a greater extent than its outcomes.

. . . There are two main types of government interest groups. The first type consists of the five general government groups: the National Association of Counties, the National League of Cities, the U.S. Conference of Mayors, the National Conference of State Legislatures and the National Governors' Association [NGA]. These groups are generalists, and are the "public interest" governmental groups. The second category are the public official organizations, associations concerned with specific government programs. . . . These include such groups as the American Public Welfare Association . . . and the National Association of Housing Redevelopment Officials . . . , groups that were involved in the passage of welfare reform and the housing bill, respectively.

[Cammisa concentrates on the former group and studies their influence and effectiveness by surveying participants in intergovernmental decision making and by analyzing a set of policy cases. She then offers some general conclusions.—Ed.]

. . . State and local government interest groups began acting as lobbying organizations during the New Deal. The first phase of intergovernmental lobbying, from then until the early 1960s, saw an increase in the prestige of urban mayors, as well as an increase in federal grants to cities. In the second phase, from the early 1960s to about 1969, the states and localities began vying with each other for federal grants. By the third phase (from about 196[9] to about 1979), the groups had established themselves as prominent lobbying organizations, and claimed revenue sharing as a policy success. . . . Donald Haider studied the lobbying effectiveness of the first three phases . . . and found that the governmental lobbies had access to the federal government and were effective on relatively narrow policy questions. The first two phases were characterized by increasing federal spending and increasing "strings" (requirements) attached to that spending. The third phase, during the Nixon administration, gave the states and localities exactly what they wanted: more money with fewer strings attached.

Since Haider's study, the policy environment has changed considerably. In the three phases that Haider describes, the federal grant system was expanding. Because states and localities are concerned with spatial issues (e.g., what government level has authority in funding and administration of programs), such a political environment is favorable to their desires. As federal grants expand, states and localities receive more money. The fourth phase differs from all three of the previous phases because the federal grant system began declining after 1979. Such a decline leads to an economic environment which is hostile to the desires of the states and local groups. . . .

The political environment throughout the fourth phase has generally been hostile to increased government social spending and, at the same time, responsive to state and local calls for increased authority. An unusual window of opportunity opened in the late 1980s, when Congress, responding to the end of the Reagan presidency, pushed for new social programs, and the "kinder, gentler" administration of President Bush went along. This may have been the last chance for state and local groups to get new or expanded federal grants. Since the early 1990s, the political environment has been conducive to decreasing federal requirements on the state and local governments (particularly with the passage of legislation restricting unfunded mandates). The end of the Reagan presidency also marked an increased prestige for the National Governors' Association. Although Reagan wanted states to take over responsibility for social programs, he had a negative view of the state and local groups, which he considered to be interested only in increasing federal government spending. Starting at the end of Reagan's term, the governors' expertise at implementing welfare programs and their role as the chief executives of states has strengthened the NGA's position. The election of President Clinton, a former NGA leader, . . . also raised the prestige of the association.

The political environment became somewhat more favorable to the state and local groups in the late 1980s, but the economic environment by that time had created new problems that . . . persisted throughout the 1990s. The federal deficit and state fiscal crises have constrained both federal and state spending. This economic environment presents great difficulties for states and localities. The subnational governments are responsible for providing services needed by constituents experiencing economic hardship, but they are finding it increasingly difficult to pay for such services. . . .

. . . The government groups reacted to the situation by both maintaining their defensive posture and pushing for some new programs. . . .

The state and local groups today face the same internal constraints and have the same characteristics that Haider described. It is difficult to achieve group consensus because membership is diverse. The governors are still an association of fifty prima donnas. The Conference of Mayors is still largely Democratic. The groups have professional staffs, and are perceived to be more legitimate than other groups by congressional staff. The groups today face a big external constraint . . . : the federal deficit, which limits federal spending on grant programs for states and localities.

. . . The groups are less effective when competing with each other (as in housing legislation) and more effective when there appears to be a groundswell of support for legislation (child care and welfare). . . .

. . . [T]he spatial role of the groups has taken on increased importance. Presidents throughout the fourth phase have focused on reinvigorating federalism and giving states more authority. The groups have taken advantage of that focus. As long as there is consensus within and among the groups, they can proclaim that a program is better run at the state and local levels than at the federal level, and national policymakers are likely to agree. . . .

If inter- or intra-group divisions are evident, the state and local groups achieve less lobbying success. . . . The level of government which receives program funding will never be trivial to state and local groups, whose interests are more spatial than functional. But if their spatial interests cause inter-group divisions, policymakers will be unable to take the groups' concerns seriously. Likewise, if there are disagreements within a group over proposed legislation, congressional actors see this as evidence of a rocky road to passage. Consciously or unconsciously, when a government group (particularly the NGA) can't come to agreement on an issue, it is taking on an obstructor role for that legislation. Time and time again, respondents said that if the governors were not satisfied with a proposal, that proposal had slim chances of passage.

The government groups are experiencing a period of change in their relationship with the federal government. They are not able to gain increased federal grants the way they once were, nor are they viewed as negatively as they were under the Reagan administration. The groups must fight to retain some programs that were once sacrosanct, but their views are nonetheless important when Congress is developing or expanding programs that will be implemented at the subnational level. If the state and local interest groups are to learn any lesson from the legislation considered in this study, it is to take advantage of a window of opportunity when it exists. . . . The opportunity to expand the grant system has passed. . . . Regardless of what phase of intergovernmental lobbying the groups are in, states and localities always wish for more money with fewer strings attached. Most of the fourth phase has been characterized by less money and, until recently, more strings. That may be changing, as conservatives in Congress see an opportunity of decentralizing social programs and spending less money on them. If decentralization means fewer strings, state and local groups will be happy, perhaps moving us into a fifth phase of intergovernmental lobbying. But if fewer strings are attached to less money, state and local groups will have a difficult time achieving the consensus necessary for lobbying success.

10

Trends and Issues in Interstate Cooperation

Ann O'M. Bowman

In the U.S. federal system, states are in the curious position of being both rival and ally to other states. This rival-ally duality creates a fragile equilibrium among the states, one that is in continuous adjustment as states compete and cooperate with each other. In one sense, competition is the natural condition, because states depend heavily on their own sources of revenue thus creating an active rivalry for economic development.[1] However, since the colonial period, states have often found that cooperation is an appropriate or necessary course of action and have created an array of interstate connections.

Basic rules for interactions among the states are set in the U.S. Constitution. The full faith and credit clause (Article IV, Section 1) binds citizens of every state to the laws and policies of other states. The interstate rendition clause (Article IV, Section 2) requires that fugitives from justice in one state who have fled to another state be returned upon request of the governor. In Article IV, Section 2, citizens of one state are guaranteed the "privileges and immunities," that is, the fundamental rights of citizens in other states. A formal provision for interstate compacts, established through Article I, Section 10 of the Constitution, provides a mechanism through which states can address shared problems. Because relationships between the states can be contentious and conflictual, Article III, Section 2 of the Constitution assigns "controversies between two or more states" to the federal judiciary for resolution. For instance, the two-centuries-old conflict between New York and New Jersey over the ownership of Ellis Island was finally resolved by the U.S. Supreme Court in 1997.[2] To maintain a system of free trade among the states, the Constitution contains a provision authorizing Congress to regulate interstate commerce (Article I, Section 8). One other important interstate principle is implicit in the Constitution: the legal equality of

From *The Book of the States 2004*. (Lexington, KY: The Council of State Governments, 2004), pp. 34–40. Reprinted by permission of the author.

each state.[3] Contemporary interstate relations have evolved from these basic provisions into a much more complex network.

Interacting States

As polities in the U.S. federal system, states can be expected to act in a self-interested manner, pursuing opportunities and resisting obstacles. Therefore, states cooperate with other states when it is perceived to be in their interest; they clash when such behavior is deemed in their interest. The assessment of self-interest is self-determined, that is, a state (or more correctly, state officials) makes the determination of self-interest, based on any number of relevant considerations.

The pursuit of self-interest puts states on a path that inevitably intersects with other states.[4] Cooperative behaviors emerge in "win-win" situations as states work together on a common problem or a shared objective. Competitive behaviors, on the other hand, develop as states vie for a prize or position in a process that typically has a zero-sum outcome. This competition can be mediated by external actors such as government institutions that determine winners and losers, as in the case of federal grant funding, or it can be unmediated, "open market" competition as when states seek tourists or firms.[5] When unmediated competition is unproductive or costly, states may reverse field and begin cooperating. For instance, in 1989 five states that had competed with each other to attract new firms pooled their efforts and created the multi-state Pacific Northwest Economic Region, a cooperative venture designed to attract investment to the region.

The pulls and pushes of competition and cooperation lead to a constantly evolving interstate equilibrium. Consider, for example, the ongoing deliberations among Alabama, Florida and Georgia over a river basin they share. At issue are water levels and allocation formulas. Each state has a preferred solution that is at least partially at odds with another state's preference. Negotiating teams for each state (and a federal commissioner who represents the interests of 10 federal agencies with a stake in the resolution of the river basin conflict) have struggled to reach agreement.[6] Complicating the resolution were partisan changes in two of the three governors' offices in 2002 and a desire by one new governor to conduct personal negotiations with his gubernatorial counterparts. . . .

Georgia and Florida were farther from the resolution of their differences than either state was with Alabama. Each wants to settle the conflict but on terms that are, if not preferential, at least acceptable to it. And each state holds a potential veto over any agreement that is reached by the other two states. In 2002, Alabama found itself in the position of broker, trying to get the other two states to compromise sufficiently to reach an accord. The presence of a federal-level official helps keep the parties at the table, because a belief shared by all three states is that a state-led solution is preferable to a federally-imposed solution. In July 2003, a memorandum of understanding was signed by the governors of the three states that set out broad guidelines for negotiators as they continue to wrestle with the details of an allocation formula. Once agreement can be achieved, a new interstate equilibrium will emerge. The larger point is quite simple: on issues that affect vital state interests, it is often difficult to reach a common accord.

Interstate Cooperation

Cooperative behaviors take many different forms including voluntary associations, optional enactment of similar laws, administrative agreements and interstate compacts.[7] In deciding whether to join other states in a collaborative venture, a state considers the anticipated costs and benefits of collective action. One can assume that a self-interested state will participate in actions in which the anticipated gains outweigh potential losses. Three specific forms of interstate cooperation are discussed in the remainder of this article: interstate compacts, multi-state legal actions and adoption of uniform laws.

Interstate Compacts

The traditional mechanism for cooperation among states is the interstate compact, a formal agreement or contract between two or more states. A state's approval of a compact (and, when necessary, congressional approval) makes the agreements legally binding on participants. A compact establishes the policies for state compliance and the terms for state withdrawal from it. Historically, compacts were primarily used to settle boundary disputes between a pair of neighboring states but over time, the substance of compacts has broadened and the number of signatory states on a given compact has increased. Other than territorial border agreements, compacts increasingly have administrative, financial, substantive and technical dimensions.[8]

Because compacts require the approval of the member states' legislatures, the compact negotiation and ratification process can bog down in intra-state politics. Of the interstate compacts in existence in 2003,

Figure [A]: State Membership in Interstate Compacts

High
> 29 compacts

9 states
N.Y., Vt., Maine, N.M., Pa., N.J., Va., Colo., Md.

High/average
28-29 compacts

7 states
Kan., Okla., Texas, W.Va., Ala., N.H., Wash.

Average
24-27 compacts

18 states
Miss., Neb., Ohio, Ore., R.I., Tenn., Ariz., Calif., Ind., Mass., Mont., Wyo., Idaho, Mo., Utah, Ark., Conn., Fla.

Average/low
22-23 compacts

8 states
Del., Ill., Ky., La., S.C., Ga., Minn., N.C.

Low
< 22 compacts

8 states
Hawaii, Wis., Alaska, S.D., Iowa, Mich., N.D., Nev.

Source: Compiled by the author from data in William Kevin Voit, Nancy J. Vickers, and Thomas L. Gavenonis, *Interstate Compacts and Agencies 2003* (Lexington, Ky: The Council of State Governments, 2003).
Note: Within each category, states range from high to low.

32 had been ratified only by one state; thus they were not in effect. For instance, Indiana was the sole signatory to the Interstate Jobs Protection Compact that, when effective, would create a commission to develop strategies to prevent the "unnecessary" interstate relocation of businesses. The compact will take effect when any two of the 18 eligible states [join] Indiana. Although proportionately fewer compacts require congressional consent, for those that do, the process is lengthened.[9] A study of Michigan and its involvement in a low-level radioactive waste compact demonstrated that states do not enter into compacts casually.[10]

To determine the number and nature of interstate compacts as well as patterns of state involvement, a report from The Council of State Governments, *Interstate Compacts and Agencies 2003*, was consulted.[11] The report identifies state members of each compact currently in existence. After excluding defunct compacts (62), border compacts (26), compacts to which only one state is a party (32) and several compacts with special considerations (e.g., no states are listed as members or the compact is U.S. state-Canadian), 155 remained. In Figure [A], states are assigned to one of five categories, based on membership in these compacts.[12]

The average rate of compact membership for states is 25.4 compacts. The lowest levels (16 compacts) are found in Hawaii and Wisconsin; the highest (32 compacts) are in Colorado and Maryland. Although the trend is for compacts to include large numbers of states, many of the extant compacts are bilateral: 57 of the 155 compacts are between two states. The New England region (Maine, New Hampshire, Vermont, Connecticut, Massachusetts and Rhode Island) has been thought of as an area especially prone to compact formation, with federalism scholar Daniel Elazar calling it "a sectional confederation within the American federal system." [13] That tendency appears to have weakened somewhat in recent years with only two of these states showing high levels of compact membership. It is true, however, that the six New England states often form regional compacts but not significantly more so than other regions.

Many compacts are nationwide in scope, e.g., all states are eligible to participate, but the data show that only approximately 10 percent of the compacts have a majority of states as members. One compact that is nearly nationwide is the Interstate Compact on Adult Offender Supervision. In 1999, its first year of existence, nine states became members of the compact; by mid-2003, 47 states had joined.[14] Two of the compacts currently in force have all 50 states as members: the Interstate Compact on the Placement of Children and the Uniform Interstate Compact on Juveniles. Still, with so few majority-state compacts in place, the promise of the compact mechanism as an instrument of national policy is muted; it appears to be more commonly a tool for more particular use.

Multi-state Legal Action

A state's willingness to enter into lawsuits with—not against—other states is another form of cooperation. Legal action by an individual state may not represent a significant challenge to a private sector firm, but action by a group of states poses more of a threat. Furthermore, by pursuing joint legal action, states are asserting and protecting their role in the federal system. In effect, a group of proactive states can beat the national government to the punch in addressing a specific problem. Notable illustrations of this approach include state-initiated lawsuits against the tobacco industry and against Microsoft during the 1990s. In the tobacco case, although a few states acted independently and reached their own settlements with tobacco companies, most litigating states relied on joint action.[15] Eventually state attorneys general were able to broker a national agreement. In the Microsoft case, 20 states filed an antitrust lawsuit in 1998, alleging illegal anti-competitive, anti-consumer actions by the corporation.

The National Association of Attorneys General (NAAG), an organization composed of the chief legal counsels of the states (and territories), has spear-headed the push for multi-state legal action. NAAG

Figure [B]:   State Involvement in Joint Legal Action

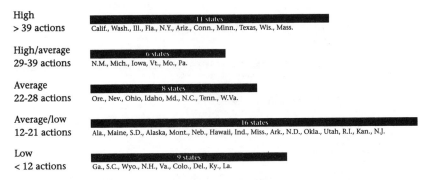

High > 39 actions	11 states Calif., Wash., Ill., Fla., N.Y., Ariz., Conn., Minn., Texas, Wis., Mass.
High/average 29-39 actions	6 states N.M., Mich., Iowa, Vt., Mo., Pa.
Average 22-28 actions	8 states Ore., Nev., Ohio, Idaho, Md., N.C., Tenn., W.Va.
Average/low 12-21 actions	16 states Ala., Maine, S.D., Alaska, Mont., Neb., Hawaii, Ind., Miss., Ark., N.D., Okla., Utah, R.I., Kan., N.J.
Low < 12 actions	9 states Ga., S.C., Wyo., N.H., Va., Colo., Del., Ky., La.

Source: Compiled by the author from data in *AG Bulletin* (Washington, D.C.: National Association of Attorneys General, various issues 1992-1999).
Note: Within each category, states range from high to low.

encourages joint state efforts regarding law enforcement and legal issues, taking policy positions and issuing guidelines but avoiding official action on issues that divide its membership.[16] Collective legal action is similar to interstate compacts in that it unites states on issues of common interest. One such common interest has been protecting consumers from fraudulent practices and products of all types. As noted above, the opportunity to join other states rather than going it alone allows the strength in numbers phenomenon to emerge.

Ascertaining the degree of interstate cooperation via legal channels involved a search of the NAAG publication, *AG Bulletin*, from 1992 through 1999. *AG Bulletin* is published 10 to 12 times per year to disseminate information to its members, especially updates on pending legal actions. In this regard, it reports which states have joined multistate lawsuits.[17] To create the database, each available issue of *AG Bulletin* was reviewed and instances of joint legal actions were noted.[18] Each case was counted only once, regardless of the number of times it was mentioned in subsequent *Bulletins*. Figure [B] shows the level of cooperation for states, as measured by their willingness to join in multistate legal actions.

During the period under study, on average, a state was a party to a multi-state legal action on 25 occasions. The lowest level of joint legal action (seven lawsuits) was found in three states, Georgia, South Carolina and Wyoming, while the highest level was in Massachusetts (51 lawsuits). One trend that is discernible in the data is an increase in the rate of multi-state lawsuits during the decade. A subset of 11 states appears to have played leadership roles, given their high rate of

Figure [C]: State Adoption of Uniform Laws

High
> 9 uniform laws

12 states
Alaska, Ark., Conn., Vt., Ariz., Colo., N.D. Minn., Mont., Hawaii, W.Va., N.M.

Average
6-9 uniform laws

28 states
Fla., Ind., Ky., N.J., Utah, Wash., Wyo., Calif., Ill., Iowa, Md., Mich., N.C. Ohio, Ore., R.I., Tenn., Del., Idaho, Maine, Neb., Nev., Okla., Texas, Ala., Kan., S.D., Va.

Low
< 6 uniform laws

10 states
Ga., Mass., N.Y., Wis., La., Miss., Mo., N.H., Pa., S.C.

Source: Compiled by the author from information found on the official website of the National Conference of Commissioners on Uniform State Laws, www.nccusl.org (October 2003).
Note: Within each category, states range from high to low.

involvement. Also, a population effect may be operative: the four states with the largest populations are in the "high" category. However, variations in state involvement may be partly attributable to an attorney general's proclivity for activism.

Uniform State Laws

A third type of interstate cooperation involves the adoption of uniform statutes. By bringing its law into conformance with other states, a state is endorsing and embracing a peer-established norm. Clearly, this form of cooperation is different from compacts and joint legal actions because it does not involve collective action per se. But the enactment of uniform laws results in a reduction of differences between states and it captures the spirit of cooperation.

The National Conference of Commissioners on Uniform State Laws (NCCUSL) was created in 1892 to draft uniform statutes and model acts. The NCCUSL, a nonprofit organization funded by state appropriations, is made up of attorneys, judges and legal experts from each state. The statute-drafting process can be lengthy, involving extensive negotiations and numerous iterations. Once a law is drafted by NCCUSL, each state has the option of enacting it and thereby conforming its law on a subject to that of other enacting states.

On its website, the NCCUSL tracks state actions as model legislation wends its way (or not) through the legislative process. To explore state adoption of uniform laws, a data set was created consisting of the uniform laws finalized by NCCUSL during the 1990s. Each state was assigned a score based on the number of uniform laws it enacted during the decade. Because the range of scores was fairly narrow, the states were grouped into three categories, as shown in Figure [C].[19]

There were 22 new uniform laws finalized by the NCCUSL in the 1990s and states, on average, adopted 7.7 of them. The average is as high as it is due to the nearly universal adoption of three new articles to the Uniform Commercial Code. The highest rate of enactment of uniform laws during the decade occurred in New Mexico, with 14. At the other end of the scale were Georgia, Massachusetts, New York and Wisconsin, which adopted four of the uniform laws during the time period.

Comparing the Types

The data in Figures [A, B, and C] suggest that for an individual state, the level of cooperative behavior tends to depend on the specific form of cooperation. Wisconsin, for example, lands in the low category in terms of interstate compact membership and uniform law adoption, but has a high level of involvement in joint legal actions. Colorado is quite the opposite: high levels of compact membership and uniform law adoption, but its rate of involvement in multi-state legal actions is low. New York displays a different pattern: the top group with regard to joint lawsuits and interstate compacts, but a low level of uniform law enactment. Thus it appears that there is some differentiation in cooperative behavior, that is, an individual state tends not to pursue all three of the types of cooperation with the same degree of enthusiasm. However, one should not take the point too far, as there is some consistency in the average category, which, regardless of the form of cooperation, includes Idaho, Ohio, Oregon and Tennessee. And at least two states, Georgia and South Carolina, display a general tendency toward limited willingness to cooperate with other states, scoring in the low category on two indicators and in the average/low on the third one. But the general conclusion is that states vary in their propensity toward cooperation.

Future Prospects

The analysis presented here yields several inferences about trends in interstate cooperation. Although the analysis itself was not longitudinal, the data collection process provided some evidence as to changes over time. In short, during the 1990s, both the frequency of multi-state lawsuits and the number of assenting states increased; thus this type of cooperation appears to be on the rise. State embrace of uniform laws is more problematic. Were it not for the Uniform Commercial Code, enactment rates of NCCUSL statutes during the decade would have been substantially lower. Therefore it does not appear that states are poised to adopt a set of laws that would bring their statutes in line with these model statutes. But the idea of greater uniformity across the states is popular among major corporate interests that do business nationally, thus putting pressure on states to conform.

Comparing the findings reported here to an earlier study, it appears that average state membership in compacts has risen by about 10 percent since the mid-1990s.[20] The increase appears to be due to the appeal of "nearly-national" compacts such as the Driver's License Compact that allows member states to exchange information about nonresident traffic law violators. Thus although only 15 compacts have a majority of states as members, this represents an increase from the earlier period. The next decade is likely to see more instances of cooperation that extends beyond the region. For example, many of the compacts that have evolved from the Low-Level Radioactive Waste Policy Act of 1980 (and a subsequent U.S. Supreme Court decision) link states in non-regional clusters.

While interstate compacts are appropriate in instances in which complex legal or fiscal issues exist, administrative agreements can be effective alternatives to them because they are easier to initiate, negotiate and amend.[21] Although definitive data are hard to come by, this trend seems to be on the upswing. For instance, in the "Southern Air Principles" in 2001, the governors of Georgia, North Carolina and Tennessee instructed their states' environmental agencies to develop a regional plan to address air pollution problems in the southern Appalachian Mountains. Another illustration of interstate administrative agreements is multi-state prescription drug purchasing pools. Three New England states, Maine, New Hampshire and Vermont, created the first coalition in 2001; within months, other states were exploring the benefits of collaborative action. These kinds of agreements may be less durable than compacts, but in a rapidly changing environment, their flexibility may be a real advantage.

The willingness of states to cooperate with each other allows what Dale Krane, quoting Daniel Elazar, called "federalism without Washington." [22] This point is well taken. If states work together, their ability to solve major national problems is enhanced. Joint state action, especially the embrace of common policies, provides an alternative to federal legislation, and could be a means of forestalling federal preemption of the states.[23] But this recalls a point made at the beginning of this article: states are not only allies; they are rivals. Furthermore, one of the premises of a federal structure is the ability of constituent units to customize policy—the inverse of uniformity. Thus, although states are increasingly interconnected, the likelihood of sustained cooperative action is tempered by competitive pressures.

Notes

1. Daphne A. Kenyon and John Kincaid "Introduction," in Daphne A. Kenyon and John Kincaid, eds. *Competition among States and Local Governments*, (Washington, D.C.: Urban Institute Press, 1991), 1–3.
2. *State of New Jersey v. State of New York*, 116 S.Ct. 1726.
3. See the discussion in Joseph F. Zimmerman, *Interstate Cooperation: Compacts and Administrative Agreements*, (Westport, CT: Greenwood Press, 2002), 19–37.
4. The possibility of noninteraction exists as well, i.e., a state may choose not to join other states in a lawsuit against the federal government or not to enter the competition for a relocating firm.
5. John Kincaid, "The Competitive Challenge to Cooperative Federalism: A Theory of Federal Democracy," in Daphne A. Kenyon and John Kincaid, eds. *Competition among States and Local Governments* (Washington, D.C.: Urban Institute Press, 1991), 87–114.
6. Stacy Shelton, "Three States Extend Deadline for Water Pact," *Atlanta Journal-Constitution* (January 7, 2003).
7. Patricia S. Florestano, "Past and Present Utilization of Interstate Compacts in the United States," *Publius: The Journal of Federalism* 24 (Fall 1994): 13–25.
8. Zimmerman, *Interstate Cooperation*.
9. Compacts considered to be of a political nature do not take effect without congressional consent.
10. Jeffrey S. Hill and Carol S. Weissert, "Implementation and the Irony of Delegation: The Politics of Low-Level Radioactive Waste Disposal," *The Journal of Politics* 57 (May 1995): 344–369.
11. William Kevin Voit, Nancy J. Vickers, and Thomas L. Gavenonis, *Interstate Compacts and Agencies 2003*, (Lexington, KY: The Council of State Governments, 2003).
12. States are grouped around the mean, with scores within one-quarter of a standard deviation on either side of the mean deemed "average." States involved in compacts at a rate that is one full standard deviation above or below the mean were categorized as high or low, respectively. Compact use that ranged between one-quarter and a full standard deviation from the mean were labeled high/average or average/low.
13. Daniel J. Elazar, *American Federalism: A View from the States*, 3rd ed. (New York: Harper & Row, 1984).

14. Other compacts with more than 40 state members include the Interstate Compact for Education, the Interstate Compact on Parole and Probation, and the Interstate Compact on Mental Health.

15. Eight states did not file a lawsuit against the tobacco industry. However, the non-filing states were included in the national agreement.

16. Joseph F. Zimmerman, "Interstate Cooperation: The Roles of the State Attorneys General," *Publius: The Journal of Federalism* 28 (Winter 1998): 71–89.

17. Despite concerted efforts, not all of the 1992–1999 issues of *AG Bulletin* could be located. NAAG's headquarters did not maintain a master file, official state libraries did not archive them, and contacting the offices of the attorneys general in all fifty states yielded several hard-to-find issues, but not all of them. Therefore this analysis is based on 70 issues of *AG Bulletin* out of the 84 published during the time period. The absence of 14 issues should not be a problem because there is no pattern to the missing issues and *AG Bulletin's* updating results in multiple mentions of the cases.

18. In a few cases, the actual cooperative act was a resolution to Congress (e.g., encouraging the passage of employment non-discrimination legislation) or the filing of comments with a federal agency (e.g., commenting on the Federal Communications Commission's proposed rules on telephone service "slamming"). These endeavors are certainly cooperative in nature; however they do not involve lawsuits, amicus briefs, or negotiated settlements. These non-legal items account for less than 15 percent of the cases.

19. Due to the limited range of scores, three categories were created. Scores less than one full standard deviation above or below the mean were considered average while the high and low categories capture scores greater or lesser than that, respectively.

20. Ann O'M. Bowman, "State-to-State Relationships in the U.S. Federal System," paper presented at the Annual Meeting of the American Political Science Association, San Francisco, California (2001).

21. See Zimmerman's chapter on formal and informal administrative agreements, 163–202.

22. Dale Krane, "The State of American Federalism, 2001–2002: Resilience in Response to Crisis," *Publius: The Journal of Federalism* 32 (Fall 2002): 1–28.

23. See the discussion in Ann O'M. Bowman, "American Federalism on the Horizon," *Publius: The Journal of Federalism* 32 (Spring 2002): 3–22.

11

The New Federalism
Donald L. Doernberg

The phrase "new federalism" surfaced in academic literature in the 1970s and 1980s,[1] but there has been a veritable explosion of attention to the concept following *United States v. Lopez*.[2] First, the Court has systematically shifted the federalism balance toward the states in its expansion of the doctrine of *Younger v. Harris*[3] through the 1970s and 1980s. Second, it has greatly increased the scope of state immunity to federal law and federal suits, with both substantive and expanded procedural components. Third, the Court has narrowed congressional power under the Commerce Clause. Fourth, it has limited congressional power under [Section] 5 of the Fourteenth Amendment. Fifth, it has circumscribed congressional power to require the states to assist in implementing federal programs. Sixth, the Court has increased immunity for sub-state level governments from certain kinds of federal law claims, particularly civil rights claims. This listing is not exhaustive, but it is surely representative.

Federalism itself is oft-misunderstood. Particularly in light of recent judicial history, one tends to think of "federalism" as shorthand for protecting states' rights from the federal government, but that is not accurate. The term properly refers to the appropriate balance of power between state and federal government, and perception of the proper balance has changed over the more than two centuries of the nation's existence. Under the Articles of Confederation, the perceived proper balance so favored the states that the central government could not function. That led directly and rapidly to the Constitutional Convention and substantial revision of the balance toward the central government. Nonetheless, the states remained the preeminent centers of power for decades. There was a clear expansion of federal power following the Civil War, largely through the Civil War amendments, and some have

Excerpted from Donald L. Doernberg, *Sovereign Immunity of the Rule of Law: The New Federalism's Choice* (Durham, NC: Carolina Academic Press, 2005), 129–32, 160–67, 176–77. Reprinted by permission of the Carolina Academic Press, Durham, NC 27701.

referred to an explosion of such power during the New Deal years.[4] The Supreme Court characterized the Civil War amendments as a substantial shift of power from the states to the federal government. Nonetheless, it was still possible in 1953 for Professors Henry Hart and Herbert Wechsler to refer to federal power as largely interstitial in character,[5] though the current editors of the fifth edition of their venerable book acknowledge that federal law has become increasingly primary in some areas.[6]

The flow of power is not all in one direction; one might see in the years since 1980 a river running in two directions at once, each driven by a different branch of the federal government. The dominant trend in Congress has been to increase federal power at the expense of the states. For example, since the elections of 1994 Congress has shown interest, under the rubric of "tort reform," in limiting the amount of recovery possible in some kinds of tort cases between private parties. Whether one thinks that such limits are a good or bad idea, it is clear that congressional legislation in the area would mark a considerable shift of power that once resided exclusively in the states. Indeed, that notion of exclusivity of state power over tort law underlay the Supreme Court's pronouncement in *Erie Railroad Co. v. Tompkins*[7] that both Congress and the federal courts lacked constitutional competence to create law in that area. Perhaps that helps to explain Congress's lack of concrete action since the idea surfaced a decade ago, although it is possible that the Commerce Clause would provide Congress with the needed constitutional shelter.

The prevailing philosophy in the Supreme Court, however, has been exactly the reverse, and the Court and Congress have clashed directly from time to time. Part of the battle over the new federalism plays out directly between the states and the federal government, but an increasingly large part surfaces as an interbranch conflict between Congress and the Supreme Court over the subtext question of which of those branches is the primary guardian of federalism. Viewing the Burger and Rehnquist Courts as engines driving a shift of power from the federal government back to the states, there are two facets to the Court's activities. First, with respect to disputes between state governments and individuals, the Court has greatly limited the federal courts' power to act as referees. One sees this aspect of the Court's focus predominantly in the abstention and the procedural Eleventh Amendment cases. Second, with respect to disputes between federal and state governments over the proper locus of power, the Court has increasingly ruled that Congress has less latitude under the Constitution than previously thought. This part of the Court's philosophy emerges most strongly in recent cases limiting the Commerce Clause, congressional authority pursuant to §5 of the Fourteenth Amendment, Congress's ability to compel state government action, and the substantive sovereign immunity case *Alden v. Maine*.[8] The combined force of these lines of cases makes up the new federalism. . . .

[The author then reviews several subjects on which, he argues, the Court has shifted power toward the states: abstention, the Eleventh Amendment, and the Fourteenth Amendment. This excerpt resumes with coverage of an additional field in which the Court has recently limited national power in favor of the states.—Ed.]

Withdrawal of Congressional Power: The Commerce Clause Cases

The Commerce Clause has long been a primary focus of federal power. As Professors Nowak and Rotunda have noted, "[t]he history of the commerce clause adjudication is, in a very real sense, the history of the concepts of federalism. . . ."[9] Commerce Clause adjudication has been so important because there was virtually no discussion of the Clause in the Constitutional Convention. In the last years of the twentieth century, Commerce Clause jurisprudence shifted significantly away from congressional power.

The Supreme Court began explicating the Commerce Clause's scope in *Gibbons v. Ogden*,[10] "one of the most important [cases] in history."[11] Chief Justice John Marshall gave the Clause an expansive reading and simultaneously gave the judiciary very limited review in Commerce Clause cases. Congressional regulation, he said, could reach not only commerce that crossed state borders, but also commerce carried on entirely within a state if it affected interstate commerce. Only intrastate commercial activity that could have *no* effect outside the state was beyond Congress's reach.

Marshall's expansive view held sway for a long time, but in the late nineteenth century, the Court began to take a narrower view. It looked at the Tenth Amendment as an affirmative limitation on congressional power. This gave rise to the concept of dual federalism, which regarded the states and the federal government as having mutually exclusive spheres of legitimate activity. As the twentieth century began and, indeed, until 1937, the Court systematically constricted Commerce

Clause power in a famous line of economic laissez-faire decisions from *Lochner v. New York*[12] through *Carter v. Carter Coal Co.*[13] limiting congressional power to regulate economic activity through the Commerce Clause. Eventually, the decisions so threatened President Franklin Roosevelt's New Deal initiatives and attempts to deal with the Great Depression that they provoked the President to propose increasing the Court's membership—the "Court-packing plan."

The proposal receives credit for causing the Court to alter its course. It is impossible to say with certainty that the causal link existed, but it is clear that beginning in 1937, the Court became noticeably more hospitable to federal commercial legislation. History tends to attribute the difference to Justice Roberts, who shifted from the conservative side of the Court to a more welcoming approach, giving the New Deal programs a 5-to-4 majority with respect to Commerce Clause challenges. As one scholar has pointed out, however, many of the negative decisions on the New Deal legislation had been by 6-to-3 votes, and it was only Roberts's shift combined with Chief Justice Hughes's that produced the difference in result.[14]

Whatever the cause, 1937 marked a significant shift in the Court's Commerce Clause approach, a shift accentuated in the years following as the conservative wing of the Court retired to be replaced by Roosevelt appointees. The Court discarded restrictive concepts that insisted that the regulated activity have some physical connection with interstate commerce and returned to Chief Justice Marshall's vision. *Wickard v. Filburn*,[15] the celebrated "backyard wheat" case, was the high water mark. Congress created a scheme to stabilize wheat prices, under which the Secretary of Agriculture placed quotas on the acreage farmers were allowed to plant with wheat. Filburn exceeded his quota, but argued that the statute was unconstitutional as applied to him because the excess wheat was for his own use, would never enter the market, and therefore was not subject to regulation as interstate commerce. The Court upheld the statute. Justice Jackson's opinion affirmed that the Court would take a practical approach, not driven by labels or categories (such as "production" versus "marketing") in deciding whether private activity touched interstate commerce. The issue was whether the activity, whether characterized as "local" or not, "exerts a substantial economic effect on interstate commerce."[16] Applying its broad approach, the Court found that Filburn's overproduction would diminish his demand for marketed wheat. "That [his] own contribution to the demand for wheat may be trivial by itself is not enough to remove him from the scope of federal regulation where, as here, his contribution, taken together with that of ma[n]y others similarly situated, is far from trivial." [17] Thus, although Filburn's impact on interstate commerce was negligible, Congress could nonetheless regulate under the Commerce Clause because of possible similar actions of people unconnected with and unknown to Filburn.

The Court thereafter did not invalidate any Commerce Clause statute for more than half a century. In 1995, however, the Court served notice that the commerce power does have limits after all. The Gun-Free School Zones Act of 1990 made it a federal crime to possess firearms in a school zone. Lopez, a Texas high school student, took a gun to school. School authorities had him arrested. He challenged his subsequent conviction on the ground that Congress had exceeded its Commerce Clause power, and the Court, albeit by the narrowest of majorities, struck down his statute. Chief Justice Rehnquist recited the Court's Commerce Clause history, including an approving reference to *Wickard.* Then however, he noted that the statute "by its terms has nothing to do with 'commerce' or any sort of economic enterprise, however broadly one might define those terms." [18] The Court did not say that Congress could never regulate noncommercial activity; instead, it ruled that when the noncommercial activity is intrastate, the Court will be less deferential than when the activity is interstate or when clearly commercial activity, whether inter- or intrastate, is involved.

The next case demonstrated that *Lopez* notwithstanding, Congress would still receive considerable deference for Commerce Clause legislation. *Reno v. Condon*[19] upheld the Driver's Privacy Protection Act of 1994, which forbids states, for the most part, to disclose personal information obtained through motor vehicle registration and driver's licensing procedures. South Carolina argued that the statute violated the Tenth and Eleventh Amendments. Under state law, any person requesting such information and certifying that it would not be used for telephone solicitation was entitled to receive it. South Carolina charged a fee for providing the information, and it allowed drivers to prohibit dissemination of data relating to them.

A unanimous Court easily concluded that state sale of data is commercial activity. Chief Justice Rehnquist also noted that the statute applies both to public and private sector actors and thus does not single out states for special treatment. The Court began with "the time-honored presumption" [20] that the statute was constitutional. It noted that the information was in demand precisely because it had commercial value. Moreover, release of such information was interstate, not merely intrastate, so the Court declined even to consider the federal government's fallback position that although the collection of motorist information was intrastate, the activity substantially affected interstate commerce, as the Court had found in *Wickard*.

The Court also rejected South Carolina's constitutional arguments. While the Justices agreed that it would take the state workers time to implement the statute and might entail other, ancillary expense, they noted that the Court had often upheld legislation that burdened the states. " 'That a State wishing to engage in certain activity must take administrative and sometimes legislative action to comply with federal standards regulating that activity is a commonplace that presents no constitutional difficulty.' " [21]

Unanimity died young. Four months later, a five-to-four Court declared in *United States v. Morrison* . . . the Violence Against Women Act (VAWA) unconstitutional as exceeding Congress's Commerce Clause power.[22] Congress had created a civil remedy "for the victims of gender-motivated violence." [23] Chief Justice Rehnquist's majority opinion found that Congress lacked the power to do that under either the Commerce Clause or the Fourteenth Amendment. The Court's rationale rested heavily on three distinctions, the first between economic and noneconomic conduct, the second between intra- and interstate activity, and the third between appropriate spheres of state and federal power.

The majority held that gender-motivated violence was certainly neither economic nor, in the vast majority of cases, interstate, conclusions with which the dissenters did not quarrel. Citing *Lopez*, the Chief Justice declined to rule that there could never be circumstances in which Congress could regulate noneconomic, intrastate activity, but was clearly skeptical. The Court would decide whether the connection was sufficiently substantial to pass constitutional muster. The majority explicitly rejected the idea that Congress can regulate noneconomic activity "based solely on that conduct's aggregate effect on interstate commerce." [24] The majority had to make that statement because Congress had assembled an impressive record documenting the effects of gender-related violence on commerce. It was impossible to say that the effects on interstate commerce were too attenuated, as in *Lopez*, so the majority had to come up with another rationale for invalidating the legislation.

Justice Souter led the dissenters. He attacked the majority's expansion of *Lopez* and criticized *Morrison's* apparent return to categorical labels. When the Court had last used what Justice Souter termed "the formalistic economic/noneconomic distinction," [25] it had done so, in his view, to further the Court's *laissez-faire* economic agenda. More to the point for present purposes, Justice Souter saw the majority's resurrection of the pre-1937 approach as in service of a different, undeclared, but clearly Court-defined agenda.

> Just as the old formalism had value in the service of an economic conception, the new one is useful in serving a conception of federalism. It is the instrument by which assertions of national power are to be limited in favor of preserving a supposedly discernible, proper sphere of state autonomy to legislate or refrain from legislating as the individual States see fit. The legitimacy of the Court's current emphasis on the noncommercial nature of regulated activity, then, does not turn on any logic serving the text of the Commerce Clause or on the realism of the majority's view of the national economy. The essential issue is rather the strength of the majority's claim to have a constitutional warrant for its current conception of a federal relationship enforceable by this Court through limits on otherwise plenary commerce power.[26]

Justice Souter reached this conclusion partly because the majority argued that criminal law is an area of traditional state concern. The Court counseled caution in approving congressional intrusion on state domains. Justice Souter countered that long-established law made clear that Congress's exercise of Commerce Clause power can either co-exist or entirely displace state law in areas ordinarily of state concern, as long as there is a substantial effect on commerce.

However, ... the *Morrison* majority may have had very real concerns unrelated to any agenda. Approval of VAWA on the basis of substantial economic effect alone might have opened the door for Congress to get pervasively involved in criminal law generally. The majority charged this would allow Congress "to completely obliterate the Constitution's distinction between national and local authority...." [27] Commentators have noted the Court's concern in *Lopez* and *Morrison* that uncritical judicial reading of the Commerce Clause, which is clearly how the majority regards the period from 1937 to [*Lopez*], would allow Congress to regulate activity ordinarily exclusively within state competence under the rubric of state policy power.

At the close of the twentieth century, the scope of the commerce power was very much under discussion. That is significant because of the terms in which the *Lopez* and *Morrison* Courts cast the discussion.

Discarding the substantial-effects test in favor of renewed focus on whether the regulated activity was economic or noneconomic, the Court focused on the clash of national and state sovereignties. Standing alone, that might not signal a broader trend, but it does not stand alone. In at least two other areas, the Court has quite discernibly limited federal power, carving out areas of state immunity from federal action. . . .

[The author then sketches the rationale and implications of two additional Court decisions, *New York v. United States* (505 U.S. 144 (1992)) and *Printz v. United States* (521 U.S. 898 (1997)), which asserted Congress's inability to compel states to implement federal programs. The reading resumes with the final section.—Ed.]

Conclusion

As so often happens at the Supreme Court level, *New York* and *Printz* were not really about disposal of low-level radioactive waste and regulation of handguns respectively. Those subjects were merely vehicles for a battle at the highest judicial level over the allocation of power in the United States that probably is essential to the country's health: the federal government versus individuals, the state governments versus individuals, and the federal government versus the states. The Framers drafted the Constitution in recognition of all three relationships, depending on division of power both between the states and the federal government and within each level of government to prevent undesirable concentrations of power subject to insufficient external controls. With respect to individuals, the Framers included numerous provisions for no purpose other than to tell government what it may not do at all or specifying how government may seek to accomplish certain things. The entire constitutional history of American government demonstrates, if nothing else, the nation's original and continuing suspicion of official power. The debates surrounding the framing and ratification of the Constitution were all about power and its allocation, and those debates have never stopped. Division of power and intractable suspicion of power were the tools the Framers sought to employ to secure liberty by ensuring the rule of law. They recognized, as Lord Acton did a century later, the incompatibility of unchecked power and the rule of law. "Power tends to corrupt; absolute power corrupts absolutely." [28] It is against this apparently universal law of human and governmental relationships that the complex of concepts known as the rule of law are set . . .

Notes

1. See, e.g., Peter Gabel, "The Mass Psychology of the New Federalism: How the Burger Court's Political Imagery Legitimizes the Privatization of Everyday Life," 52 *Geo. Wash. Law Rev.* 263 (1984).
2. 514 U.S. 549 (1995).
3. 401 U.S. 37 (1971).
4. See, e.g., Richard E. Levy, "*New York v. United States:* An Essay on the Uses and Misuses of Precedent, History, and Policy in Determining the Scope of Federal Power," 41 *Kan. Law Rev.* 493, 495 (1993).
5. See Henry M. Hart, Jr. & Herbert Wechsler, *The Federal Courts and the Federal System* 435 (1ˢᵗ ed. 1953).
6. See Richard H. Fallon, Daniel J. Meltzer & David L. Shapiro, *Hart and Wechsler's the Federal Courts and the Federal System* 495 (5ᵗʰ ed. 2003).
7. 304 U.S. 64 (1938).
8. 527 U.S. 706 (1999).
9. John Nowak & Ronald D. Rotunda, *Constitutional Law.* West Publishing Company (6ᵗʰ ed. 2000).
10. 22 U.S. 1 (1824).
11. 22 U.S. (9 Wheat.) 1 (1824).
12. 198 U.S. 45 (1905).
13. 298 U.S. 238 (1936).
14. See, e.g., Jed Handelsman Shugerman, "A Six–Three Rule: Reviving Consensus and Deference on the Supreme Court," 37 *Ga. Law Rev.* 893, 520–21 (2003).
15. 317 U.S. 111 (1942).
16. *Id.* at 120.
17. *Id.* at 127.
18. *United States v. Lopez,* 514 U.S. 549, 561 (1995).
19. 528 U.S. 141 (2000).
20. *Id.* at 148.
21. *Id.* at 150–51 (quoting *South Carolina v. Baker,* 485 U.S. 505 (1988)).
22. *United States v. Morrison,* 529 U.S. 598 (2000).
23. *Id.* at 601–2.
24. *Id.* at 617.
25. *Id.* at 644 (Souter, J., dissenting).
26. *Id.* at 644–45 (Souter, J., dissenting).
27. *Id.* at 615 (citing *United States v. Lopez,* 514 U.S. 549, 564 (1995)).
28. John Emerich Edward Dalberg Acton, *Essays on Freedom and Power* 364 (Gertrude Himmelfarb ed., 1949).

12

State Autonomy in Germany and the United States

Daniel Halberstam and Roderick M. Hills Jr.

In his dissent in the 1995 decision of *Printz v. United States*,[1] Justice Breyer embarked on a rare judicial excursion into comparative constitutional law. *Printz* held that the federal government could not require state governments' executive officials to regulate private persons according to federal standards. The decision extended the 1992 holding of *New York v. United States*,[2] which held that the federal government could not commandeer the state legislature by requiring the state to enact a program for the storage of privately generated nuclear waste. Thus, after *New York* and *Printz*, state governments may refuse to comply with the federal government's commands that state and local governments regulate private persons according to federal standards. We will call this power of state and local governments the "*Printz* entitlement."

In his criticism of the *Printz* entitlement, Justice Breyer argued that the experience of other federal regimes showed that it was not necessary for protecting federalism. As Justice Breyer observed, "The federal systems of Switzerland, Germany, and the European Union, for example, all provide that constituent states, not federal bureaucracies, will themselves implement many of the laws, rules, regulations, or decrees enacted by the central 'federal' body."[3] As Justice Breyer observed, these federal regimes give their component states the power but also the obligation to execute federal policy "because they believe that such a system interferes less, not more, with the independent authority of the 'state,' member nation, or other subsidiary government, and helps to safeguard individual liberty as well."[4] This comparison with foreign constitutional regimes led Justice Breyer to ask the majority a pointed question: "Why, or how, would what the majority sees as

From Daniel Halberstam and Roderick Hills, *Annals of the American Academy of Political and Social Science* (574/March 2001) pp. 173–184, Copyright © 2001 by Sage Publications. Reprinted by permission of Sage Publications, Inc.

a constitutional alternative—the creation of a new federal . . . bureaucracy, or the expansion of an existing federal bureaucracy—better promote either state sovereignty or individual liberty?" [5]

This article attempts to take up Justice Breyer's question by comparing U.S. and German constitutional rules regarding state autonomy.
. . . Although differences in political culture make such comparisons
hazardous, we will tentatively suggest ways in which (1) the German
system provides greater protection for state independence in implementing federal law but (2) the U.S. system avoids some of the problems of inefficiency familiar from the German experience.

I. Cooperative Federalism: German and American Systems Compared

According to an oft-repeated cliché, the German and American
systems of federalism are radically different from each other. The
Germans divide power between federation and *Länder* vertically, giving the federation the primary prerogative of enacting legislation and
the *Länder* the prerogative of executing such legislation. By contrast,
the U.S. Constitution is said to divide powers horizontally, giving the
federal government and the states separate legislative jurisdictions in
which each can enact and execute their own distinct policies free from
interference from the other.

This conventional contrast between the German and American
systems of federalism, however, is misleading. At least since the U.S.
Supreme Court decided *Wickard v. Filburn*[6] in 1942, the U.S. Constitution has not reserved much exclusive jurisdiction to state governments to legislate free from federal interference. Moreover, since the
New Deal, the U.S. government has enlisted the states to play the
primary executive role in implementing dozens of important federal programs, including unemployment insurance, poverty assistance, environmental protection, worker health and safety, public housing, community
development, maintenance and construction of interstate highways,
and so on. This is not to say that the German and American systems of
cooperative federalism do not differ in important ways. Indeed, there
are three salient differences that merit discussion.

First, the Grundgesetz (the German Constitution, or Basic Law)
provides for the formal representation of state governments in the federal legislative process through the Bundesrat. Each *Land* government
sends members of its cabinet to represent the interests of the *Land* in

the Bundesrat. As these officials are simultaneously delegates to the Bundesrat and officers of the *Land* government and can be instructed and recalled by the *Land* government, their representation of *Land* interests is more direct than the U.S. senator's representation of state interests even prior to the ratification of the Seventeenth Amendment, when Senators were chosen (but not instructed or recallable) by state legislatures. In return for this closer representation of the *Länder* governments in the Bundesrat, however, the German framers of the Grundgesetz who favored federalism had to limit the jurisdiction of the Bundesrat (Golay 1958, 50). The Bundesrat does not have the same capacity as the U.S. Senate to stop federal legislation but instead can veto only those laws that affect the administrative duties of the *Länder*.

Since the ratification of the Seventeenth Amendment (and probably before then as well), the American states have lacked any such direct and formal power to veto collectively federal laws imposing administrative duties on states. The *Printz* entitlement, however, gives them an analogous power: the power of individual states to refuse to implement federal statutes within that state's borders. The *Printz* entitlement could be characterized as a more individualistic version of the Bundesrat: whereas the Bundesrat gives the *Länder* the power *collectively* to veto federal imposition of administrative duties on the *Länder*, the *Printz* entitlement gives each *individual* state a similar power to veto federal administrative duties. . . .

The second respect in which the German and U.S. constitutional rules regarding cooperative federalism differ is that, apart from those areas enumerated in Article 87 in the Grundgesetz in which the federation must maintain its own implementing bureaucracy, the Grundgesetz gives the *Länder* a monopoly on the implementation of federal law, either as the agents of the federation or as a matter of their own concern. The federation can take measures to ensure that the *Länder* execute federal laws faithfully, but, when the *Länder* execute such laws as a matter of their own concern, the measures available to the federation are strictly limited by Grundgesetz Article 84. In particular, the federation cannot create its own federal field offices or send commissioners to any but the highest *Länder* authorities without the consent of the Bundesrat.

The United States gives Congress a different weapon by which to induce faithful state implementation of federal law. Since at least *McCulloch v. Maryland*,[7] the United States has the constitutional power to create an unlimited array of federal agencies to implement federal law. Under no obligation to involve the states at all in the implementation of federal laws, Congress may bypass the states entirely if they do not carry out federal laws in the manner demanded by Congress, using agencies designed according to Congress's specifications. In addition, Congress may condition a state's continued ability to regulate in a given area on that state's assistance in the implementation of federal regulatory policies.[8] Thus Congress can secure state cooperation whenever (1) Congress can make a credible threat to preempt state law by creating a federal agency to regulate a field in place of the states unless the states regulate according to federal standards and (2) state politicians value the right to continue the state's regulatory presence in the preemptible field more than they dislike the conditions that Congress places upon their continued presence in that field. Finally, Congress may also condition a state's receipt of federal funds on that state's regulating according to federal standards and will secure state assistance as long as state politicians value the federal funds more than they dislike the federal conditions (Hills 1998).

A third difference between the U.S. and German systems of federalism is that the *Länder* have much more limited capacity to initiate their own tax and regulatory policies absent federal authorization, because the German doctrine of field preemption is broader than the analogous American doctrine. Article 72(1) of the Grundgesetz provides that *Länder* may exercise concurrent powers "only so long as and to the extent that the federation does not exercise its right to legislate." This provision has been construed to forbid the *Länder* from imposing taxes that are also imposed by the federation (Isensee and Kirchhof 1990). As a result, Article 106 of the Grundgesetz precisely specifies the taxes that each level of government can impose, leaving the *Länder* with the relatively unimportant sources of revenue enumerated in Article 106(2) (Currie 1994, 53–54).

This is not to say that the *Länder* are financially impoverished, because Article 106(3) provides that revenue from income, corporation, and sales taxes shall be shared by both the federation and the *Länder*. Such taxes are imposed only with the consent of both *Länder* (through the Bundesrat under Grundgesetz Article 105(3)) and federation, however, with the result that no single *Land* can generate much revenue through its own solitary efforts. Aside from the strict limit on taxing authority, the *Länder* are fiscally hobbled by Article 107(2) of the Grundgesetz, which imposes a requirement of *Finanzausgleich*, or financial equalization between rich and poor *Länder*, requiring wealthy *Länder* to provide financial assistance to poorer *Länder* to ensure substantial equality of living conditions and state resources (Larsen 1999). Both provisions limit the capacity of *Länder* to generate own-source revenue or, if they can generate such revenue, to retain it. In the United States, by contrast, states are permitted to levy any tax concurrently with the federal government so long as the federal government does not expressly preempt such taxation and so long as the tax complies with fairly lenient constitutional limits (for example, the tax must not be legally incident on, or discriminate against, a federal agency and must not discriminate against or unduly burden interstate or international commerce). As a result, states have much more flexibility to come up with and retain extra money through state-imposed taxes in the United States than the *Länder* do in Germany.

In the U.S. system, aside from greater powers of concurrent taxation, the states also have greater capacity than the *Länder* have in Germany to regulate private activity when federal law does not expressly preempt such law. . . .

II. The Practical Effects of Different Constitutional Structures

We will suggest that two general consequences plausibly follow from the differences in constitutional structure. We stress that these are tentative hypotheses that can be confirmed only through more careful empirical work. Indeed, it is quite possible that the effects of, for example, the political culture or the political party system overpower any appreciable effects of constitutional structure. To the extent that the constitutional structure has practical effects, however, we speculate that (1) the U.S. system of federalism is likely to provide states with less effective protection from the federal government than the Grundgesetz provides to the *Länder* but (2) the German protections for the *Länder* arguably impose a greater cost than the American system in terms of efficient and flexible administration of national laws.

Our first hypothesis is that the *Printz* entitlement is likely to be less effective in protecting state autonomy than the structures created by the Grundgesetz. There are two reasons for this inference. First, the *Printz* entitlement will provide little practical benefit to state governments if the federal government can easily bypass the state governments by federalizing activities using purely federal agencies. In such a case, as several scholars have noted, the state governments would enjoy a useless autonomy, because their fields for autonomous activity would be preempted. Justice Breyer seems to endorse this view when he suggests that the alternative to commandeering is "the creation of a new federal . . . bureaucracy, or the expansion of an existing federal bureaucracy." [9] The *Printz* entitlement poses no direct obstacles to such bypass of the states and preemption of state law. By contrast, Articles 83–86 of the Grundgesetz give the *Länder* the right and duty to administer all federal policies not enumerated in Article 87, making it impossible for the federal government to bypass the *Länder*.

Second, the *Printz* entitlement gives states only an individual rather than collective veto: each state has the power to refuse to implement federal regulation of private persons within its own borders. The exercise of such a power by a single state is likely to be politically difficult because, by declining to implement federal policy, the state's voters would forfeit federal grant revenue while still paying the same federal taxes that would finance the federal program in acquiescing states. The payment of federal taxes for the benefit of neighboring states is not likely to be a political winner (Baker 1995). By contrast, the Grundgesetz gives the *Länder* a collective veto over federal policy in the form of the Bundesrat: if the *Länder* exercise this veto, then the federal policy is not implemented in any *Land*. The *Länder* that oppose a federal policy through the Bundesrat, therefore, need not fear that the policy will give a competitive advantage to those *Länder* that do not oppose it. In this sense, the Bundesrat functions as something like a legally protected cartel of the *Länder* from which defection is impossible.

We do not wish to overstate the barriers to the effective use of the *Printz* entitlement. The states have some compensating legal advantages that may mitigate the risk that the federal government will implement federal laws with federal agencies whenever states exercise their *Printz* entitlement. In particular, field preemption in the United States appears to be narrower than German field preemption with the consequence that, compared to the German *Länder*, states under the U.S. Constitution appear to retain broader powers to initiate policies that supplement federal laws and federal revenues even when Congress is deadlocked over controversial policy proposals. [10]

The states may exploit this power to initiate programs as a practical means to counteract Congress's constitutional authority to federalize policy areas. . . . One result is that state policy initiatives may be quite influential in the federal lawmaking process by providing the initial impetus and sometimes even blueprint for federal action (Elliot, Ackerman, and Millian 1985). To bypass or overrule the states, not only must Congress often demonstrate that its proposed regulatory scheme is politically desirable, but it must do so by arguing specifically against the continued existence of active state regulation.

It is not surprising, therefore, that when Congress enters new policy areas, the resulting federal statutes pay substantial deference to the existing state schemes and often carve out a special place for them in the federal scheme.... Congress will have considerable incentive to make concessions to state officials simply to get control over state matching funds that would be lost if states declined federal grants. Consider, for instance, the considerable concessions that the Social Security Administration made to induce California to place state revenue in the federal Supplemental Security Income program (Derthick 1990, 105–9). The *Printz* entitlement, at a minimum, prevents Congress from simply taking over the states' bureaucratic structures cost-free for its own policy programs. Instead, Congress either has to undergo the political risk and fiscal expense of creating its own structures or must pay the state governments a grant acceptable to them in return for the states' services (Hills 1998).

Nevertheless, one might respond that this description of the *Printz* entitlement rests on empirical assumptions too tentative to justify confidence that the entitlement will protect state autonomy as effectively as German law does. How can one be sure that the vagaries of intergovernmental deal-making will ensure that the states will be left with enough discretion to implement federal law? Perhaps Congress will bypass states and use federal agencies even when it is inefficient to do so, simply because Congress has a self-interested desire to monopolize patronage or credit-taking opportunities (Chubb 1985, 284–85; Conlan 1988, 38; Anton 1989, 111). By contrast, German federalism gives the *Länder* the surer protections of a constitutional entitlement to administer federal statutes and a collective rather than individual veto over federal mandates (Halberstam forthcoming). In short, it seems hard to argue with the conclusion that German law protects state autonomy more reliably than U.S. federalism does.

This extra protection of federalism, however, comes at a price. Our second hypothesis is that, when compared to the U.S. system of cooperative federalism, the German system tends to produce what Fritz Scharpf (1987) has described as a "joint decision trap"—the tendency in German federalism to require consent from multiple actors for political action, resulting in the obstruction of clear and effective policy-making. By giving the *Länder* a collective veto (through the Bundesrat) and a monopoly (through Articles 83–86 of the Grundgesetz) over the implementation of federal law, the German system locks the two levels of government—*Länder* and federation—into a position in which neither can dispense with the other in executing any policy of significance (Halberstam forthcoming). This collective veto over federal lawmaking gives the *Länder* far greater capacity to hold federal lawmaking hostage to their demands for policy concessions or simply for more revenue, even when this is not justified by their superior regulatory performance. ... The federation, therefore, must enter into lengthy, complex, and publicly invisible negotiations with the byzantine networks of appointed and elected officials of the *Länder* to secure passage and faithful implementation of the law (Leonardy 1991).

The U.S. system of intergovernmental relations mitigates this obstacle to national legislation by not giving state governments any legal monopoly over the power to implement national laws and by allowing each state to withhold its implementing services separately rather than collectively through the individual exercise of the *Printz* entitlement. With the states' lack of any monopoly on implementation, the upper limit of money and discretion for which a state can bargain is determined not by constitutional procedure but by the opportunity costs that the federal government faces by forgoing state services—namely, the creation of a potentially inefficient federal agency, which might become an embarrassment to Congress and result in the loss of the matching funds that the state government would otherwise supply (Hills 1998). ... We suggest that this ad hoc method of determining the state role in implementing federal legislation mitigates the joint decision trap faced by the German federation while still preserving a significant role for states in implementing (and resisting) federal policy.

A second potential cost of the German system of federalism is that the assignment of implementation duties to the *Länder* is remarkably inflexible. The responsibilities of federation and *Länder* bureaucracies are defined ex ante by the Grundgesetz; thus the German system does not allow for greater or fewer enforcement responsibilities to be allocated to the *Länder* based on any *Land's* track record of enforcement. This rigidity may prevent more generally what Albert Breton (1996) calls "vertical competition," that is, competition between the state and federal bureaucracies to determine which level of government can administer a function more efficiently (233–39). The essential idea underlying Breton's theory is that the performance of one level of government in delivering services in one jurisdiction can serve as a benchmark for citizens to appraise how well another level of government is delivering the same services in another jurisdiction. . . .

One might argue, then, that the Grundgesetz's constitutional division of labor inflexibly prevents citizens from gaining information about the relative competence of the different levels of government by observing their performance and withdrawing responsibility from inefficient agencies. The need for vertical competition might be especially great in Germany given that bureaucratic section heads (*Referenten*) in charge of implementing federal policy tend to be overly risk averse and hostile to efficiency-promoting reform (Mayntz and Scharpf 1975, 69–76). The degree to which *Länder* politicians will combat these bureaucratic tendencies may be uneven. . . .

In sum, contrary to conventional wisdom, the U.S. and German systems of federalism both enlist component jurisdictions to implement national policies. The difference between the two regimes is not whether but how the enlisting occurs. There is reason to believe that the structure of German intergovernmental relations has some costs that the American system avoids, such as potential inefficiencies of collaborative decision making and diminished possibilities for checking inefficiencies in policy implementation through vertical competition. Conversely, the German system may better protect the significance of the *Länder* by providing categorical and collective protection within the constitutional structure. If elected federal legislators have a self-interested bias in favor of centralized administration, then the U.S. system may inadequately protect the states' role in administering federal law. While the Grundgesetz eliminates the danger of the underuse of the *Länder* posed by such perverse incentives, it appears to do so with a cleaver rather than a scalpel, imposing *Länder* implementation even when such a system might be excessively costly. The challenge, in this case, would be to discover a mechanism for eliminating federal politicians' perverse incentives to underuse subordinate jurisdictions without eliminating some of the flexibility of ad hoc arrangements characteristic of the U.S. system.

References

Anton, Thomas J. 1989. *American Federalism and Public Policy: How the System Works*. New York: Random House.

Baker, Lynn. 1995. Conditional Federal Spending After *Lopez. Columbia Law Review* 95:1911–89.

Beamer, Glenn. 1999. *Creative Politics: Taxes and Public Goods in a Federal System*. Ann Arbor: University of Michigan Press.

Breton, Albert. 1996. *Competitive Governments: An Economic Theory of Politics and Public Finance*. New York: Cambridge University Press.

Chubb, John. 1985. Federalism and the Bias in Favor of Centralization. In *The New Direction in American Politics*, ed. John Chubb and Paul Peterson. Washington, DC: Brookings Institution.

Conlan, Timothy. 1988. *New Federalism: Intergovernmental Reform from Nixon to Reagan*. Washington, DC: Brookings Institution.

Currie, David P. 1994. *The Constitution of the Federal Republic of Germany*. Chicago: University of Chicago Press.

Derthick, Martha. 1990. *Agency Under Stress: The Social Security Administration in American Government*. Washington, DC: Brookings Institution.

Elliot, E. Donald, Bruce Ackerman, and John C. Millian. 1985. Toward a Theory of Statutory Evolution: The Federalization of Environmental Law. *Journal of Law, Economics, & Organization* 1:313–40.

Golay, John Ford. 1958. *The Founding of the Federal Republic of Germany*. Chicago: University of Chicago Press.

Halberstam, Daniel. Forthcoming. Comparative Federalism and the Issue of Commandeering. In *The Federal Vision*, ed. Kalypso Nicolaidis and Robert Howse. Oxford: Oxford University Press.

Hills, Roderick M. 1998. The Political Economy of Cooperative Federalism: Why State Autonomy Makes Sense and "Dual Sovereignty" Doesn't. *Michigan Law Review* 96:801–944.

Isensee, Joseph and Paul Kirchhof. 1990. *Handbuch des Staatsrechts*. Heidelberg: C. F. Müller.

Larsen, Clifford. 1999. States Federal, Financial, Sovereign, and Social: A Critical Inquiry into an Alternative to American Federalism. *American Journal of Comparative Law* 47 (Summer): 429–88.

Leonardy, Uwe. 1991. The Working Relationships Between Bund and Länder in the Federal Republic of Germany. In *German Federalism Today*, ed. Charlie Jeffery and Peter Savigear. Leicester: Leicester University Press.

Mayntz, Renate and Fritz Scharpf. 1975. *Policymaking in the German Federal Bureaucracy*. New York: Elsevier.

Rose-Ackerman, Susan. 1980. Risk Taking and Reelection: Does Federalism Promote Innovation? *Journal of Legal Studies* 9:593–619.

Sabato, Larry. 1983. *Goodbye to Good-Time Charlie: The American Governorship Transformed*. 2d ed. Washington, DC: Congressional Quarterly Press.

Scharpf, Fritz. 1987. The Joint-Decision Trap: Lessons from German Federalism and European Integration. In *Law and State: A Biannual Collection of Recent German Contributions to These Fields*. Tübingen: Institute for Scientific Cooperation.

Notes

1. 521 U.S. 898 (1997).
2. 505 U.S. 144 (1992).
3. *Printz v. United States*, 521 U.S. 898, 976 (Breyer, J., dissenting) (citations omitted).
4. Id. at 976–977 (citations omitted).
5. *Printz*, 521 U.S. at 977–78.
6. 317 U.S. 111 (1942).
7. 17 U.S. (4 Wheat.) 316 (1819).
8. *New York*, 505 U.S. at 167–69.
9. *Printz*, 521 U.S. at 978.
10. As Susan Rose-Ackerman (1980) has noted, state politicians might hang back, waiting for others to take successful risks that the latecomers can then imitate. But, in practice, the advantages of being the first to succeed with a policy seem sufficient incentive for ambitious state politicians to engage in creative policymaking in order to make a national name for themselves (Sabato 1983; Beamer 1999).

13

Ways of Achieving Federal Objectives
Martha Derthick

The Federal Government in State Politics

In giving grants and attaching conditions to them, the federal government becomes an actor in the state political system. It is a peripheral actor rather than an integral one, for it has no legitimate role within that system—no formal right to make decisions and no recognized informal right to function as a lobby. Nonetheless, it alters the environment within which the integral actors function, alters the distribution of influence among them, and thus itself becomes an actor in state politics.

The selection of subjects for the public agenda—of "issues" for consideration—is the first step in determining the content of public policy, and it is at this point in the process of state politics that federal influence begins to be felt. By offering grants for specified activities, the federal government places an item on the political agenda: should the aided activity be undertaken or not? The setting of conditions works in parallel fashion. By saying to the state that it will not give money unless a certain rule is adopted (or, if the grant program is already under way, by saying that money will cease to be given), the federal government causes the state to consider whether the required action should be taken. An issue is raised that might not have been raised in the absence of federal action. Strictly speaking, of course, the federal government does not itself place the question on the agenda of state politics. What it does is to stimulate proposals by actors integral to the state political system, such as elected executive or legislative officials, party officials, appointed administrators, or executives of pressure groups. For state political actors who independently share some or all of the federal goals, federal action creates opportunities ("excuses") for the making of proposals.

Reprinted by permission of the publisher from "Prospects for the Grant System" in *The Influence of Federal Grants: Public Assistance in Massachusetts* by Martha Derthick, pp. 201–214, Cambridge, Mass.: Harvard University Press, Copyright © 1970 by the President and Fellows of Harvard College.

For these elected officials and for appointed administrators—who together are ultimately the objects of federal influence because they are possessors of authority to act within the state government—federal sponsorship reduces the cost of making a proposal and taking the subsequent action. Not only are monetary costs transferred to the federal level; if opposition arises, state officials may be able to transfer political costs as well, by imputing responsibility to the federal government. Moreover, federal action increases the cost of inaction—that is, the cost of *not* proposing or taking the actions the federal government seeks to stimulate. Officials who do not respond to federal stimuli become vulnerable to criticism for failing to act—for "failing to take advantage of federal funds" or "failing to meet federal standards."

Federal influence continues to operate as consideration of the federally stimulated proposal proceeds. The terms of the federal offer or requirement affect the content of proposals and discussion within the state. The proponents or action takers have as one important resource of influence, perhaps their principal resource, the claim that action is desirable or necessary because it will secure federal funds. The "normal" distribution of influence among political actors in the state—that is, the distribution that would prevail in the absence of federal action—thus is altered to the advantage of those with whom the federal government is allied.

In summary, the federal government exercises influence in large part by stimulating demands from groups within the state and by placing "extra" resources of influence at their disposal. It works through allies.

The State Agency as Federal Ally

Temporary allies—that is, more or less accidental allies, intermittently active for limited purposes—may contribute substantially to the attainment of federal objectives. In Massachusetts the federal public assistance administration has at various times and for limited purposes been allied with the old-age lobby (the two have also been at odds) and with professional and good-government groups such as the National Association of Social Workers and the League of Women Voters. But the dependence of the federal government on support within the state is such that it needs a permanent ally, one always organized and prepared to take action, always receptive to federal communications, and having interests thoroughly consistent with those of the federal administration. From the perspective of the federal administrative agency, this is ideally the role of its state counterpart. As the formal recipient of federal funds, the formal channel for federal communication with the state, and a possessor of authority within the state government, the state agency has a combination of obligations to the federal administration and assets of influence at the state level that make it by far the most suitable and efficacious of potential federal allies. Much federal activity—some of it designed for that purpose and some not—contributes to making the state agency into an ally, an organization not simply accountable to the federal agency (responsible for the state's conduct and capable of reporting on it), but also *responsive* to it (disposed to make state conduct conform to federal preferences). Such activity is one of the major techniques of federal influence.

The first step in creating a state-agency ally is often to call an agency into existence. Many state and local administrative agencies, especially those in urban renewal, public housing, and antipoverty programs, have been created for the purpose of receiving and administering federal grants. The next step (likely to be more difficult with an established agency than a new one) is to shape its values and conceptions of purpose so that they are consistent with federal objectives, and to enhance its power and autonomy at the state level. To the extent that the state agency shares federal goals, is willing to commit its power to attaining them, and has power so to commit, the probability that federal goals will be achieved is greatly enhanced.

Federal patron agencies and their state counterparts might be expected to have shared values and goals without the federal agency's taking steps to assure this, if only because they share programmatic functions. The sharing of functions, however, is not necessarily sufficient to assure the congruence of a wide range of values among a high proportion of administrators in numerous governments, the governments themselves being representative of diverse value systems and regional subcultures. If federal preferences are to prevail, then, the core of shared values and goals that federal and state administrators derive from the sharing of a function must be elaborated and perfected, in ways of federal choosing, until a high degree of congruence has been achieved. The professionalization of personnel, through which a common body of values and doctrines is disseminated, has been the principal means of doing this.

To the extent that the federal effort to bring about a sharing of values between governments is successful, difficulties of obtaining conformance are much reduced. The state agency becomes highly responsive to federal preferences, and responsive for what federal administrators can only regard as the right reasons. That is, it responds not just because it seeks to maximize the receipt of federal funds (and thus is willing to act as if it shared federal goals); rather, it responds because it does in fact share them. Indoctrination of the state agency is the federal administrators' only defense against the persistent and pervasive problem that arises from the tendency of state governments to agree to federally stipulated actions because doing so will enlarge the flow of federal money. At most, the spread of professionalism at the state level may altogether eliminate the problem of nonconformance. If state agencies come to share federal values and have power to embody them in state policy, they become something more than responsive partners of the federal agency. They also undertake to pursue shared goals independently. The values expressed through public action at the state level then become identical to those that prevail within the federal administration. The result is the elimination of federal-state conflict and hence the elimination of the necessity for the exercises of federal influence. The federal effort to professionalize and to render autonomous the state agency is thus in a way the ultimate adaptation to limits on that influence.

Federal action contributes to state-agency power and autonomy in various ways, of which the most obvious, in the public assistance program, has been the "single state agency" requirement. On the basis of this statutory provision, federal administrators have insisted that the agency possess enough authority to assure that federal conditions are met. Very early in the federal grant program, this resulted in amendments to Massachusetts law that much increased the rule-making powers of the state welfare department.

In the case of the "single state agency" requirement, enhancing the counterpart's power is the primary end of federal action. Although most federal actions obviously do not have this as their major goal, virtually all federal-state interaction through the grant system incidentally yields that result.

As the recipient of federal grants, the counterpart is endowed with resources that would not otherwise be available to it and that come to it more or less independently of action by the governor or legislature, upon whom it would otherwise be altogether dependent for monetary support. How much power the agency thereby gains depends on how much discretion it has in the use of federal money.

This use may be closely circumscribed by federal action or by the action of the state legislature. In the Massachusetts public assistance program, the state welfare department was more a passive channel for the routinized flow of federal funds to local agencies (and ultimately to assistance recipients) than an independent allocator of the funds, the crucial decisions about allocation having been made by the legislature (once the cost-of-living formula was passed, at least). Nevertheless, the result of federal grants was to increase, in a subtle way and to an unspecifiable degree, that state agency's power vis-à-vis local agencies. The agency gained leverage in its role as rule maker and supervisor of administration, since its right to function in this role depended both on grants of authority from the state legislature and on the state's sharing of assistance costs.

And the "state" share of costs, from the perspective of local agencies, was the equivalent of the state *and* federal shares combined, for the state welfare department disbursed federal grants to local agencies and had authority to supervise their spending. "Federal" money, having been so channeled, from the local perspective acquired the character of "state" money.

The stipulation of federal conditions or rules to accompany grants had the same effect. Given the nature of a federal system, federal rules can be effective within the state only after being reincarnated as state rules. Therefore the making of federal rules for the grant program stimulates the making of state rules; it stimulates the usage of the counterpart agency's authority. Again, whether the result of this process is to increase state-agency "power" depends on the particular circumstances of the rule making and the particular relationship of power. When the state rule simply repeats verbatim a federal rule and does not entail the use of state discretion, state-agency power in relation to the federal administration is decreased. On the other hand, whether the state agency exercises discretion itself (typically the case) or merely repeats what the federal administration has stipulated (less often the case), its rule-making authority within the state political system has been enhanced by usage. In Massachusetts, for the perspective of the local agencies to which public assistance rules were addressed . . . , all rules were state rules no matter what the origin of their content. All were experienced and interpreted as manifestations of state authority. All therefore tended to enhance state power as it was exercised in relation to local agencies.[1]

An alliance between federal and state administrative agencies, formed and perfected through the working of the grant system, can become a powerful force in state politics, perhaps the dominant force in the making of policy for the program in question. When federal and state agencies work together, each reinforces the influence of the other, the state agency gaining as a result of the federal partnership, the federal agency being compensated for deficiencies in its ability to exercise influence directly in state affairs. The result is that a relationship of mutual dependence develops such that each accommodates itself, perhaps unconsciously, to the interests of the other. What the federal agency undertakes depends in part on what its state counterpart desires or can be expected to concur in, for the state agency's cooperation is essential to the realization of any federal goal. Similarly, a state agency learns to accommodate its goals to federal ones. Where, as in Massachusetts before 1968, a state agency has little independent strength within the state political system, its dependence on federal patronage becomes very great. It must rely on federal action to create opportunities for action and on the justification of "federal requirements" or the "availability of federal funds" to rationalize and legitimize all that it does. Whatever power and autonomy the Massachusetts welfare department possesses derive very largely from the relationship with its federal patron.

Federal influence, in summary, operates mainly through the agency that receives grants, and with the agency's self-serving cooperation. It operates by enhancing the role that the agency plays in the state political system and by shaping the agency's values, goals, interests, and actions. It operates primarily on the structures and processes of policymaking and administration rather than directly on the substance of policy. This may be a critical limitation, but if the influence on structures and processes is extensive and enduring enough, the result must be to influence policy outcomes as well—*all* policy outcomes, not just those in which the federal government is actively interested. If the federal government can influence the locus of policymaking authority in the state government, how the policymakers perceive opportunities for action, what values prevail among the policymakers, and what resources of influence are at their disposal, it has gone far in influencing the content of policy. It has, in any case, increased the disposition of the state to respond to federal action and to undertake, independently, actions consistent with federal preferences.

The Withholding of Funds

The ultimate resource of federal influence is the withholding of the grant, but this is almost impossible to use, for withholding serves no one's interests. Objections are bound to come from Congress.[2] Although Congress agrees with the administration on certain general statements of federal conditions when the effects on particular constituencies are impossible to foresee, withholding is a specific act, threatening to a particular constituency; this automatically brings a response from that constituency's representatives in Congress and evokes the sympathetic concern of other congressmen, who are made aware of a potential threat to their own constituencies. Even apart from the possible difficulties with Congress, administrators are reluctant to withhold funds because of the damage it might do to program goals and to relations with state governments. Given the limits on its influence, the federal administration is—or at least perceives itself to be—heavily dependent upon maintaining their good will and disposition to cooperate. Partly for this reason, it seeks to avoid direct, hostile confrontations with state governments such as the withholding of funds entails. Above all, it wishes to avoid public sanctions against the state agency (which, at least *pro forma*, must be the object of withholding), for one way of maintaining the state-agency alliance is to avoid embarrassing the agency in public.[3]

These objections to the manipulation of funds as an enforcement technique apply to the withholding of the entire grant, which in principle is the penalty for nonconforming policies or recurrently nonconforming administrative practices, more than to the taking of audit exceptions, which in principle is the penalty for specific nonconforming acts of expenditure. Because they are more feasible to use than withholding, the federal administration is sometimes tempted to use audit exceptions on a large scale as a substitute for withholding; that is, audit exceptions may be applied to a whole class of expenditures in an effort to bring about change in a nonconforming policy or practice, as when the regional representative decided to apply them in Massachusetts in the later 1940s to the salaries of elected board members who were engaged in administration. However, using audit exceptions in this way is subject in some degree to most of the same objections, and to others besides. An audit exception is inconvenient to administer, and as a *post hoc* action that applies only to particular acts of expenditure (selected acts, in the normal case, for not all expenditures are audited) its range of effectiveness is limited. It is particularly difficult to apply to acts of omission. The difficulties of withholding or of taking audit exceptions on a large scale help to explain why the whole aim of federal enforcement activity is to bring about compliance in advance and thus to avoid confrontations in which financial penalties will have to be invoked. Federal administrators consider that they have done their jobs well when the volume of audit exceptions is low.

It would be wrong, however, to infer that the federal ability to withhold funds is of no effect. It is in fact one of the major resources of federal influence—but it is of use mainly as a potential resource. It lies at the foundation, as a weapon in reserve, of all federal enforcement activity, and the nature of that activity is such as to make the best possible use of it.

Federal enforcement is a diplomatic process. It is as if the terms of a treaty, an agreement of mutual interest to the two governmental parties, were more or less continuously being negotiated. In these negotiations, numerous diplomatic forms and manners are observed, especially by the federal negotiators. Typically they are in the position of having made a démarche. Negotiations become active when a new federal condition is promulgated or an old one is reinterpreted, or when a federal administrative review has revealed a defect in the state's administration. Negotiations are carried on privately. The federal negotiators refrain from making statements in public, for they want to avoid the appearance of meddling in the internal affairs of the states. They refrain from making overt threats. They are patient. Negotiations over a single issue may go on steadily for several years and intermittently for decades. They are polite. In addressing state officials, they are usually elaborately courteous. They make small gestures of deference to the host government, as by offering to meet at times and at places of its choosing.

The objective of the negotiating process is to obtain as much conformance as can be had without the actual withholding of funds. Because federal requirements are typically stated in general terms, administrators have a high degree of flexibility in negotiating terms of conformance. Within the broad guidelines they have laid down, they have been able to adapt to the political and administrative circumstances of each state. If the constraints of the situation so require it, federal administrators may consider conformance to have been achieved even if state action falls considerably short of the federal ideal. As long as federal requirements are vague and general, conformance, though difficult to prove, is equally impossible to disprove. The federal administration may therefore avoid outright defeat no matter what concessions it makes to state political and administrative realities. (The situation changes, of course, if federal requirements are highly specific. Federal administrators then may feel compelled to accept merely formal proofs of conformance that falsify reality and that they *know* to falsify reality, as with caseload standards in Massachusetts.)

The function of intergovernmental diplomacy in a federal system, like that of international diplomacy, is to facilitate communication and amicable relations between governments that are pretending to be equals by obscuring the question of whether one is more equal than the other. In the case of federal-state relations in the United States, that question is obscure in any event, and the function of diplomatic processes may merely be to keep it that way or to obscure, and thereby facilitate, changes in power relations. That this be done is important primarily to the federal government, for it is the aggressive, the states the defensive, actor in intergovernmental relations. It has the greater interest in seeing that change is facilitated. But perhaps the principal advantage of a diplomatic style to federal administrators (and the choice of that style is essentially their choice) is that this mode of behavior makes the best possible use of the technique of withholding funds. It enables federal officials to exploit, without actually using, this basic resource. In cases of federal-state conflict, federal negotiators keep open the possibility of withholding during the process of negotiation, referring to it in oblique and subtle terms. They seek to obscure the low probability that they will actually use it. By not making overt threats to withhold, federal administrators protect their credibility; the state is kept guessing. Diplomatic behavior is thus an adaptation to the impracticability of withholding, as well as to other constraints on federal influence, especially the widespread belief that the federal government ought not to interfere in state and local affairs. By relying so heavily on private negotiations, federal officials avoid "meddling" in public. At the same time, they avoid exposing the state agency to public embarrassment or more tangible federal penalties so that the agency's disposition to cooperate is not discouraged.

It might seem that, as time passes, the federal administration's failure to withhold funds would undermine its credibility and render withholding useless even as a negotiation weapon. In fact, the federal willingness to withhold funds itself diminishes with time. It is much easier to withhold (or delay the granting of) funds at the outset of a grant program, when the volume of the grant is low and the program not yet routinized. In the first five years of the public assistance program, the federal administration did make several attempts to withhold funds, and it was not altogether implausible, when a dispute with Massachusetts arose in 1939–40 over the merit system requirement, that it would try to do so again. The welfare commissioner, apparently believing that it would, gave in to the Social Security Board very quickly. Ten years later, when the issue over board member-administrators arose, it was much less plausible that withholding should be tried, and by 1964–65, when the dispute over the educational requirement developed, withholding was altogether implausible. But not everyone knew this (many state legislators did not), and some people who did know it, especially the welfare commissioner, preferred to pretend that they did not. Withholding would probably not remain effective as a resource of influence were it not for the federal alliance with the state agency; when the two cooperate in pursuit of a shared goal, the state agency exploits the possibility of federal holding and vouches for the credibility of it.

The fact that the state agency is the sole official recipient of federal communications and the official interpreter of them within the state gives it an important advantage. It can make decisions about dissemination and interpretation in such a way as to facilitate attainment of its own ends. This is likely to mean, as in the dispute over the educational requirement, that the state agency will encourage the belief that a serious threat of federal withholding exists. The federal administration, which alone might provide an accurate interpretation of its own intent, refrains from doing so as a tactical necessity. Attempts to elicit clear statements of intent are unavailing, whether they come from the state agency or other sources. But whereas the federal agency refrains from issuing threats of withholding itself, it does nothing to dispel threats that others issue in its name. Its interests will best be served if those statements are believed. In these circumstances, federal intentions may be difficult for anyone to evaluate, even those who, like state administrative officials, have direct access to the federal agency and experience in the administration of grant programs. For others, such as state legislators, who have no such access and no such experience, federal intentions are virtually impossible to evaluate. In any case, it is always impossible for the opponents of federally sponsored action to demonstrate that the federal administration will *not* withhold funds.

The limited capacity of state legislators to appraise federal intentions with respect to withholding is one advantage the state agency has whenever it undertakes an action with federal sponsorship. It might be supposed, however, that opponents of federally sponsored action would get help from Congress, which is thought to be responsive to the appeals of parochial interests and skilled at overturning the acts of federal administrators. Judging from the Massachusetts experience, however, appeals to Congress appear to bring few results to those who make them. When federal and state agencies act cooperatively, they have much protection, individually or together, against unwanted intervention from legislatures at either or both levels of the federal system.

They have, of course, the usual assets of administrators confronting legislators: they are the full-time specialists in their function, while legislators have only a part-time interest in that function. For a congressman to intervene successfully once the federal administration has committed itself to a particular action in a particular state requires an intense and sustained interest in the matter and a great mastery of administrative detail. The Massachusetts case suggests that these conditions will rarely be met. Although congressmen, in response to constituents' requests, at critical times inquired of the federal administration about its intentions in Massachusetts, these inquiries almost without exception were routine and perfunctory. The letter from the constituent was forwarded to the administration with a form letter from the congressman requesting a response. A response—couched in oblique, noncommittal language that tended to minimize the degree of disruption being experienced within the state and the degree of the federal administration's responsibility for it—then went to the congressman, who presumably relayed it to the inquiring constituent as proof that he had acted on the constituent's request. Typically, these congressional inquiries revealed little knowledge or specialized interest in the case on the part of the congressman, and the replies from the administration were designed to avoid increasing either.

The only important exception to this pattern was the activity of Congressman [John] McCormack with respect to the directive on educational requirements. If ever there was a situation in which congressional intervention might be effective, this seemed to be it. Here was a congressman—the Speaker of the House, no less—who was opposed to an important action of the administration, an action profoundly damaging to the career prospects of perhaps eight hundred local government employees in his state. His objection was largely spontaneous and strongly enough felt to produce protests to the secretary and the undersecretary of health, education, and welfare. But in the end it had very little effect on the administration's action. None of this means that federal public assistance administrators are not subject in profoundly important ways to congressional controls. What the administrators undertake to do depends heavily on what Congress has authorized and on the administrators' guess of what Congress will tolerate. Contrary to what is perhaps the usual impression of Congress' performance, the evidence from public assistance suggests that Congress is more effective in making broad policy than in doing "casework" for particular individuals or groups of aggrieved constituents.

In addition to the defenses that administrators normally have against legislators, the grant system offers special ones, a result of the diffusion of responsibility it entails. When called to account for controversial actions, administrative agencies at both federal and state levels can escape responsibility vis-à-vis their own legislatures by attributing responsibility to a counterpart at the other level. In parallel fashion, each legislature can escape responsibility vis-à-vis its own constituents. The ability of all major official actors to deny responsibility very much reduces the chances of successful opposition.

Notes

1. From the perspective of the state agency, federal efforts to enhance the agency's authority and to stimulate exercise of that authority are not unambiguously beneficial. How welcome they are depends on how highly the state agency values the ends prescribed by the federal administration; on the amount of resistance that pursuit of them is likely to provoke within the state; and on the federal ability to endow the agency with resources of influence to overcome the resistance. The danger is that federal action will force the state agency into situations of conflict without sufficiently compensating it.

2. See U.S. Senate, *Proposed Cutoff of Welfare Funds to the State of Alabama*, Hearings before the Committee on Finance, 90th Cong., 1st sess. (1967), for [an] example.

3. In doing research for this book, I found that the one restriction on the cooperation of federal regional officials was a concern that their relations with state officials might be damaged. I was given access to federal files with the understanding that I would not use them to attack or gratuitously embarrass the state agency. I was asked to use the material "objectively," a condition that I was of course happy to accept. When the completed manuscript was made available for comment, the federal office did not ask for any deletions.

Part II

Review Questions

1. What intergovernmental policy implications follow from the fact that American government structures are bewilderingly diverse? Are rational action and reform possible in such an intergovernmental system? In your answer, consider Reischauer's discussion of the negative consequences of this diversity; can you suggest any positive ones?

2. What political and structural impediments stand in the way of efforts to attempt equalization of governments' resources through the grant system, even if budgets were not as tight as they have been in recent years?

3. Describe the shifts in position and tensions felt by the main PIGs during recent years. What seem to be the sources of their potential strengths and weaknesses? What political behavior would one expect to see on the part of the PIGs if a president were to propose a wholesale shift of funding from categoricals to block grants and a further cutback in total assistance? Why would PIGs react this way?

4. Why do opponents of systemic intergovernmental change have a strategic advantage in intergovernmental politics?

5. In what ways have states been seeking to exert influence with the federal government in the intergovernmental system in recent years? Through associations of public officials? Via actions taken by the states themselves, either singularly or in coalition with others—as Bowman outlines? What possibilities and limits exist regarding the ability of states to exert their influence intergovernmentally?

6. Interpret the models of the intergovernmental system, presented by Wright in Part I, in light of the evidence on patterns of interstate cooperation presented by Bowman, on a "new federalism" in the Supreme Court by Doernberg, and on the relative advantage of the U.S. system in encouraging flexibility in cooperative intergovernmental relations by

Halberstam and Hills. If states are not now largely reactive, or passive, in the complex network, which model most satisfactorily interprets current activity? Is a new model needed?

7. If Doernberg is correct that Congress has been a centralizing political institution in the intergovernmental system while the Supreme Court has generally been moving in the opposite direction, what are the likely implications for coherent intergovernmental political deliberation and cooperative intergovernmental ties?

8. If there were a new Constitutional Convention in the twenty-first century United States, and if you were a delegate to the gathering, would you suggest modifications to the U.S. constitutional rules to encourage any changes in the operations of intergovernmental politics? In particular, does the German case, as sketched by Halberstam and Hills, carry any implications that should be considered in the United States?

9. Derthick claims that the federal government hardly ever cuts off funding for a grant program, despite the fact that states and locals frequently fail to meet federal requirements. Does this mean that the threat to eliminate funding is an empty one?

10. Derthick says, "The function of intergovernmental diplomacy in a federal system, like that of international diplomacy, is to facilitate communication and amicable relations between governments that are pretending to be equals by obscuring the question of whether one is more equal than the other." Is this analogy to diplomacy reasonable? Why or why not?

11. Compare Derthick's analysis of the troubling implications of the pattern of influence in intergovernmental politics to Grodzins's more sanguine assessment. Be sure to analyze the topics of diffusion of responsibility and bureaucratic barriers to outside influence. In your view, whose portrayal is more accurate today? Does the system operate with an impressive variety of access by many parties to key decisions? Or does it resemble an opaque and difficult to penetrate morass?

Part III

FISCAL ASPECTS OF
INTERGOVERNMENTAL RELATIONS

Money may or may not make the world go 'round, but there may be no better way of seeing the interdependence and complexity of today's intergovernmental system than by "following the money trail," or examining the fiscal aspects of the network. Power and control, after all, flow from money. And even though, as Part II makes clear, not *all* forms of intergovernmental influence are directly tied to fiscal links, it remains true that financial instruments—especially the grant-in-aid—are one of the most important ways by which American governments at all levels are tied together in a bewilderingly intricate and dense sets of obligations, opportunities, and dependencies.

As of fiscal year 2003, for instance, and despite cutbacks in aid—particularly for the nation's largest cities—federal dollars constituted roughly 32.5 percent of state revenues, and local governments in general relied on state and national grants for more than 40 percent of their budgets.[1] The pattern has been undeniably complex, with increases for certain policy sectors and programs and reductions and delays for others. The picture is one of feast, or at least substantial support, in the midst of famine, or cutbacks; and greater pressure on states and localities to find ways to support their own programs, even as intergovernmental assistance for individuals has mushroomed. Clearly, then, these indicators suggest considerable financial interdependence and complexity.

The readings in Part III document some of the fiscal developments in the system during recent years, explain the significance and purposes of intergovernmental fiscal instruments, consider how urban governments are affected as they are enmeshed in a larger pattern, and analyze some of the donor and recipient behavior generated by intergovernmental fiscal activity and the influence of financial instruments. Once again, however, it will prove impossible to cover these aspects of the American system without paying considerable attention to other features, especially the *political* significance of fiscal mechanisms. Thus, a lesson in this section, as in the preceding one, is that the various dimensions of the intergovernmental pattern are inextricably related.

This section provides a suggestive sampling, but not a fully comprehensive overview. Even with the wide range of issues and topics addressed in the readings that follow, some important issues receive less attention. For instance, although some coverage of a few key sectors is included, the great differences across intergovernmental programs are not dealt with in detail. Further, while cities and economic development are discussed, the contentious topic of urban-suburban fiscal disparities is touched upon relatively little.

The introductory chapter of this part provides highlights from a recent analysis of the fiscal features of the intergovernmental system. The Organisation for Economic Co-operation and Development, or OECD, is an institution supported by thirty member countries committed to democratic government and market-based economies. The OECD encourages responsible discussion about good governance, sensible policy, and economic growth. Its studies and reports are read widely and often considered a sound source of information regarding social and economic developments around the world. The excerpt (no. 14) from their recent analysis of the U.S. economy sketches some of the basic fiscal dimensions of American intergovernmental relations. This reading makes clear the volume, trend, and basic composition of intergovernmental aid in the United States at this time, the ways in which different U.S. governments depend on quite different revenue sources, and some of the emerging fiscal issues. The excerpt also offers brief reviews of some of the largest and most important intergovernmental grant programs in the country.

Various forms of intergovernmental assistance have been significant in the development of the intergovernmental system. The next two readings address some of the economic and political dimensions of these tools. George Break classifies fiscal mechanisms according to their expected economic effects (no. 15). Grounded in economic theory, his discussion is especially helpful because it treats not only fiscal mechanisms employed by the national government but also the economic impact of state aid to local governments.

But one can also examine empirically the actual operations of the fiscal instrumentalities and assess the overall state of affairs of the fiscally interdependent system. The next reading (no. 16), by Phillip Monypenny, does so by comparing the conventional justifications for aid with the aid's practical impact. In his frequently quoted essay, the effects of the intergovernmental grant system are analyzed in toto. Writing during an earlier debate about the intergovernmental network and its future, Monypenny finds that the oft-cited economic and fiscal ends attributed to the grant system are not supported by the data. In other words, most of these justifications for the system are unfounded. He then argues that this system of fiscal instruments actually serves some political functions. His logic supports the view, advanced in the introductory chapter of this book, that American intergovernmental relations constitute an amalgamated pluralism and that indisputable links exist between fiscal and political aspects of the system.

The form of fiscal instrument, however, does matter. Whereas many analyses implicitly assume that a review of different types of grants is sufficient, the two articles following Monypenny's (nos. 17 and 18) offer evidence in regard to the importance of different types of fiscal instruments. They also demonstrate that a broad conception of "instrument" may be necessary to capture some of the fiscal aspects of the system.

A number of scholars in recent years have investigated the circumstances in which U.S. cities have sought, often competitively with other U.S. urban settings, to attract business, capital, jobs, and thus economic development. To this end, among other efforts, cities can borrow funds and invest for their futures. Some researchers have offered provocative analyses emphasizing the considerable degree to which, in doing so, cities in the United States are dependent on and vulnerable to a number of influences over which they have little control, most particularly market forces in the nation's political economy.[2] Alberta Sbragia (no. 17) offers a fascinating study of an underemphasized aspect of cities' links with the broader world: the roles of other governments, particularly other levels of government, in shaping and reshaping the choices that cities make. She shows that all instruments of borrowing matter, not simply those that provide grants via intergovernmental aid. The ways in which cities act to maximize their own freedom of action, including creating new, nonelected special-purpose governments as a way of circumventing intergovernmental constraints on borrowing and spending, are part of an elaborate "politics of circumvention" that raises serious questions about who controls public choices and whether the people can hold decision makers accountable.

Beyond debt instruments and other subtle instruments that shape intergovernmental finance are the kinds of grants made available to governments. And despite frequent proposals by many, including many presidents, for simplifying the nation's grant structure by establishing several major block grants, the system is dominated by categorical aid and is likely to remain so for the foreseeable future. Why? Part of the reason is found in the excerpt from a study conducted by the Advisory Commission on Intergovernmental Relations (no. 18). This analysis examines economic and political inducements to adopt this form of financial assistance.

The next two essays (nos. 19 and 20) return to the subject of local governments and how they are financed and influenced by other levels. David Brunori (no. 19) reviews how these thousands of governments fund their activities and indicates that forces now beyond their immediate control, including the ceding of authority to the state level, have seriously limited local autonomy and independent decision making. In particular, he sees efforts to reinvigorate local use of the property tax as a key to vigorous local government. Pietro S. Nivola (no. 20) also takes aim at the limited ability of local governments to make their own timely, wise, and adaptive decisions. He concentrates on the large cities, and his focus is on how national decisions severely constrain effective urban action. Part of the story is clearly fiscal, as he documents, and part has to do with the regulatory constraints emanating from Washington.

Both readings document some of the ways in which the interdependence of the system affects local actors and perspectives, and both raise serious questions about whether and how even the most representative and accountable local decision makers can make policy choices in the interests of their communities. These readings therefore connect the issues of complexity and interdependence, as they manifest themselves on the fiscal dimension, with one of the most important political challenges: finding ways to achieve democratic governance. They also demonstrate that in addition to their implications for politics, the fiscal dimensions of the system are directly connected to questions of administration.

Notes

1. For details, see the excerpt from the 2005 OECD *Economic Survey of the United States* included later in this part.
2. See, for instance, Stephen L. Elkin, *City and Regime in the American Republic* (Chicago: University of Chicago Press, 1987; Paul E. Peterson, *City Limits* (Chicago: University of Chicago Press, 1981); and Martin Schefter, *Political Crisis/Fiscal Crisis: The Collapse and Revival of New York City* (New York: Basic Books, 1985).

14

Fiscal Relations across Levels of Government
Organisation for Economic Co-operation and Development

The history of fiscal federalism in the United States dates back to the founding of the Union in 1789. Already prior to the establishment of the federal government, the states had exercised their powers to levy taxes and provide certain services, and the tenth amendment to the US constitution expressly reserves to "the States or to the people" all powers "not delegated to the United States by the Constitution, nor prohibited by it to the States". Over the century following the Civil War the responsibilities of the federal government and its involvement in the fiscal affairs of lower levels of government expanded substantially. More recently, however, there has been some devolution of programmes back to the states, reflecting in part dissatisfaction with the economic effects of several large federal programmes. Besides substantial changes over time in the federal-state relationship, fiscal policies vary considerably among state and local governments, making the United States a particularly interesting case for the study of the decentralisation of fiscal functions and instruments with the aim of "combining the different advantages which result from the magnitude and the littleness of nations" (Tocqueville, 1980, p. 163). . . .

Main features and trends shaping fiscal relations across the levels of government

The current extent of decentralisation

Historically, states have enjoyed a substantial degree of fiscal autonomy, as expressed in the tenth amendment, reflecting the fact that the states historically preceded, and transferred only limited powers to, the Union. States are largely free in their choice of tax bases and rates, subject to only few limitations imposed by the federal constitution, notably that taxation of exports and imports is a federal activity and that their power to tax interstate commerce is limited. On the expenditure side, most major spending functions are located at the state or local government level, important exceptions being national defence and pension and health insurance for the elderly and disabled. As in the case of taxes, allocation of expenditure functions to the sub-national level involves substantial or even complete state autonomy in programme design, as opposed to mere delegation of federally-controlled budgetary functions. Another important aspect of state prerogatives is their autonomy in organising local governments within their own boundaries. Local government structures vary greatly across states, with different functions performed by county, municipal, school district and special district governments. Moreover, several state constitutions include "home rule" clauses that confer on municipal governments the right to create their own charters as well as considerable autonomy in conducting their affairs.

Federal government total expenditures trended up until the early 1980s and have since declined to about 20% of GDP (Figure 14-1). Except for a surge in the late 1990s and subsequent sharp decline, federal government receipts have shown little trend over the period, averaging about 18%. State and local receipts and expenditures trended up until the mid-1970s and have remained fairly stable since then at around 14% of GDP. While revenues and expenditures of sub-national governments have tended to be in balance, this has clearly not been the case at the federal level. The implications for net government saving (the difference between current receipts and current expenditures) and net government lending (which includes the balance of capital receipts and expenditures) are shown in the lower panel of Figure 14-1. On either measure sub-national budgets have been close to balance. Most obviously, their net saving has been almost always positive, which likely reflects discipline imposed by capital markets, and perhaps also the effectiveness of their balanced budget requirements discussed below. By contrast, since the mid-1960s the federal government has almost always run budget deficits, which may result from the combination of its greater ability to borrow in financial markets, the inability to achieve lasting deficit reduction through fiscal rules, and its greater role in and ability to achieve cyclical stabilisation.

Total expenditures of local governments are almost as large as those of state governments, while federal expenditures are nearly twice as large (Figure 14-2). Apart from interest payments on federal debt, most of federal expenditures are for defence, social benefits (primarily pension

Figure 14-1. Government total receipts and expenditures
Per cent of GDP

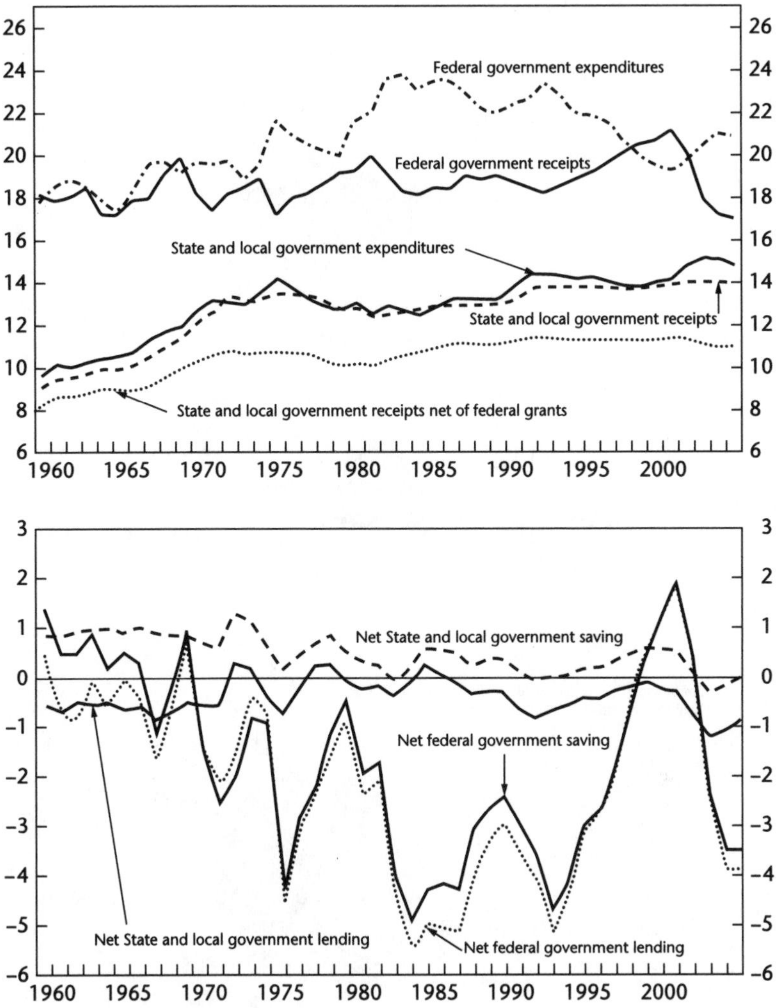

Source: Bureau of Economic Analysis.

and health benefits for the elderly and disabled) and grants to sub-federal governments. Only little more than 10% of federal expenditures, or about 2% of GDP, is spent on non-defence consumption and investment. At the state level, grants to local governments are the single largest spending category, followed by social services (such as income support and the Medicaid health-care programme for the indigent) and

Figure 14-2. Decomposition of government expenditures

A. Decomposition of federal government expenditures, 2002-03 (1)
Total expenditures : $2232.6 billion

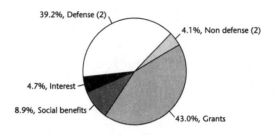

B. Decomposition of state government expenditures, 2002-03
Total expenditures : $1359.0 billion

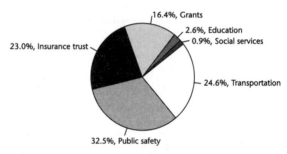

C. Decomposition of local government expenditures, 2002-03
Total expenditures : $1194.9 billion

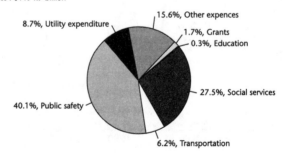

1. Fiscal year 2002 Q3 to 2003 Q2
2. Including consumption expenditures and gross government investment
Source: Bureau of Economic Analysis and Bureau of the Census.

education, overwhelmingly higher education. Finally, primary and secondary education is by far the largest expenditure component of local
governments, comprising nearly 40% of their total expenditures. Other

Figure 14-3. Decomposition of government revenues

A. Decomposition of federal government revenues, 2002-03 (1)
Total revenues : $1895.7 billion

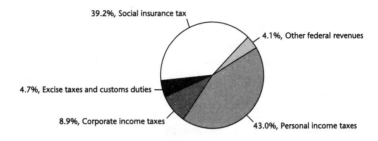

39.2%, Social insurance tax

4.1%, Other federal revenues

4.7%, Excise taxes and customs duties

8.9%, Corporate income taxes

43.0%, Personal income taxes

B. Decomposition of state government revenues, 2002-03
Total revenues : $1295.7 billion

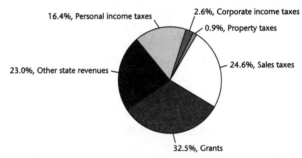

16.4%, Personal income taxes

2.6%, Corporate income taxes

0.9%, Property taxes

23.0%, Other state revenues

24.6%, Sales taxes

32.5%, Grants

C. Decomposition of local government revenues, 2002-03
Total revenues : $1140.6 billion

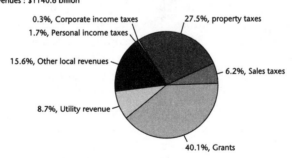

0.3%, Corporate income taxes

27.5%, property taxes

1.7%, Personal income taxes

15.6%, Other local revenues

6.2%, Sales taxes

8.7%, Utility revenue

40.1%, Grants

1. Fiscal year 2002 Q3 to 2003 Q2
Source: Bureau of Economic Analysis and Bureau of the Census.

important local government functions are social services (such as hospitals and other health services), utilities and public safety.

The composition of revenues is quite different across the three levels of government (Figure 14-3). Within taxes, over time a broad division of tax bases has developed by which the federal government relies almost exclusively on income taxation in the form of personal and corporate income and payroll taxes, the states on sales and, to a lesser extent, personal income taxes, and the local government level on property taxes. Notably, the federal government does not levy a general tax on consumption, like a sales tax or value-added tax (VAT), nor a property tax, and most states' involvement in property taxation is negligible. Also, corporate income is a small revenue source for state and local governments. Thus, there are only two major tax bases that are shared between levels of government: personal income between the federal and state governments, and sales between state and local governments. While virtually all federal revenues are raised in the form of taxes, taxes account for only 44% of state revenues. Nearly one-third of state revenues are derived from federal government grants; the remaining quarter is derived from various sources, including nearly 10% from user charges, for example for hospital services and higher education. Finally, local governments raise only about one-third of their revenues in the form of taxes. Grants, mostly from state governments, account for another third of their revenues, and most of the remaining third is derived from user charges and utility revenue.

As mentioned above, the organisation of the local government sector is at the discretion of the states. The structure of the local government sector is therefore quite diverse across states, so that it is difficult to make generalisations concerning the functions of the various forms of local government. Table 14-1 provides some indications as to the assignment of functions. The three major forms of local government are counties, municipalities (including cities) and school districts. Within each of these categories there is vast heterogeneity; for example, there are more than 3000 counties in the United States, ranging in population from less than 200 to more than nine million. Counties dominate in the local government provision of social services and income maintenance, where they account for over 60% of spending in this category by all local governments. Other important county functions are transportation and public safety, but municipal governments are the most important providers in these two areas as well as in environment and housing and in utilities. Utilities are also the major role of so-called special district governments. These are organised to provide a variety of services including water, sanitation, parks and transportation. They may overlap several municipal jurisdictions or be a subset of a single jurisdiction. Finally, school district governments perform practically no other function than operating public schools, but because of the

Table 14-1. Local government expenditures by type of government and function, 2001-02

	County government	Municipal government	Township government	Special district government	School district government	% of total local government expenditure
Total direct expenditure ($ billions)	254	359	34	120	361	1 129
Per cent of total local government expenditure	22.5	31.8	3.0	10.7	32.0	100.0
Government's share in total local government spending on:						
Education	8.7	8.8	2.2	0.5	79.8	39.0
Social services and income maintenance	61.0	21.4	0.5	17.1	0.0	10.6
Transportation	30.6	49.8	6.5	13.1	0.0	5.6
Public safety	34.7	57.6	4.7	3.0	0.0	9.1
Environment and housing	18.1	53.8	4.1	24.0	0.0	9.3
Utility expenditure	5.0	52.3	1.5	41.2	0.0	10.6
Other	35.3	47.4	5.0	6.7	5.6	15.8

Source: U.S. Bureau of the Census, 2002 Census of Governments, available at http://www.census.gov/govs/www/estimate.html.

importance of this function at the local government level, they account for one-third of total expenditure by local governments. On the revenue side, county, municipal and school district governments share the major local own-source revenue, property taxes, roughly in proportion to their expenditures. Municipal governments receive most local sales and income taxes, while school district governments benefit from by far the largest share of intergovernmental transfers, almost all from their state government. Direct transfers from the federal to local governments, which totalled $43 billion in 2001-02, are small in comparison both to federal transfers to state governments ($318 billion) and state government transfers to local governments ($356 billion).

Recent trends and future forces

While the decades between the Great Depression and the 1980s saw several large expansions of the federal government's size and role, which to some extent entailed federalisation of functions previously performed by sub-national governments, this trend has been reversed in several areas since the mid-1980s. Programmes whose operation has been devolved to lower levels of government, however, often still require funding from the federal government. One common feature has been a change in the trade-off between lower governments' autonomy in programme design on the one hand and their financing responsibilities on the other, notably through a switch from open-ended matching grants to earmarked, lump-sum grants (referred to as block grants in the US context, despite their earmarked nature). The switch from matching to block grants suggests that the intention of these grants is of a paternalistic kind rather than to correct for spill-over effects. The most important example of this development, the welfare reform of 1996, will be discussed in the following section. While devolution of programme responsibility appears to have produced efficiency gains through experimentation at the state level, it has also shifted greater financial risk to the states, raising the question whether they would be able to avoid welfare-reducing cyclicality in spending on core services if block grants were extended into areas such as health.

Sub-national governments' capacity for setting spending and revenue levels and for bearing the risk of cyclical fluctuations in spending and revenues has been reduced since the late 1970s by the widespread adoption or strengthening of tax and expenditure limitations. Virtually all states operate under some form of balanced budget rule enacted in state laws or enshrined in the states' constitutions. However, these balanced budget rules . . . did not prevent the growth in the size of state and local government during the 1960s and early 1970s, evident in Figure 14-1, and the concomitant upward drift in various tax rates. The "tax revolts" of the late 1970s and early 1980s saw many states adopting rules which typically restrict the growth in state and local governments' revenues and/or expenditures from one fiscal year to the next. While the strictness of tax and expenditure limitations varies across states, in some instances they have had the effect of shrinking the size of government in relation to the economy, as intended by their proponents. Problems arose, however, because for various reasons the entire spending restraint tended to fall on a few budget items, leading to outcomes that were certainly unintended. The design of fiscal rules that properly balance a desirable degree of sub-national fiscal flexibility against the risks of undesired perpetual government expansion and potential fiscal crises and bailouts remains a challenge.

Potentially the most important forces increasingly impacting on intergovernmental fiscal relations emanate from the ageing of the population. This is most obvious on the expenditures side of the ledger, where health and other age-related spending is on the rise. While many of the most strongly affected programmes are located at the federal level, there are substantial old-age-related expenditures at the sub-national level as well, primarily through the Medicaid programme. Moreover, ageing affects not only expenditures, but also the trend growth of revenue sources at different levels of government. In particular, some retirement income that is part of the growing share of benefits and transfer receipts in personal income is sheltered from personal income taxation. Also, older people tend to spend a smaller share on goods and services that are subject to sales tax, and more on those that are exempt, notably health services and pharmaceuticals. Ageing therefore threatens to reduce the main revenue sources of both the federal and the state governments; the main own-source revenue of local governments, the property tax, is less affected. The shift towards ageing-related expenditures that are mostly redistributive in nature is particularly problematic for states. Usually the funding of redistributive spending is achieved through progressive income taxation. But because of taxpayer mobility, states' ability to levy progressive income taxes is quite limited, and their other main revenue source, the sales tax, tends to be regressive. An important challenge going forward will therefore be to adjust the spending responsibilities of the various levels of government to their capacity to raise the required revenues in a manner that is desirable both on efficiency and equity grounds.

Issues concerning the allocation of spending responsibilities

The argument for providing at the sub-national level public goods and services whose consumption is limited to the providing jurisdiction is that preferences for public services differ across jurisdictions, and that governments at lower levels know best the preferences of their constituents (Oates, 1972). Leading examples of these goods and services are elementary and secondary as well as higher education, public safety and basic infrastructure such as roads and transportation, sewerage and utilities. There appears to be considerable variation in the scope and amount of goods and services provided by local governments across the country, some of which reflects differences in population density and economic structure. However, the conclusion that decentralised governments will provide the efficient level of public goods rests on a number of assumptions. The presence of spill-over effects can lead to sub-optimally low provision of public goods, while grants from higher levels of government can have the opposite effect. The question whether the level of public goods provision by *local* governments is efficient has received considerable attention, with several studies concluding that it is (Brueckner, 1982; Gramlich and Rubinfeld, 1982). These findings are consistent with the evidence that both property taxes and services benefits are capitalised into property values, as the benefits of most services provided by local government accrue to property owners (Oates, 1969; Weimer and Wolkoff, 2001). However, not all the conditions for efficient local public-goods provision under "Tiebout sorting" appear to be met, as there is substantial redistribution across local governments in the context of school finance, presumably reflecting the importance of externalities associated with basic education. There also appear to be strong spill-over effects at the *state* level, at least for certain services such as medical spending (Brueckner, 1998; Baicker, 2005). Policy responses to the risk of undesirably low provision of redistributive and health services by state governments are discussed below.

The remainder of this section discusses in greater detail four areas in which intergovernmental relations play an important role in programme design and funding. Programmes in these four areas—income support, medical care for the indigent (Medicaid), highway construction and education—illustrate the diversity of the current structure of grants. Jointly they account for about two-thirds of total federal grants to state governments (Figure 14-4), and education alone accounts for more than half of

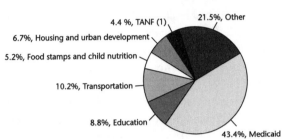

Figure 14-4. Federal grants to state and local governments
Fiscal year 2004

1. Temporary Assistance for Needy Families
Source: Office of Management and Budget (2005), Budget of the US
Government, Fiscal Year 2006, Historical Tables.

total grants from state to local governments. Although, as mentioned earlier, all of these grants are earmarked, there is considerable variation across programmes in the freedom the receiving governments have in allocating these funds. Related to this variation in the lower level's competence for programme design and allocation are other dimensions along which different grants are distinct, such as whether they are capped at a specific amount or open-ended, and whether they are matching grants or lump-sum "block" grants (which are nonetheless earmarked) of a fixed size.

Welfare

Federal legislation enacted in August 1996 fundamentally changed the structure of public assistance programmes to low-income families. In terms of relations between the federal government and the states, its most important effect was to replace the previous open-ended federal matching grant under Aid to Families with Dependent Children (AFDC) by a capped block grant under Temporary Assistance for Needy Families (TANF). At the same time as imposing an upper limit on the federal contribution to welfare spending, the welfare reform removed many federal eligibility and payment rules, thus devolving to states much greater authority in programme design. The 1996 reform was the culmination of a process that had started in the 1980s, when growing dissatisfaction with AFDC had led an increasing number of states to seek federal waivers from the AFDC rules (Blank, 2002). By the time that the welfare reform was enacted, 27 states had major state-wide waivers in place, most of which were designed to enforce work requirements for welfare recipients more stringently. These waiver programmes had to be approved and administered by the Department of Health and Human Services and had to be thoroughly evaluated. The experiences gained under these waivers were a critical element in shaping the 1996 reform legislation with its strong emphasis on work requirements (both work trigger rules and minimum work participation rates) and time limits. . . . The size of the federal block grant was fixed for each state at the level of its 1994 receipts under AFDC and two smaller programmes. To prevent states from substantially reducing their welfare programmes and diverting block grant funds to other purposes, the legislation included a "maintenance-of-effort" requirement by which states have to maintain at least 75% of their 1994 spending on programmes replaced by TANF, including AFDC-related child care.

The most important overall effect in terms of programme design has been the reorientation of support from non-working to working families through the combination of (federally mandated) work requirements, subsidies for work-related expenses (notably child care) and strengthening of work incentives through lower benefit reduction rates. States have also made wide use of their new discretion under the reform legislation. Although the multi-dimensional character of state welfare programmes under TANF complicates the evaluation of the effects of individual welfare reform measures on recipient behaviour (Blank, 2002), the welfare reform is generally credited with being the main reason for the dramatic decline in caseloads during the second half of the 1990s (Figure 14-5). The nation-wide caseload, which had peaked under AFDC in March 1994 at 5.1 million families, declined through December 2000 to 2.2 million, with the bulk of this decline occurring between 1995 and 1999. During the same 1994 to 2000 period the percentage of children in families receiving AFDC or TANF benefits declined from 14.3% to 6.1%. Moreover, the decline in caseloads continued, although at a slower pace, through nearly the entire period of economic weakness during recent years, with the number of families receiving benefits in June 2004 (the latest available data) falling below 2 million. . . . Overall, the experience suggests fairly stable integration of marginal populations into the labour market. Helped by the clause that caseload reductions are treated as equivalent to work participation rates, all states achieved the 50% all-family work target for 2002, and all but four states met the two-parent work target.

Figure 14-5. Welfare caseloads
Total number of families, calendar years, monthly average

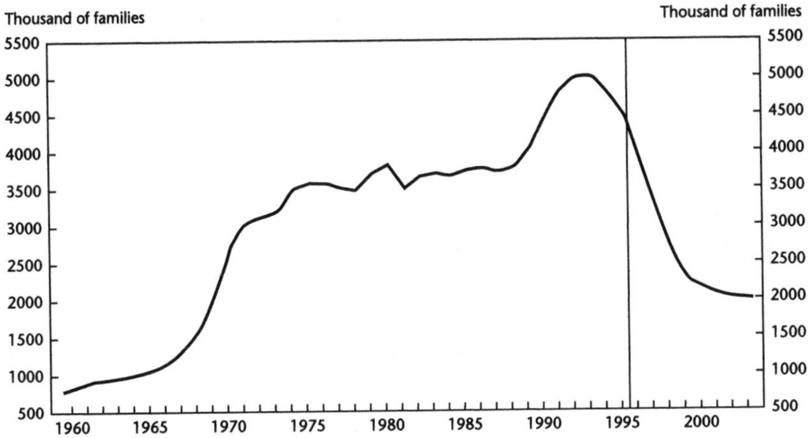

Source: US Department of Health and Human Services.

The traditional concern in the literature about allocating responsibility for welfare to the sub-national level is that it may lead states to engage in a "race to the bottom" with the result that welfare provision is ultimately much below the level that would prevail under a national welfare system (*e.g.* Brown and Oates, 1987)....A number of empirical studies have arrived at conflicting results concerning the importance of welfare migration (see Brueckner (1998) for a survey of older results). More recent studies suggest that a modest amount of welfare migration exists, but that it is unlikely to reduce significantly the level of benefits offered by states....

Medicaid

Medicaid, the medical insurance programme for the indigent, is by far the largest programme shared between the federal government and the states. Total Medicaid spending in FY 2003 was $275 billion ($2^{1}/_{2}$ per cent of GDP), of which $160 billion, or 58%, was funded by the federal government and the remaining $115 billion by state governments. The federal contribution to Medicaid accounts for slightly more than 40% of total federal grants to state and local governments. In contrast to the welfare programme discussed above, Medicaid is an open-ended entitlement under which every person meeting eligibility

Table 14-2. Medicaid enrolment and expenditures by group, FY 2002

	Enrolment[1]		Expenditures[2]	
	Millions	Per cent	$ billion	Per cent
Total	39.9	100.0	214.9	100.0
Aged and disabled	11.7	29.3	147.5	68.7
Dual eligibles[3]	6.7	16.9	91.1	42.4
Other aged and disabled[3]	5.0	12.4	56.4	26.3
Adults	9.8	24.6	24.1	11.2
Children	18.4	46.1	34.3	16.1

1. Enrolment measured in person-years.
2. Items do not add up to total because the attribution of 4% of expenditures ($8.6 billion) is unknown.
3. Breakdown of enrolment of aged and disabled in dual eligibles and others was obtained by applying proportional size of these two groups estimated by Bruen and Holahan to most recent CMS enrolment data for FY 2002.
Source: Centers for Medicare and Medicaid Services, 2003 Data Compendium, available at http://www.cms.hhs.gov; Bruen, B. and J. Holahan (2003), "Shifting the Cost of Dual Eligibles: Implications for States and the Federal Government", Kaiser Commission on Medicaid and the Uninsured, Issue Paper #4152, November.

criteria has a right to receive services promised under the programme. Also unlike TANF, Medicaid is a matching grant under which the federal matching rate varies between 50 and 77%, depending on state income *per capita*. To be eligible for federal funds, states are required to provide Medicaid coverage to certain "mandatory eligibility groups", notably low-income families who would have met a state's eligibility requirements for AFDC as of July 1996. However, states can extend Medicaid coverage to optional groups, which are divided into "categorically needy" and "medically needy"....

When Medicaid was created in 1965, it was intended as the medical care complement to income support under AFDC, and AFDC served as the gateway programme through which most beneficiaries signed up. By 2003, spending for optional services or populations accounted for almost two-thirds of total Medicaid spending, reflecting strong political pressures over past decades to extend Medicaid coverage beyond the initial target group. The importance of the shift in Medicaid's focus for the overall cost of the programme is illustrated in Table 14-2. Working-age adults and their children together still account for more than 70% of enrolment, but for little more than one quarter of total expenditures. By contrast, the aged and disabled, most of whom

Table 14-3. Average annual changes in Medicaid enrolment and
spending, 2000-03

	Enrolment (millions)			Spending per enrolee ($)			Total spending ($ billions)		
	2000	2003	Average per cent change	2000	2003	Average per cent change	2000	2003	Average per cent change
Aged and disabled	9.9	10.8	2.9	11 879	14 122	5.9	117.3	151.9	9.0
Families	22.3	29.8	10.1	1 988	2 403	6.5	44.4	71.6	17.3
All enrolees	32.2	40.6	8.0	5 023	5 512	3.1	161.7	223.5	11.4

Source: Holahan, J. and A. Ghosh (2005), "Understanding the Recent Growth in Medicaid Spending,
2000-2003", Health Affairs, Web Exclusive W5, 52-62.

belong to optional groups, account for less than 30% of enrolment but
nearly 70% of expenditures. More than half of the aged and disabled are
so-called "dual eligibles", persons who are entitled to Medicare and are
eligible for some level of Medicaid benefits due to low incomes and
assets. Although Medicare covers much of their acute-care costs, Medicaid pays for Medicare premiums, co-payments and deductibles, for
prescription drugs (until 2006), and for certain services not covered by
Medicare, most importantly long-term (including mental) care. Recent
years have seen the combination of two major sources of cost pressure
on the programme, which have greatly contributed to the fiscal distress
of the states (Boyd, 2003). One source is that, as Medicaid eligibility
became increasingly decoupled from welfare eligibility during the
1990s, states have extended coverage much higher up the income distribution. Combined with the ongoing decline in employer-sponsored
health insurance coverage (Wiatrowski, 2004), this has had the effect
of sharply increasing Medicaid enrolment in the wake of the recent
economic downturn (Table 14-3). The second source is the ageing of
the population and hence the secular growth of the number of Medicaid beneficiaries with very high medical expenditures, largely because
Medicaid is the only source of government assistance for long-term and
nursing home care. . . .

At the same time as most states considerably expanded Medicaid
eligibility during the 1990s, they searched for strategies to contain
increases in costs per enrolee, principally through increased reliance on
managed care. The need for cost containment measures became much
more acute over the past four years, when Medicaid enrolment surged
while state tax revenues dropped sharply. These measures focused on

freezing or cutting Medicaid payment rates to providers (*i.e.* hospitals, physicians, managed care organisations or nursing homes), reducing optional benefits, and developing preferred drug lists (Smith *et al.*, 2004). Reductions in Medicaid eligibility have not been used extensively, however. . . .

Debate about reform of Medicaid finances has focused on three issues. The first concerns states' use of certain intergovernmental transfers and financing mechanisms which, although legal when taken in isolation, can be combined in ways to raise the federal share of total Medicaid funding above the statutory federal matching rate or to make federal matching funds available for purposes other than purchasing health care services covered by Medicaid for eligible persons. Efforts to strengthen Medicaid's fiscal integrity by cutting down on these mechanisms have been under way since the late 1990s, and the Administration's FY 2006 budget proposes further steps in this direction. A second issue is whether a more fundamental reform of the programme should be achieved in a fashion similar to the change from AFDC to TANF, by combining devolution of programme design with the replacement of the current open-ended federal matching grant by a capped federal contribution. It seems questionable whether greater devolution to the state level would lead to more efficient programme design. . . . A final issue is whether to shift all services currently provided to dual eligibles by *Medicaid*, including long-term care, to the federal level (Bruen and Holahan, 2003; National Governors Association, 2005). This would imply combining in *Medicare* the provision of means-tested benefits with those that are not. The rationale would be that the federal level is the appropriate one for addressing policy challenges that are as comprehensive as the cost pressures associated with the ageing of society. . . .

Highway spending

Highway construction is one of the largest areas of capital expenditures by state and local governments. Total highway expenditures by all levels of government in 2000 amounted to $127 billion, with about 62% spent by state governments and 37% by local governments. Direct federal spending on highways contributed only 1.5% of the total. However, the federal government's role in financing highway expenditures is substantially larger. In 2000, federal matching grants earmarked for highway programmes accounted for $31 billion, or 24% of total highway spending. The principal vehicle through which the federal government finances these grants is the Federal Highway Trust Fund, which is overwhelmingly financed by federal tax receipts on motor fuel. Congress has for some time passed multi-year authorising legislation, which establishes upper limits for funds that can be made available to states for highway funding. About 90% of the funds are allocated to states at the beginning of each federal fiscal year according to a formula provided by law called apportionment; the remaining 10% are allocated by Congress on a discretionary basis throughout the fiscal year. The use of apportioned funds by each state is further restricted by assigning the funds to different programmes, such as interstate highway maintenance or national highway construction. States that incur expenses for qualifying projects are reimbursed afterwards at the federal matching rate which varies across programmes, but is no lower than 80% and oftentimes as high as 95%. When the Federal Highway Trust Fund was created in the mid-1950s, the intention was to provide states with an incentive to create an integrated nation-wide highway network without relying on tolls for its financing. However, this network having been established, the very low price of spending on new highways from the states' perspective creates the risk of excessively high spending on qualifying projects (Roth, 2005). . . .

Education

All state constitutions identify the role of the state government in establishing and operating a public school system that is free to all students. While the exact arrangements differ, state governments have historically issued regulations and laws governing schools and then delegated responsibility for school operation to local governments. Although there is wide variation across states, state and local governments typically share funding responsibilities. . . . The federal government's role in primary and secondary education has historically been small. Federal government funding in FY 2004 amounted to $38 billion, or 8% of aggregate nation-wide expenditures for primary and secondary schools of about $500 billion, while the state and local share was 83% (Department of Education, 2005). Most of the federal contribution is targeted at economically disadvantaged students under Title 1 of the Elementary and Secondary Education Act (ESEA) of 1965 and at students with disabilities under the Individuals with Disabilities Education Act. ESEA launched a comprehensive set of programmes, including federal aid to disadvantaged children, to address the problems of poor urban and rural areas. The No Child Left Behind Act of 2001 (NCLB) is the most recent re-authorisation of ESEA. Compared to previous law, NCLB drastically expands testing requirements and establishes new accountability requirements that states have to meet in order to remain eligible for federal grants. Concerning testing, the central requirement is to annually test the reading and mathematics proficiency of students in grades 3 through 8 in all public schools, not only those in schools receiving ESEA Title 1 funds, using achievement standards developed by each state and approved by the Department of Education. . . .

The key debate about NCLB in the context of fiscal relations is whether, and to what extent, the law is an "unfunded mandate" in the sense that it imposes financial burdens on state budgets without adequate federal funding. The Administration has argued that there exist no federal mandates in the context of federal programme obligations because states are free to forgo federal grants (Department of Education, 2005). By contrast, the National Conference of State Legislatures (NCSL) has calculated that the $12.3 billion of federal funds provided in FY 2004 for the implementation of NCLB was $9.6 billion less than the amounts for mandated activities that states must implement to comply with NCLB, bringing the cumulative under-funding up to that year to $27 billion (National Conference of State Legislatures, 2004). . . .

Summary

To summarise this section, current grants from the federal to state governments are all earmarked, but there is considerable variation concerning how specific federal rules are and how open-ended the federal contribution is. Neither revenue sharing nor fiscal equalisation across states exist, leaving differences in the size of TANF block grants and in federal matching rates for Medicaid as the only significant elements of re-distribution across states. Given the substantial degree of autonomy which states have to determine their spending patterns, grants are the main mechanism through which the federal government can influence spending decisions at the state level. But the main argument in the literature for grants serving allocative purposes, namely to correct for spill-overs of benefits across jurisdiction borders, does not seem to explain the existing federal grant structure well: where grants are matching grants, matching rates are often too high (*e.g.* Medicaid and especially highway funding) to purely reflect corrections for spill-overs. Conversely, the recent trend towards earmarked but closed-ended block grants is likely better understood as a means to make greater devolution of programme design to states politically acceptable without giving up the paternalistic motivation of inducing states to provide a minimum level of certain services, rather than as an attempt to adjust matching rates for the purpose of correcting for spill-overs (Inman and Rubinfeld, 1997). In the context of welfare reform, this devolution has contributed to the remarkable decline in caseloads by encouraging experimentation in programme design, and here, as well as in the area of education, tendencies to restrict states' flexibility in adapting programmes to their needs should be resisted or reversed. There are stronger tensions, however, between states' desire to extend Medicaid coverage to certain populations and their ability to finance their share of the resulting costs. This raises the question whether coverage of some populations should be taken over entirely by the federal government in view of states' more limited ability to raise funds. . . .

Bibliography

Baicker, K. (2005), "The Spillover Effects of State Spending", *Journal of Public Economics*, Vol. 89.

Blank, R. (2002), "Evaluation Welfare Reform in the United States", *Journal of Economic Literature*, Vol. 40.

Boyd, D. (2003), "The Current State Fiscal Crisis and Its Aftermath", Kaiser Commission on Medicaid and the Uninsured, Report #4138, September.

Brown, C. and W. Oates (1987), "Assistance to the Poor in a Federal System", *Journal of Public Economics*, Vol. 32.

Brueckner, J. (1982), "A Test for Allocative Efficiency in the Local Public Sector", *Journal of Public Economics*, Vol. 19.

Brueckner, J. (1998), "Welfare Reform and Interstate Welfare Competition: Theory and Evidence", The Urban Institute, Occasional Paper No. 21, December.

Bruen, B. and J. Holahan (2003), "Shifting the Cost of Dual Eligibles: Implications for States and the Federal Government", Kaiser Commission on Medicaid and the Uninsured, Issue Paper #4152, November.

Department of Education (2005), "10 Facts About K-12 Education Funding", available at http://www.ed.gov/print/about/overview/fed/10facts/index.html.

Gramlich, E. and D. Rubinfeld (1982), "Micro Estimates of Public Spending Demand Functions and Tests of the Tiebout and Median-Voter Hypotheses", *Journal of Political Economy*, Vol. 90.

Inman, R. and D. Rubinfeld (1997), "Rethinking Federalism", *Journal of Economic Perspectives*, Vol. 11.

National Conference of State Legislatures (2004), *Mandate Monitor*, Washington, D.C., March.

National Governors Association (2005), *Medicaid Reform: A Preliminary Report*, Washington, D.C., June.

Oates, W. (1969), "The Effects of Property Taxes and Local Public Spending on Property values: An Empirical Study on Tax Capitalization and the Tiebout Hypothesis", *Journal of Political Economy*, Vol. 77.

Oates, W. (1972), *Fiscal Federalism*, Harcourt Brace Jovanovich, New York, NY.

Roth, G. (2005), "Liberating the Roads: Reforming U.S. Highway Policy", Cato Institute, Washington, D.C., March.

Smith, V., R. Ramesh, K. Gifford, E. Ellis, R. Rudowitz and M. O'Malley (2004), "The Continuing Medicaid Budget Challenge: State Medicaid Spending Growth and Cost Containment in Fiscal Years 2004 and 2005", Kaiser Commission on Medicaid and the Uninsured, Report #7190, October.

Tocqueville, A. (1980), *Democracy in America*, Vol. 1, Vintage Books Random House, New York, NY.

Weimer, D. and M. Wolkoff (2001), "School Performance and Housing Values: Using Non-Contiguous District and Incorporation Boundaries to Identify School Effects", *National Tax Journal*, Vol. 54.

Wheaton, W. (2000), "Decentralized Welfare: Will There Be Underprovision?", *Journal of Urban Economics*, Vol. 48.

Wiatrowski, W. (2004), "Medical and Retirement Plan Coverage: Exploring the Decline in Recent Years", *Monthly Labor Review*, Vol. 127.

15

The Economics of Intergovernmental Grants

George F. Break

... Grants-in-aid may be classified in numerous ways.[1] The classification in table 15-1 highlights both the flexibility of grants as a fiscal instrument and the diversity that complicates the assessment of the effects of different grant programs. Four basic types of grant are widely used.

Categorical grants of the open-ended matching variety (3e) have the economic effect of stimulating state and local expenditure in designated functional areas (1d) by lowering the price at which grantees can acquire the program benefits; grantees are free to buy as much as they like at that lower price. The grants are allocated by formula with administrative checks on their use (2c). Federal grants for public assistance and medicaid, which accounted for about 18 percent of total federal grant expenditures in [an earlier year], fall in this category. State matching grants of any kind are rare.

Unconditional general grants allocated by formula fall at the opposite end of the economic spectrum. Their effect is to increase the money income of recipient governments but not to change the prices at which they can purchase goods and services for their citizens. Though there are no examples of a completely unrestricted federal general grant (1a, 2a, 3a) in the United States, general revenue sharing (1b, 2b, 3b) [came] close.[2] About 10 percent of state grant funds goes for general support of local government.

Fixed-amount grants for specified purposes are the most popular type of grant in the United States. . . . This category includes the traditional federal categorical matching closed-end grant (1d, 2c, 3cd), federal block grants (1c, 2bc, 3b), and most state grants for education and highways.[3] Though messy in the eyes of many economists because they combine income and price effects in ways that are difficult to disentangle, these fixed-sum special-purpose grants have numerous attractions.

From George F. Break, *Financing Government in a Federal System* (Washington, D.C.: Brookings, 1980), 73–76.

Table 15-1   The Many Dimensions of Intergovernmental Grants

---

1. How funds are used by recipient
   a. Unrestricted
   b. General, with limited restrictions
   c. Block, within broad program areas
   d. Categorical or functional, within narrow program areas
2. How funds are allocated to recipient
   a. Formula, unrestricted
   b. Formula, subject to limited restrictions
   c. Formula, with administrative checks
   d. Competitive applications by grantees (project grants)
3. Degree of participation by grantor
   a. None (beyond provision of grant funds)
   b. Administrative oversight
   c. Technical services; cooperative management
   d. Grantee matching requirements up to the limit of grantor funds (closed-end matching grants)
   e. Grantee matching requirements with unlimited grantor funds (open-ended matching grants)

Not the least of these may be their ability to conciliate appearance and reality, seeming to support some function close to the heart of the grantor while in reality allowing the grantee to use the funds for any local purpose desired. Closed-end grants have the further advantage of greatly simplifying the budgetary and administrative problems of the grantor. Open-ended grants, in contrast, create budgetary uncertainties by committing the grantor to the provision of whatever funds grantees choose to match. And if the aided activities are not tightly defined, recipients may exert explosive pressures on spending levels by diverting open-ended grant funds to programs the grantor had neither intended nor wished to support.[4]

Project grants are distinguished by the requirement that donees compete for the available funds by submitting detailed plans concerning their use (2d). Some potential recipients may choose not to compete, either because they lack the technical expertise needed to prepare the required plans or because they regard the risks of failure as too high to justify the costs of applying. For the grantor, on the other hand, project grants provide welcome opportunities to reject low-priority proposals and to adjust the terms of support for others so as to maximize the public benefits to be obtained from the funds expended. . . .

The greater importance of project grants in the federal grant system [vis-à-vis state grants] suggests that the relationship between the two parties to a transaction may have a significant impact on grant design. The degree and type of controls exercised by grantors might well be different on grants between two independent powers than on grants between superior and subordinate powers or grants involving a mixture of independent and subordinate powers.

Notes

1. See, for example, Jesse Burkhead and Jerry Miner, *Public Expenditure* (Aldine, 1971), p. 285; ACIR, *Federal Grants, Their Effects on State-Local Expenditures, Employment Levels, Wage Rates: The Intergovernmental Grant System: An Assessment and Proposed Policies*, Report A-61 (GPO, 1977), pp. 25–29.
2. In Canada, federal–provincial tax equalization grants fall in the completely unrestricted category. Australia also uses unconditional financial assistance grants. See ACIR, *In Search of Balance: Canada's Intergovernmental Experience* (GPO, 1971); David B. Perry, "Federal–Provincial Fiscal Relations: The Last Six Years and the Next Five," *Canadian Tax Journal*, vol. 20 (July–August 1972), pp. 349–60; James A. Maxwell, "Revenue-Sharing in Canada and Australia: Some Implications for the United States," *National Tax Journal*, vol. 24 (June 1971), pp. 251–65.
3. In states with separate school districts, education grants looked at from the point of view of the state government are grants restricted to one function; but from the point of view of the school district, they are general-purpose grants unless their use is restricted to particular education programs.
4. Martha Derthick, *Uncontrollable Spending for Social Services Grants* (Brookings Institution, 1975).

16

Federal Grants-in-Aid to State Governments: A Political Analysis

Phillip Monypenny

The federal system is always in danger and it is always rising anew from the ashes of its earlier existence. . . . Though [reports and studies] contribute a great deal of information about the current state of federal-state relations, it cannot be said that they settle any of the questions currently in dispute, in particular the question of whether the position and significance of the states as policy making centers has been significantly changed by the changing scope of the activity of the national government. . . . It is to the scope and character of the grants system, and to its political conditions, that this paper is directed. Incident to this discussion there may be an opinion, if not a conclusion, as to the effect of the grant system on the policy making freedom of state government.

[The author analyzes developments in the grant system, documents the patterns of grants-in-aid, and then compares the results with some of the most frequently cited justifications for the American system of fiscal interdependence.—Ed.]

. . . The picture presented, both in terms of the distribution of aid among the states, and the apparently arbitrary selection of purposes for which aid is extended do not square very well with the textbook justifications for a grant-in-aid system. The classic case for the extension of financial assistance by one government to another is that it provides money for local units which need it in order to support essential activities at a minimum level. This implies a larger measure of support for some units than for others, depending on the relative ability of units to finance the programs supported. No *major* federal grant is based primarily on an equalization factor, and those which include such a factor do not begin to produce a uniform level of service. . . . Perhaps the most

From *National Tax Journal* 13 (March 1960): 1, 11–16. Reprinted by permission of the National Tax Association.

comprehensive justification of the federal grant system would be that it provides a measure of service which national interest requires without complete federal assumption of the function. . . . Every grant, from the construction of wildlife refuges to the piddling expenditures for civil defense, serves some purpose which its defenders regard as properly national. The only difficulty is that the attributes of matters of national concern are by no means obvious. . . .

The stimulation of state and local activity in fields of national interest is often cited as a proper basis of federal aid. Apart from civil defense, in which the national expenditure is minute, there are no grant fields which had not developed prior to the grants as activities of state governments under their inherent powers. This is true of higher education, of the agricultural . . . extension service, of orthopedic care for crippled children, of state financing of highway construction, of unemployment compensation, or whatever. It is true that federal aid may have been a factor in persuading the less-ready states to undertake what had already been undertaken elsewhere. It is hard to make a case for federal aid as a pioneering measure.

Finally, the difficulties which state and local governments face in raising revenue are often urged as a basis for increased federal assistance. The enormously wide variations in the ratio of resources to populations among the states make this absurd if it requires aid to all states on a uniform basis. Admitting the greater difficulty of tapping wealth in a smaller area than a large one, in dealing with a national system of production and distribution, most of the difficulties of the states in raising revenue are self-imposed. The states increased revenue drastically in the middle of the depression, at a time when it would seem to have been economic folly to raise taxes, and expanded their own scale of operations equally drastically. If a tax on real estate remains the prime resource of local governments to support their ever more expensive functions, this is the doing of the states, not the federal government. Those cities whose fiscal difficulties are most prominently displayed house the greatest concentrations of wealth.

The claim of greater administrative competence on the part of federal authorities may be viewed with some skepticism. Wisconsin supplied key members of the federal staff in the early days of employment security, and the states have contributed a considerable contingent of public health officers to the U.S. Public Health Service. It is true that the federal service escapes some of the impediments which hamper administrators of state programs. They are freer of the fear of political reprisals from minor political figures, and they are able to handle the recruitment and assignment of personnel with far less concern about the patronage obligations of executive and legislative leaders. On the other hand, the introduction of federal aid administration imposes another administrative and legislative layer, and to that extent dilutes responsibility, slows action, and increases the necessity of documentation. A great many states could probably build highways just as well without the oversight of the [federal bureaucracy], and administer unemployment compensation and the public employment services without the watchful eye of the [national agency responsible].

Nevertheless, federal aid is here to stay and it is not likely to become any more consistent from one program to another. The balance of federal to state authority, which varies from one program to another, is not likely to shift very much.

The standard explanation of taxpayers' organizations for the federal aid programs is that they represent the triumph of expenditure without responsibility. There is an element of truth in that, but it is not the whole story. It is obvious that many states choose to spend less than others in the very fields in which federal aid pays the highest bonuses for state expenditure. A dollar raised from taxes is still a dollar, whether it brings additional money in federal grants or not. The pressure against the tax is just as heavy by those who have no interest in the expenditure. Obviously, too, Congress has not escaped the need to tax to support these programs, and what its members stand to gain by satisfying demands for larger grants, they lose by imposing taxes. The increase in state tax revenues has been dramatic, and it has been incurred to meet increasing state responsibilities in the very fields in which federal aid has been least available—public education, mental hospitals, and, in the wealthier states, [public] assistance.

Nor is there much evidence that federal aid causes costs to be incurred for certain purposes despite a lack of interest in them by people in the state. In many of the fields where state expenditure is relatively low, ... federal grants have been unsuccessful in luring increased expenditure. Where there is local support for the activity as in highways and vocational education, expenditures in many states are far larger than the minimum that would be required just to match federal allotments. On the other hand, in the fields in which excessive expenditure is alleged to be created by federal aid, public assistance, especially for the aged, there is the strongest local support for large expenditure, and the state programs long preceded federal grants.

It is unlikely therefore that the prospect of free expenditure by the states without the assumption of concomitant tax obligation is the chief root of the grants system. What is then the root of this apparently contradictory phenomenon of patchwork assistance to states in which each field of activity has its own basis for granting money and its own set of administrative requirements, varying from very stringent to very undemanding? It must be sought in the political system of the United States itself, which refuses to conform to the nice legal distinctions of a federal system, or to the logical consistencies of the advocates of executive responsibility and responsible party government.

That system has been adequately sketched in other places and by more skillful hands than those which shape these paragraphs. The population of the United States is divided by loyalties to a thousand different causes. People look to the complex fabric of government for means to pursue these causes, acting at points which are responsive, whatever the formal jurisdiction of the officials who respond. Groups within the population use their influence in one part of the fabric to negate the influence of their opponents at other points, to impose controls, or to escape them. The population acts through political parties and outside of them; it divides in elections for office, and recombines in pursuit of more particular goals. It uses the weapons of numbers, or of status, of publicity, or of intensity of organization, of money, or of familial and personal connection, as they are appropriate.

For such a population the federal grant-in-aid is a made-to-order device for securing unity of action without sacrificing the cohesiveness which is necessary for political success. The great obstacle to effective political action in a country such as the United States is the particularity of the ends of a great part of the politically active public. There are political organizations which will gladly lose national elections if they can keep their hold on local office, and followers of a national leader who are indifferent to the local office base of the party leadership whom they wish to enlist in their campaign. There are local labor organizations which will sacrifice any doctrinal commitment which their parent organizations may have if they can maintain their jurisdiction over jobs which members hold in public employment or in the work under government contract. There are wheat farmers who see farm programs in terms of wheat, and growers of perishable commodities who are more interested in the financing of production and distribution and in cooperative marketing than they are in price supports. Specificity of aim limits the possibility of getting sufficient support to outweigh opposition.

Commitment to a political party as a means of political action is not binding enough to make parties a means of achieving unity of program.

Action through a single government, whether it be state, nation, or local unit, obviously requires some specificity of aim. Legislation must be drafted so as to embody with some precision the aims of those who promote it. Once drafted, it is apt to estrange some of those who were linked in the coalition when it had only partially defined aims. Once drafted, the legislation also defines the opposition, which before lacked a firm base of coalition. The course of legislation may unite persons of very different views because of what they dislike.

The situation changes at once when it is proposed to act through grants to another governmental unit rather than by direct action. By state grants to local units, as in the field of education, a minimum state program is assured, but wide room may be left for differences of local emphasis. The obstacle to the realization of educational goals which lies in local tax limits is the common problem of persons with very divergent educational goals. They can unite to escape this common problem without reconciling their divergences on program.

If this is so in the states, where there is an extensive legal power of regulating the policy, as well as the structure and finance of local units, it is the more so in the federal government. The fiscal power of the federal government can be invoked without bringing to play its policy-making powers, except for that minimum on which those desiring the fiscal assistance can agree. This does not imply that those who support federal financial assistance escape the problem of levying taxes to support the expenditure they sponsor. At the federal level, however, they can both spend and tax; at the state level claims on fiscal resources are less successful. It is possible to get unemployment compensation on a virtually national basis without battling to the wall every combination of employers determined to pay for no more than a minimum program, and yet get a more extensive program in those states where there is support for it. It is possible to get the semblance of a national highway program while still enabling each state to decide whether it will support a more extensive or an intensive program of highway construction; to have many miles of roads to a less high standard, or fewer to a higher. It is notable that in approving the interstate system, which is built with 90 percent federal money, and very extensive federal controls over routes and design, Congress attempted to box in the [federal agency charged with execution] with requirements of Congressional approval of specific administrative decisions not present in earlier highway legislation.

It can be asserted therefore that politically speaking, federal aid programs are an outcome of a loose coalition which resorts to a mixed federal–state program because it is not strong enough in individual states to secure its program, and because it is not united enough to be able to achieve a wholly federal program against the opposition which a specific program would engender. In this connection the uneven responsiveness of governmental units to various population segments undoubtedly plays a part in the resort to federal or to state action, or to a combination of both. Mayors expect Congress to support housing programs which do not get sympathetic attention in state legislatures.

Water, wildlife, forest, and soil conservationists generally look to Washington rather than to the states. Characteristically taxpayers' federations concentrate their attention on state governments, and resist the transfer of questions from that arena to another in which they have less confidence.

Viewed in this light, the grant-in-aid programs make sense. Each is the product of a specific coalition, and the terms of that coalition are evident in the statute and in the administrative practices which result from it. . . .

. . . The grant-in-aid system is by no means an undermining of federalism, but rather a refinement of it. It corresponds to a pragmatic pluralism, which has long been remarked as a characteristic of politics in the United States. It has built into it the characteristically different policy tendencies of states and of the national government. It is scarcely a means of enforcing similarity between them. Although direct administration by either government would have the advantage of political and administrative clarity and consistency, the choice of federal aid schemes as an alternative to either is sufficient evidence that these simpler measures were not a practical means for the attainment of political objectives whose achievement was only possible if they were not too minutely specified.

17

Entrepreneurial Cities, U.S. Federalism, and Economic Development

Alberta M. Sbragia

Each American government moves through a universe made up of tens of thousands of other governments. Each of these governments has, in Fritz Scharpf's terms, an "institutional self-interest" that is defended, enhanced, and pursued vis-à-vis other governments.[1] When governments pursue their institutional self-interests, they are engaging in politics. They are political actors in that universe.

The interest of a government as an institution can be pursued in various ways, each of which has its own appeal. In financing public works and economic development, local governments have used the strategy of circumvention to increase their discretion and flexibility. The price of this strategy is clear: discretion now is bought by narrowing discretion in the future.

The politics of circumvention—and the cost of that type of politics—have shaped the way that local public investment occurs within the American federal system. Judges, the bond market, and the actions of both federal and subnational governments have molded federalism throughout the past two centuries. In the nineteenth century, economic entrepreneurship was dominant. State and local governments took their turn as entrepreneurs until they were stopped. They then began establishing the legal and financial channels that would let them resume activist policies. The process . . . is one of entrepreneurship, restriction, and circumvention (which in turn allowed a renewal of entrepreneurship followed most recently by restriction).

State governments, local governments, and state courts have been central players: the federal government has permitted, and ultimately redirected, this process in the twentieth century through granting tax exemption. In the nineteenth century, the federal government in general played a secondary role, but the Supreme Court made rulings that helped to establish the municipal bond market. Subnational governments subsequently used this market as a pawn in their chess game.

Such a historical view is not always taken, however. Scholars usually stress the independence of the municipal bond market, relative to the capital investment sponsored by states and cities. The market for these scholars is a privileged player. They attribute the bond market's influence to a general phenomenon—the power of markets over public authority. My argument is that, looked at historically, the relationship between public authority and private money has been such that governments have actually shaped the investment system. The reason for the bond market's influence over the finances of American cities has little to do with the imperatives of capital markets or the notion that money talks. It has a great deal to do with the historical choices made by public authorities, including the courts.

The municipal bond market, subnational governments, and Washington, D.C., form a triangle. Although market judgments about the creditworthiness of local borrowers do affect what borrowers can borrow and at what terms, the market's power derives from the public investment system itself—a system that has moved through the pattern of entrepreneurship, restriction, and circumvention. . . . A capital market operating within a different investment system would not have the same kind of influence as the American municipal bond market.

The American market has power over subnational borrowers partly because the federal government does not guarantee debt. Risk concentrates the mind and calls for measured judgments about local government borrowers as much as about corporate borrowers. The market's power also derives from its legal status under tax law. Tax law and the municipal bond market are inextricably intertwined. Tax law controls access to the municipal bond market and is therefore an instrument with profound implications for American federalism. To assert its control over state and local entrepreneurship in the 1980s, in fact, Congress found it necessary to change tax law. Washington—not bankers or lenders—ultimately determines how much power the municipal bond market has over cities. Conversely, the cities' access to the bond market is also controlled by Washington, not by bankers or lenders.

Within the federal system, however, the importance of the bond market has lain primarily in the possibilities for evasion offered to local governments. The market allows subnational governments to circumvent the numerous restrictions imposed by state law on their borrowing. In other words, the municipal bond market allows local governments to evade state governmental constraints. The market allows local officials to "push the limits." It is the instrument that allows the politics of circumvention to proceed—as long as state rather than federal law is being circumvented.

The market's role in the strategy of circumvention shows how public-private institutional networks undergird the system of public investment in the United States. The private sector facilitates the political strategy pursued by local governments, while imposing its own costs and demands (such as credit ratings) on local borrowers. The market was an integral part of the strategy developed by governments trying to cope with the present under the constraints imposed by the past.

Interactions between governments, courts, and capital markets changed the options and opportunities available to each actor in the system. And this interaction led to the creation of a new actor in the system—the public authority. The creation of the authority represented an essential tactic in the strategy of circumvention. It was an act of intergovernmental politics. Once in place, public authorities then became important actors in the next phase of intergovernmental politics. The odyssey of public authorities in the American system is instructive in that it shows how intergovernmental politics in one period shape such politics in a subsequent phase.

Historical analysis also shows that the opportunities open to officials at any level of government are neither fixed nor infinite. Any equilibrium reached within the federal system is transient. Governments—local governments in particular—have used both law-based and market-based strategies to achieve greater maneuverability in a particular system. Yet the cost of obtaining such maneuverability was often paid by local officials in subsequent generations.

Once cities had been definitively subordinated to the states, they could not overcome their status. However, they did try to maintain an aggregate level of investment activity that was greater than was permitted by the state's limitations. Debt limits (including the requirement of electoral approval) were viewed as constraints on desired investment and were therefore circumvented. In many states, the creation of a new institution—the public authority—provided one answer to local government's dilemma.

The authority diluted the power of city government, but it also allowed the provision of badly needed public services. In the postwar period, it allowed local governments to engage once again in economic development. The elected government had been the investor and entrepreneur in the nineteenth century, whereas the public authority, in many states, played that role in the postwar period. Given the tenuous relationship between many elected municipal governments and the public authorities that control significant investment in the cities' territorial boundaries, this might be viewed as a problematic bargain. Nonetheless, that bargain is essential to understanding the compartmentalized nature of politics in capital-intensive sectors.

Entrepreneurship has thus occurred twice at the subnational level—in the nineteenth century and in the 1970s and 1980s. In these periods, state and local governments used public capital investment extensively for purposes of economic development. Entrepreneurship has in turn been followed by measures designed to restrict local government activism.

The creation of authorities relied heavily on local governments' being able to use the financial market to their own ends. Governments and markets depend on—and use—one another over time. But using the market as an instrument can only occur as the law permits it. Capital markets are profoundly dependent on the legal order, for it is that order that structures the contours of markets. It is ironic, then, that state courts were critical actors in the fashioning of the strategy of circumvention. State judges ultimately decided whether the law could be evaded by local government borrowers. The market was there to be used by governments, but it could be used only if the state courts so permitted.

Once the authority was in place, the competition between local governments to attract industry and to promote economic development generally led to an expansion of borrowing. Economic development efforts boomed during the 1970s and early 1980s as authorities used their powers in creative ways. The federal government then moved to restrict such entrepreneurial activity in the mid-1980s by using tax policy to make local borrowing more expensive.

Subnational governments have not reacted to economic or social forces impinging upon them within a political/administrative vacuum. Their entrepreneurship in the nineteenth century was certainly inspired by technological change, as well as by the desire for economic growth. But politicians invent and manufacture within their own realm. In this case, their entrepreneurship involved positioning themselves in both the federal system and the economy as it evolved over time. Their response to economic change is so shaped by the federal system that they could not address such change without simultaneously thinking about how to manipulate or work around the federal system. The concepts of "urban political economy" and "political economy of federalism" are interwoven.

The resulting system is an extraordinarily complex one. Governments are far from acting simply as the forum for interest-group competition or as access points or veto points for contending interest groups. Yet neither are government officials autonomous actors choosing from a portfolio of policy choices that are unconstrained by the legacy of previous choices. Strategies and choices in the public investment portfolio vary with context; they are different in the 1830s, the 1960s, and the 1990s.

Subnational officials in the United States work within a system in which their predecessors have made Faustian bargains. In order to circumvent state restrictions, while benefiting from the federal tax exemption on local borrowing, they created new governmental entities that qualified for the tax exemption. However, in so doing, they fragmented their own power. The landscape of local government in the United States, therefore, looks far different from the one portrayed in most textbooks. General-purpose governments have become surrounded by special-purpose entities, which are often insulated from the pressures of decision making that are intrinsic to general-purpose governments accountable to electorates. In a political landscape where taxes are transformed into user fees and citizens into users, the electorates are more remote.

The contemporary pattern of policy making in American public investment is the unanticipated consequence of a process that began with the earliest debates over the appropriate national role in the provision of internal improvements. The range of choices that contemporary policy makers face are not those they would necessarily prefer. It is a range that historical forces have handed them.

Elected officials who wish to improve their chances of reelection, build coalitions, and reward political friends must work within relatively narrow limits. In the capital investment arena, many political choices are simply not available. Elected officials need to address constituency demands and simultaneously maneuver within the constraints and opportunities provided by the legal system that regulates both their behavior and the market within which they borrow.

That market, however, is hypersensitive to law and politics, for it is founded on property rights as defined by courts and on tax law set by the Supreme Court and Congress. Officials, therefore, are affected by law both directly (as it affects their maneuverability) and indirectly (as it shapes the market from which they borrow). Whether investing for infrastructure or for economic development, local officials are operating within an elaborate legal framework. The legal order lies at the heart of the investment system.

Public authorities, unaccountable to electorates, play a different game, one that is neither acknowledged nor understood by either citizens or scholars. Given how little scholarly research there is on these entities, it is difficult to analyze their role in the evolution of the federal system. Their very existence, however, constrains the choices available to elected officials.

Public authority officials also need to maneuver within legal and market constraints, but their insulation from the electorate and their relative invisibility gives them a privileged position. This study has examined the foundation of the public authority system, but future work on federalism, urban politics, metropolitan politics, and state and local government will need to develop our analytic understanding of the role of public authorities.

The American system is characterized by a loose-jointedness that, perhaps paradoxically, makes it difficult to "erase history." It is difficult to mobilize the political resources necessary to change restrictions and laws; circumvention is an easier strategy than a frontal assault on a constitutional provision or statute. The powerful role of the judiciary facilitates that circumvention.

The loose-jointed nature of the American system also binds the public and private sectors together in a symbiotic relationship. Public-sector officials can use private-sector resources to maneuver within a system that is not well articulated administratively. Maneuverability and the capacity for discretion within the public sector, however, is paid for by dependence on private-sector resources. . . . A lack of centralization may well correlate with high levels of public-private cooperation and dependency.

Historical analysis of public investment reveals an enduring characteristic of the American federal and policy-making systems. Circumvention is cheaper than change, even though its outcomes may well be far from ideal. The complexity of the system increases over time: when new circumventory mechanisms are invented, the mechanisms of the past are retained rather than eliminated.

It is in this context that the municipal bond market was important. It has allowed local governments to fashion a strategy of circumvention that has tempered the need to attack anachronistic state restrictions directly. The use of the private sector allowed the public sector to create public authorities and thereby to become ever more Byzantine in structure. The state courts acted as the bond market's allies. Without the bond market, the revenue bond would not have been born, but without the state courts' validation, the revenue bond would not have survived. Thus, the state courts, the municipal bond market, and the general strategy of circumvention were inextricably bound together—with the result that the system of state and local capital investment became ever more convoluted as the creation of public authorities added a final touch.

But the strategy of circumvention shaped state-local relations only. The intervention of the federal government in the 1980s added another dimension to the intergovernmental politics of local capital investment. Washington did not change state restriction or the fragmentation of local government. Rather, it added new restrictions, which could not be circumvented as state limits had been. Local governments could not use the market to circumvent federal limits, for those same limits shaped the market itself. The municipal bond market, based as it is on the federal tax exemption of local borrowing, can provide an escape from state limits but not from their federal counterparts.

Washington's intervention was an example of intergovernmental politics at its most visible. The use of tax reform to limit the maneuverability of subnational officials was not primarily an example of partisan politics, but it is still politics, in that national legislators imposed on subnational officials their idea of the proper way to carry out economic development.

Governments act politically toward each other. Much public policy making involves politics between governments, as well as more traditional politics rooted in state-society relations and expressed through interest groups and political parties.

Democracy and Territorial Politics

The conventional view of politics involves elected officials and interest groups; the picture of politics sketched here involves judges' allowing governments to circumvent other levels of government as well as national legislators' forcing state and local borrowers to change their ways. Governments are politicians in their dealings with other governments.

This view of politics requires us to treat intergovernmental politics as seriously as politics that involve social groups. Politics based on the interests of governments as institutions coexist with politics based on the organization and representation of societal interests. To treat federalism as a structural characteristic—as a static feature—of the American political system rather than viewing it as a political dynamic is to diminish the complexity of American politics and policy making.

The intergovernmental form of politics is a less democratic version of politics than that rooted in state-society relations. Electorates are often simply uninvolved and unaware. Some of the governments involved—public authorities in particular—are not elected governments. Even when elected officials engage in intergovernmental politics, they may not be responding to pressures from citizens or (societally based) interest groups. In fact, so-called technical policy areas—which typically do not interest the participants in electorally based politics—are generally those most likely to be the object of intergovernmental politics.

Technical matters are precisely those that are likely to affect the institutional self-interest of governments. Government operations—widely viewed as technical—can be marginal to politics as conceived according to the state-society model but at the very core of intergovernmental relations as discussed in this analysis. The use of the revenue bond, the legitimation of that bond by state courts, and the creation of public authorities are not, and have not been, important to political discourse as traditionally defined in any city or state government. They are invisible on the political map as conventionally drawn. Yet they have changed the face of American subnational government and the system of financing and have transformed taxpayers into ratepayers.

Further, the channels through which action and conflict take place are not those specified in democratic theory. The role of the courts in this form of political dialogue is particularly difficult to analyze using traditional categories. And the use of the market as an instrument does not fit into our categories of politically relevant action. Yet, simply because the activities identified within the general realm of intergovernmental politics do not fit within our notions of how the exercise of political action is linked to the exercise of democracy does not justify ruling out intergovernmental politics as an important part of the American political dynamic.

Conflict between governments is sometimes viewed as being of more relevance to students of public administration than to students of political science. Relations between governments are not viewed as "politics" because they are not rooted in state-society relations; that is, social or economic or racial groups are not involved in influencing the government. Yet, the outcomes of intergovernmental politics set the parameters of choice for traditional political actors.

If we generalize from the sector of public investment, it seems that intergovernmental politics in the United States have at least three important features. The first has to do with "horizontal politics." This element manifests the competitiveness that is intrinsic to American federalism. American state and local governments have been competing with each other for over two centuries now, and this competition has been ferociously intensified by the ease of incorporation in the United States. As new states entered the union and as local governments proliferated within both new and existing states, the number of competitors constantly increased. It is this competitive element that drives a great deal of intergovernmental politics at the subnational level and that dominates the pursuit of economic development. Whereas German federalism has developed rules that are designed to minimize competition among territorial units, the history of American federalism—and of horizontal relationships among states and among local governments—has been based on competition for economic growth.

Second, intergovernmental politics in the area of economic policy (especially in the post–World War II period) are driven by two different views of the American economy and of economic growth. Washington tends to think in macro-economic terms, and more recently micro-economic views (those focusing on specific industrial sectors) have become more prominent. Yet subnational officials view the economy spatially; they think territorially. Seen from Washington, D.C., it does not matter where a business firm locates, pays taxes, and hires workers (as long as it does not move abroad), but in the dynamic of territorial politics that locational decision is all-important. It is the collision between views of the economy viewed through the lens of macro-economic indicators (including federal revenues) on the one hand and through the lens of territory on the other, which leads to such disparate positions of what is appropriate policy in the area of economic development.

Third, this conflict will encourage the development of strategies that are intended to increase the discretion of local officials, even as the structural limits that impinge upon them become more stringent. Such strategies will use private-sector institutions and "non-political" institutions such as courts to stretch the bounds of the restrictions that state and local officials find themselves facing. At their end, federal officials will continue to use a variety of mechanisms—including tax laws, mandates, and a wide variety of regulatory measures—to assert control.

Conclusion

American federalism is not a static feature of American politics and policy making. It shapes a territorially based politics, which coexists with that socially based dynamic traditionally defined as "politics." Governments are central actors in the "politics of federalism." Indeed, governments act toward other governments much as interest groups relate to government. Governments drive a political process that involves shifting coalitions, changes in the importance of the main actors, the introduction of new actors, the development of strategies, the use of unexpected instruments such as tax law, the creation and sustenance of public-private networks, judicial intervention, and the erosion of the influence of the electorate and electorally based politics. Intergovernmental politics in the United States are not marginal to politics and policy but, rather, form part of the very fabric of American governance.

The opportunities and constraints that confront a government are not constant over time. The opportunity structure that faces local governments in the present has evolved over nearly two centuries and is deeply rooted in the historical legacy of governmental intervention in the American economy. The development of that structure has been driven by governments' jostling and competing for position, authority, jurisdiction, and finance. The creation of the structure we now find in situ has been fraught with intergovernmental conflict, and its shape has been defined by the winners and losers of those battles. In many cases, the arbiter of such conflict has been the judiciary—both the state courts and the U.S. Supreme Court.

In a federal system, roles and responsibilities can never be completely fixed or defined. They are constantly being challenged by one governmental unit or another. The options available to any single government are typically unclear enough so that officials from any unit may find it worthwhile to push against the boundaries. Federalism, far from being a static property of the American political system, packages the conflict between governments. It lays some of the ground rules and provides the ammunition for all participants in the never-ending game of intergovernmental politics.

Intergovernmental politics coexist with the kinds of politics that are grouped under the rubric "state-society" relations. Governments qua institutions must be thought of as political actors—as politicians—in their own right. They do not simply respond to interest-group pressures or provide the incentives for individual office holders or administrators. They also act within a universe of other governments, peers if you will. They maneuver within that universe over time, using strategies that are designed to increase the range of discretion and the number of vantage points suitable for action.

It matters whether one uses the prism of intergovernmental politics or the prism of state-society relations to analyze politics and policy. The two models emphasize different actors, different motives, different time frames, and different channels of action. This study argues, for example, that the politics of circumvention played a key role in the intergovernmental politics of local capital investment. Governments are viewed as purposive, capable of using the legal and financial system to achieve their institutional ends. Territorial units rather than functionally organized interests are central to the analysis. A wide range of institutions—including the judiciary—play important and interdependent roles. Rather than focusing on specific investment decisions, this type of analysis focuses on the constraints and opportunity structure within which any individual decision is taken. The focus is on understanding the parameters within which political choices, as traditionally understood, are made.

By contrast, a study of local public investment based on the state-society model would focus on the local political coalitions that affected local choices about investment. Local officials would be seen as responding to certain pressures rather than others, and the focus would be on elections and electorates, majors, campaign contributors, organized interests, and the imperatives of the municipal bond market. In this type of analysis, the existence of the revenue bond and the public authority would be taken as givens, as would the fact that capital-intensive services charge user fees.

Intergovernmental politics enjoy an ironic quality. They are invisible, yet they are entrenched in the American political system. They can seem bloodless, when compared to politics as conventionally understood. In short, intergovernmental politics seem to lack the human interest that makes traditional accounts of urban politics so fascinating. Certainly, the creation of the revenue bond is not as stirring a story as the political battles that have raged around specific investments such as convention centers. The electorate was not involved in the creation of the revenue bond except as a factor to be excluded.

The tenuous link of intergovernmental politics to traditional democratic politics, however, does not diminish the impact of the former. The decisions made by the intergovernmental style of politics are rarely challenged by traditional political actors. The issues over which territorial politics are fought are rarely on the first page of any newspaper, yet they help define what can be done and by which governments. Finally, it is both significant and troubling that so much of what a government does and will be able to do in the future is shaped by other governments rather than by citizens.

Note

1. Scharpf, "The Joint-Decision Trap: Lessons from German Federalism and European Integration," *Public Administration* 66 (autumn 1988), p. 242.

18

Why Categorical Grants?

U.S. Advisory Commission on Intergovernmental Relations

The development of American federalism since the Civil War, which settled the most fundamental issues, is in large part the story of an expanding system of categorical aids....

These features of American federalism were not, in any clear sense, preordained. Other advanced democracies having a federal constitution have followed different developmental patterns.[1] Among the most obvious historical alternatives that might have been, but were not, adopted are: a pattern of financial self-sufficiency on the part of state and local governments; direct performance by the national government of all its domestic functions; a clear distinction between national and subnational services and responsibilities; and the use of broad-gauged general support and functional (or block) grants for the equalization of fiscal capacities and service levels among the states. In the light of such alternatives, the question to be considered is: Why was the development of the American federal system characterized by the extensive use of categorical assistance programs rather than by the alternative federal-state-local relationships?

Possible answers to this query... suggest the importance of at least three factors: (1) economic and fiscal considerations; (2) the constitutional and philosophical traditions of the United States; and (3) features of the decision-making process in the American political system....

Economic and Fiscal Factors

[Most of the economic and fiscal factors covered by the author, including the tax structure at various levels of government in the United States, the depression, and the economic diversity of the country, were

From U.S. Advisory Commission on Intergovernmental Relations, *Categorical Grants: Their Role and Design* (Washington, D.C.: ACIR, 1977), 49, 51, 53–57. Footnotes have been renumbered.

summarized in the introductory chapter to this volume. This excerpt resumes with a discussion of one economic-fiscal factor not explicitly covered thus far in this book.—Ed.]

Some economists have suggested another conceptual framework for the growth of categorical aids. This explanation involves recognition of the "spillovers" or "externalities" that occur in the provision of many state and local government services. The benefits flowing from public programs are not necessarily restricted to residents of the jurisdiction that provides and finances them through its taxes. Some spill over to the residents of nearby areas or to the general public. Wastewater treatment is one clear case; the beneficiaries of cleaner water often are those who live downstream from a source of pollution, not those whose effluent is treated. Highways that carry a large volume of interstate traffic are another obvious example of a state service that benefits nonresidents. Higher education, because of the frequency with which college graduates migrate to other states, might be a third instance.

The danger in these situations is that the amount of public services provided will be inadequate, because local voters and taxpayers have no incentive to pay for activities that benefit others. One solution is to have a share of the costs proportional to the actual distribution of benefits borne by a higher level of government, which can be accomplished by a properly designed grant-in-aid. . . . George F. Break concluded that:

> . . . external benefits, which will probably continue to grow in importance, are already pervasive enough to support a strong prima facie case for federal and state functional grants to lower levels of government.[2]

Grants aimed at correcting these spillovers usually are categorical and would be necessary even if a state or locality possessed a strong fiscal base.

This theory, although accepted by many experts in public finance, is subject to certain criticisms. First, it is based upon the somewhat tenuous assumption that state and local governments know the needs or preferences of their citizenry and act to maximize their residents' economic welfare.[3] Other economists, although accepting the basic argument in certain instances, suggest that many existing grants are not actually based upon the externality principle. Concerning this interpretation, Charles L. Schultze concludes that externality

. . . is not very useful for analyzing most of the existing social grants. Rather, many of these grants are a means by which the federal government uses state and local governments . . . as agents or subcontractors to produce centrally determined amounts and kinds of collective goods, since, for a number of reasons, principally historical and political, the federal government itself virtually never delivers collective goods or services at the local level.[4]

. . . One set of estimates of the importance of the externalities involved in various functional fields [indicates that] the federal government makes financial contributions to some fields in which externalities are slight (police protection, libraries), while the states and localities retain substantial fiscal burdens in activities that involve the largest externalities (education, welfare). Moreover, as Schultze adds, most federal grants do not have the specific characteristics that the externality theory suggests are desirable. . . .

[Constitutional and historical factors, which are discussed next, have been summarized in the introductory chapter.—Ed.]

Political Factors

The categorical grant program also appears to many analysts to be an expression of basic American political patterns and institutions. Important influences may be found in the operations of interest groups, the attitudes of federal officials, the structure and procedures of Congress, and the social and political diversity of the population.

Interest Group Influences

A political interpretation of grants-in-aid, based on observations about interest group activities, was offered several years ago in an article by Phillip Monypenny. Monypenny found that the growing grant system largely failed to satisfy the standard textbook justifications for federal aid. It did not provide for substantial fiscal equalization among the states, for example, and the programs did not appear to fall into areas of special national interest or concern by any consistent definition.

Monypenny believed that the actual source of the grant programs lay in features of the political system. A sharing of program responsibility, using federal fiscal resources but offering some discretion through administration by the states, was produced when an interest group lacked sufficient strength to gain all of its objectives in either the state capitals or Congress. . . .

Federal Distrust

The use of categorical aid programs also has been encouraged by a set of attitudes shared by many officials in the national legislative and executive branches. In its most moderate form, this attitude appears in the view that the government that raises money via taxation should also control the expenditure of that money. A preference for categorical aid reflects the judgment that this instrument maximizes accountability in the use of federal funds. Not infrequently, however, a more extreme position is taken, based upon a deeply felt distrust regarding the intentions, performance, and general competence and representativeness of state, municipal, and county governments.

The 1955 report of the Kestnbaum Commission highlighted the need for accountability through categorization, concluding that:

. . . when federal aid is directed toward specific activities, it is possible to observe the effects of each grant, to evaluate the progress of aided activities, and to relate the amount of financial assistance to needs. There is more assurance that federal funds will be used to promote the nation's primary interests.[5]

More recently, a congressional committee professional staff member, Dr. Delphis C. Goldberg, has described this position from the legislative perspective, contrasting categorical programs with broader-purpose grants:

There are practical disadvantages to assistance mechanisms that carry few or no conditions. The federal government may become locked into supporting ineffective and inefficient activities, and the information needed to evaluate programs becomes difficult or impossible to obtain. In discharging its responsibilities, Congress generally desires more than assurance of fiscal probity; it wants to know how well the money is spent and who benefits.[6]

Distrust or actual hostility toward subnational governments was indicated in the views expressed by Wilbur J. Cohen, a former secretary of the Department of Health, Education and Welfare [since reorganized as the Department of Health and Human Services and the Department of Education—Ed.], in an interview in 1972. Secretary Cohen described his comments on the revenue-sharing proposal to a group of Democratic mayors.

I told them, I found it hard to argue—in fact I am very unsympathetic with all you fellows asking for this federal revenue sharing when most of you run political machines that don't allow competent people to administer programs and you're shackled to a lot of political hacks.[7]

Only the federal government, in Secretary Cohen's view, could guarantee rapid action on pressing social problems.

. . . I think in the nature of problems we face in our society, there's no question in my mind that we wouldn't be where we are today if there were no federal people pushing civil rights, desegregation or equal treatment for women. Take big, social-economic-ideological problems, and if left to just disorganized state and local action, or citizen action, I'm not saying that they might never get done, but they might take 100, 200 years. Whereas, the federal government action in the problems, whether it's against mental retardation, old-age assistance or whether it's building libraries—take any of the categories—I think have resulted in faster, more effective meeting of the nation's social problems.[8]

Historically these criticisms have had both administrative and political dimensions. In the 1920s and 1930s, the former was paramount, and federal aid was widely credited with improving the administrative practices of the states.[9] Many grant requirements were directed specifically toward this end. The Kestnbaum Commission, along with many other students of government, concluded that, "When used effectively, the (categorical) grant not only has increased the volume of state and local services, but also has promoted higher standards both in service and administration. . . ."[10]

In the 1960s and 1970s certain political issues received greater stress. States were regarded as unrepresentative and unresponsive to urban needs, encouraging the development of direct federal-local project grant programs.[11] Yet many policymakers believed that cities also neglected the interests of their least fortunate citizens. As noted by Edward R. Fried and his associates . . . :

. . . states and localities may fail to meet the needs of some groups of citizens, especially those with little power and status in the community. Although a few states and localities have at times been more progressive than the national government, most have been relatively unresponsive to the needs of the poor minorities. Disadvantaged groups (for example, labor unions in the 1930s and the blacks and the poor in the 1960s) have often turned to the federal government for help after failing to arouse state and local governments to awareness of their plight. The goal of providing more nearly equal opportunities for the disadvantaged—which was a growing national concern in the 1960s—cannot be met by relying on the highly unequal resources of state and local governments or on their willingness to provide the services that the disadvantaged require.[12]

One expression of this critical view under the Great Society was the provision of federally funded services through limited-purpose governments and private nonprofit organizations, thus bypassing the traditional state-local system entirely.

The federal government, however, has sometimes stepped into fields in which states actually have served as innovators, as well as those in which they seem to have lagged. Morton Grodzins has pointed to instances in the historical record (such as unemployment compensation, aid to the aged and blind, and road construction) in which the federal government has acted as an emulator of state programs by making national programs of their successes. Thus, he notes, "the states can lose power both ways."[13]

Congressional Influence

Certain features of the structure and milieu of the national legislature also encourage the heavy use of categorical grants. Students of the legislative process indicate that specialization is a dominant feature of the modern Congress, particularly the House of Representatives. Power is concentrated at the committee and subcommittee level, while the central organs of leadership have limited control over activities in either chamber. Individual congressmen are expected by their peers to become expert in some narrow, particular field of public policy, normally a field related to their committee or subcommittee assignments. In this manner Congress as a whole gains the expertise necessary to deal with complex social and economic issues.

This norm of legislative specialization is accompanied by another—that of deference. Next to their own personal judgment, congressmen rely most heavily in determining their issue positions on the opinions of their colleagues. Those thought to be most expert in a field, quite naturally, are usually the members who sit on that particular area's committee or subcommittee, and their views are respected.[14] Deference goes beyond this respect for one's colleagues, however. At least in the past, freshman legislators were expected to refrain from even speaking out on matters outside their committee work unless their home district was affected directly.[15]

Specialization also is tied to the practice of decisionmaking by "logrolling." Individual congressmen generally seek committee assignments that relate to the interests of their constituents and, therefore, their own reelection prospects. For this reason they often have a direct stake in the promotion of new and beneficial programs. Other congressmen hesitate to undercut the electoral base of their colleagues and expect this favor to be returned.

A consequence of these practices is that in many fields, the basic decisions are made at the committee or subcommittee level and are seldom challenged on the floor. This situation appears to have had a direct impact on the development of the grants system. The fragmentation of responsibility in Congress inclines it toward the creation of a large number of specialized grants, which may provide duplicative or even conflicting services. Harold Seidman stated:

> It's no accident that we have four different water and sewer [grant] programs, because these come out of four separate committees of Congress. These are very important programs for a Congressman's constituency, and a Congressman wants to be sure that it will remain in an agency under the jurisdiction of his committee.[16]

Similarly, the weakness of central legislative organs means that each committee is largely free to follow its own inclinations regarding procedural matters, such as planning requirements, recipient administrative organization, matching and allocation formulas, and so forth. As a consequence grant programs vary greatly in these administrative particulars.

Although some specialization is certainly necessary in dealing with complex legislative problems, the fragmentation of Congress fails to provide for an equally urgent requirement—the task of integrating the manifold activities of government. As Samuel P. Huntington has stressed, the complex modern environment requires both a high degree of specialization and a high degree of centralized coordinative authority. Congress has adjusted only half-way by accommodating the former but not the latter function.[17]

Although establishing a direct cause-and-effect relationship would be difficult, the dispersion of authority in Congress has increased over the course of this century along with the expansion of the intergovernmental grant system. The increased development of categorical aid during the

World War I era followed a revolt in 1910–11 against Rep. Joseph G. "Boss" Cannon, who as Speaker of the House had acquired extensive control over the House of Representatives. The effect of this revolt was to strengthen the position of committee chairmen.[18] The post–World War II growth of assistance occurred after another set of reforms embodied in the *Legislative Reorganization Act of 1946*. That act, which reduced the number of congressional committees and was intended to strengthen them, had what was in many respects the contrary result, because it led to a proliferation of subcommittees and actually intensified the dispersion of power. At the same time congressional committees acquired their first permanent professional staff positions.[19]

The number of subcommittees grew steadily in the 1950s and their autonomy increased. Earlier struggles for control between committees and the central legislative leadership were replayed between the subcommittees and committee chairmen. As in 1910 the forces for dispersion proved the more powerful. By 1962—just before the period of the most rapid increase in categorical programs—it could be said that, "given an active subcommittee chairman working in a specialized field with a staff of his own, the parent committee can do no more than change the grammar of a subcommittee report."[20]

This trend has continued. In the 94th Congress (1975–76), 144 subcommittees were in existence, a significant increase from the 83 functioning 20 years [earlier]. Moreover, each subcommittee now possesses some staff. Most authorization hearings in recent years have been held at the subcommittee level, rather than by the full committee, as had been the practice in the past.[21] According to a recent observer, the problem of overlapping jurisdictions has increased. Duplication in hearings and frequent legislative delays occur, and a situation has arisen in which legislation is drafted in isolated environments that may not reflect the views of the membership at large.[22]

The growth of the modern executive bureaucracy has paralleled the structure of congressional subcommittees established since 1946.[23] The administrative agencies, in turn, reinforce the pattern of congressional organization. Bureaus and subcommittees closely work together and with the interest groups concerned with their specific policy areas. These "subgovernments," as they have been termed, are the spawning ground of many new aid programs. They form "iron triangles," which have often been criticized for operating beyond the control of the congressional leadership, the presidency, and the public-at-large.[24]

Social Pluralism

The great social diversity of the United States also has had an impact upon the nature of its public policy. The nation is composed of a very large number of cultural and economic groups, each possessing different political objectives and concerns. As a consequence the existence of a large national majority actively committed to any specific major social policy change would be unusual. This fact is reflected in Congress, where modest, incremental programmatic steps, typified by the smaller categorical grant programs, are most readily accepted. Gary Orfield, an analyst of Congress, indicates:

> For a number of readily understandable reasons, Congress is far more responsive to the need for new (categorical) programs than to basic fiscal or social rearrangements. Redressing general social or economic imbalances always means helping some while denying to others a portion of their goods or of their social objectives. ... Most new grant programs, on the other hand, give additional benefits to some groups while seldom disturbing the others. When a Senator fights for more housing or better health care for old people, or for better education benefits for veterans, he usually gains strength from a segment of his constituency without deeply offending anybody else.[25]

Education provides an example. This field was the first area of federal assistance, and it is one in which programs have been particularly numerous. The current variety of categorical education programs reflects the inability in past decades of the supporters of federal aid to education to agree upon a system of general education support. Legislation to create a program of general assistance for education was considered repeatedly by Congress after 1870, with bills introduced into the House or Senate during most sessions over this period of nearly a century.[26] However, division among the advocates of aid—especially those within the Democratic party—made passage impossible, with religion and race the most divisive issues.[27] The result was that consensus could be reached on the desirability of programs for specific education purposes but not for general aid. Jesse Burkhead has commented:

> Specific grants for special purposes can be devised which avoid the problems that block the approval of [general] federal aid [to education]. The past experience has been that pressures for federal aid have most frequently found expression in the passage of just such specialized programs. The agitation of the 1870s and 1880s was

capped by the enactment of a vocational education law. The struggles of 1948 and 1949 brought educational legislation for impacted areas. And the 1956–57 House battles culminated not in a construction bill, but in the [National Defense Education Act].[28]

Similarly in the early 1960s, attention was initially focused on assistance for higher education, which generated less opposition than aid to elementary and secondary schools.[29]

Social pluralism and divergent interests also abet the enactment of comprehensive bills, including a number of distinct programs. Title after title is added in the process of building a supportive coalition. The 1965 *Elementary and Secondary Education Act* (ESEA) provides an example. In five titles ESEA provided aid to the educationally disadvantaged, authorized funds for school textbooks and libraries, established supplementary education centers for adults and children, developed a national network of regional educational laboratories, and assisted the strengthening of state departments of education. U.S. Commissioner of Education Francis Keppel, who served as a "broker" among various interests in developing the legislation, developed a coalition that fit together as intricately as a "Chinese puzzle."[30]

Notes

1. See R. J. May, *Federalism and Fiscal Adjustment*, London, Oxford University Press, 1969.
2. George F. Break, *Intergovernmental Fiscal Relations in the United States*, Washington, D.C., The Brookings Institution, 1967, p. 63. Break's text provides a full discussion of the externality rationale for categorical grants. See especially pp. 63–68.
3. Wallace E. Oates, *Fiscal Federalism*, New York, Harcourt Brace Jovanovich, Inc., p. 73. Oates comments that although these weaknesses are such that some might believe that the Pigovian prescriptions for intergovernmental grants to correct spillovers should be rejected entirely, his own view is that a case for such grants does remain in many instances.
4. Charles L. Schultze, "Sorting Out the Social Grant Programs: An Economist's Criteria," *American Economic Review*, 64, May 1974, pp. 182–83. He defines "collective goods" as "those goods actually produced and distributed free (or at highly subsidized prices) by governmental organizations."
5. *Commission on Intergovernmental Relations*, U.S. House of Representatives, 84th Cong., 1st Sess., June 28, 1955, p. 122.
6. Delphis C. Goldberg, "Intergovernmental Relations: From the Legislative Perspective," *Annals of the American Academy of Political and Social Science*, 416, November 1974, p. 63.
7. "Wilbur J. Cohen: A Defender of Categorical Grants," *National Journal*, Dec. 16, 1972, p. 1912.

8. Ibid.

9. For example, see V. O. Key, Jr., *The Administration of Federal Grants to States*, Chicago, Ill., Public Administration Service, 1937, pp. xiv, 368.

10. *Commission on Intergovernmental Relations, op. cit.*, p. 126.

11. For a summary of this view, see Roscoe C. Martin, *The Cities and the Federal System*, New York, Atherton Press, 1965, especially Chapter 3.

12. Edward R. Fried, et al., *Setting National Priorities: The 1974 Budget*, Washington, D.C., The Brookings Institution, 1973, p. 173.

13. Morton Grodzins, *The American System: A New View of Government in the United States*, Chicago, Ill., Rand McNally & Co., 1966, p. 317–18.

14. Charles L. Clapp, *The Congressman: His Work as He Sees It*, Washington, D.C., The Brookings Institution, 1963, p. 149.

15. Ibid., pp. 20–24.

16. Seidman's remarks are contained in Douglas M. Fox, "A Mini-Symposium: President Nixon's Proposals for Executive Reorganization," *Public Administration Review*, 34, September/October 1974, p. 489.

17. Samuel P. Huntington, "Congressional Responses to the Twentieth Century," *The Congress and America's Future*, David B. Truman (ed.), 2nd Ed., Englewood Cliffs, N.J., Prentice-Hall, Inc., 1973, p. 22.

18. Gary Orfield, *Congressional Power: Congress and Social Change*, New York, Harcourt Brace Jovanovich, Inc., 1975, p. 16.

19. Michael J. Malbin, "Congressional Staffs—Growing Fast, but in Different Directions," *National Journal*, July 10, 1976, p. 958.

20. George Gordon, Jr., "Subcommittees: The Miniature Legislatures of Congress," *American Political Science Review*, 56, September 1962, p. 596.

21. Bruce I. Oppenheimer, "Subcommittee Government and Congressional Reform," *DEA News Supplement*, Summer 1976, p. S-8.

22. Ibid., p. S-11.

23. Richard E. Neustadt, "Politicians and Bureaucrats," *The Congress and America's Future, op. cit.*, p. 120.

24. The "subgovernment" system is discussed in Chapter I of another Commission report in this series: Advisory Commission on Intergovernmental Relations, *Improving Federal Grants Management* (A-53), Washington, D.C., U.S. Government Printing Office, February 1977.

25. Orfield, *op. cit.*, p. 262.

26. Jesse Burkhead, *Public School Finance: Economics and Politics*, Syracuse, N.Y., Syracuse University Press, 1964, pp. 237–38.

27. Orfield, *op. cit.*, pp. 126–27.

28. Burkhead, *op. cit.*, p. 265.

29. Ibid.

30. Jerome T. Murphy, "The Education Bureaucracies Implement Novel Policy: The Politics of Title I of ESEA, 1965–72," *Policy and Politics in America: Six Case Studies*, Allan P. Sindler (ed.), Boston, Mass., Little, Brown and Co., 1973, pp. 162–65.

19

Financing Local Government in a Changing World
David Brunori

Capital is mobile, and people and business will move to places where they can keep more of it.

—Indianapolis Mayor Stephen Goldsmith, 1997

The federal system places inherent limitations on the extent and choice of taxes that American cities, towns, and counties can impose on their residents. Because individuals and firms can relocate to other areas, jurisdictions must offer competitive services and reasonable tax burdens. Local governments compete for business investment, in particular. This competition limits the taxation of mobile tax bases and the use of the tax laws to redistribute wealth.

In addition to the competitive pressure to keep taxes low, myriad political and legal limitations have constrained local taxing authority. The tax revolts of the 1970s and 1980s led to constitutional and statutory restrictions on local government taxing authority. An antitax bias has also characterized the political process at all levels of government. This bias has further restrained government financing options. Finally, many taxes that local governments rely on have inherent limitations. Sales taxes face a continually shrinking base. Personal income taxes face profound political opposition. And business taxes, many of which fall on a mobile base, have never been considered a viable source of local government revenue.

The future may very well pose even greater challenges to local government finance—and thus to local government autonomy. At the beginning of the 21st century, technological advancement, international trade, and the deregulation of utilities will magnify the traditional legal and political constraints on local tax policy. Moreover, local governments will operate in an environment shaped by constantly changing demographics.

While the world has changed rapidly, the tax systems that support all levels of governments have largely stayed the same (see, for example, Brunori 1998). The underlying taxes that support local governments were designed and implemented in a different time and for a different economy. The sales tax was first used as a temporary revenue measure during the Great Depression. Income taxes, both personal and corporate, were adopted a generation before that. The property tax has existed since the colonial period in America. With a few exceptions, these taxes have not changed significantly since their inception.[1] Most scholars believe that without radical changes, many types of taxes cannot continue raising sufficient revenue in the 21st century (Brunori 1998).

Not surprisingly, the changing economy has prompted government leaders, business leaders, and scholars to review how state and local government[s] finance public services (see, for example, Neubig and Poddar 2000). The most significant local government review has been undertaken by the National League of Cities. In 1997, the National League of Cities launched the Municipalities in Transition Project to identify and study the economic, political, and social changes that would affect American local government. The National League of Cities has commissioned several studies on the future of local government finance (see, for example, Tannenwald 2002).

This chapter describes some of the problems and challenges posed by a rapidly changing society and economic environment as well as their likely effects on the ability of local governments to raise revenue.

Globalism

Increased international trade will continue to have profound effects on local government taxing powers. The trend of constantly increasing international trade among the nations of the world will no doubt continue (Neubig and Poddar 2000). The United States has worked diligently to encourage international trade by entering into agreements that will reduce trade barriers and encourage commerce across national borders. Local government officials are well aware of the fact that globalization will result in profound changes. As the National League of Cities (1997) reported, an American city may conduct more trade with Hong Kong than with a direct neighbor.

Part of the increase in international trade is attributable to increases in individual and capital mobility. Falling trade barriers and dramatic reductions in communications and transportation costs have significantly increased capital mobility. The potential sites for investment and business activity have increased tremendously over the past several decades (Thomas 2000). The ability of companies and individuals to sell products and services around the world makes compliance and administration of some taxes, particularly those imposed on mobile bases, more difficult and expensive.

The problem is that most local taxes depend on physical location, even as location becomes less and less important to how people and firms do business. Income taxes are imposed according to where a person lives or works. Business taxes are imposed according to the location of sales, operations, or property. Sales and use taxes (and all consumption-based excise taxes) are determined by where the sale takes place or where the product or service is consumed. The property tax is defined by place.

International trade and ever-broadening global markets have two distinct effects on local tax policy. First, they expand competition between local governments to include foreign nations. ... [S]tate and local governments work to entice firms from neighboring states or localities to relocate. The potential to enter into bidding wars for firms exists because of the mobility of capital and lack of trade barriers within the American federal system.

The global trading network is now more open, and mobility has never been greater. Therefore, local governments are now actively involved in international economic development activities (Liou 1999). The goal of many local governments is to lure foreign companies interested in investing in the United States.

International competition extends to all levels of government. For example, counties now vigorously pursue foreign investment. More than half of all counties actively engage in enticing foreign business to their communities through trade missions and advertising campaigns aimed at foreign nationals (Pammer 1996).

International competition for business will likely center on tax policy. As in domestic competition, state and local governments will use various "selling" points to lure foreign investors. In addition to offering quality public services, particularly transportation, local governments will paint a picture of a competitive tax environment.

Local governments are aware that "in a world of mobile tax bases, interjurisdictional tax differentials can influence the location of such bases" (Oakland 1994, 202). Indeed, as in the case of domestic competition, the widespread perception is that lowering tax burdens, especially those related to business activities, is imperative to get foreign nationals to invest in a particular jurisdiction. Many local governments are willing to surrender tax options as part of a strategy to enhance development through increased foreign investment (Liou 1999).

State governments are competing on the international economic scene as well. State competition for foreign investment may cause additional problems for local governments. When state governments pursue companies or industries looking for investment options, the states routinely offer tax incentives. These tax incentives often consist of property tax benefits. The problem ... is that while states are happy to compromise the local tax base, they are less excited about reimbursing local governments for their loss. In the end, the effects of competition on the way local governments raise revenue may pale in comparison to the effects of international competition.

The second issue confronting local governments in the new global marketplace is the proliferation of international trade agreements and treaties. By design, such agreements diminish or eliminate trade barriers and increase commercial activities across national borders. In doing so, however, these agreements place restrictions on the use of tax policy to finance government, particularly as tax policy relates to economic development.

Some evidence suggests that the major trade agreements signed by the United States, including the North American Free Trade Agreement (NAFTA) and the General Agreement on Tariffs and Trade (GATT), restrict state and local taxing power (Aune 2001; McLure and Hellerstein 2002). NAFTA, the World Trade Organization, GATT, and Mercosur have increased trade competition but reduced tax competition (Youngman 1999). State and local government officials are concerned not only about a reduction in competition but also about the likelihood that state and local taxes will be challenged under international trade agreements (Carlson 1996; Hope 1994).

Finally, the idea of state and local governments competing in the international economic arena has led to calls for increased federal preemption for trade policy. Some scholars and policymakers believe that the federal government should prevent, or at least limit, state and local government involvement in international economic development (Thomas 2000). Specifically, they have called for the federal government to preempt states and local governments from pursuing foreign businesses. Although such preemption does not seem likely, it reflects the anxiety and concerns that many policymakers and political leaders have with international trade and local government finance.

The primary effect of growing international trade will be recognition that taxation of mobile capital and people is an inefficient and ineffective means of raising local government revenue. Similar to concerns over domestic competition, concerns over international competition will likely lead to the conclusion that only property taxes and user fees are capable of efficiently supporting local government.

Technological Advances

Like globalization, technological advances will continue to have profound effects on local government finance. The high-technology economy will change the way local governments raise revenue. Technology is creating new business structures, new services, and more "remote" activities (Neubig and Poddar 2000). For example, the Internet makes it possible for relatively small businesses to expand their base and to sell goods and services throughout the United States. These businesses are highly mobile and have few geographic constraints. Small and medium-sized businesses are no longer limited to local markets.

. . . The ability to purchase goods and services through the Internet has sharply reduced reliance on sales taxes. Although this problem is much more serious for state than for local governments, it calls into question whether local governments can view sales taxes as an adequate source of revenue. Local governments are expected to lose tens of billions of dollars a year in sales tax revenue (Bruce and Fox 2001).

Electronic commerce will also make it much more difficult to impose business taxes. Technological developments have made businesses increasingly mobile. Businesses today are no longer as dependent on plants and equipment. Thus, relocating to another jurisdiction, while still a significant undertaking, is much easier today than it was a decade ago. This mobility will prevent expanded reliance on business taxes and will likely result in an eventual elimination of all local business taxes, as governments realize that such taxes are perceived to hurt their competitiveness. Local governments will not be able to rely on business property tax revenue to the extent they once did.

Technology will affect personal income and wage taxes as well. The age of electronic commerce has resulted in more people working from remote locations. The Internet, personal digital assistants, cell phones, and laptop computers allow employees in many industries to perform their responsibilities away from the employer's main office. Remote workers may pose challenges to local governments relying heavily on wage taxes. Employees and employers may have opportunities to avoid wage and payroll taxes. If the local government imposes taxes according to the location where the employee performs work, such opportunities will certainly exist.

To the surprise of many, the high-technology economy is also affecting local property taxes. When heavy manufacturing dominated the American economy, a large portion of the property tax base consisted of business land, plants, and equipment. Factories and heavy equipment, as well as extensive business ownership of land, have filled the coffers of local government for much of the 20th century.

Modern businesses, which tend to rely on computers and technology, have fewer plants and less equipment relative to large manufacturing firms (Bonnet 1998). These businesses do not own significant amounts of real property; this lack of ownership leads to a decrease in business property tax revenue. It also leads to a shift in property tax burdens from business to residential property (Strauss 2001).

The new economy creates another problem for the property tax. Capital-intensive firms (that is, those with relatively large amounts of plants and equipment) now incur a larger burden of the property tax than high-technology or service-centered businesses (Green, Chevrin, and Lippard 2002). That inequity ultimately undermines support for the tax, particularly within the business community. Such inequities lead to calls for lower tax burdens on capital-intensive firms.

Most commentators agree that changing technology will increase the limitations on local taxing authority (Break 2000). For this reason, researchers have cited growth in technology as one of the major factors affecting American local governments in general, and cities in particular (National League of Cities 1997).

Deregulation

Deregulation of key industries,[2] such as electricity, gas, telecommunications, and financial services, is also forcing changes in state and local business tax systems (Bonnet 1998; Burling 2000; Cline 2002; Hassell 2000; Neubig and Poddar 2000). The era of deregulation presents several issues for local government finance.

First, compared with unregulated businesses, regulated industries have traditionally been subject to higher property and other tax burdens. Local governments collect tax on gas, electric, and telecommunications utilities that are set at more than double the rate imposed on other industries (Walters and Cornia 1997). Local governments had the opportunity to impose higher tax burdens because the regulated industries were monopolies that faced little or no threat from lower-priced competitors. Utilities usually passed on the tax burdens to consumers through government-sanctioned price increases.

Today, however, deregulated industries such as power and telecommunications companies are demanding lower tax burdens more in line with the taxes paid by their new, unregulated competitors (Bonnet 1998). Moreover, falling utility prices have depressed the value of utility-owned land across the United States (Walters and Cornia 1997). This decline in value has, in turn, depressed property tax revenue across the United States. Future declines are predicted to be significant, particularly on property that is taxed to fund public education (Walters and Cornia 2001).

Second, . . . many local governments own and operate utilities that provide services, usually electricity, to their residents. Most electric utilities operating in the United States are owned by cities, and the profits of the operations are used to fund general government services. Tallahassee, Florida, for example, finances 40 percent of its budget through a city-owned utility that sells electricity. The deregulation movement threatens the existence of such locally owned utilities. For those utilities that remain in operation, deregulation will change. Even if local governments maintain ownership and operation of utilities, competition from private companies is likely to decrease the revenue yield.

Finally, increased competition from the private sector will force local governments to revisit their policies concerning rights-of-way and franchise fees. Such fees and charges generate significant amounts of revenue for many localities. The inability to collect such fees will have a significant effect on nontax revenue collection (Bonnet 1998; Green et al. 2002).

Overall, the deregulation movement will likely reduce utility revenue as well as curb property tax revenue. The expected reduction in overall local government revenues will be modest, but any additional undermining of already weak traditional local tax bases could cripple local governments' ability to finance services (Walters and Cornia 1997).

An Aging Population

In addition to international trade, technology, and deregulation, the rapid aging of the U.S. population will challenge the financing capacity of local governments. Declining birth rates and longer life spans are the primary reasons for increases in the average age of Americans. In

1980, 11 percent of the U.S. population was over the age of 65. By 2030, projections show that 20 percent of the population will be older than 65 (Bonnet 1998).

Traditionally, older citizens have been thought to harbor animosity toward taxes in general, and property taxes in particular. Their animosity toward the property tax is well known (Green et al. 2002). Real estate values, and the attendant increased property tax burdens, often increase at faster rates than income, especially for elderly homeowners on fixed incomes. The property tax imposes a greater, and more visible, burden on senior citizens than any other levy.

In addition to the financial burdens imposed, property taxes are unpopular with senior citizens because of the fear that they will lose their homes if they are unable to pay property taxes. One way to enforce the property tax is to seize the property. A home, often the most valuable financial asset owned by senior citizens, has immeasurable psychological and emotional value. The thought of losing such an asset adds to homeowners' dislike of the property tax.

There has also been a widespread perception that most senior citizens are unwilling to support elementary and secondary public education. The underlying theory is that because senior citizens do not have children in the schools, they have less at stake in educational outcomes. School taxes, of course, account for the majority of property taxes. Senior citizens are thought to oppose candidates who advocate higher school taxes. Moreover, in many states, particularly in the Northeast, school budgets must be approved by a referendum of voters. Historically, the elderly have voted at far higher rates than the rest of the population. . . . [I]f the property tax is not viewed as a principal source of finance for public schools, a main rationale—and public support—for the tax evaporates. To the extent that the increasingly aging population is unwilling to support public education, that population can be expected to oppose property tax increases.

. . . [M]any of the problems that gave rise to the elderly's dislike of the property tax have been addressed by policymakers. Circuit breakers, homestead exemptions, deferrals, and other programs have significantly reduced the tax burdens on senior homeowners, particularly those with low and fixed incomes. Despite the varied relief programs, however, senior citizen animosity toward the tax continues.

Policymakers have access to few additional policies that would provide senior citizens with property tax relief. Current relief measures are already becoming increasingly expensive. Tax relief measures were instituted during a time when senior citizens had higher poverty rates than the rest of the nation. Today, however, senior citizens have the lowest poverty rates of any age group in the United States.

Tax Policy in the New Economy

The changing economy will have significant effects on local government taxation. International trade and the high-technology economy place a premium on mobility and intangible property. Local governments have never succeeded in raising money from taxing mobile capital, services, or intangibles. And no local government has devised a workable method for taxing these components of the new economy in the future.

Globalization, international trade, and technological developments will make it more difficult to rely on sales and income taxes. These developments will also make it virtually impossible for local governments to tax business activity. Business tax bases have grown far too mobile. Cities and counties are not likely to try to impose additional sales, income, and business taxes; rather, they will likely concentrate on raising revenue from immobile tax bases. One noted observer drew an analogy between the modern technological revolution and the economic transformations of the late 1800s: "It is not a paradox that the rising importance of intangible property in the 19th century led not to greater inclusion of intangibles in the tax base, but to just the opposite—restriction of the property tax base to tangible property and immobile tangible property at that" (Youngman 1999, 1897).

In this regard, the rising importance of mobility will likely lead to increased efforts to tax immobile bases. The difficulty in taxing mobile tax bases leaves only property taxes and user fees as viable sources of revenue for local governments. These sources of revenue allow fiscal—and political—autonomy. But the tax on real property is the only tax capable of raising revenue that can sustain local government operations. As one leading theorist explains, "Real property offers one of the few tax bases that cannot be realistically shifted to another jurisdiction" (Youngman 1999, 1898).

The changing world order, however, presents challenges to the property tax system as well. Deregulation will have a serious, albeit relatively short-term, impact on local government tax revenue. The greater challenge will come from an aging population, because older people have traditionally opposed property taxes.

In 1997, two American political scientists observed that "The hyper mobility of capital, the international division of labor, and the 'death of distance' due to information technologies appear to undermine local autonomy" (Clarke and Gaile 1997). Without the ability to increase reliance on the property tax, local autonomy will likely continue to erode.

Notes

1. Perhaps the most significant change occurred with respect to the property tax. Until the early 20th century, the tax was levied on all property, including personal and intangible property. The "general" property tax was widely criticized as unworkable in an increasingly mobile society; this view led to widespread reforms. The property tax is now almost exclusively levied on land and improvements.
2. The most significant changes with respect to electric utilities occurred with the passage of the Federal Energy Policy Act of 1992, which requires owners of transmission lines to allow others to use their lines (Cappellari 1999). The most significant change with respect to the telecommunications industry was the enactment of the Federal Telecommunications Act of 1996 (Richman 2002).

References

Aune, Katie. 2001. "Enforcing the Standards of GATT/WTO in Challenges to State Taxes." *State Tax Notes* (December 24): 1015–20.

Bonnet, Thomas W. 1998. *Is the New Global Economy Leaving State and Local Tax Structures Behind?* Washington, D.C.: National League of Cities.

Break, George. 2000. "The New Economy and the Old Tax System." *State Tax Notes* (March 6): 767–71.

Bruce, Donald, and William E. Fox. 2001. "E-Commerce and Local Finance: Estimates of Direct and Indirect Sales Tax Losses." *Municipal Finance Journal* 22 (fall): 24–47.

Brunori, David. 1998. *The Future of State Taxation.* Washington, D.C.: Urban Institute Press.

Burling, Philip. 2000. *Impacts of Electric Utility Deregulation on the Property Tax.* Cambridge, Mass.: Lincoln Institute of Land Policy.

Cappellari, John. 1999. "Electric Utility Taxation under Deregulation." *State Tax Notes* (January 18): 177–94.

Carlson, Keith. 1996. "Implications of GATT and NAFTA for Minnesota's Sales and Use Tax." *State Tax Notes* (February 19): 599–603.

Clarke, Susan, and Gary Gaile. 1997. "Local Politics in a Global Era: Thinking Locally, Acting Globally." *Annals of the Academy of Political and Social Science* 551 (May): 28–43.

Cline, Robert. 2002. "Can the Current State and Local Business Tax System Survive the New Economy Challenges?" *State Tax Notes* (April 15): 241–46.

Green, Harry A., Stan Chevrin, and Cliff Lippard. 2002. "The Local Property Tax in Tennessee." *State Tax Notes* (May 27): 851–77.

Hassell, Daniel C. 2000. "Public Utility Real Estate Tax in Pennsylvania." *State Tax Notes* (April 10): 1301–8.

Hope, Heather. 1994. "GATT May Disrupt Balance of Free Trade and Federalism, Says MTC's Bucks." *State Tax Notes* (January 17): 157.

Liou, Tom Kuotsai. 1999. "Symposium on Local Economic Development Financing: Issues and Findings." *Journal of Public Budgeting, Accounting, and Financial Management* 11 (fall): 386–97.

McLure, Charles E., and Walter Hellerstein. 2002. "Does State-Only Apportionment of Corporate Income Violate International Trade Rules?" *State Tax Notes* (September 9): 779–86.

National League of Cities. 1997. *Major Factors Facing America's Cities.* Washington, D.C.: National League of Cities.

Neubig, Thomas S., and Satya Poddar. 2000. "Blurred Tax Boundaries: The New Economy's Implications for Tax Policy." *State Tax Notes* (October 9): 965–73.

Oakland, William. 1994. "Fiscal Equalization: An Empty Box?" *National Tax Journal* 47(1): 199–209.

Pammer, William. 1996. "Economic Development Strategies among Counties." In *The American County: Frontiers of Knowledge,* edited by Donald E. Menzel (184–202). Tuscaloosa: University of Alabama Press.

Richman, Roger. 2002. "Local Government, Federalism, and the Telecommunications Revolution." *State and Local Government Review* 34(2): 133–44.

Strauss, Robert. 2001. "Pennsylvania's Local Property Tax." *State Tax Notes* (June 4): 1963–83.

Tannenwald, Robert. 2002. "Are State and Local Revenue Systems Becoming Obsolete?" *State Tax Notes* (April 8): 143–59.

Thomas, Kenneth. 2000. *Competing for Capital: Europe and North American in a Global Era.* Washington, D.C.: Georgetown University Press.

Walters, Lawrence C., and Gary C. Cornia. 1997. "The Implications of Utility and Telecommunications Deregulation for Local Finance." *State and Local Government Review* 29(3): 172–87.

Walters, Lawrence C., and Gary C. Cornia. 2001. "Electric Utility Deregulation and School Finance in the United States." *Journal of Education Finance* 26(4): 345–72.

Youngman, Joan M. 1999. "Property Taxes in an Age of Globalization." *State Tax Notes*(June 7): 1897–900.

20

Tense Commandments:
Federal Prescriptions and City Problems

Pietro S. Nivola

Each year the U.S. government publishes a report called *The State of the Cities*. The final year of the twentieth century was a very good one. Thanks to "the Clinton-Gore economic policies and effective empowerment agenda," the end-of-the-millennium edition proclaimed, "most cities are showing clear signs of revitalization and renewal."[1] Yet, the authors conceded, even in that time of great prosperity the nation's central cities still faced "challenges."

Challenges? During the 1990s dozens of large cities—including such major centers as Baltimore, Cincinnati, Cleveland, Milwaukee, Philadelphia, Pittsburgh, St. Louis, and Washington, D.C.—continued to shed inhabitants. Sprawling suburban subdivisions still accounted for more than three-quarters of all new metropolitan growth.[2] Although many other cities finally managed to regain population, few kept pace with the growth of their suburbs.[3]

Disparities in growth between the metropolitan core and its outlying counties remained wide by other measures as well. Despite thousands of acres of abandoned land at the cores of the thirty-nine largest metropolitan regions, permits issued for construction of new housing units in 1998 were still down from their level in 1986. The volume of permits outside the core areas was about four-and-a-half times larger.[4]

Suburbs captured the bulk of employment growth. One study of ninety-two metropolitan areas found that, although 52 percent of their central cities began netting some increase in private sector jobs between 1993 and 1996, 23 percent did not, and fully 82 percent of the cities recorded a declining share of private employment in relation to the rest of their respective regions.[5] The nation's capital, for example, started the 1990s holding at least a third of its metropolitan area's jobs. Seven years later the city held less than a quarter. Although Atlanta by comparison was a thriving city, its share of jobs also dropped dramatically, from 40 percent in 1980 to 24 percent by 1996. From 1994 to 1997 the central business districts in Ohio's seven major cities had a net increase of only 636 jobs. The suburbs of these cities added 186,410 new jobs.[6]

In absolute terms the enclaves of poverty left behind in the inner cities by the unending dispersal of people and jobs to distant peripheries shrank in the 1990s.[7] This was no small accomplishment, but it scarcely changed the fact that poor people remained a substantial percentage of the resident populations of many cities. At long last the strain of sustaining these dependents had diminished almost everywhere, including urban counties where dependency declined by more than 40 percent between 1994 and 1999.[8] But it remained no less true that cities were still the locus of disproportionate caseloads in comparison with surrounding communities. Orleans Parish in which the city of New Orleans is located was home to just 11 percent of Louisiana's population but 29 percent of its welfare recipients. Philadelphia County had 12 percent of Pennsylvania's people but 47 percent of all Pennsylvanians on welfare. Baltimore accounted for 56 percent of Maryland's welfare cases. Nearly two-thirds of all welfare recipients in the Washington metropolitan area were clustered inside the District of Columbia.[9]

The depopulation, impoverishment, and decay of much of urban America, however, had abated. Whether the decline would be durably halted, let alone lastingly reversed, is another matter. For the calamity of September 11, 2001, dealt a severe setback not only to New York and Washington, D.C., but to cities across the land. The terrorist assaults, arriving as the national economy had already started to falter, wiped out almost 80,000 jobs in New York and sent the unemployment rate in the District of Columbia toward double digits.[10] The economic shock waves rippling out from "ground zero" would also shatter hopes of robust growth through 2002 for places as far away as Miami or San Francisco.[11] Even if none of this had happened, the central fact of the urban scene in the United States remains as unmistakable today as ever: far more Americans, when choosing where to live and work, still locate outside old cities rather than inside them. If anything, save for anomalies like New York in recent years, the margin of difference continues to widen, not narrow.

Most of the underlying causes of this country's urban predicament are familiar. Among them are disproportionate poverty—hence crime and blight—in the inner cities, some lingering barriers to racial or class assimilation in the suburbs, a cultural preference for the suburban way of life, stiff city tax rates heightened by the costs of supporting large unionized bureaucracies and the unsatisfactory public services some of them deliver. Less recognized is the distinct possibility that sometimes the regulatory policies of the federal government—the rules and rulings that its judges and bureaucrats, as well as its lawmakers, impose—further disadvantage the cities, hobbling their ability to attract residents and businesses. . . .

Arguably the burden of what a former mayor of New York had called the federal "mandate millstone" may have diminished a little by the end of the 1990s thanks to attempts at self-restraint by policymakers in Washington but also because municipal economies were mostly faring better.[12] How much weight was really lifted, and whether alleviating more of it would have left the cities in an even stronger position today, remains an open question.

"Shift and Shaft"

City governments in the United States, unlike municipal administrations in most of Europe, must largely support themselves; they collect approximately two-thirds of their revenues from local sources.[13] German localities derive less than one-third of their income from local revenues.[14] Britain's local councils are now responsible for as little as a fifth of their budgets for basic functions.[15] The locally sourced share is even less in the Netherlands and, until recently, Italy.

In principle the relative self-sufficiency of local government in America is a virtue; municipal taxpayers ought to pay for the essential services they use. But in practice these taxpayers are also asked to purchase plenty of other costly projects, many of which federal law prescribes. A handful of national rules bore down on local governments before 1965. By the 1990s hundreds were weighing down on them.[16] Meanwhile federal aid to large cities was shrinking. Mayors became alarmed by the confluence of these trends and so was the U.S. Advisory Commission on Intergovernmental Relations: "The financial burdens imposed by federal laws and regulations," the commission stressed in a 1993 report, "have been increasing faster than the growth of federal aid since 1986."[17] While affluent jurisdictions absorbed this cost shifting with minimal disruption, communities of lesser means—notably many old central cities in the Northeast and parts of the Midwest—experienced difficulties.

Cities with large concentrations of low-income households and shaky sources of taxable wealth, of course, are squeezed the worst.[18] A few

Figure 20-1. Federal Aid to Large Cities, 1980–98

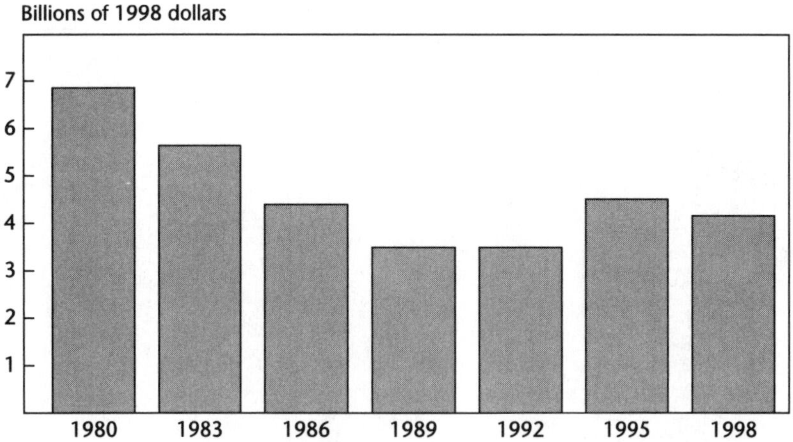

Billions of 1998 dollars

Sources: U.S. Department of Commerce, Bureau of the Census, *Statistical Abstract of the United States, 1982–83*, p.300; *1986*, p.290; *1989*, p.288; *1991*, p.302; *1994*, p.317; *1998*, p.328; and *2001*, p.290 (various years).

Note: Cities include Austin, Baltimore, Chicago, Cleveland, Columbus, Dallas, Detroit, El Paso, Houston, Indianapolis, Jacksonville, Los Angeles, Memphis, Milwaukee, Nashville, Philadelphia, Phoenix, San Antonio, San Francisco, San Jose, Seattle, and Washington, D.C.

of these desperate places (Bridgeport, Connecticut, for instance) became insolvent.[19] The extreme exceptions aside, however, bankruptcy has not been the first problem that the profusion of federal prescriptions typically posed. Rather, their cumulative, lower-profile effects have complicated basic municipal management decisions, including those pertaining to taxing and borrowing. According to a study by the National League of Cities, nearly 40 percent of the hundreds of cities it surveyed reported that their financial needs had become harder, not easier, to satisfy at the end of the 1990s.[20] Evidently the era's economic boom had not generated sufficient growth of local revenues in about one out of five of these cities, so property tax rates rose yet again in 1998.[21] That year a group of prominent mayors repeated their long-standing complaint about how Washington's unfunded mandates tended to "destabilize" municipal budgets.[22]

The following figures tell a good deal of the fiscal side of the story. Federal aid to large cities declined in constant dollars between 1980 and 1998, the last year for which reliable data are currently available (figure 20-1). To be sure, support from state governments and increases in locally collected revenues helped offset the federal reductions, but at least in large

Figure 20-2. General Revenue in Large Frost Belt Cities, 1980–98

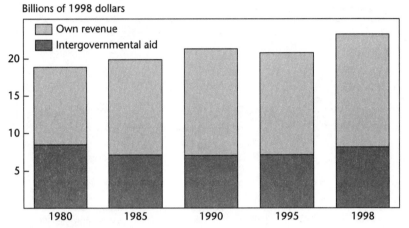

Billions of 1998 dollars

Sources: U.S. Department of Commerce, Bureau of the Census, *Statistical Abstract of the United States, 1997*, p.302; *1982–83*, p.300; *1988*, p.278; *1992*, p.302; *1998*, p.328; *1999*, p.326; and *2001*, p.290.

Note: Cities include Chicago, Philadelphia, Baltimore, Indianapolis, Washington, D.C., Milwaukee, Cleveland, Boston, Columbus, and Detroit.

Frost Belt cities through 1998 the local increases were not large—and in some cases, not large enough (figure 20-2). Meanwhile, externally imposed claims on municipal resources often outpaced the latter's modest increases in these cities. Glance at one example: municipal wastewater treatment. Adjusting for inflation, local expenditures to build and run treatment plants up to federal standards ballooned from about $7.5 billion a year in 1978 to more than $23 billion a year in 1998.[23] Federal funding to offset this kind of huge annual invoice dwindled (figure 20-3).

The strain in certain cities was much greater than the aggregated figures suggest. Revenues in constant dollars available to Detroit, for example, had contracted until 1998, even as this troubled city faced new multimillion dollar expenses piled on by federal and state authorities (figure 20-4). And as revenues sagged, so did bond ratings. Thus cities such as Detroit remained hard pressed not only to defray their new obligations directly but also to meet them by borrowing.

Increases in federally mandated expenses exacted a toll in more prosperous places too. Before New York City's financial health was battered in the fall of 2001 the city estimated it would have to finance at least $8 billion in mandatory capital expenditures for water-quality projects alone in the next ten years.[24] New York will have to pull off investments of this

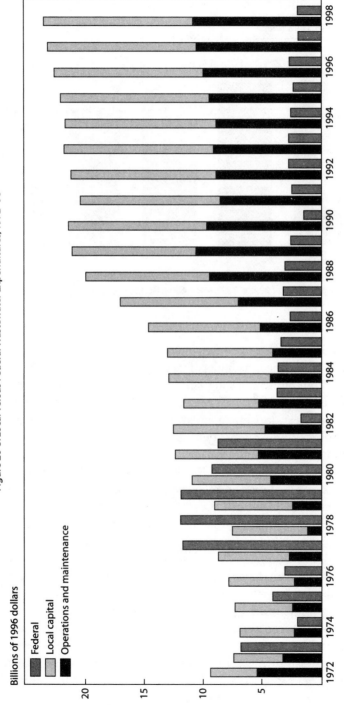

Figure 20-3. Local versus Federal Wastewater Expenditures, 1972–98

Billions of 1996 dollars

Federal
Local capital
Operations and maintenance

Source: Association of Municipal Sewage Agencies, The Cost of Clean (Washington, 1990).

Figure 20-4. Distribution of General Revenue in the City of Detroit, 1980–98

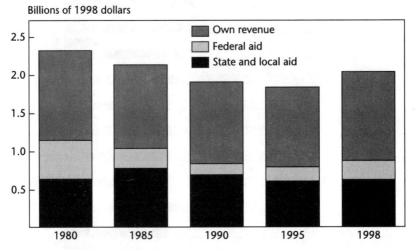

Billions of 1998 dollars

Sources: U.S. Department of Commerce, Bureau of the Census, *Statistical Abstract of the United States, 1997*, p.302; *1982–83*, p.300; *1988*, p.278; *1999*, p.326; and *2001*, p.290.

magnitude amid already mountainous debts and with a tax system that probably has reached the limits of its capacity.[25] At a minimum the added financial commitments facing cities like New York seem likely to force municipal officials to forgo further rounds of badly needed tax reductions.

Finances aside, some mandates impinge directly on local administration of routine services, tying the hands of managers and at times thwarting improvements that the beleaguered taxpayers in cities consider past due. For middle-class households and businesses contemplating where to locate in metropolitan areas, these circumstances do not enhance the allure of the central cities.

Exemplifying the Problem

America's urban public schools are perhaps the clearest example of a crucial local service beset by bureaucratic rules and legal sanctions, including numerous federal directives. Few other advanced nations, if any, devote as large a share of their total public education expenditures to nonteaching personnel.[26] There may be several excuses for this lopsided administrative overhead, but the growth of government regulation, and the throngs of academic administrators needed to handle the red tape, is almost certainly at least one explanation.

For decades, U.S. urban schools systems labored under forced busing orders. Many of them had the unwanted result of stimulating "white flight" to the suburbs. Even as these legal pressures gradually subsided, newer ones mounted. Increasingly the schools would need to supply various specialized services. Local authorities, for example, must set aside tens of billions of dollars a year to meet the needs of students with learning disabilities.[27] Congress, which fashioned this expensive program known as special education, has never reimbursed even a quarter of its yearly bill. Meanwhile, the number of clients swells as definitions of disability take in behaviors that in an earlier time were not considered clinical abnormalities—and as teachers, parents, and administrators dump their faltering students into the program.

Compliance costs are especially onerous for city schools, where the concentrations of learning-disabled pupils are high and the means to support them low. The District of Columbia is forced to spend roughly a third of its entire education budget on students eligible for special education, a clientele that constitutes 15 percent of the school system's overall enrollment.[28] In 1997 just over 17 percent of Baltimore's school children qualified for the program, reportedly costing the Baltimore school district as much as $221 million—again, one-third of the city's school budget.[29] Chicago's public schools enroll more than half of all the special education students in the state of Illinois.[30] Federal and state aid has fallen far short of what is needed to support this overload. And when a school system has to hire legions of counselors, therapists, administrators, and lawyers, how can it also afford to recruit what it needs most: competent teachers? The Chicago school district had to dig deep into the pockets of its taxpayers for many hundreds of millions of dollars in property tax increases between 1988 and 1993.

Wretched schools have been among the main reasons why American families have fled, or avoided, old cities. It is hard enough for distressed city school systems, which struggle to impart even rudimentary reading and arithmetic skills, to compete with their wealthier suburban counterparts. The hardship is surely compounded by federal entitlements that without adequate recompense increasingly divert the scarce resources of cities from better serving the majority of their citizens. Amid the centrally directed priorities and their fiscal impacts, it often becomes harder for local school boards to undertake essential innovations. Not long ago an in-depth study of six large urban school districts—Boston, Memphis, New York, San Antonio, San Francisco, and Seattle—found that reform-minded city officials were stymied first and foremost by inadequate financial capacity and flexibility.[31]

. . . There are many good reasons for federal policymakers to be telling city governments what they must or must not do, even if city officials deem many of these strictures unaffordable or overbearing. Although the local objections frequently are to be taken seriously, sometimes they turn out to be decidedly unconvincing—and an overall assessment cannot help but be fraught with debatable judgments as to how competing values ought be traded off, empirical evidence weighed, and urban impacts quantified.[32] . . .

Underlying such [instances] are the political pressures that, in varying degrees, thrust federal regulators into local governance. The incentives to intervene from the top are complex and somewhat different from those in other democracies and have gained momentum that has been at best only mildly suspended in recent years. . . .

Notes

1. U.S. Department of Housing and Urban Development, *The State of the Cities 1999: Third Annual Report* (Government Printing Office, 1999), p. 3.
2. See Bruce Katz and Jennifer Bradley, "Divided We Sprawl," *Atlantic Monthly*, December 1999, pp. 26–42.
3. Atlanta was illustrative: it gained 12,300 residents in the 1990s and was able to reverse the population losses it had experienced in the 1980s. But the city's gains were trivial compared with those of its surrounding counties, which expanded by 647,100 people. Brookings Center on Urban and Metropolitan Policy, *Moving Beyond Sprawl: The Challenge for Metropolitan Atlanta* (Brookings, 2000), p. 9.
4. Brookings Center on Urban and Metropolitan Policy, *Housing Heats Up: Home Building Patterns in Metropolitan Areas* (Brookings, 1999), p. 3.
5. The estimate is based on an analysis of ninety-two large metropolitan areas by John Brennan and Edward W. Hill, *Where Are the Jobs? Cities, Suburbs, and the Competition for Employment* (Brookings Center on Urban and Metropolitan Policy, November 1999), p. 1.
6. Bruce Katz, "Enough of the Small Stuff! Toward a New Urban Agenda," *Brookings Review*, vol. 18 (Summer 2000), p. 5.
7. While poverty had declined in central cities in absolute terms, urban rates of poverty were still twice as high as suburban poverty rates, 18.8 percent as against 9 percent in 1997. In 1989 suburban median income was 58 percent higher than the median income in central cities. By 1996 the gap had widened to 67 percent. See Katz, "Enough of the Small Stuff!" p. 8. The proportion of the nation's welfare families that live in the one hundred largest U.S. cities went from 48 percent to 58 percent between 1994 and 1999.
8. "Mean Streets," *Economist*, July 22, 2000, p. 31.
9. Brookings Center on Urban and Metropolitan Policy, *A Region Divided: The State of Growth in Greater Washington, D.C.* (Brookings, 1999), p. 3.

10. Leslie Eaton, "Big Job Losses Add to New York Economic Gloom," *New York Times*, November 16, 2001, p. A1; and Spencer S. Hsu, "Forecast Is Gloomy for District Economy," *Washington Post*, November 16, 2001, p. B1.

11. By the end of September 2001, the twelve-month forecast for economic growth in Miami suddenly plunged from 2.44 percent to –0.65 percent. San Francisco's outlook went from 2.72 percent to –0.36 percent. The situation in the rest of the country changed dramatically almost everywhere as well. Mary William Walsh, "Urban Pain, From Sea to Sea," *New York Times*, September 30, 2001, p. C2.

12. Edward I. Koch, "The Mandate Millstone," *Public Interest*, no. 61 (Fall 1981), p. 13.

13. Dennis R. Judd, *The Politics of American Cities: Private Power and Public Policy*, 3d ed. (Scott, Foresman, 1988), p. 201.

14. See Hartmut Haubermann, "The Relationship between Local and Federal Government Policy in the Federal Republic of Germany," in Chris Pickvance and Edmond Preteceille, eds., *State Restructuring and Local Power: A Comparative Perspective* (London: Pinter Publishers, 1991), pp. 92, 93, 99.

15. "Local Difficulties," *Economist*, May 9, 1998, p. 55; and Manfred Konukiewitz and Helmut Wollman, "Physical Planning in a Federal System: The Case of West Germany," in David H. McKay, ed., *Planning and Politics in Western Europe* (St. Martin's Press, 1982), p. 75.

16. Clyde Wayne Crews Jr., *Ten Thousand Commandments: An Annual Policymaker's Snapshot of the Federal Regulatory State, 2000 Edition* (Washington: Competitive Enterprise Institute, 2000), p. 48.

17. U.S. Advisory Commission on Intergovernmental Relations, *Federal Regulation of State and Local Governments: The Mixed Record of the 1980s* (July 1993), p. 7.

18. Cities in general bear a disproportionate burden for poverty-related public expenditures, including police, fire, courts, and administrative functions. See, for instance, Janet Rothenberg Pack, "Poverty and Urban Public Expenditures," *Urban Studies*, vol. 35, no. 11 (1998), pp. 1995–2019.

19. Bridgeport's formal bankruptcy in 1991 was imputed to the impact of unfunded mandates emanating largely from the state of Connecticut, not the federal government. However, the state itself had been hammered by Washington's mandates. Residents of Connecticut, more than taxpayers in any other state, have been paying more in federal taxes than they receive back in federal spending. Inevitably, much of the pressure from this imbalance passes down from the state to the local level. States in the Northeast and Great Lakes regions have experienced intergovernmental deficits more commonly than states in the Sun Belt and Great Plains. See Jay H. Walder and Herman B. Leonard, *The Federal Budget and the States, Fiscal Year 1997* (Harvard University, John F. Kennedy School of Government, September 30, 1998), p. 1.

20. Michael A. Pagano, *City Fiscal Conditions in 1998* (Washington: National League of Cities, June 1998), pp. 1–2.

21. The rate of growth in city revenues was approximately 30 percent less than the growth rate of the nation's gross domestic product during the period 1988–97. Pagano, *City Fiscal Conditions*.

22. Stephen Goldsmith and others, *Markets Not Mandates: A Request to Congress for a New Contract with America's Cities* (Washington: Cato Institute, 1998), p. 1.

23. The figures are in 1996 dollars and include SRF capitalization, plus annual local operations and maintenance costs. See Association of Metropolitan Sewerage Agencies, *The Costs of Clean* (Washington, March 1999).

24. Office of Management and Budget, *Preliminary Ten-Year Capital Strategy: Fiscal Years 2002–2011* (New York, January 24, 2001), p. iii.

25. In 1997 New York City's bond rating was just slightly better than Philadelphia's, no better than Detroit's, and worse than that of St. Louis and Baltimore. New York had $42 billion in loans outstanding as of early 2002. This debt burden was much larger than that of the entire state of California ($25 billion). Richard Pérez-Peña and James McKinley Jr., "A Mountain of Boom-Time Debt Looms as New York Feels Pinch," *New York Times*, February 21, 2002, p. A1. Until Mayor Rudolph Giuliani managed some reductions, the overall tax rates had reached the point that further increases were likely to yield diminishing returns. For a careful analysis comparing New York's precarious position to that of several other cities, see Andrew Haughwout and others, "Local Revenue Hills: A General Equilibrium Specification with Evidence from Four U.S. Cities," *National Bureau of Economic Research*, Working Paper 7603 (Cambridge, Mass.: National Bureau of Economic Research, March 2000). Although the Giuliani administration scaled back a number of the city's manifold taxes (including most notably the commercial rent tax), others, including the personal income tax, did not seem to come down much below the level prevailing at the end of 1989.

26. See Pietro S. Nivola, *Laws of the Landscape: How Policies Shape Cities in Europe and America* (Brookings, 1999), p. 81.

27. Tom Loveless and Diane Ravitch, "Broken Promises: What the Federal Government Can Do to Improve American Education," *Brookings Review*, vol. 18 (Spring 2000), p. 20.

28. "Coming Up $80 Million Short," *Washington Post*, September 8, 2001, p.A20. Cost overruns in special education caused the program's expense for the city to jump 41 percent from 1998 to 2001.

29. Kalman R. Hettleman, "Special-Ed Funding Isn't Fair to All Students," *Baltimore Sun*, May 17, 1998, p. 1L.

30. Paul G. Vallas, "Saving Public Schools," *Manhattan Institute Civic Bulletin*, no. 16 (March 1999), pp. 1–2, 9.

31. Paul T. Hill, Christine Campbell, and James Harvey, *It Takes a City: Getting Serious about Urban School Reform* (Brookings, 2000), chap. 2.

32. A large body of work has attempted, with mixed success, to evaluate the effects of federal urban programs. To pay full homage to that literature would require a footnote of unwieldy length. For an early, and thorough, compendium that reviews methodological complexities, as well as some particular programs, see Norman J. Glickman, ed., *The Urban Impacts of Federal Policies* (Johns Hopkins University Press, 1980). . . .

Part III

Review Questions

1. What are the relative strengths and weaknesses of the different types of intergovernmental aid mechanisms—for instance, formula, project, categorical, and block grants? Be sure to include both economic and political considerations.

2. Analysts of American intergovernmental relations frequently allude to the interdependence of units in the system. Document this interdependence using fiscal data. In particular, consider local decision making.

3. "Welfare reform" in the 1990s resulted in a shift in intergovernmental programs and responsibilities that replaced the heavily federally supported (and partially regulated) Aid to Families with Dependent Children (AFDC) program with a block grant to the states, Temporary Assistance to Needy Families (TANF). In what ways might many state officials conclude this change constitutes an improvement? In what ways might it seem problematic? Consider, in particular, states prone to wide economic fluctuations as well as states that may find many of their citizens in need at present or in the future.

4. George Break says that fixed-amount grants for specified purposes may "conciliate appearance and reality" because they seem to support functions deemed important by the grantor while allowing grantees to use the funds for any local purpose. Explain this effect of the fixed-amount grant. Does the coverage by Nivola support or contradict this thesis?

5. What are open- and closed-ended grants? What are their relative advantages and disadvantages?

6. Imagine that a presidential election has just taken place. The winner has campaigned on the issue of reforming the system of intergovernmental aid so that public functions would be sorted out by level of government. "Matters of national concern should be handled at the national level," the president-elect says, "and matters of more limited concern should be

handled by the state and local governments. One of my first priorities is to redirect the system in this fashion." The new national chief executive calls on you, an expert in intergovernmental relations, for advice on how to carry out this program. What do you say? Consider Monypenny's analysis of the political functions of fiscal assistance, as well as the ACIR's discussion of the attractions of categorical grants and Nivola's analysis of urban settings. What advice would you proffer regarding national grant programs in the fields of welfare, Medicaid, highways, and education (see the OECD coverage)?

7. In an essay in Part II of this book, Reischauer explains how the diversity among American governmental structures and functions impedes any efforts to design rational fiscal instruments. Monypenny seems to imply that the prevalence of grants is in large measure the *result* of diversity. Are these two claims necessarily inconsistent? Discuss.

8. In an era of cross-cutting mandates (similar or identical strings, such as nondiscrimination requirements, attached to many different grants offered in divergent policy sectors), does Monypenny's assertion that narrow coalitions are responsible for individual programs still seem valid? Do other kinds of coalitions in the modern system complicate the picture? Explain.

9. Some critics of the American system of intergovernmental relations claim that the current pattern of categorical grants constitutes an aberration from the fundamental features of the American political system, like governmental accountability. Is this a valid criticism? In your answer, include reference to the forces that encourage the establishment and maintenance of categorical programs.

10. In seeking their own financing for economic development, U.S. cities have been reliant on other levels of government. The reasons have partly to do with the system of grants-in-aid, but not completely. According to Sbragia, how do states and the federal government constrain and shape the development opportunities pursued by cities?

11. Municipal bonds and independent public authorities are among the technical and financial subjects that influence the actions of cities in the United States as they develop their economies. How are these technical topics also political ones? Use Sbragia's analysis in your response.

12. Sbragia suggests that intergovernmental politics, in particular as seen in the efforts by cities to pursue economic development, exhibits characteristics worrisome from the perspective of democracy. How? Why? Do you agree? What do the readings offered by Brunori and Nivola infer about the effectiveness of the governance of local officials even if this issue is resolved?

13. Changes in federal intergovernmental aid can have a more than proportionate impact on state and local spending. How? Consider the analyses offered by Break, as well as by Nivola.

14. Some analysts, for instance those considering the challenges faced by the PIGs in recent years (see Part II of this book), emphasize the dominance of federal cutbacks and budget constraints in limiting what local governments can decide. What does Brunori's analysis suggest about the validity of this idea?

Part IV

ADMINISTRATIVE ASPECTS OF INTERGOVERNMENTAL RELATIONS

In one policy sector after another, intergovernmental administrative arrangements are responsible for many of the most significant public decisions and the consequences of those decisions. Yet these arrangements are relatively obscured from public view. Even the most prominent bureaucratic units within individual governments, such as the cabinet-level agencies in Washington, can be almost incomprehensible to the citizenry. Their Byzantine procedures, obscure jargon, and legions of specialists often make them seem remote and intimidating. Complexity and misunderstanding are magnified when the administration of programs takes place in operations that span two or more government levels.

A survey of some intergovernmental administrative activities indicates how important, if confusing, this topic is. Many of these activities are aimed at implementing general policy, usually established in broad outline at the national level. Converting this general intention into specific actions, while also incorporating state and local objectives, may entail a set of formidable tasks. At the national level, administrative actors may be deeply involved in deciding which government units are to receive how much aid—if indeed financial assistance is to be part of the intergovernmental program—as well as in developing program regulations, mediating and negotiating with state and local agencies, reviewing plans and operations of other levels of government, and coordinating intergovernmental programs handled by various federal agencies. At other levels, intergovernmental administration includes such activities as drafting plans (and seeking support for them within the community, the government, and higher levels of administration), negotiating with other governments, managing programs (which can involve designing, staffing, and evaluating complex efforts), dealing with program beneficiaries and their representatives, and attempting to coordinate state and local programs with one another and with other state and local activities.

Not all of these activities, of course, can be investigated through the readings in Part IV. Indeed, it is useful to note that some of the challenges and routines of intergovernmental administrative action are illuminated in other readings in earlier sections of this book [see, in particular, the selections by Derthick (no. 13), the Advisory Commission on Intergovernmental Relations (no. 18), and Nivola (no. 20) in Parts II and III]. But the readings included next bring into focus some of the most salient developments in the administrative sphere of intergovernmental relations; three general comments can be made about them. First, of course, the articles illustrate the links among political, fiscal, and administrative aspects of the American intergovernmental pattern. Many administrative problems and opportunities in the system are tied to aid programs and regulatory efforts, and very often administrative disputes between and among governments reflect political disagreements. Second, these articles (and, in fact, most studies of administrative aspects of intergovernmental relations) understandably focus on negative topics—problems and tensions of the system. Still, it is important to recognize that in many policy areas much of the time calm, workable arrangements have developed—as the last reading in the current part suggests. The fact that the system often works can be obscured by both political rhetoric and the network's very complexity.[1] Third, much of today's debate about intergovernmental relations lays the blame for the weaknesses in the system, including the costliness of operations and the frequent lack of coordination, on the federal government. Some of the readings in this part do reflect this perspective, but others suggest that this explanation is somewhat oversimplified. The federal government is surely not free of blame for intergovernmental administrative difficulties, yet neither is it the sole culprit or causal agent. Solutions to these problems do not lie with a simplistic castigation of national decision makers.

Part IV emphasizes some of the front-burner issues of recent national debate. Indeed, the first three readings frame an administrative-political controversy that has made front-page news in recent years: intergovernmental regulation and mandating. The intergovernmental system of grants-in-aid, long a route to encourage incentive-based bargaining across levels of government during program implementation, has always contained its share of "strings" imposed by "donor" governments—those on the giving end of the purse strings. From the 1980s and continuing on to the present, however, the quantity and perceived intrusiveness of intergovernmental regulation have accelerated. A major instrument of influence across levels will continue to be grants, as the analysis in this book has shown. However, large policy agendas in combination with constrained budgets have encouraged governmental decision makers to address issues without making commitments of their own to substantially higher levels of spending. During this period, federal mandates increased significantly for state and local governments; states themselves, pressed to achieve ever more and faced with their own fiscal limitations, have expanded their regulation of local units. Reformers have responded by seeking ways to control the burdens and excesses of these conflictual intergovernmental links. The last several years have seen great turbulence, and some action, to deal with this set of developments. The perspectives and forces fueling the debate and the reform efforts are reflected in these selections.

The first of these readings (no. 21) is excerpted from a study by the Advisory Commission on Intergovernmental Relations (ACIR), *Regulatory Federalism,* which focuses on the increased regulatory activity in the intergovernmental system. In this excerpt the commission distinguished various types of regulatory mechanisms used in intergovernmental administration. Some of these varieties of regulation are associated with grants-in-aid, whereas others are imposed through federal laws or rules divorced from any aid program. The ACIR report was published as the controversy about regulation was beginning to heat up.

The Unfunded Mandates Reform Act (UMRA), enacted in 1995, sought to constrain Washington's ability to impose costly and potentially burdensome requirements on other governments. The next two readings (nos. 22 and 23) provide insights about that effort. The UMRA required the ACIR to conduct a study of nationally created mandates and identify candidates for elimination or modification. The ACIR staff produced a draft report (no. 22) that, in turn, caused a firestorm of protest by groups concerned that national commitments and requirements in a whole range of policy sectors might be weakened. The tone of the ACIR draft suggested that a real war on mandates might be about to erupt, and great pressure was placed on the commission, even by the Clinton administration, not to adopt the report as an official set of recommendations. The excerpt printed here includes the general line of argument by the commission staff and a sampling of the laws and requirements that they proposed changing. Most of these proposals did not result in changes to the mandates themselves, and the draft report was never approved by the full commission. The ACIR itself closed its doors, thanks in significant measure to the controversy, shortly thereafter.

What did the UMRA actually produce, then? In some senses it may still be too early to tell for sure. But Paul Posner has written the most thorough analysis of that question to date and has shown, as well, that the roots of the unfunded mandate "problem" are far more complicated than many observers recognize. Posner finds that some, but only modest, limitations have been placed on mandates through the UMRA, that mandates are just as much a Republican- as a Democratic-initiated phenomenon, and that complex political forces continue to shape the structure and context for intergovernmental administration. This excerpt builds on his analysis of detailed empirical evidence to sketch broad and provocative conclusions about the mandating phenomenon.

The final reading in this part, by Robert Agranoff and Michael McGuire, reminds us that administrative aspects of intergovernmental relations comprise much more than mandates, constraints, and friction. In fact, the day-to-day action across governmental boundaries is handled by public managers adept at bargaining and negotiating with each other, and in multiple directions. Furthermore, although—as we have seen—the operation of grants programs typically provides a key forum for administrative negotiation, the bargaining and negotiations typical in today's intergovernmental management range far beyond such programs and reach into the nitty-gritty details of handling contracts, dealing with audits, managing cooperative agreements, and procuring goods and services and other key functions.

Taken as a group, these readings show the importance of administrative themes in the intergovernmental system, the serious issues decision makers must face in trying to effect improvements, and the multiple causes that must be considered if effective change is to be made.

Note

1. Paul Peterson, Barry G. Rabe, and Kenneth K. Wong, *When Federalism Works* (Washington, D.C.: Brookings, 1986).

21

The Techniques of Intergovernmental Regulation
U.S. Advisory Commission on Intergovernmental Relations

As was noted previously, an element of *compulsion* is one key feature of the new intergovernmental regulation that distinguishes it from the usual grant-in-aid conditions. The requirements traditionally attached to assistance programs may be viewed as part of a contractual agreement between two independent, coequal levels of government. In contrast, the policies which the new intergovernmental regulation imposes on state and local governments are more nearly mandatory. They cannot be sidestepped, without incurring some federal sanction, by the simple expedient of refusing to participate in a single federal assistance program. In one way or another, compliance has been made difficult to avoid.

A variety of legal and fiscal techniques has been employed by the national government to encourage acceptance of its regulatory standards. Four major strategies—direct orders, crosscutting requirements, crossover sanctions, and partial preemption—are described below and are summarized in table 21-1.

Direct Orders

In a few instances, federal regulation of state and local government takes the form of direct legal orders that must be complied with under the threat of civil or criminal penalties. For example, the *Equal Employment Opportunity Act of 1972* bars job discrimination by state and local governments on the basis of race, color, religion, sex and national origin. This statute extended to state and local governments the requirements imposed on private employers since 1964. Similarly, the *Marine Protection Research and Sanctuaries Act Amendments of 1977*

From U.S. Advisory Commission on Intergovernmental Relations, *Regulatory Federalism: Policy, Process Impact and Reform* (Washington, D.C.: ACIR, February 1984), pp. 7–10.

Table 21-1   A Typology of Intergovernmental Regulatory Programs

Program Type	Description	Major Policy Areas Employed
Direct orders	Mandate state or local actions under the threat of criminal or civil penalties	Public employment, environmental protection
Crosscutting requirements	Apply to all or many federal assistance programs	Nondiscrimination, environmental protection, public employment, assistance management
Crossover sanctions	Threaten the termination or reduction of aid provided under one or more specified programs unless the requirements of another program are satisfied	Highway safety and beautification, environmental protection, health planning, handicapped education
Partial preemptions	Establish federal standards, but delegate administration to states if they adopt standards equivalent to the national ones	Environmental protection, natural resources, occupational safety and health, meat and poultry inspection

prohibit cities from disposing of sewage sludge through ocean dumping. Court orders based on constitutional provisions, like those banning segregated schools, are similar in nature.

For the most part, however, Washington has exempted subnational governments from many of the kinds of direct regulatory statutes that apply to businesses and individuals. Hence, although state governments may administer the *Occupational Safety and Health Act,* they (and local governments) are exempt from its provisions in their capacity as employers—as is the federal government itself. Politics often has dictated this course, but there also are some constitutional restrictions on the ability of Congress to regulate directly. The wage and hour requirements imposed on state and local governments by the 1974 amendments to the *Fair Labor Standards Act* were greatly circumscribed by the Supreme Court in *National League of Cities v. Usery* (1976).[1] The Court's ruling held that the law interfered with their "integral operations in areas of traditional governmental functions," and thus threatened their "independent existence."

In this respect, the relationship of the federal government with the states and localities must be contrasted with that of the states and their own local subdivisions. Because local governments are creatures of state law, state "mandating" through direct orders is both legally permissible and very frequent.[2]

Much more commonly, then, Washington has utilized other regulatory techniques to work its will. These may be distinguished by their breadth of application and the nature of the sanctions which back them up.

Crosscutting Requirements

First, and most widely recognized, are the crosscutting or generally applicable requirements imposed on grants across the board to further various national social and economic policies. One of the most important of these requirements is the nondiscrimination provision included in Title VI of the *Civil Rights Act of 1964*, which stipulates that

> No person in the United States shall, on the ground of race, color, or national origin, be excluded from participation in, be denied the benefits of, or be subjected to discrimination under any program receiving Federal financial assistance.[3]

Since 1964, crosscutting requirements have been enacted for the protection of other disadvantaged groups (the handicapped, elderly, and—in education programs—women). The same approach was utilized in the environmental impact statement process created in 1969, as well as for many other environmental purposes. It also has been extended into such fields as historic preservation, animal welfare and relocation assistance.[4] A total of some 36 across-the-board requirements dealing with various socio-economic issues, as well as an additional 23 administrative and fiscal policy requirements, were identified in a 1980 OMB inventory.[5] . . . Of the former group, the largest number involve some aspect of environmental protection (16) and nondiscrimination (9). Two-thirds of the 59 requirements have been adopted since 1969.

Crosscutting requirements have a pervasive impact because they apply "horizontally" to all or most federal agencies and their assistance programs. In contrast, two other new forms of intergovernmental regulation are directed at only a single function, department or program. Thus, both can be described as "vertical" mandates.[6]

Crossover Sanctions

One approach relies upon the power of the purse. It imposes federal fiscal sanctions in one program area or activity to influence state and local policy in another. The distinguishing feature here is that a failure to comply with the requirements of one program can result in a reduction or termination of funds from another, separately authorized and separately entered into, program. The penalty thus "crosses over."

The history of federal efforts to secure the removal of billboards from along the nation's major highways illustrates the use of the traditional financial "carrot" along with this new financial "stick."[7] Beginning in 1958, the federal government offered a small bonus in the form of additional highway funds to states that agreed to regulate billboard advertising along new interstate highways. By 1965, however, only half of the states had taken advantage of this offer—not enough to suit the Johnson White House.

A dramatic change occurred with the adoption of the *Highway Beautification Act of 1965*. The bonus system was dropped, and Congress substituted the threat of withholding 10% of a state's highway construction funds if it did not comply with newly expanded federal billboard control requirements. Despite the bitter opposition of the outdoor advertising industry, 32 states had enacted billboard control laws by 1970, though only 18 of these were judged to be in full compliance. Nearly all of the rest of the states fell quickly into line when Congress made appropriations to compensate for part of the cost of removing nonconforming signs, and the Federal Highway Administrator stepped up his pressure on them.

A similar fiscal penalty subsequently was employed in a number of other programs. In the wake of the OPEC [Organization of Petroleum Exporting Countries] oil embargo, federal officials urged the states to lower their speed limits and the Senate adopted a resolution to that effect. Twenty-nine states responded to this effort at "moral suasion." But these pleas were quickly replaced by a more authoritative measure: the *Emergency Highway Energy Conservation Act of 1974*, which prohibited the Secretary of Transportation from approving any highway construction projects in states having a speed limit in excess of 55 mph. All of the remaining states responded within two months.

Partial Preemption

The crossover sanctions, like the crosscutting requirements, are tied directly to the grant-in-aid system. Federal power in these cases derives from the Constitutional authority to spend for the general welfare. A final innovative technique, however, has another basis entirely. It rests on the authority of the federal government to preempt certain state and local activities under the supremacy clause and the commerce power.

Yet, this is preemption with a twist. Unlike traditional preemption statutes, preemption in these cases is only *partial*. Federal laws establish basic policies, but administrative responsibility may be delegated to the states or localities if they meet certain nationally determined conditions or standards.

The *Water Quality Act of 1965* was an early example of this strategy, which one analyst describes as the "if-then, if-then" approach. The statute was the first to establish a national policy for controlling pollution. Although the law allowed each state one year to set standards for its own interstate waters, the Secretary of Health, Education, and Welfare was authorized to enforce federal standards in any state that failed to do so. That is,

> . . . if a state does not issue regulations acceptable to the U.S., then a federal agency or department will do so, and if the state does not adopt and enforce these regulations, then the federal level of government will assume jurisdiction over that area.[8]

This same technique—which others have called the "substitution approach" to federalism[9]—has since been extended to a variety of other areas. For example, the OSHA law asserts national control over workplace health and safety but permits states to operate their own programs if their standards are "at least as effective" as the federal ones.

The most far-reaching applications, however, are in the *Clean Air Act Amendments of 1970*. This path-breaking environmental statute set federal air quality standards throughout the nation, but required that the states devise effective plans for their implementation and enforcement. Its compass is great: for example, [the] EPA can require states to change their own transportation policies (perhaps by giving additional support to mass transit) or to regulate private individuals (as in establishing emission-control requirements and inspection programs for automobiles).[10] Two close observers comment:

Of all the intergovernmental mechanisms used to nationalize regulatory policy, none is more revolutionary than the approach first applied in the Clean Air Act Amendments of 1970. It is an approach minimizing both the voluntariness of state and local participation and the substantive policy discretion provided for officials in subnational governments. In fact, it is a mechanism which challenges the very essence of federalism as a noncentralized system of separate legal jurisdictions and instead relies upon a unitary vision involving hierarchically related central and peripheral units. . . . [I]t is an approach allowing national policymakers and policy implementors to mobilize state and local resources on behalf of a national program. As preliminary measures, these resources can be mobilized using technical, financial, or other forms of assistance, but underlying this mechanism is the ability of national officials to formally and officially "draft" those resources into national service. We call this legal conscription.[11]

Applications and Combinations

These four techniques—direct legal orders, crosscutting requirements, crossover sanctions and partial preemption—are the major new statutory tools in the federal government's kit for the regulation of states and localities. Each has distinctive characteristics, and poses special problems of policy, law, administration, finance and politics.

. . . Among the major regulatory statutes examined, crosscutting requirements (18) and partial preemptions (13) clearly are relatively numerous, while crossover sanctions (6) and direct orders (6) are relatively rare.

It also should be noted that these devices have sometimes been combined. A good example is provided by the 1970 *Clean Air Act Amendments*. Basically, the law relies upon the technique of partial preemption. States must prepare State Implementation Plans (SIPs), which will control pollution to the extent necessary to achieve federal air quality standards. These must be approved by the Environmental Protection Agency. If the EPA judges a SIP to be inadequate, it must disapprove the SIP. In the event that a state fails to make necessary revisions, [the] EPA is required to promulgate an adequate SIP.

This, however, is not the only sanction imposed by the act. More teeth are added by Section 176(a), which bars both the EPA and the Department of Transportation from making grant awards in any air quality control region which has not attained primary ambient air quality standards and for which the state has failed to devise adequate transportation control plans. This, of course, is a tough crossover sanction. Furthermore, Section 176(c) prohibits any agency of the federal government from providing financial assistance to any activity which does not conform to a state SIP. This provision uses the crosscutting requirement approach to strengthening SIP implementation.

Fund termination, as in crossover sanctions, also is used to enforce compliance with a number of the crosscutting requirements relating to nondiscrimination. Discriminatory actions can result in the cutoff of aid, not only in the program area in which discrimination was found, but to an entire institution or jurisdiction.

Notes

1. *National League of Cities v. Usery*, 426 U.S. 833 (1976).
2. For a discussion of state practices, see Advisory Commission on Intergovernmental Relations, *State Mandating of Local Expenditures*, A-67 (Washington, D.C.: U.S. Government Printing Office, 1978).
3. PL 88-352, title VI, section 601, July 2, 1964.
4. See ACIR, *Categorical Grants: Their Role and Design*, A-52 (Washington, D.C.: U.S. Government Printing Office, 1978), chapter VII.
5. Office of Management and Budget, *Managing Federal Assistance in the 1980s, Working Papers, Volume I* (Washington, D.C.: U.S. Government Printing Office, 1980).
6. Catherine H. Lovell et al., *Federal and State Mandating on Local Governments: An Exploration of Issues and Impacts* (Riverside, Calif.: Graduate School of Administration, University of California, Riverside, 1979), p. 35.
7. See Roger A. Cunningham, "Billboard Control under the *Highway Beautification Act of 1965*," *Michigan Law Review* 71 (June 1973), pp. 1295–1374.
8. James B. Croy, "Federal Supersession: The Road to Domination," *State Government* 48 (Winter 1975), p. 34. Emphasis added.
9. Frank J. Thompson, *Health Policy and the Bureaucracy: Politics and Administration* (Cambridge, Mass.: The MIT Press, 1981), p. 240.
10. Congressional Budget Office, *Federal Constraints on State and Local Government Actions* (Washington, D.C.: U.S. Government Printing Office, 1979), p. 7.
11. Mel Dubnick and Alan Gitelson, "Nationalizing State Policies," in *The Nationalization of State Government*, Jerome J. Hanus, ed. (Lexington, Mass.: D. C. Heath and Company, 1981), pp. 56–57.

22

The Role of Federal Mandates in Intergovernmental Relations: Draft Report

Staff of U.S. Advisory Commission on Intergovernmental Relations

Introduction

The *Unfunded Mandates Reform Act of 1995* (P.L. 104-4) represents a bipartisan agreement that something is wrong with American federalism as it has evolved in recent years. The law directs the Advisory Commission on Intergovernmental Relations (ACIR) *"to investigate and review the role of federal mandates in intergovernmental relations"* and to make recommendations to the President and Congress as to how the federal government should relate to state, local, and tribal governments. In this preliminary report, ACIR proposes for public review and comment recommended changes in federal policies to improve intergovernmental relations while maintaining a commitment to national interests.

Changes in the Federal System

The mandate issues examined in this report arose because American federalism no longer has clearly defined responsibilities for federal, state, and local governments. One result of this lack of defined roles has been increased federal involvement in activities historically considered to be state and local affairs. Federal involvement usually began with financial aid to achieve national goals. In recent years, federal involvement has taken the form of direct orders to meet federal requirements, often with no federal financial assistance. The extensive and complex nature of this involvement is illustrated by the following examples:

- More than 200 separate mandates were identified to ACIR by state and local governments, involving about 170 federal laws reaching into every nook and cranny of state and local activities.

Draft report approved for public review and comment January 1996; ultimately not adopted by the U.S. Advisory Commission on Intergovernmental Relations, July 23, 1996. Washington, D.C.: ACIR. Pages 1–6, 7–8, 11–13.

- [An ACIR report] ... identified 3,500 decisions involving state and local governments, relating to more than 100 federal laws.
- State and local officials must comply with 33 federal laws to receive non-construction federal grants.

These numbers provide a dramatic picture of the cumulative effects of federal laws on state and local governments. They also confirm the need for better definition of the appropriate working relationships between the partners in the federal system. Relief from existing federal mandates will be especially important if state and local governments are to assume greater responsibilities from federal devolution.

Determining the Appropriate Federal Role

In *Garcia v. San Antonio Metropolitan Transit Authority* (1985), the Supreme Court made it clear that constitutionally the Congress is responsible for determining the precise scope of national authority over state and local governments. The court recognized that clear lines defining the appropriate scope of federal activities could not be drawn and, instead, left it to the political process to determine appropriate governmental roles.

Historically, the political process has determined that some activities are so important to national interests that a federal role is generally accepted as necessary. Among the most obvious is legislation protecting civil rights granted by the Constitution. In an earlier period, the economic emergency of the 1930s produced federal programs to alleviate national economic and social problems. In other instances, national policy is necessary because the problems transcend state lines, such as when dirty air or dirty water from one state intrude on another state. As a result, some federal government mandates on state and local governments are an acceptable feature of the U.S. federal system.

In recent years, however, the Washington tendency has been to treat as a national issue any problem that is emotional, hot, and highly visible. Often, this has meant passing a federal law that imposes costs and requirements on state and local governments without their consent and without regard for their ability to comply. Such actions, even though they may have broad public support, are damaging to intergovernmental comity. The challenge facing the federal government is to exercise power to resolve national needs while, at the same time, honoring state and local rights to govern their own affairs and set their own budget priorities.

The wide diversity of federal mandates makes it difficult to establish uniform ways to determine whether a mandate is proper or improper from an intergovernmental perspective. Nevertheless, ACIR has been charged with making determinations about existing mandates as they affect state and local governments. In reaching its conclusions, the Commission considered several key questions:

- Does the national purpose justify federal intrusion in state or local affairs?
- Are the costs of implementing the mandate appropriately shared among governments?
- Is maximum flexibility given to state and local governments in implementing the mandate?
- Are there changes that can be made in the mandate to relieve intergovernmental tensions while maintaining a commitment to national goals?

The ACIR Review of Existing Mandates

As required by the *Unfunded Mandates Reform Act,* ACIR started its review process by adopting criteria describing mandate issues of significant concern and the types of problems to be analyzed. ... Information about mandates meeting the criteria were [*sic*] solicited from state and local governments, federal agencies, and the public. ACIR also relied on a variety of efforts by others to help in identifying mandates needing attention:

- The National Governors Association requested each governor's office to list the mandates of most concern in their states.
- A general appeal was made in the magazines and newsletters of national and state groups representing state and local governments.
- A survey of small rural governments was conducted by the National Rural Development Partnership.
- Officials attending national and state association meetings were asked to identify troubling mandates.

Information was received from over half the states, eight municipal leagues, four state associations of counties, the national associations representing state and local governments and their officials, and directly from a variety of local government officials.

ACIR selected 14 mandates for analysis. The 14 mandates selected constitute only a small portion of the over 200 identified, but they illustrate the diverse, complex, and troubling challenges that federal mandates pose for the intergovernmental system. While only 14 mandates are reviewed in this report because of time and resource limitations, the Commission believes that many more of the over 200 mandates identified need to be evaluated. ACIR urges that a review of additional mandates be authorized as soon as possible.

The selection of the 14 mandates was based on:

(1) The preponderance of communications identifying the mandates as troubling to state and local governments;
(2) The significance and diversity of issues posed for intergovernmental relations; and
(3) The criteria published by the Commission. . . .

Basis of Recommendations

In considering its recommendations on the intergovernmental role of federal mandates, the Commission was guided by the published criteria. The criteria defined mandates of significant concern as those that: (1) require state or local governments to expend substantial amounts of their own resources without regard for state and local priorities; (2) abridge historic powers of state and local governments without a clear showing of national need; (3) impose requirements that are difficult or impossible to implement; and (4) are the subject of widespread objections. The 14 mandates subjected to intensive review in this report meet one or more of these criteria.

The criteria also identified a number of specific conditions for which ACIR should make relief recommendations. The specific conditions were: requirements not needing national action or, if needing national action, not federally funded; unnecessarily rigid; unnecessarily complex or prescriptive; unclear goals or standards; contradictory or inconsistent provisions; duplicative provisions; obsolete provisions; lacking in adequate scientific and economic basis; lacking in practical value; or would create undue financial difficulties for the governments.

ACIR recognizes that mandate issues are more than disagreements between political scientists about which government has the *right* to make a decision. Instead, mandate issues relate to the nuts and bolts of government operations that are necessary to provide effective protection and efficient services. This means evaluating how the mandate will affect not only costs but routine government operations as well.

In examining the individual mandates, the Commission considered the fundamental intergovernmental issues associated with the mandate, and did not evaluate the specific mandate requirements. We urge those reviewing these analyses and the accompanying recommendations to give similar attention to the roles of federal, state, and local governments as they relate to the mandate.

Common Issues

ACIR's review of existing mandates found a number of common issues that are troubling federal, state, and local government relations. These issues and ACIR's proposed recommendations to address them include:

1. *Detailed procedural requirements.* State and local governments are not given flexibility to meet national goals in ways that best fit their needs and resources. The imposition of exact standards or detailed requirements, in many instances, merely increases costs and delays achievement of the national goals. The federal role in implementation should be to provide research and technical advice for those governments that request it, but, in general, state and local governments should be permitted to comply with a mandate in a manner that best suits their particular needs and conditions.

2. *Lack of federal concern about mandate costs.* When the federal government imposes costs on another government without providing federal funds, the magnitude of costs is often not considered. If the federal government has no financial obligation, it has little incentive to weigh costs against benefits or to allow state and local governments to determine the least costly alternatives for reaching national goals. The federal government should assume some share of mandate costs as an incentive to restrain the extent of the mandate and to aid in seeking the least costly alternatives.

3. *Federal failure to recognize state and local governments' public accountability.* State governments often are treated as just another interest group, as private entities, or as administrative arms of the federal government, not as sovereign governments with powers derived from the U.S. Constitution. Local governments, despite the important role they play in delivering government services, have been given even less consideration. Non-governmental advocacy groups' views have sometimes been given more attention than

those of state and local governments. Federal laws should recognize that state and local governments are led by elected officials who must account to the voters for their actions, just as the President and Members of Congress.

4. *Lawsuits by individuals against state and local governments to enforce federal mandates.* Many federal laws permit individuals or organizations to sue state and local governments over questions of compliance, even though a federal agency is responsible for enforcement. Federal laws, however, are often written in such broad terms, it is not clear what is required of federal, state, and local officials. In these circumstances, permitting litigation brought by individuals subjects state and local governments to budgetary uncertainties and substantial legal costs. Because the federal agency is not directly involved with the costs and problems of this litigation, it has little incentive to propose amendments that would clarify the law's requirements. Only the federal agency responsible for enforcement of a law should be permitted to sue state and local governments.

5. *Inability of very small local governments to meet mandate standards and timetables.* The requirements for many federal mandates are based on the assumption that all local governments have the financial, administrative, and technical resources that exist in large governments. Many very small local governments have only part-time staffs with little technical capability and very limited resource bases. Extending deadlines or modifying requirements for these small governments may have minimal adverse effects on the achievement of overall national goals but may make it possible for such governments eventually to comply. Deadlines should be extended and requirements modified for very small local governments.

6. *Lack of coordinated federal policy with no federal agency empowered to make binding decisions about a mandate's requirements.* There are mandates that involve several federal agencies. This has resulted in confusion about what the law requires and how state and local governments can know when they are in compliance. In addition to making state and local governments aware of mandate requirements, federal agencies should explain the reasons for the mandate and should assist in taking the actions necessary for implementation. A single federal agency should be designated to coordinate each mandate's implementation and to make binding decisions about that mandate.

Summary of Recommendations on Individual Mandates

ACIR's proposed recommendations for individual mandates can be summarized into three categories.

The Commission finds that the following mandates as they apply to state and local governments do *not* have a sufficient national interest to justify intruding on state and local government abilities to control their own affairs. While the Commission does not take issue with the goals of these mandates, it believes that achieving those goals can be left to elected state and local officials. Thus, ACIR recommends repealing the provisions in these laws that extend coverage to state and local governments.

> *Fair Labor Standards Act*
> *Family and Medical Leave Act*
> *Occupational Safety and Health Act*
> Drug and Alcohol Testing of Commercial Drivers
> Metric Conversion for Plans and Specifications
> Medicaid: Boren Amendment
> Required Use of Recycled Crumb Rubber

The Commission finds that the following mandates are necessary because national policy goals justify their use. However, the federal share of the costs should be increased or the stringent requirements and deadlines imposed on state and local governments should be relaxed. These mandates impose substantial costs on state and local governments as a result of requirements that are unnecessarily burdensome. Thus, ACIR recommends retaining these mandates with modifications to accommodate budgetary and administrative constraints on state and local governments.

> *The Clean Water Act*
> *Individuals with Disabilities Education Act*
> *Americans with Disabilities Act*

The Commission finds the following mandates are related to acceptable national policy goals, but they should be revised to provide greater flexibility in implementation procedures and more participation by state and local governments in development of mandate policies. Thus, ACIR recommends revising these mandates to provide greater flexibility and increased consultation.

The Safe Drinking Water Act
Endangered Species Act
The Clean Air Act
Davis-Bacon Related Acts

Summary of Each Mandate

[The ACIR draft report includes summaries for all the mandates mentioned above. Three from the total, each representing one of the categories listed above, are included here. The rest are omitted for reasons of space.—Ed.]

Occupational Safety and Health Act

The *Occupational Safety and Health Act of 1970* (OSHA) (29 U.S.C. 651–678) establishes standards for safe, healthy, and productive work environments. State governments and their political subdivisions, as well as the United States government, are specifically *excluded* from the definition of "an employer" under the act. In the case of state governments and their political subdivisions, OSHA has no requirements unless a state volunteers to participate in the federal program. States that volunteer to administer the federal OSHA program within their jurisdiction are required to extend federal requirements to all public employees in the state.

Twenty-three states have assumed responsibility for operating the federal OSHA program. Two additional states have federally approved OSHA plans only for state and local government employees. Even in the remaining states, however, there may be an impact, or a perception of an impact, because some OSHA requirements are replicated in state laws or are perceived as mandatory even though they are not.

Numerous complaints expressed about OSHA policies in both participating and non-participating states attest to the widespread misunderstanding about the law's coverage and the substantial compliance costs. Making all states, not just the non-participating states, exempt from OSHA would allow all states to set their own health and safety standards, taking into consideration their priorities and budgetary constraints. Such a policy would give states flexibility similar to that given federal agencies.

RECOMMENDATION: Repeal the provisions extending OSHA coverage to public employees in participating states.

Americans with Disabilities Act

The *Americans with Disabilities Act of 1990* (ADA) (P.L. 101–336) prohibits discrimination against individuals with disabilities in employment, public services, and public accommodations. Any state or local government policies found to be inconsistent with ADA provisions are to be modified as soon as feasible. Each government program is to be examined for physical barriers to access and for remedial measures that need to be taken.

ADA provides important and necessary social benefits, but it is creating problems for state and local governments because of expensive retrofitting and service delivery requirements, confusing and ambiguous statutory language, and insufficient technical assistance provided by the federal government. Further, virtually no federal funding has been appropriated to cover most state and local compliance costs. With tight budgets and limited time to correct structural obstacles to improve public accommodation, it has been difficult for many governments to implement the extensive changes required. Structural changes to existing buildings to meet "program accessibility" requirements were to be made by [a certain date], a deadline not met by many state and local governments.

Also, the use of the terms "reasonable accommodation," "undue hardship," "readily achievable," and countless other broad expressions in the law has subjected state and local governments to numerous lawsuits over legal interpretations of ADA. The penalties for noncompliance are severe, and legal costs can be substantial.

Federal enforcement of ADA is uncoordinated, with eight federal departments having some enforcement power. The prime responsibility for processing complaints under ADA are the Justice Department and the Equal Employment Opportunity Commission. The Federal Communications Commission manages telecommunications issues. The National Council on Disability is an independent federal agency that identifies emerging issues and recommends disability policy to the President and Congress. The Architectural and Transportation Barriers Compliance Board provides some educational and technical assistance regarding accessibility.

RECOMMENDATION: Either provide increased federal funding to state and local governments to assist in compliance, including funding for paratransit, or modify some deadlines and requirements to let state and local governments meet ADA goals in a manner that recognizes state and local technical and budget constraints without abridging the national commitment to the rights of individuals with disabilities. In addition, a single federal ADA enforcement and assistance agency should be designated to coordinate enforcement and technical assistance, and legal action against state and local governments should be limited to actions brought by the federal government.

The Safe Drinking Water Act

The *Safe Drinking Water Act* (SDWA) regulates drinking water standards for the 58,530 waterworks serving 25 or more persons on a regular basis. It establishes maximum levels for contaminants known to occur in public water systems, establishes wellhead protection programs, certifies and specifies appropriate analytical and treatment techniques, and establishes public notification procedures. It requires drinking water suppliers to assume a wide range of responsibilities, including monitoring of the water supply.

The safety of drinking water is a public health issue. Prior to 1974, states had responsibility for the safety of drinking water, but they generally relied on standards set by the Public Health Service. Since drinking water endangers not only the residents of a local community and state but also those traveling interstate, the regulation of drinking water may be justified as a national concern. It should be recognized, however, that other vital public health concerns, such as restaurant inspections, are the responsibility of state and local governments.

State and local concerns over the *Safe Drinking Water Act* hinge on what constitutes safe drinking water and how to achieve it in the most cost-effective way. These governments do not object to assuming the costs of providing safe drinking water, but some do object to incurring costs that in their opinion do not improve water quality. The existing law overreached in the standards and compliance requirements it imposed on local water systems.

Amendments recently approved by the Senate will repeal some of the most onerous provisions, including mandatory additional tests for contaminants, tests for contaminants not a threat in local areas, and eased provisions for treatment of surface water supplies. The Senate amendment also authorizes funding for state capitalization loan funds to reduce interest costs of compliance. The amendments, however, do not alter intergovernmental relationships in the SDWA.

RECOMMENDATION: Enact amendments similar to those approved by the Senate and establish a long-term goal of returning to the states full responsibility for safe drinking water standards.

23

The Politics of Unfunded Mandates

Paul L. Posner

Have mandates joined death and taxes as one of the inevitable certainties of life? It is hard to imagine, but before 1960, this question would have been greeted with puzzlement, as a presumption was shared by both parties against the national regulation of state and local governments. Yet, in the 1970s and 1980s, mandates came to be embraced by both parties as an efficient tool to achieve national objectives that leaders felt compelled to promote. The shift from voluntaristic to coercive tools of federal action marked a significant departure in our federal system.

The passage of mandate reform in the 1990s can be seen as a collective expression of national remorse over these trends and may presage a period where federalism casts a larger shadow over policy debates. However, mandates have deep roots in our political system. Many of the factors underlying the earlier shift to coercive federalism are still with us today, notably the continuing pressure on leaders to champion new national initiatives implicating state and local governments. Moreover, changes in our political system eclipsing congressional deference to state and local interests now require those governments to mobilize their membership to protect federalism interests in Congress, an uncertain prospect that is constrained by the ambivalence of state and local groups toward certain mandates. Thus, the passage of mandate reform, although signaling a renewed commitment to federalism, will require other changes in national political forces before a sustainable change in governance will emerge, characterized by a systemic forbearance and observance of federalism principles.

From *The Politics of Unfunded Mandates: Whither Federalism?* (Washington, DC: Georgetown University Press, 1998), 211–222. Reproduced by permission of the publisher.

Implications of the New Policymaking Process

Classic notions of both federalism and policymaking suggested that Congress would show a great deal of deference to state and local governments in formulating national policy. Historically, state and local governments enjoyed considerable deference in the process, resting on the very real dependence of national office holders on state and local parties for their jobs.

This institutional deference was reflected in a presumption against coercive federal mandates and preemptions on the state and local sector that had been accepted as one of the rules of the game by all actors in the system prior to the 1960s. ... [T]his influence was bolstered by a system that was widely viewed as stacked against major policy initiatives and grounded in policy incrementalism and the numerous veto points within Congress, and in the broader system as well, that tended to frustrate bold policy changes.

Classic political science literature suggested that mandate legislation would spark heated conflict within Congress. Major policy change was said to invariably prompt major conflict, with conflict rising as the stakes increase.[1] Consensus was expected in areas where the stakes were either small or where policy monopolies prevented the emergence of groups with conflicting perspectives, but regulatory policies were said to inspire a high level of conflict among interest groups.[2] As narrow interests facing concentrated costs from regulation, state and local governments would be expected to mobilize themselves more effectively than would advocates representing the more diffuse interest of regulatory beneficiaries.[3] The conflict could be expected to become partisan, as Republican allies of states and localities in particular would mobilize to oppose increased federal power over the states.

The congressional adoption of mandates and preemptions over the past twenty years is clearly at odds with these models of our system.[4]

... [M]andates have become a major instrument of national policy, relied on by leaders of both parties at various times to support differing policy goals. The legitimation of mandates began in the 1970s and continued, surprisingly, into the 1980s and early 1990s, even in a purportedly conservative era of governance. ... [N]otable mandate restraint and rollback occurred in 1996, but the record was mixed as Congress nonetheless enacted some significant new mandates and preemptions.

The rapid passage of many mandates chronicled in this study reflects the emergence of a new style of policymaking at the federal level. The adoption of far-reaching, nonincremental policy reforms became more commonplace during this period. Ideas that were purveyed by influential experts and policy entrepreneurs found increasingly fertile ground in a more open, activist Congress that was anxious to take credit for legislation appealing to broadly shared values championed by an all-pervasive media.

The change in congressional incentives was perhaps most important. Most studies suggest that members of Congress, freed from their state and local party moorings, became anxious entrepreneurs in search of new policy ideas and profiles to gain media attention and political support. The competition for policy leadership has had a profoundly nationalizing and centralizing effect on policymaking in Congress, as congressmen from both parties were compelled to sponsor national programs and policies, albeit serving different interests and ideas.[5] Most domestic programs embraced by national leaders, such as improving education or reducing crime, involve functions traditionally performed by state and local governments and thus invariably implicate them in new national initiatives.

Nationalization of policy became a logical response to this new environment, but why mandates? ... [W]e as a nation are loathe to empower federal bureaucracies to both fund and deliver domestic programs and services, particularly in well established areas of state and local jurisdiction. Accordingly, the federal government sought to either entice state and local involvement through grants or compel their participation through some form of mandate.

At the outset, the federal role often began with grants, reflecting in part the relative weakness of advocacy coalitions supporting new programs as well as diffuse resistance to the use of mandates as a policy tool.[6] Over time, however, the grant program served to strengthen the beneficiary coalitions and generate support from state and local bureaucracies and leaders as well. As these programs took root at the state and local level, the nation's tolerance eroded for differences among states' approaches and gaps in services to various groups, while the legitimacy of the federal role took hold. Accordingly, mandates came to be seen as a logical and appropriate tool to promote greater national uniformity.

But this logic was underscored by the growing political strength of beneficiary coalitions, which enabled them to succeed in convincing policymakers to choose more coercive policy tools such as mandates. Remarkably, these coalitions were strong enough to gain both adoption of mandates and substantial federal funds to underwrite state and local compliance during a time when federal budget deficits reached peacetime highs in the 1980s and early 1990s. This pattern supports the conclusion of John Kincaid who argued that the era of cooperative federalism characterized by reliance on grants helped promote a more coercive federal role epitomized by the use of mandates.[7]

Perhaps more surprising than the passage of mandates was the frequent adoption of some of the most fiscally burdensome mandates in a consensual process rather than the kind of conflictual, deliberative process portrayed in traditional views of regulatory policymaking. State and local groups were not frequently mobilized to oppose this legislation, and Congress often proceeded to enact expensive mandates by unanimous acclamation or consensus. Far from a policymaking process paralyzed by gridlock, congressional policymaking, if anything, exhibited a race to claim credit on these issues.

A key factor was the success of mandate advocates in defining proposed mandates as politically compelling causes that could not be publicly opposed by either conservatives or state and local interest groups. Having successfully defined the scope of conflict in terms of benefit, not cost, the legislation moved through the congressional obstacle course at a rapid pace.

Recent literature suggests this pattern is not limited to intergovernmental mandates. Baumgartner and Jones posit a "punctuated equilibrium" model to explain how policy areas dominated by policy monopolies and seemingly unshakable programs suddenly can become unhinged and replaced by a new political and policy regime. Importantly, they suggest that major policy changes are often accomplished as waves of enthusiasm sweep over the system, typically driving out any serious opposition or countermobilization.[8] Such new policies are buttressed by an unassailable policy idea that legitimate political actors oppose only at their own peril. In Baumgartner and Jones' model, the political system "lurches" from one equilibrium to another, with the process of change often happening rapidly and by acclamation.[9]

This dynamic is similar to the issue-attention cycle posited by Anthony Downs. Downs wrote that nonincremental policy change occurs through a process of alarmed discovery and euphoric enthusiasm. Often after objective indicators of a problem have peaked, strong public pressure emerges to "solve" the problem.[10]

The types of issues in which "Downsian" mobilization [is] most likely to occur are what they call "valence" issues, for which only one side of the debate is perceived as legitimate.[11]

... [I]t is difficult for affected interests to mobilize against these issues once they attain agenda status. But, as tempting as it is for politicians to vote for them, they are also difficult to solve, giving rise to the cycle observed by Downs in which politicians and the public lose interest over time.

Indeed, some suggest that national elected officials are more vulnerable to bandwagon politics than ever before.[12] Thanks to the erosion of allegiances to party or to state and local government leaders, members of Congress are said to be more atomistic and thereby feel less protected if they are on the wrong side of a publicly compelling issue. Furthermore, they are also increasingly operating in a transparent environment, with an increasingly omnipresent media feeding back images of their performance to their constituencies. Faced with this increasing pressure, public officials are increasingly anxious to avoid being perceived as being on the wrong side of issues, causing them to shun politically infeasible policies and support those that are politically compelling, regardless of ideology or party position.

What happened, though, to the constraints in our system that were thought to prevent this nationalization dynamic? The foregoing suggests that one of the major factors prompting rapid adoption of mandates in [recent decades] was the neutralization or weakening of actors and constraints expected to limit the expansion of federal power in our system. Beginning in the 1930s, the Supreme Court provided the rationale for an expanded federal role in domestic policy and, until the 1990s, generally ruled that state and local governments had to look to the political process, not the 10th Amendment, to protect their jurisdictional prerogatives. Essentially, the Court's rulings enabled Congress to achieve its policy goals through mandates and preemptions.

During this period, Republicans, although supporting federalism principles, often engaged in a competition to avoid being blamed for defeating politically compelling mandates that were defined in valence terms or actually championed mandates when they implemented higher priority policy goals. Unless they could prevent mandate bills from coming to the agenda in the first place, Republicans often were consigned to the role of "reluctant mandators," supporting the overall mandate in formal votes but working behind the scenes to modify their stringency. In other cases, they endorsed mandates when other party goals and principles were at stake, as shown by [a] roll call analysis revealing Republican support for mandates that advance party objectives in such areas as moral policy, business preemption, and welfare.

This finding reinforces the views of Timothy Conlan, who observed that, like most Americans, national political leaders have a philosophical allegiance to federalism but are often unwilling to sacrifice more specific policy goals calling for federal action. He cites polling data that indicate public support for political conservatism on general issues of federal power but that also show public support for a wide range of new federal policy interventions.[13]

State and Local Governments and Mandates

State and local governments might have been expected to be the most significant restraint on the passage of mandates. After all, if they cannot defend their institutional interests and prerogatives, how can we expect other actors to speak effectively on their behalf?

In earlier eras, federalism enjoyed a presumptive status as one of the universal rules of the game, and the assertion of new federal powers required major mobilization of interests and ideas sufficient to justify departing from this political norm. The decline of the endemic political ties between federal, state, and local officials and the apparent erosion of federalism as a widely shared value has required the mobilization of state and local governments themselves to protect their interests through their interest group organizations in Washington. Unlike in earlier eras, federalism is no longer the default option, but rather it requires for its protection the active mobilization of state and local interests in orchestrated lobbying campaigns. . . .

[W]hen state and local government interest groups marshalled an intense grassroots lobbying campaign, they enjoy[ed] some success in defending themselves on mandate issues, as Justice Blackmun's *Garcia* opinion envisioned.[14] . . .

Internal Conflicts among State and Local Officials

However, all too often mandates disarmed state and local government interest groups and prevented the mobilization necessary for the protection of federalism interests in the current era. Frequently, state and local government interest groups themselves were not able to generate the requisite internal consensus needed to marshall active grassroots campaigns that were necessary to protect federalism interests in the face of politically compelling mandate goals.

The mandate goals proved to be compelling not only to congressional officials, but often to state and local officials as well. ... [S]tate and local government groups were often neutral or even supportive of individual mandates and concentrated their lobbying on winning concessions or on federal funding to ease implementation. And ... the federal funding carrot exerts a pervasive, albeit more subtle, nationalizing influence on state and local policy priorities.

Achieving unity on any contentious policy issue is not easy for organizations comprised of state and local elected officials of different political persuasions and parties. The broad political appeal of many mandates made it even more difficult for elected officials across the political spectrum to agree to oppose them. Like congressional conservatives, they risked public blame by opposing these programs. And, like members of Congress, some were policy entrepreneurs anxious to make a mark on the national stage. Absent a consensus, these organizations were often silent on the fundamental policy question pertaining to the need for a federal mandate. Instead, they chose to focus on the need for funding and flexibility in implementing mandates—issues that more readily garnered internal agreement among their politically diverse memberships.

The political appeal of most mandates was accentuated because the benefits of new mandates appeared immediate and concrete, whereas the costs and implementation challenges were difficult to visualize until the regulations specified the requirements. ... The Advisory Commission on Intergovernmental Relations concluded that this pattern of delayed state and local reaction is common for mandates with broad symbolic appeal, including the handicapped access requirements (Section 504 of the 1973 Rehabilitation Act) and Endangered Species Act.[15]

In contrast, state and local groups were likely to be more vigilant in attacking existing mandates whose costs have become salient to their members. ... [T]he groundswell of support for mandate reform was prompted at least in part by the delayed impacts of the regulations issued a number of years after the passage of such legislation as the 1986 safe drinking water mandate and asbestos in schools mandate, which state and local groups initially did not oppose. Although public policy analysts would like costs and benefits to be considered together when major regulatory programs are established, often costs are dealt with serially and separately from benefits, as Congress uses the litmus test of experience to assess the need to modify regulatory statutes to deal with cost claims.[16]

Mandates also served a political function for state and local officials in gaining leverage—in policy struggles within their own governments, as well as in competition with other states or localities for economic development. Within their own governments, state and local officials found mandates to be a useful tool to accomplish their own policy agendas in the face of recalcitrant local political actors. . . . [S]tates and localities also engage in competition with other jurisdictions for economic development, and federal mandates essentially provide a floor to prevent competition from degenerating. States or localities seeking to regulate in certain areas such as gun control or commercial truck drivers can see their efforts undermined if some jurisdictions benefit from inaction or refuse to adopt a common regulatory framework.

Intergovernmental Roots of Mandates

Ironically, as the foregoing suggests, state policy activism can prompt federal mandates every bit as much as can state policy inaction. This is a seemingly counterintuitive point since most advocates justify nationalization of policy to correct state policy inaction or inequities. In this view, the best way for states to ward off federal mandates would be to become policy activists and innovators.[17]

From this standpoint, states have earned greater federal forbearance by their modernization of administrative and fiscal systems and by their increased programmatic leadership over the past thirty years.[18] States threw off the yoke of segregation that for many years clouded their "states' rights" claims; revenue systems were expanded; bureaucracies became more professionalized; legislatures were reapportioned and became more responsive to policy demands; and interest groups representing a more diverse range of constituencies found their way to state capitols. Thanks in part to these trends, states have become policy activists, leaders, and innovators in many areas. States increased their spending in many programs that were originally started with federal grants to become senior fiscal partners, and they replaced many of the federal funding cuts of the early 1980s.[19]

However, in many cases the very policy maturity, activism, and diversity celebrated by federalism observers has helped lay the foundation for federal mandates. Most of the significant mandates passed in the 99th Congress were preceded by similar programs in a number of states, as both federal and state officials supported nationalization of policies initiated by the states for different reasons. Indeed, the growth of federal regulatory activism coincided with periods of state policy activism as well. This apparent puzzle can be resolved by accepting the view that state activism is positively linked to and prompts federal regulatory activism.

Traditionally, it has been acknowledged that state innovations sow the seeds for national adoption by testing policy ideas and approaches in "laboratories of democracy." However, state innovations also provide *political* incentives for nationalization of these policies. They inspire policy advocates to extend the policies of some states to all states. . . .

The intergovernmental environment itself, then, came to be an important factor prompting policies' federal adoption. In an increasingly national political system, diversity among states' policies tends to be viewed, not as a cause for celebration of the strengths of our federal system, but as a reason for alarm and a rationale for centralizing policy mandates or preemptions. An infrastructure of nationalized media, interest groups, and entrepreneurial national and state political leaders combines to accelerate the diffusion and nationalization of state policy innovations in a process that has probably accelerated in recent years. . . .

Equally important, in a society whose economics, culture, and communications have increasingly [become] nationalized, state and local governments themselves have also become less insulated from national trends in both governance and programs.[20] . . .

Politically, as one observer said, state legislatures are becoming increasingly "congressionalized," as state political leaders rely less on party labels and gubernatorial coattails and become more like policy entrepreneurs running candidate-centered campaigns in search of visibility, campaign financing, and votes.[21] Governors too have had to establish candidate-centered campaigns independent of party, prompting them also to become more like policy entrepreneurs in search of new ideas to champion.[22] Interest groups have carried national ideas to the states by increasing their organizational presence in state capitols, and the kinds of groups represented in states have become more diverse and include public interest groups similar to those proliferating in Washington.[23] Over the years, federal grant programs have helped institutionalize national values and interests in state governments as bureaucracies and interest groups have coalesced around these programs in the states.

All of this suggests that policy problems increasingly are presented in similar ways at both national and state levels. And it means that state and local leaders are becoming every bit as vulnerable to the same publicly compelling causes and policy stampedes as are national leaders. . . .

Viewed in this light, mandates are not only a tool of coercion applied by the federal government against protesting state and local officials. Rather, their increasing prevalence reflects the growing interdependence of national and state and local political cultures and political systems that redefines how state and local officials define their political interests in our federal system. Most important, state and local officials have become crosspressured by overlapping allegiances to nationally pervasive values. . . . Programmatic values have frequently assumed the primary place in the debate at all levels, often rendering concerns over federalism and governmental process in general to the back burner.[24]

Cooperative Mandating?

This is not to say that state and local governments have not opposed certain mandates and achieved some success in modifying them. As discussed earlier, they were particularly successful in mounting vigorous assaults on existing mandates whose costs and frustrations are well known by their members. However, although they made mandates more cooperative and flexible, state and local governments, wittingly or unwittingly, helped legitimize mandates themselves.

Internally, it was often easier for state and local groups to obtain membership support for public positions seeking mandate modifications, flexibility, and federal reimbursement of costs than for positions in total opposition to the proposed mandate itself. Externally, modifications and funding were more readily accepted by the programmatic and functionally based policy networks in command of policymaking in our system. Unlike federal grant funding issues, state and local governments and beneficiaries often had conflicting interests when it came to the creation of a mandate. . . .

Modifications and funding to assuage state and local interests were also quite appealing to members of Congress pushing mandate legislation. A Congress averse to conflict will more likely embrace legislation that mollifies all significant interests. This type of legislation gives members the ability to claim credit for both the mandate benefits and for saving their states and localities from its worst effects.

From the federalism perspective, the successful modification of mandates helped blunt their state and local impact and surely made these seemingly coercive programs more cooperative in design and implementation. State and local success in achieving flexibility and funding of mandates confirms the relevance of the overlapping author-ity or cooperative model of federalism. . . . This outcome suggests that state and local governments still have substantial political resources that limit the scope of the federal role when activated. Some observers conclude that this state and local influence over the design and imple-mentation of federal programs is the most certain protector of their interests in a new federalism characterized by an ever-growing and increasingly pervasive national community.[25]

Ironically, the very success state and local governments enjoy in modifying mandates helped legitimize the federal regulatory presence itself.[26] Federal mandate programs were arguably strengthened and made more effective by promoting state and local cooperation in their implementation. State and local authority over the delivery of federal-ly mandated programs were enhanced by it. However, the authority and autonomy of state and local governments over their own public services and values [were] ultimately undermined, as federal programs have grown to encumber a growing share of state and local resources and legal authority. This confirms the validity of the inclusive authority or coer-cive federalism model. . . .

Participation in federal programs, although better than unilateral projection of federal power, does not protect the structural integrity of state and local governments from federal encroachment. The coopera-tive approach to mandates helped promote federalism values in choos-ing *how* to mandate, but it did not generally inform the decision about *whether* to mandate—a decision that may be best explained by the coercive model of federalism.

Notes

1. Robert A. Dahl, *Democracy in the United States,* 2nd edition (Chicago: Rand McNally, 1972), p. 303.
2. Theodore Lowi, "American Business, Public Policy, Case-Studies and Political Theory," *World Politics* 16 (July, 1964), pp. 677–715.
3. James Q. Wilson, *The Politics of Regulation* (New York: Basic Books, 1980).
4. The term mandate used in this chapter . . . include[s] both conditions of aid and preemptions, as well as direct order requirements.

5. David Mayhew, *Congress: The Electoral Connection* (New Haven: Yale University Press, 1978). Also, see Burton Loomis, *The American Politician: Ambition, Entrepreneurship, and the Changing Face of Political Life* (New York: Basic Books, 1988).

6. Some analysts suggest that grants are created by groups too weak to gain their goals at either level of government alone. See Thomas J. Anton, *American Federalism and Public Policy: How the System Works* (New York: Random House, 1989), pp. 82–84.

7. John Kincaid, "From Cooperative to Coercive Federalism," *Annals* 509 (May, 1990), pp. 139–152.

8. Frank R. Baumgartner and Bryan D. Jones, *Agendas and Instability in American Politics* (Chicago: University of Chicago Press, 1993).

9. Ibid., p. 12.

10. Anthony Downs, "Up and Down with Ecology: The Issue Attention Cycle," *Public Interest*, 28 (Summer, 1972), pp. 38–50.

11. Frank R. Baumgartner and Bryan D. Jones, *Agendas and Instability in American Politics*, chapter 5.

12. Anthony King, "The American Polity in the 1990's," in *The New American Political System*, 2nd edition, ed. Anthony King (Washington, D.C.: American Enterprise Institute, 1990), pp. 287–307.

13. Timothy Conlan, "Federalism and Competing Values in the Reagan Administration," *Publius: The Journal of Federalism* 16 (Winter, 1986), p. 45.

14. *Garcia v. San Antonio Metropolitan Transit Authority*, 105 S. Ct. 1005 (1985).

15. Advisory Commission on Intergovernmental Relations, *Regulatory Federalism: Policy, Process, Impact and Reform* (Washington, D.C.: ACIR, 1984), p. 117.

16. This classic pattern was viewed as a consequence of the politics of speculative augmentation, wherein Congress deliberately sets goals stretching current implementation capacity, with concessions made to reality over time should these goals prove to be impractical. See Charles Jones, *Clean Air: The Policies and Politics of Pollution Control* (Pittsburgh: University of Pittsburgh Press, 1975), p. 176.

17. Michael Reagan expresses the classic formulation when he observes that the reasons for federal preemption of states is that states are either not doing a good job or not doing the job at all. See his *Regulation: The Politics of Policy* (Boston: Little, Brown, 1987), p. 186.

18. For assessment of state modernization and capacity, see Advisory Commission on Intergovernmental Relations, *The Question of State Governmental Capacity* (Washington, D.C.: ACIR, 1985).

19. Paul L. Posner and Margaret T. Wrightson, "Block Grants: A Perennial, but Unstable, Tool of Government," *Publius: The Journal of Federalism* 26, No. 3 (Summer, 1996), p. 100.

20. States have been converging on per capita income, party competition, and voter participation at least since the early 1950s. For example, the coefficient of variation for party competition in gubernatorial elections declined from 42 to 18 percent between 1952 and 1984. Hofferbert reports steadily decreasing socioeconomic and policy variation among the states since 1890. See his "The Nationalization of State

Politics," in Richard Hofferbert and Ira Sharkansky, ed., *State and Urban Politics* (Boston: Little, Brown, 1971).

21. Stephen A. Salmore and Barbara G. Salmore, "The Transformation of State Electoral Politics," in Carl Van Horn, ed., *The State of the States*, 3rd edition (Washington, D.C.: Congressional Quarterly, 1996), pp. 51–76.

22. John F. Bibby and Thomas M. Holbrook, "Parties and Elections," in *Politics in the American States*, ed. Virginia Gray and Herbert Jacob (Washington, D.C.: Congressional Quarterly, 1996), pp. 78–121.

23. Clive S. Thomas and Ronald J. Hrebenar, "Interest Groups in the States," in *Politics in the American States*, pp. 122–158.

24. Edward W. Weidner, "Decision-Making in a Federal System," in *American Federalism in Perspective*, ed. Aaron Wildavsky (Boston: Little, Brown, 1967), p. 238.

25. Michael Reagan and John Sanzone, *The New Federalism*, 2nd edition (New York: Oxford University Press, 1981), p. 170.

26. American business also enjoyed success in modifying regulatory programs by accepting those programs only in principle. Richard A. Harris, "Politicized Management: The Changing Face of Business in American Politics," in *Remaking American Politics*, ed. Richard A. Harris and Sidney M. Milkis (Boulder, Co.: Westview Press, 1989), p. 275.

24

Another Look at Bargaining and Negotiating in Intergovernmental Management

Robert Agranoff and Michael McGuire

Lost within the recent attention given to network management and collaboration is the continuing importance of bargaining and negotiation in intergovernmental relations and management. The field of public management has been learning a great deal about the many links between local governments and nongovernmental organizations, the development of local partnerships and contractual agreements with private firms, and the importance of intercommunity activity in metropolitan areas. As a result, our conceptions of managerial behavior and governing are evolving rapidly (McGuire 2002). Also important are the growing conjunctions of federal and state government administrators with nongovernmental organizations in networks that negotiate policy adjustments. Such studies are expanding the concepts of nonhierarchical management in the public sector (Agranoff 2003b). However, the types of mutual adjustment and joint activity we see in such horizontal environments have existed in the vertical, intergovernmental context for decades, and such activity reigns in significance even today. Indeed, much of the horizontal activity we study exists as a result of federal/state, federal/local, and state/local programming (Walker 2000). The sheen of network management is brighter today, but bargaining and negotiating across governments provide a venerable model of (and the context for) collaborative and cooperative public management.

We argue that a renewed focus on "old-fashioned" bargaining and negotiation in intergovernmental relations is needed. As such, the primary emphasis in this article is on administrative rather than political bargaining. Administrative federalism in the United States is highly transac-

From *The Journal of Public Administration Research & Theory* Vol. 14(4) 2004, pp. 495–512, by Robert Agranoff and Michael McGuire, "Another Look at Bargaining and Negotiating in Intergovernmental Relations." Reprinted by permission of Oxford University Press.

tional. To manage intergovernmentally is in many respects a function of both jurisdictional and functional imperatives, which opens the process to reaching negotiated settlements across boundaries. In many different programs, all involved government agencies work together to work out many details that meet the approval of affected parties. Local officials sometimes must comply with the letter of the law, but more often than not they are able to find common ground with state and federal officials. Managerial activity of this kind not only has been the theoretical precursor to current discussions of network management but continues to provide the framework within which networks emerge and operate.

We make our case for another look at bargaining and negotiation in three ways. First, we revisit the notion that the U.S. federal system is, by design, a fertile field for administrators to make intergovernmental adjustments through bargaining. We identify the preconditions or "pillars" of the system that define bargaining and negotiation in intergovernmental programs. This "open field" for negotiations over programs is a product of the noncentralized nature of the American federal system (Elazar 1984). The propensity to bargain or to seek mutual adjustment occurs within a social and political context that defines administrative federalism in ways that interact and even compete with legal concerns that govern federal processes. Although such administrative behavior has gained visibility since the days of federal program expansion in the United States in the 1960s, public administrators representing different governments have been able to use bargaining and negotiation as frontline approaches in the implementation of intergovernmental programs for most of U.S. history. As a result, the American public administrator operates in a setting that invites local innovative management through bargaining and adjustment through negotiation. Not only can the local manager seek favorable treatment in intergovernmental programs, but the system of intergovernmental relations in America encourages such activity.

Second, we demonstrate that bargaining and negotiating extend far beyond grant-in-aid programs. Just as there has been a tendency to view intergovernmental relations "predominantly if not exclusively in terms of fiscal relationships" (Wright 1988, 121), so too is there a propensity to equate bargaining and negotiation in terms of grants management. Our understanding of managing intergovernmental relations is derived almost exclusively from its application to grants-in-aid and the importance of bargaining between the financial donor and the recipient of the funds. As a result, this "monetary myopia and fiscal fixation" (Wright 1988, 121) in the managerial context provides an important but incomplete picture of contemporary intergovernmental management. We provide recent evidence of vertical intergovernmental administrative activity that includes regulatory, contractual, audit, and many other transactions.

Third, we suggest a set of research issues that heretofore have been unexamined. The public management field needs to broaden its understanding of the degree to which mutual adjustment contributes to program performance, either positively or negatively. There is a great deal more to bargaining and negotiating across governments than working out details of a grant program, but with few exceptions (e.g., Bardach 1977; Church and Nakamura 1993; Williams 1981) empirical documentation of such activity is minimal. . . .

Pillars of Bargaining and Negotiation

In this section we show that the prevalence of vertical interaction [is] based in four preconditions or pillars of administrative bargaining: (1) the importance of territory or place, (2) the tradition of a limited national bureaucracy, (3) the long-standing practice of simultaneous action across levels of government, and (4) consequent reciprocal, interactive administrative action.

The Importance of Place in American Politics and Administration

An elementary component of American political culture involves place or territory as the basis for political expression. Jurisdiction is conceived in terms of a specific territory with well-defined boundaries that are organized, in theory, to serve equally all of its residents. Elazar's (1994) study of the impact of space and culture in American government reveals that the United States never had the premodern experience of organizing on any other basis but on the principle that equality of political attachments should prevail within every territorial jurisdiction. He maintains that territorial democracy has been instrumental in offering opportunities for maintenance of necessary and proper diversity in the United States. It has also enabled elements of discrimination, thus bringing on the need for change through intergovernmental interaction, sometimes antagonistically and sometimes cooperatively.

State governments are the clearest examples of the impact of place. Once territorial colonies, their governments played key roles in the formation of the union and admission of new states under the Constitution. After admission to statehood each state was entitled to the same rights and powers as the original states, a de jure symmetry. They became the primary domestic policy and program engine, save a few functions like foreign affairs and defense, the monetary system, and interstate commerce. Even when the federal government became involved in a program area that affected states, their territorial imperatives were respected. For example, the building of the National Road in the first third of the nineteenth century, a federally funded project, paid maximum respect to state wishes in routing, and the states carried out the actual contracting and construction. Although there were many contested differences and negotiations, virtually all were settled with maximum respect for state-based concerns and interests (Wood 1996). The same pattern holds some two centuries later, and although the federal government has come to use its fiscal and legal powers more frequently to cut more deeply into state affairs, states and their administrators must still be recognized and respected as jurisdictions representing places within the federal system (Walker 2000).

Local administrations require a closer look, in that they do not possess the same constitutional status as states. Nevertheless, by tradition and practice, their space also engenders measures of respect. In his classic public administration textbook, first published in 1926, Leonard White reminds us that the historical roots of the American administrative system are found in the English institutions of local government, based on minimal functions and simple structures, in which "the great bulk of administrative work was done by the localities, not by the central state authorities" (1939, 18–19). Most administrative work was performed originally at the local level. Tocqueville observed that this local tradition is reflected as far back as the 1650s in New England. He described how "the independence of the township was the nucleus round which the local interests, passions, rights, and duties collected and clung. Inside the locality there was a real active political life that was completely democratic and republican" (1969, 44). Local control is thus a deep-seated American tradition.

Prefederation state constitutions recognized local control: "Far from valuing complete independence in a state of nature, Americans above all valued the communities in which they lived" (Lutz 1988, 71). Localities were expected to regulate safety and security within their borders. Most economic and social practices, even morals, were locally controlled. Everything from the heights of fences to the rights of individuals to live in communities was subject to local government intervention. As the nation transformed colonies into states and became federated in 1789, even more governments were created within governments (e.g., counties and special districts), and the sense of place emerged as an important value while governments necessarily interacted. . . .

[R]ecent research documents [s]how many cities operate collaboratively almost entirely in terms of how such activity benefits the jurisdiction (Agranoff and McGuire 2003a). Such jurisdiction-based management in the intergovernmental system is a clear manifestation of the relevance of place in American federalism and the effect of territory on administrative activity. Jurisdictional borders and influences are certainly intergovernmentally permeated, but they remain real. Because each unit in the federal system is to some degree a legally independent jurisdiction (or a legally chartered organization), it logically follows that some power is retained within a unit that has a program role. Many cities act on that power administratively for its own benefit.

Some observers suggest that the definition and meaning of place and territory are changing, perhaps even becoming less important for administrative affairs (Frederickson 1999). The theory of administrative conjunction argues that we are experiencing a redefinition of the relationship between citizens and their government, resulting in the declining relationship between jurisdiction and public management. The borders of jurisdictions increasingly are porous, so the problems that citizens want addressed are seldom contained in a single municipality. Residents often work in one city, shop in another city, and vote in still another; thus they have little social, political, or financial commitment to the jurisdictions in which they live. However, even as jurisdictional borders are becoming less relevant in defining problems, political leadership within jurisdictions is still more important than political leadership between the jurisdictions. It is this local, political linkage that maintains the stature of place and territory in intergovernmental administrative relations.

As a result, "place" has important meaning in the American system; it symbolizes community and reinforces the fragmented nature of American federalism. Indeed, to the extent that jurisdiction represents place, many "places" have been created: states, counties, municipalities and villages, special districts and rural townships. Each is a "fragment" and potential player in the game of administrative federalism.

Limited National Bureaucracy

The story of American historical ambivalence in concentrating political authority in the executive is well known. Neither the Jeffersonian model of dual but separate tiers nor the Hamiltonian top-down model completely won out. Americans' concerns, argues James Q. Wilson (1975), were over England's subversion of liberties, unjust taxation, weakening of the judiciary, stationing of standing armies, and extensive use of royal patronage at colonial expense. Except for taxation, which raised questions of representation, these grievances invoked administrative abuses of power. The reaction was a weakening of executive powers (Lutz 1988), legislative supremacy, and the separation of powers so that each branch could check the usurpation of the other. This system, Wilson concludes, went essentially unchanged in theory and unmodified in practice throughout the nation's first century. The federal government was mostly devoted to routine tasks (e.g., postal, customs) or temporary crises like military emergencies. Indeed, Tocqueville observed that Europeans who were accustomed to the close and constant presence of officials interfering into everything would experience "the absence of what we would call government or administration" and predicted that "the hand directing the social machine" would eventually go unnoticed by citizens (1969, 72).

Federal and state government changed in the nineteenth century. The "hidden" profile changed by the dawn of the twentieth century because of the growth, at congressional behest, of federal client-serving and regulatory agencies based in Washington and in the field. It was the early beginning of the American version of the welfare state (Skocpol 1995). In spite of the obvious growth in the size and scope of the national government, it was also, as historian Jon Teaford's (2002) study concludes, a period of state-level growth and centralization. When federal programming accelerated from the 1930s to the 1970s, federal requirements and federal program management further encouraged professionalization at the state level. As patronage was precluded for federal programs, education requirements for administrative offices and program workers were imposed, and in some cases these standards were extended to the local level (Derthick 1970). Furthermore, the municipal reform movement emerged within the first few decades of the twentieth century, making the United States among the first countries to professionalize local administration. The local government forms that emerged from this period were more responsive to diversity and more sensitive to client needs, including citizen participation, administrative decentralization, community relations, and social equity (Ross and Levine 2001, 187). The national bureaucracy is no longer as "limited" as it was during the first century of the American republic, but neither has it usurped the public preference for subnational action.

Americans continue to be "ambivalent about 'the state' and have never allowed the possibility for any such comprehensive regime" (Skocpol 1995, 33). The United States has never had a prefectural tradition, with its use of *tutelage* or prior approval power by the central state administration over local decisions. As Stephen Skowronek (1982) concludes, the U.S. national structure remains decentralized because national administrative structures have rarely supplanted the powers of state and local government and because Congress, with its state and local constituencies, has reinforced legislation that implements national policies at the state and local levels. Members of Congress traditionally fear central control and opt for the funding "carrot" or the remote controls of regulations, rather than have the federal government assume primary responsibility. The federal government thus follows the state/local highway model more than the central control exemplified by the postal service and its concentrated authority in Washington (Teaford 2002, 7). This multilayered model brings on the need for cooperative action.

Multilevel, Simultaneous Actions

The tradition of place and limited national bureaucracy does not mean that program responsibilities are strictly divided among territorial levels. Quite the contrary, since the 1960s when intergovernmental relations was made prominent by groups of scholars at the University of Chicago (Grodzins 1966) and the University of Minnesota (Anderson 1960), the concept of cooperative federalism and its successors laid dual federalism to a final rest (Agranoff 2001). The U.S. system has always been not only multilayered but also interdependent[.] ...

Elazar's (1962) historical study confirms that both federal grant and regulatory programs, along with interactive relations among government, were quite notable throughout the nineteenth century. The work of Skocpol (1995) on the development of U.S. social welfare policies indicates that targeted programs for veterans were enacted as far back as after the Civil War, well before national social security in the 1930s. Similar programs for women were created early in the twentieth century across the states. These programs also generated actions at various levels.

Reaching back to the years of settlement, Ylvisaker says that local government was a complex of local, state (territorial), and national action and that "at no time has either the state or the federal government retired from the field and left local units to enjoy complete or unremitted control over the community's affairs" (quoted in Grodzins 1966, 18). The resultant condition is the continuing need for action by two or more governments operating within the same program sphere[.] ... A more active federal government and the aforementioned state centralization have ensured that the federal and state governments have a presence in virtually every community, if not by their offices, then clearly by their programs and their legal/regulatory functions. The need for some forms of mutual (if not cooperative or joint) action often arises. ...

Reciprocal Administrative Action

The matrix-like character of the American situation, coupled with localism and the absence of a large federal bureaucratic presence, inevitably means that some actions will have to be worked out administratively. Many actors working in the same spheres implement federal and state programs. ...

Clearly the era of cooperative federalism represented a management based on federal (and state) specified funding, standards, and minimal supervision over state and local planning and performance. ...

Grodzins (1966) concludes in his work on recreation administration that local contacts with state and federal administrators led to considerable variation in action and treatment, leaving wide avenues of administrative discretion. To a considerable degree, local success in advancing the interests of local government depends on local officials taking advantage of what the federal government has to offer and is willing to advance and accept. The opportunity is universal, but not every local administration partakes[.] ... In this regard, local officials and administrators, working with local citizens and groups, played five essential reciprocal roles: (1) acquirer of external aid for local needs; (2) adapter of external government functions and services to local conditions; (3) experimenter with new functions and services (or new versions of traditional ones); (4) initiator of governmental programs that spread across state and nation; and (5) underlying the others, provider of a means by which a local community can pay the "ante" necessary to "sit in the game"—that is, to secure an effective voice in governmental decisions of local impact (Elazar 1961, 24–28). It is exercising that voice as a function of administrative federalism that brings on the reciprocal action. To the extent that differences arise, even minor ones, bargaining and negotiation come into play.

Bargaining and Negotiating Beyond Grants

Many jurisdictions play the game of bargaining and negotiation on a frequent basis. Such activity occurs in many different contexts and for many different purposes. The most common types of intergovernmental bargaining activity take place within the context of a grant or contract program, although it is very much alive in regulatory and other programs. We have referred elsewhere to this type of management as "donor–recipient" management (Agranoff and McGuire 2003). Bargaining can be large scale, where stakes are high and political action is just as important, if not more so, as administration. Jurisdictions also bargain over daily, routine problems, which are no less significant for the manager.

Grants management has provided the primary focus and locus of intergovernmental management in the literature. It emanated from the expanded system of grants-in-aid in the 1960s. Conceptually, Jeffrey Pressman (1975) initially captured this type of management in his study of federal aid to cities. He reminded us that "donor and recipient need each other, but neither has the ability to control fully the actions of the other. Thus, the aid process takes the form of bargaining between partly cooperative, partly antagonistic, and mutually dependent sets of actors" (1975, 106–7). Helen Ingram's (1977) study of environmental programs concluded that programs are not necessarily instruments of federal control but, rather, opportunities to bargain. Similarly, Liebschutz (1991) depicts an intergovernmental fiscal system in New York as one defined by bargaining and negotiation. Whereas federal officials would like to bind state and local program managers to federal policy, subnational governments seek the maximum possible leeway to pursue their own separate goals and objectives with federal help. In social services programs, as Richard Elmore concludes, "this give and take has become a managerial strategy in the implementation process. [The] bargain is a two-way affair, inherently different from hierarchical control. A contract is not an instrument of coercion" (1985, 36). It is a managerial game that, according to Walter Williams's study of manpower and community development, "requires . . . subtle skill and much knowledge about the roles, the players, and available strategies in the federal–local bargaining situation" (1981, 197). . . .

Management research based solely in grants and the relationship between the donor and the recipient stands in contrast to historical evidence from Daniel Elazar's (1962) research on federal–state cooperation in the nineteenth century. . . .

A 2002-2003 disagreement regarding Medicaid is illustrative of high-stakes intergovernmental bargaining (Agranoff 2003a). In early 2003, the Bush administration proposed a basic change to the Medicaid program: states would have the option to enter into a new flexibility agreement. Although mandatory recipient coverage for the poor and handicapped would remain, states would have broader powers to expand, reduce, or eliminate benefits for the other recipients, particularly those identified as "medically needy." States would be given flexibility to design private health plan "buy ins" for these Medicaid-eligible recipients. Funding for those states that opted into the program change would be increased by a total of $3.25 billion for fiscal year 2004 and a total of $12.7 billion over seven years. These amounts then would be tied to a fixed state allocation. If program costs go down, the states would benefit from the added payments. In exchange for the flexibility, however, states would have to give up the existing open-ended funding allocations to meet their spending.

At the National Governors Association Winter Meeting in Washington, D.C., in February 2003, there was not great enthusiasm for the Bush proposal. Governors estimated that the long-sought-after flexibility to reduce costs would only affect about 15 million of the 45 million Medicaid recipients. They also expressed concern that the proposal would eventually cap federal Medicaid contributions, leading to large financial burdens for the states at the end of the seven-year period. Medicaid costs, it was pointed out, are unlikely to go down because of the rising costs of prescription drugs, medical technology, and elderly and disabled care. Most states, while picking up around half of all costs, thus wish to maintain the open-ended nature of Medicaid funding. Republican governors argued that more recognition should be given to the fact that every dollar in state cuts would save the federal treasury one to two dollars, thus complete flexibility should be handed over immediately. One Republican governor suggested that the federal government allow the states to keep the federal money they save and that Medicare, a social insurance program primarily for the elderly, should assume the entire cost of health care for those elderly who are on Medicaid (about six million people). Some Democratic governors and members of the House and Senate have called for temporary increases in the federal share of Medicaid. The governors could not agree on a Medicaid reform position at the meeting, so they established a bipartisan committee of eight governors to negotiate with the administration and Congress on Medicaid revisions. After months of negotiating, the committee agreed that its disagreements were too fundamental to come up with a proposal. Nevertheless, the Medicaid negotiations represent one of the most visible examples of high-stakes bargaining.

Intergovernmental bargaining and negotiation can also be less visible and more routine. The No Child Left Behind Act of 2001 changed the distribution of 1965 ESEA (Elementary and Secondary Education Act) funds from a broad-based distribution program to a performance-based standards program backed up by penalties, in order to achieve testing, accountability, and transferability levels. To many states it amounts to a shift from broad age-based funding to a mandated single model for performance testing, which essentially constitutes a direct order that reduces state discretion over their educational systems (Krane 2002). States are already bargaining with the U.S. Department of Education to retain testing procedures that are more stringent than the federal model, other states are bargaining to test in more areas than in reading and math, and still others are asking to test in the school years they are currently testing. Their negotiating aim is to maintain the integrity of their preexisting systems and to avoid unnecessary costs. Along with "maximum flexibility," states are also asking for more funding, because only about one-half of the amount proposed by the administration has been appropriated.

In one local government study many examples of this kind of bargaining behavior emerged (Agranoff and McGuire 2003). The city of Garfield Heights, Ohio, was known by Cuyahoga County Community Development Block Grant program officials for submitting more than the limit of two local project applications, year after year. When the mayor and city grant coordinator were called on to reduce the normal submitted number down from as [many] as six applications to the required two, Garfield Heights officials took the opportunity to ensure they received both grants (whereas other cities normally received one of two submissions) and to negotiate the most favorable terms for each of the two allotted. In a more lighthearted example, Ithaca, Michigan, once allowed [the] U.S. Environmental Protection Agency to do some experimental water testing that the agency had requested. After the testing, [the] EPA in Chicago wrote city officials a letter informing them that the testing was completed, that they would hear the results in some months, and that [the] EPA "might charge the city a fee for the testing." The mayor and city manager fired back a letter that included the following sentence: "Ithaca reserves the right to charge EPA for the water run through the testing source, as metered by our public utilities department." Other than the test results, there was no further EPA contact with the city.

Often the stakes are considerably higher. Woodstock, Illinois, engaged in substantial interaction with the U.S. Environmental Protection Agency regarding a Superfund Unilateral Executive Order that designated the city as the "Potentially Responsible Party" of a municipal-owned landfill containing contaminated materials. After reaching an agreement with Allied Signal Company to pick up the major out-of-pocket costs for the cleanup, the city hired a consultant who prepared a proposal containing over fifty of its own mitigation measures and sent them to [the] EPA in a letter. [The] EPA rejected the city's solution out of hand and maintained that the original order had to be followed. Then the city's attorney requested a consultant–city manager–city attorney face-to-face meeting with officials in Chicago. Several meetings and detailed negotiations followed until an agreement was reached several months later. The city would absorb the costs of initial site preparation and clearing and subsequently through "pump and treatment of the waste and maintenance of the site" for twenty years. City crews instead of a private contractor could do the work. The city manager estimated that the repeated exchanges led to a solution that was just under half of the cost of the initial EPA order. . . .

A Renewed Research Agenda

The brief examples of the kinds of intergovernmental bargaining and negotiation that occur suggest that such activity is inherent in the U.S. federal system. As demonstrated, a rich literature of empirical, largely descriptive research developed throughout the twentieth century, but a great deal more must be known about the role and impact of bargaining and negotiation. [The authors then sketch the kinds of research they think would be most valuable.—Ed.]

Conclusion

Intergovernmental administration has become a mighty complicated exercise in the United States. To the seasoned manager it is much more involved and protracted than the federalism stories of grantsmanship, regulatory burdens, and an occasional audit exception. Managing also includes contracts, loans, cooperative agreements, reciprocal services agreements, shared or joint investments, procurement of goods and services, personal and political contacts, and lobbying for program and policy changes. As a result, this type of administration is part of the theory of governance that "comprehends lateral relations, interinstitutional relations . . . and a general institutional fragmentation" (2003, 226), which Fredrickson and Smith say call for comprehension within the disarticulated state. Its strength, they conclude, is the attempt to create an explicitly empirical explanation of the situation. It is in this spirit and orientation that an explicit focus on bargaining and negotiation within the U.S. intergovernmental system can add to public administration theory.

The paradox of the study of intergovernmental bargaining and negotiation is clear. A vast literature exists on the historical and contemporary prevalence of bargaining as quintessentially American—or at least highly "contextual"—yet some administrators are not aware of its potential, and many scholars still view intergovernmental activity in terms of seeking grants and complying with regulations exclusively. The literature documents the long-standing significance of bargaining, but few systematic data exist to make the kinds of generalizations that are needed to advance understanding of this aspect of public management, in either the frequency and nature of the undertaking or how it operates. The body of knowledge that involves cross-agency, cross-jurisdictional management should include the theory and practice of intergovernmental bargaining. The field of public management has jumped headfirst into studying interdependence, adjustment, and joint activity in horizontal policy networks, yet such characteristics of the vertical intergovernmental system persist and are relatively ignored.

In 1938, Jane Perry Clark, an astute observer of the intergovernmental system, argued that "much of the cooperation between the federal and state governments has been found in the sea of governmental activity without any chart, compass, or guiding star, for cooperation has been unplanned and uncorrelated with other activities of government even in the same field" (1938, 7). Her assessment still applies to intergovernmental relations today. Although she was somewhat hopeful that general patterns of intergovernmental activity could be discerned, there is more to intergovernmental bargaining than meets the eye, and there is still so much more to learn about it.

References

Agranoff, Robert. 2001. Managing within the matrix: Do collaborative intergovernmental relations exist? *Publius: The Journal of Federalism* 31 (2): 31–56.

———. 2003a. Fiscal policies and a weak economy fray the American federal fabric. *Federations* 3:7–10.

———. 2003b. *Leveraging networks: A guide for public managers working across organizations*. Arlington, VA: IBM Endowment for the Business of Government.

Agranoff, Robert, and Michael McGuire. 2003. *Collaborative public management: New strategies for local governments*. Washington, DC: Georgetown University Press.

Anderson, William. 1960. *Intergovernmental relations in review*. Minneapolis: University of Minnesota Press.

Bardach, Eugene. 1977. *The implementation game*. Cambridge, MA: MIT Press.

Church, Thomas W., and Robert T. Nakamura. 1993. *Cleaning up the mess: Implementation strategies in superfund*. Washington, DC: Brookings.

Clark, Jane Perry. 1938. *The rise of a new federalism*. New York: Columbia University Press.

Derthick, Martha. 1970. *The influence of federal grants*. Cambridge, MA: Harvard University Press.

de Tocqueville, Alexis. 1969. *Democracy in America*. Trans. George Lawrence. Ed. J. P. Mayer. New York: Doubleday.

Elazar, Daniel J. 1961. *Illinois local government*. Urbana: University of Illinois Press.

———. 1962. *The American partnership: Intergovernmental co-operation in the nineteenth century United States*. Chicago: University of Chicago Press.

———. 1984. *American federalism: A view from the states*. New York: Crowell.

———. 1994. *The American mosaic*. Boulder, CO: Westview Press.

Elmore, Richard F. 1985. Forward and backward mapping: Reversible logic in the analysis of public policy. In *Policy implementation in federal and unitary systems*, ed. Kenneth Hanf and Theo A. J. Toonen, 33–70. Dordrecht, the Netherlands: Martinus Nijhoff Publishers.

Frederickson, H. George. 1999. The repositioning of American public administration. *P.S. Political Science and Politics* 32 (4): 701–11.

Frederickson, H. George, and Kevin Smith. 2003. *A public administration theory primer*. Boulder, CO: Westview Press.

Grodzins, Morton. 1966. *The American system*. Chicago: Rand McNally.

Ingram, Helen. 1977. Policy implementation through bargaining: The case of federal grants-in-aid. *Public Policy* 25 (4): 499–526.

Krane, Dale. 2002. The state of American federalism, 2001–2002: Resilience in response to crisis. *Publius: The Journal of Federalism* 32:1–28.

Liebschutz, Sarah F. 1991. *Bargaining under federalism: Contemporary New York.* Albany: State University of New York Press.

Lutz, Donald S. 1988. *The origins of American constitutionalism.* Baton Rouge: Louisiana State University Press.

McGuire, Michael. 2002. Managing networks: Propositions on what managers do and why they do it. *Public Administration Review* 62 (5): 599–609.

Pressman, Jeffrey L. 1975. *Federal programs and city politics: The dynamics of the aid process in Oakland.* Berkeley: University of California Press.

Ross, Bernard H., and Myron A. Levine. 2001. *Urban politics.* 6th ed. Itasca, IL: F. E. Peacock.

Skocpol, Theda. 1995. *Social policy in the United States: Future possibilities in historical perspective.* Princeton, NJ: Princeton University Press.

Skowronek, Stephen. 1982. *Building a new American state: The expansion of national administrative capabilities.* New York: Cambridge University Press.

Teaford, Jon C. 2002. *The rise of the states: Evolution of American government.* Baltimore, MD: Johns Hopkins University Press.

Walker, David B. 2000. *The rebirth of federalism.* 2d ed. New York: Chatham House.

White, Leonard D. 1939. *Introduction to the study of public administration.* Rev. ed. New York: Macmillan.

Williams, Walter W. 1981. *Government by agency: Administering grants-in-aid programs.* New York: Academic Press.

Wilson, James Q. 1975. The rise of the bureaucratic state. *The Public Interest* 41:77–103.

Wood, Joseph S. 1996. The idea of the National Road. In *The National Road*, ed. Karl Raitz, 93–122. Baltimore, MD: Johns Hopkins University Press.

Wright, Deil S. 1988. *Understanding intergovernmental relations.* 3d ed. Belmont, CA: Wadsworth.

Part IV

Review Questions

1. The ACIR commission rejected its draft report on mandates by a 13–7 vote. Among those in opposition to the proposed changes included in the report was Citizens for Sensible Safeguards, a coalition of approximately 250 organizations interested in enforcing the requirements of federal policy on such subjects as the environment, disabilities policy, and labor standards. Why would such a group oppose the suggested mandate changes? OMB Watch, another opposition group, argued that

   > federal "mandates" are widely misunderstood in today's political climate. In the abstract, they are often condemned as burdensome, inflexible, and generally unneeded. But when the debate shifts from generalities to the specifics of particular programs, public support for wholesale deregulation usually shifts dramatically. Everyone favors eliminating burdensome and unneeded regulations. No one is for eliminating needed public protections that safeguard our livelihoods, environment, health, and safety.

   Explain this statement.

2. What does the fate of the ACIR recommendations suggest about the relative strength in national politics of functional interest groups vis-à-vis the public interest groups that represent the interests of state and local governments?

3. Does the controversy in regard to mandates show that any effort to separate intergovernmental "politics" from "administration" is bound to be unsuccessful? Why or why not?

4. Posner argues that *many* actors and forces have contributed to a shift in the system of intergovernmental relations from "voluntaristic" to "coercive" tools of federal action. What does he mean by these types of tools? What actors and forces were significant to this shift? Why?

5. In fact, Posner argues that state and local officials themselves have been complicit in the accretion of mandates over time. How so? Link this line

of analysis to Derthick's explanation of how influence is exercised via grants (see Part II).

6. Using Posner's analysis, as well as some of the readings from Part III, develop a prognosis about the longer-term impact of the Unfunded Mandates Reform Act of 1995. Explain the reasons behind your expectations.

7. Posner indicates that policy "nationalization" has developed, in particular, through *mandates* for reasons specific to the United States. What is the logic behind his statement? He suggests that burdensome mandates have nevertheless been the products of "consensual" politics. Why and how? How does this picture fit with ideas about how policy is made in this country? Are there ways that the appeal of the Republican "Contract with America" of the 1990s, containing a commitment to *end* unfunded mandates, might also provide evidence for the kind of politics *driving* mandate creation? What are the implications for the models of federalism and intergovernmental relations sketched in Part I, including those outlined by Wright?

8. Some argue that the unfunded mandates emanating from Washington over the years are a product of the myopic priorities of the political party in control of Congress during most of that period, the Democrats. Others suggest that the main problem is that "Washington" seems uniquely blind to the costs and challenges faced by other levels of government. Consider Nivola's depiction of the challenges faced by U.S. cities (reading no. 20 in Part III). In light of the readings in this part, what does the evidence he offers indicate about which depiction is more correct?

9. Agranoff and McGuire depict an administrative terrain of intergovernmental relations in which thousands, if not millions, of public managers operate in several directions on technically complex programmatic issues. Is this reality a reassuring triumph of expertise in addressing issues of extraordinary complexity and interdependence or does it represent the victory of bureaucrats over citizens and political leaders in the struggle for control of the intergovernmental pattern? Can both conclusions be correct?

Part V

EMERGING INTERGOVERNMENTAL
ISSUES AND CHALLENGES

The readings presented thus far document the persistent salience of intergovernmental matters in American public life. A few of the authors have also offered hints and a bit of speculation about what might happen in the near- to mid-term future. This is not so surprising, since a number of developments have raised the topic of intergovernmental relations to a prominent position in domestic policy discussions today.

The initial chapter of this book provides a review of many of these. The selections in this final part focus in particular on a set of large and important intergovernmental issues that surely must be addressed in the years ahead.

The first two readings deal with two of the kinds of challenges to the intergovernmental system that have been capturing front-page attention in recent years: large natural disasters and threats from terrorism and related "homeland security" concerns. In both cases, there is a natural tendency for policymakers to consider centralizing more power at the national level—particularly given the need for coordinated responses and the fact that the consequences of mistakes can be horribly costly.

In the first selection (no. 25), Jonathan Walters and Donald Kettl review the intergovernmental system's handling of the Hurricane Katrina episode as it devastated New Orleans and surrounding areas in 2005. Walters and Kettl suggest that the Katrina fiasco serves as a high-profile example of how the several kinds and levels of government respond to "cataclysmic events"—whether caused by avian flu, earthquake, hurricane, or terror. They document the potential for disaster in such cases and note the irony that the political party traditionally associated with decentralization from Washington proposed in this instance a militarization of disaster response. They point to the need for a balanced consideration of the capacities and responsibilities of the many governments involved and emphasize the critical place of that much-ballyhooed goal—coordination—in crafting the right kind of intergovernmental design for such troubling challenges.

The second reading (no. 26), also by Donald Kettl, moves the focus explicitly to the broad terrain of homeland security. He notes, correctly, that everyone cares about this subject but few discuss or consider its specifically intergovernmental dimensions. Much of the public consideration of threats to security occurs in and around Washington, and while the nation now has a huge cabinet-level Department of Homeland Security, a great deal of the action must necessarily take place at subnational levels, especially in and by localities: first responses, planning for schools and school systems, local public health, and the like. The scope and complexity of the issue strain both governmental capacity and possibilities for coordination, and Kettl outlines some of the steps that he believes are necessary to build an effective intergovernmental approach.

The third excerpt (no. 27) moves to the context and implications of another large-scale development: the increasingly globalized pattern of worldwide interdependence—of business, markets, economies, standards, information, and political forces. Partly as a product of these shifts and partly due to increased recognition of the global impact of decisions made by individual governments recently, a whole series of international agreements on matters like trade policy, economic cooperation, and environmental protection have begun to extend the already complicated American array of ties further—to countless others around the world. And as transnational influences expand, our understanding of the nature and dynamics of intergovernmental links from a U.S. perspective must also undergo reformulation.

Laurence J. O'Toole Jr. and Kenneth I. Hanf show how extensively the internationalization of governance has shaped today's problem-solving responses at national, state, and local levels. Indeed, they suggest that the "system" has now become a complex web with a diffuse additional level, as the United States and other nations bind themselves with other countries in the interest of collective problem solving for challenges that cannot be confined by national borders. They emphasize in particular how the increasingly dense global links shape and are shaped by the actions of public administrators, but the more general theme is that decision makers of all sorts and even those in the most local of settings are now insinuated into an extraordinarily complex, yet sometimes effective, pattern of far-reaching ties with others. Their analysis reframes many of the inherited ideas about U.S.-style federalism and intergovernmental relations and implicitly raises questions about how we should think about the pattern, its consequences, its appropriate management, and its possible improvement.

Given these sorts of enormous issues, and the pressing domestic agenda on such diverse and divisive matters as health care, social policy, environmental protection, sustainable energy, tax policy, and economic growth, how can the nation map a huge and growing agenda onto a sensible overall intergovernmental design? Jonathan Walters (no. 28) approaches this tough question by noting that, perhaps somewhat paradoxically, intergovernmental challenges emerge everywhere but are rarely considered systematically anywhere—or at least anywhere prominent and influential enough to attract the attention of most key stakeholders. He documents the ways that myriad policy arenas, like welfare reform or environmental regulation or Medicaid funding, tend to generate significant repercussions for other governments and their citizens, but in rather haphazard fashions. Walters notes the absence of the right kind of forum for focusing attention on the shape of the intergovernmental forest, for all the issue-specific trees that demand urgent, immediate, and repeated consideration. Whereas the old U.S. Advisory Commission on Intergovernmental Relations performed this task for a few decades, it became the victim of its own nonpartisan attention to the system itself rather than to the coalitions of political actors who collectively negotiate the details. In the twenty-first century, Walters argues, a respected forum for intergovernmental analysis is urgently needed, and he considers where and how such a platform might be constructed. In asking, "Does Anyone Care?" he offers a challenge and call to action to all bound together in this modern, or postmodern, version of James Madison's "compound republic."

25

The Katrina Breakdown
Jonathan Walters and Donald F. Kettl

When Hurricane Katrina hit New Orleans, only one thing disintegrated as fast as the earthen levees that were supposed to protect the city, and that was the intergovernmental relationship that is supposed to connect local, state and federal officials before, during and after such a catastrophe.

In sifting through the debris of the disaster response, the first question is why intergovernmental cooperation broke down so completely. While it's hard even at this point to get an official accounting of exactly what happened, clearly there were significant communication and coordination problems at all levels of government. At the moment, much time and effort is being spent assigning culpability—for a lack of preparation, delayed decision making, bureaucratic tie-ups and political infighting—to individuals and agencies. But in the end, such investigations may produce little that is of widespread practical use.

What is more critical, and has significant implications for the future of emergency management in the United States, is the need to explicitly and thoroughly define governments' roles and responsibilities so that officials in other jurisdictions don't suffer the same sort of meltdown in the next natural or man-made disaster. The lurching tactical responses to the terrorist attacks of 2001 and [2005 's] rash of major hurricanes only underline the truly fundamental issue: how to sort out who should do what—and how to make sure the public sector is ready to act when the unexpected but inevitable happens.

It won't be easy. Some in the federal government clearly feel that if they're going to be blamed for failures—failures that they ascribe at least in part to state and local officials—then they'd prefer a system where the federal government has the option of being much more preemptive in

From *Governing*, December 2005, 20–25. Reprinted with the permission of the authors.

handling large-scale domestic disasters. States as a whole, though, are not going to go along with any emergency management plan that involves the feds declaring something like martial law. They would much prefer that existing protocols be continued and the Federal Emergency Management Agency regain its independence from the Department of Homeland Security and be led by experienced professionals rather than political appointees.

A Growing Federal Role

In fact, the history of disaster response and recovery in the United States has witnessed an ever-increasing federal role. On April 22, 1927, President Calvin Coolidge named a special cabinet-level committee headed by Commerce Secretary Herbert Hoover to deal with the massive flooding that was ravaging communities up and down the Mississippi River Valley that year. The scene, described in John M. Barry's highly topical chronicle, "Rising Tide: The Great Mississippi Flood of 1927 and How It Changed America," arguably represents the beginning of the modern era of intergovernmental disaster response. (It also represents the first clear attempt to politicize federal disaster response, with Hoover consciously riding his performance during the disaster all the way to the White House.)

In 1950, the federal government began trying to formalize intergovernmental roles and responsibilities through the Federal Civil Defense Act, which defined the scope and type of assistance that the federal government would extend to states and localities after certain kinds of disasters or emergencies (although Congress had been offering financial aid to states and localities in a piecemeal fashion since the early 1800s). In 1979, President Jimmy Carter created the Federal Emergency Management Agency, largely in response to governors' complaints about the fragmented nature of federal disaster planning and assistance. And in 1988, Congress passed the Robert T. Stafford Disaster Relief Act, which outlined the protocols for disaster declaration and what sort of intergovernmental response would follow.

From 1989 to 1992, a succession of disasters, including the Loma Prieta earthquake in California and hurricanes Hugo in South Carolina and Andrew in Florida, put the whole issue of intergovernmental emergency response in the public hot seat, notes Tom Birkland, director of the Center for Policy Research at the Rockefeller College of Public Affairs and Policy. In particular, the disasters highlighted the federal government's slow-footed and bureaucratic response in the wake of such catastrophic events. (To be sure, such events were also teaching state and local governments plenty about *their* emergency response capabilities.) That, in turn, led to a major turnaround at FEMA, with the appointment of James Lee Witt, the first FEMA director to arrive on the job with actual state emergency management experience.

In general, two things were going on around the increasing federal role in emergency readiness and response, Birkland says. States and localities were getting hooked on federal money—especially for recovery. But American presidents were also discovering the political benefits of declaring disasters, which allowed them to liberally sprinkle significant amounts of cash around various states and localities in distress. "That spending grew considerably under the Clinton administration," says Birkland. "And it created the expectation of federal government largesse. Federal spending, however, was always meant to supplement and not supplant state and local spending."

Local Response

But if the federal role in disaster response and recovery has increased—along with expectations of federal help—emergency management experts at all levels still agree on the basics of existing emergency response protocol: All emergencies are, initially at least, local—or local and state—events. "For the first 48 to 72 hours, it's understood that local and state first responders are principally responsible," says Bill Jenkins, director of the Homeland Security and Justice Issues Group, which is currently looking into the intergovernmental response to Katrina. "The feds come in as requested after that."

The extent to which the local-state-federal response ramps up depends on a host of factors, including the size of the incident and what plans and agreements are in place prior to any event. It also very much depends on the capacity of the governments involved. Some local and state governments have the ability to deal with disasters on their own and seem less inclined to ask for outside help. Others seem to hit the intergovernmental panic button more quickly. But whichever it is, say those on the front line of emergency response, how various governmental partners in emergency response and recovery are going to respond shouldn't be a surprise-filled adventure. Key players at every level of government should have a very good idea of what each will be expected to do or provide when a particular disaster hits.

Most important to the strength of the intergovernmental chain are solid relationships among those who might be called upon to work closely together in times of high stress. "You don't want to meet someone for the first time while you're standing around in the rubble," says Jarrod Bernstein, spokesman for the New York City Office of Emergency Management. "You want to meet them during drills and exercises." In New York, says Bernstein, the city has very tight relationships with state and federal officials in a variety of agencies. "They're involved in all our planning and all our drills. They have a seat at all the tabletop exercises we do."

During those exercises, says Bernstein, federal, state and local officials establish and agree on what their respective jobs will be when a "big one" hits. Last summer, for example, the city worked with FEMA, the U.S. Department of Health and Human Services, the Federal Bureau of Investigation and New York State health and emergency response officials on an exercise aimed at collecting 8 million doses of medicine and distributing them throughout the city in a 48-hour window. "What we were looking at is how we'd receive medical stockpiles from the federal government, break them down and push them out citywide. There is a built-in federal component to that plan," Bernstein says.

No Plan B

While pre-plans and dry runs are all well and good, they're not much use if not taken seriously, however. In 2004, FEMA and Louisiana's Office of Homeland Security and Emergency Preparedness conducted a tabletop exercise, called Hurricane Pam, that simulated a Category 3 storm hitting and flooding New Orleans. It identified a huge gap in disaster planning: An estimated 100,000 people wouldn't be able to get out of the city without assistance. As is standard in emergency management practice, it is the locality's responsibility—at least initially—to evacuate residents, unless other partners are identified beforehand.

Critics of Mayor Ray Nagin say he failed to follow up aggressively on the finding. Last spring, the city floated the notion that it would rely primarily on the faith-based community to organize and mobilize caravans for those without cars or who needed special assistance getting out of the city. The faith-based community balked, however, citing liability issues. The city never came up with a Plan B.

Meanwhile, the Department of Homeland Security had great confidence in its 426-page "all-hazards" National Response Plan. Unveiled last January, it "establishes standardized training, organization and communications procedures for multi-jurisdictional interaction; clearly identifies authority and leadership responsibilities; enables incident response to be handled at the lowest possible organizational and jurisdictional level; ensures the seamless integration of the federal government when an incident exceeds state or local capabilities; and provides the means to swiftly deliver federal support in response to catastrophic incidents."

Katrina was its first test. And in the wake of the Category 4 storm and subsequent flooding, the city's vital resources—communications, transportation, supplies and manpower—were quickly overwhelmed. But DHS Secretary Michael Chertoff waited until 24 hours after the levees were breached to designate the hurricane as an "incident of national significance—requiring an extensive and well-coordinated response by federal, state, local, tribal and nongovernmental authorities to save lives, minimize damage and provide the basis for long-term community and economic recovery."

The nation—indeed the world—bore painful witness to its failure. "There are mechanisms and protocols set up as part of the National Response Plan, and those were not followed," says John R. Harrald, director of the Institute for Crisis, Disaster and Risk Management at George Washington University. Harrald notes that under the response plan, one of the first things that's supposed to happen is the rapid activation of a joint operations center to coordinate the intergovernmental response. In Louisiana, that didn't happen quickly enough, he says.

Calling in the Troops

As a result of Katrina, and to a lesser extent hurricanes Rita and Wilma, the general citizenry and elected leaders at all levels of government, as well as emergency responders up and down the chain of command, are demanding a comprehensive review of how local, state and federal governments work (or don't work) together.

Part of that discussion has to include what to do when a state or local government's ability to prepare, respond or to ask for help is either impaired or wiped out altogether. "The question is what do you do when state and local capacity fails for one reason or another, either because they're overwhelmed or they're incompetent," says GWU's

Harrald. "Do we have a system that allows us to scale up adequately or do we need a system where we can bring the military in sooner but that doesn't give away state and local control?"

Bill Leighty, Virginia Governor Mark Warner's chief of staff, who volunteered to spend two weeks in Louisiana helping manage the state response to Katrina, says he thinks there needs to be a serious intergovernmental discussion about when, for example, it might be appropriate to involve the military more directly in a domestic crisis. It is a position born of watching FEMA in action, versus what he saw of the military while he was in New Orleans. FEMA's bureaucratic approach to every item it provided or action it took was, at times, brutally exasperating, says Leighty. "But when you tell the 82nd Airborne, 'Secure New Orleans,' they come in and they know exactly what to do and it gets done."

Even some long-time New Orleans residents, who watched helplessly as looters rampaged through parts of the city, say they wouldn't have minded at all if the military had stepped in to restore order. "There are times when people are overwhelmed," says Frank Cilluffo, director of the Homeland Security Policy Institute at George Washington University, "and they don't care what color uniform is involved in coming to the rescue—red, blue or green."

However, both Kathleen Babineaux Blanco, the Democratic governor of Louisiana, and Haley Barbour, the Republican governor of Mississippi, strenuously objected to requests from the White House to give the Pentagon command over their states' National Guard troops. And President George W. Bush's suggestion of a quick resort to the military in future disasters stunned many observers, including those in his own party. In a television address from New Orleans, he argued that only the armed forces were "capable of massive logistical operations on a moment's notice."

But governors were aghast at the idea that the military would become America's first responders. In a *USA Today* poll, 36 of 38 governors (including brother Jeb Bush) opposed the plan. Michigan Governor Jennifer Granholm put it bluntly: "Whether a governor is a Republican or Democrat, I would expect the response would be, 'Hell no.'" For one blogger, the worry was "How long before a creek flooding in a small town in Idaho will activate the 82d Airborne Division?"

Bush grabbed the military option in part because of the poor performance of state and local governments. Indeed, everyone breathed a sigh of relief when Coast Guard Admiral Thad Allen arrived to assume command.

Part of the explanation also lies in public opinion polls. A Pew Research Center survey just after the storm revealed that nearly half of those surveyed believed state and local governments had done a fair or poor job—and there was no partisan difference on that conclusion. That meant the smart political play for Bush, although he didn't fare much better in the poll, was to suggest that the military might have to do what state and local governments could not.

That idea, of course, could scarcely be further from the strategy the Republicans had spent a generation building. The Richard Nixon–Ronald Reagan model of new federalism revolved around giving the states more autonomy and less money. But faced with the need to do something—and lacking any alternative—Bush reached back to Lyndon Johnson's Great Society philosophy of an expanded role for the federal government.

But Bush's plan to push the military into a first-response role was clearly less a broad policy strategy than a tactic to find a safe haven in the post-Katrina blame game. That became clear in November, when he announced his avian flu initiative. In that plan, he penciled in a heavy role for state and local public health officials.

Control and Contention

Some believe there is a middle ground when it comes to issues of authority and autonomy. James A. Stever, director of the Center for Integrated Homeland Security and Crisis Management at the University of Cincinnati, says he and colleagues had forwarded a paper to the former head of Homeland Security, Tom Ridge, outlining the concept of "homeland restoration districts." The idea is to have established criteria for when a more robust federal disaster response might be appropriate. Recovery districts would allow for ad hoc federal takeovers of specific geographic areas when appropriate, says Stever, rather than creating some new, overriding national response protocol that calls for broad federal preemption of local and state authority.

But sifting through such ideas—and the others that are sure to surface—is going to mean rekindling the sort of conversation about intergovernmental coordination and cooperation that Washington hasn't seen in a long time. Whether the current Congress and administration will be willing to conduct that conversation isn't clear. State and local officials, for their part, have been called in by Congress to testify on how the intergovernmental response to disasters ought to go.

But such sessions have frequently had the familiar ring of both state and local tensions over who controls federal funding, as well as a little tin-cup rattling.

For example, in testimony before the House Homeland Security Committee, David Wallace, mayor of Sugar Land, Texas, argued that the first lesson learned in the wake of Katrina is that local governments should have more control over how federal homeland security first-responder money should be spent. "There was a real concern from the beginning that an over-reliance by the federal government on a state-based distribution system for first responder resources and training would be slow and result in serious delays in funding reaching high-threat, high-risk population areas." Wallace concluded his testimony with a request for federal funding for what he describes as Regional Logistics Centers, designed to bring local regional resources to bear in the immediate aftermath of disasters.

Nor is it only touchy issues of funding and control related to readi-ness and response that need discussing, points out Paul Posner, who spent years as a GAO intergovernmental affairs analyst. "There's other knotty issues that cause a lot of intergovernmental friction, like federal insurance policies, local building codes and state land use policies." These are key issues that Posner points out all influence how vulnerable certain places are to disasters in the first place.

From hurricanes and pandemics to earthquakes and terrorism, the United States is grappling with the prospect of a host of cataclysmic events. Taken individually, most communities face a small chance of being hit, but experts agree that it's not a matter of "if" but "when" another large-scale disaster will occur somewhere in the United States. As Katrina so powerfully illustrated, a fragmented intergovernmental response can be disastrous.

26

Homeland Security: The Federalism Challenge
Donald F. Kettl

The Role of Local Government in Homeland Security

. . . [T]he one piece that strikes me as the missing link in the discussions at the federal level about homeland security is the question of federalism. I say that . . . because all homeland security problems begin initially as an issue of first response by first responders and, therefore, all homeland security issues are by definition, local. Any homeland security system that's going to be effective has got to be, at its core, an intergovernmental system.

My great concern about the new department is this: The people in Washington working on it are so preoccupied by the tremendous difficulty of the structural issues that the intergovernmental issues—which, in many ways, are the hardest pieces of the puzzle—are likely to get either short shrift or little attention at all in the discussion.

Suppose, however, that we did want to pay careful attention to what the federalism component of homeland security really means. . . . [W]hat would looking at the "home" in homeland security mean? I want to share with you some of the findings that we've come up with as a result of the work that we've been doing as part of the Century Foundation's project on federalism and homeland security. . . . I want to try to summarize what we found and suggest some strategies that might make some sense.

If you look at what state and local governments have done so far, it's fair to say that the primary focus of homeland security has been on *response*, not on prevention, although there has been an increased emphasis on prevention because of federal arguments about the need to try to be more alert. But, as we know, a primary complaint by state and local officials is that the federal government will say, "The terror level

Reprinted in edited form from a series of colloquia on homeland security sponsored by the Nelson A. Rockefeller Institute of Government, 411 State Street, Albany, NY 12203.

is now orange; be more careful." What, where, how, about what? Often the state of intelligence is not sufficiently good to tell anybody more than just to be careful, to which state and local officials say, "But we're already doing that. Asking us to do more of what we're already doing is hard because we're already stretched as far as we can be. There's only so much time we can spend putting people on overtime, having them drive by bridges and dams and power plants, and so on." So, in short, an effort to try to focus more on deterrence is an effort that has to be centered at the federal level. For better or worse, most of the effort at the state and local level has been—and will continue to be—focused on response.

What is Homeland Security?

Let me try to explain what the homeland security system looks like. We talk about homeland security as if we know what it means. In practice, however, there is a surprising level of confusion, disagreement, or, at the very least, differences in emphasis among state and local governments about what "homeland security" is. In part, that's a political issue because when most local officials are discussing homeland security they will say, "Look, we know what to do. It's primarily a matter of preparing our response. We know how to respond. Give us the money that we need; we know what to do." On the other hand, there are those who from the top down say, "What we need to do is to create an integrated, seamless response system so that we don't run the risk of having problems fall through the cracks." This creates a tension in homeland security. Those who study issues of federalism will recognize this as one of your deep and historic tensions between those who say, "Give local governments flexibility and more money to create a better system from the bottom up" and those who argue the need for a more integrated system from the top down. I'll come back and talk about some of this a little bit later. At the core of the problem of homeland security is some disagreement about what homeland security is, who ought to be in charge of it, and how it ought to work.

An Examination of What has been Accomplished Since September 11, 2001

Another question is, "What have [we] actually accomplished since September 11?" It is undoubtedly the case that local governments in particular and state governments as well have worried much more about since September 11. There has been, in particular, a lot more emphasis spent simply on trying to put together plans at the state and local level, which, in many cases, were desperately needed.

One problem is that preparedness plans have, in many parts of the country, not been accompanied by much action. There are a lot of reports; there are a lot of plans; there is a lot of saying, "Here's what we'll do if—" but the pieces and the components required to put the plans into action in many parts of the country have not adequately been put into place. Let me give one example of that.

Everybody knows as a result of what happened, both with September 11 and as a result of the Anthrax attacks that followed soon afterwards, that public health has to be a key component of the first response system and the first response system has got to be quick and first on the scene.

In one of the states that we examined, which shall go nameless for reasons that will be obvious as I tell the story, there was this suspicious little bit of white powder that was discovered in October 2001. This was in a part of the country where it gets a little cold that time of year, so they called the first responders out who arrived on the scene and proceeded to take people outside, have them strip down to their underwear, and hose them down to make sure that they'd be decontaminated—a rather unpleasant experience.

About forty-five minutes into this event, it dawned on somebody that maybe they ought to call the public health people: It took forty-five minutes to determine that public health people ought to be part of the first-response process. The public health people came, but then they were not allowed into [the] command post. The health workers said, "We're here; we're here as part of the first response system." As it turns out, it was the public health workers that A) knew what to do in case of that kind of issue and B) would have advised something differently, C) weren't called, and D) when they arrived, they weren't let in. I've been assured that this problem has since been cleared up so it won't recur. But one wonders in how many parts of the country that still is an issue.

First Responders: The Role of Local Public Health

One of the crucial issues with the first response system is an effective and a strong public health system. If there's any weakness anywhere at the local level in terms of homeland security, it seems to be in public health. The fact is that in most states and most localities that public health has not been carefully integrated into an effective first-response system. There may be plans for doing so, but whether or not it would work in case of crisis is something that nobody really knows for sure. There have been some unsettling tests of this so far that suggest, in practice, that it might not work so well. Sooner or later the pressure of events tends to solve some of these problems. The problem is: How much pressure of which events would be required to solve which problems? The whole point of having an effective first response system is to make sure that important minutes and hours are not lost as people try to figure out the right thing to do. This delay can cause problems, and in part because the first instincts may not be correct and they're hard to correct after the fact.

First Responders: Schools

Another example that shows the role of local players deals with the local schools. In this example, a local school had done some things to respond to FEMA's [Federal Emergency Management Agency's] suggestion that all local schools ought to have a plan put in place in case suspicious powder was found. The question was: What should be done? What was the plan? A local fire chief I talked to had spoken to school officials and said, "What in fact is the plan?" It turns out the school officials had received the directive, but had not quite gotten around to figuring out what they ought to do. They hadn't gotten around to figuring out whether or not the best thing to do was to evacuate the school and run the risk that children would walk past the room where the suspicious powder was, each of them taking a good inhalation of it, and running the risk of sending it right to their lungs—or whether it was better to keep them in their classrooms and running the risk that the ventilation system would produce the same result. One of those alternatives is probably better than another, but the school had not figured out which.

Variations in Preparedness at the Local Level

The third issue is widespread variation. The fact is that the level of attention to this issue has varied tremendously around the country. It is no secret, of course, that New York and Washington are widely viewed to be the most significant, likely targets and therefore have the most preparation in place. If there is any piece of luck—and I hesitate even to use the word in connection with September 11—but if there was any piece of luck about what happened that awful morning, it was that the events happened in two of the communities in the country best prepared to deal with the consequences. There were a lot of other communities where such things, had they occurred, would have been met with much less effective results, including, as it turns out, the District of Columbia across the Potomac, where local officials took considerably longer to implement their emergency response plan than the people in Arlington who had to respond to the crash at the Pentagon.

The fact is that in many smaller communities, the level of preparedness is much lower. That raises an important question. Those communities most likely to be at risk are the ones that often tend to be best prepared, and the places that are least likely to be affected are the ones that have tended to pay less attention to security. . . . There is widespread variation around the country, and many state and local governments have simply not taken the issue as seriously.

Coordination

Another is coordination. We all know that coordination is important. In many ways, the defining administrative strategy of homeland security is coordination. The whole reason why we created this new federal department is to secure better coordination among federal entities that have a piece of the homeland security puzzle. At the state and local level, this is largely a matter of coordination as well, whether it's through mutual aid agreements, whether it's through a strategy to integrate public health into the first-response system, whether it's to enhance the ability of fire departments to come to each other's aid—a whole variety of issues that are, at their core, about federalism.

When you think of homeland security, you need to think of interorganizational, intergovernmental coordination. Homeland security is, at its foundation, an issue of coordination. Anyone who is even a casual student of federalism knows that this is one of the crucial problems in making homeland security work effectively. Coordination is not federalism's strong suit. In particular, if coordination is going to work effectively with the wide variation in local preparedness, it requires communities to work closely with each other.

In one state, it turns out that local governments from smaller communities are very nervous about entering into mutual aid agreements because larger governments refuse to guarantee that they would in fact respond if in fact a problem occurs. Smaller local governments have an inadequate base of revenues and expertise to mount effective systems on their own. In fact, it's foolish for all communities to develop the same level of expertise when coordination among them is by far more efficient and more effective. However, that requires smaller communities and larger communities to work together. Communities have found that very difficult in practice.

People in Washington may often forget these challenges because they look at homeland security with tunnel vision. For local communities, coordination is important to solve homeland security problems— but they are often, at the same time, fighting with the same partners over other issues. They might be fighting with each other over water and sewer permits, over expansion plans, over economic development strategies, over who gets the new Wal-Mart. Coordination is at the heart of what are some of the nastiest and most enduring conflicts in the American system. These conflicts tend to spill over from other problems into homeland security and, in the process, they make homeland security problems far harder to solve. . . .

Communication

Another issue is communications systems. On the morning of September 11, we discovered just how difficult communication systems can be and how important they are. As it turns out, the police department had better information about the condition of the World Trade Center towers than did the firefighters on the inside, because the police department had a helicopter circling overhead. They radioed the information to police commanders. But the police commanders were not in touch with the fire commanders, and the fire commanders in the lobbies of the World Trade Center did not have access to the TV pictures that all the rest of the world was watching. Not only did they have difficulty communicating to the firefighters on upper floors, they also had trouble communicating among related agencies.

We've discovered that for homeland security to work, especially in cases of attack and terrorist events, effective communication is crucial. We also know that there are many, many local communities around the country where radio systems are not inter-operable. . . . Overall, . . . we have significant problems of communication that frustrate and complicate the problems of coordination.

Funding

Another issue is money. Local government officials are saying, "If we really want to solve these problems, what we need is more money. We can't come up with the cash ourselves." It must come from the federal government, because state governments are in the middle of "the biggest fiscal crisis since World War II." The federal government is saying, "We'll make more money available," but the actual flow of funds has been at a far lower level than what was originally promised. There is no doubt that local governments desperately need more money to help buy some of the communications equipment, to buy first responder suits so that local governments are prepared for dealing with emergency response to chemical and biological contamination. The simple fact is this: Simply putting more money into the system wouldn't necessarily produce higher levels of homeland security. More money would, in all likelihood, only replicate, in larger measure, all the problems we already have—because more money put into the system would not secure more coordination.

If you listen carefully to [what] local governments are saying, they're saying, "Give us more money because we need to buy more radios, more equipment, more trucks, more hazardous material vehicles, more of all these things." But you tend not to hear local governments saying, "Give us more money and we'll work better with our neighbors." You also hear local governments saying, "Whatever you do, don't give the money to the states because we don't want the state governments putting their fingers into this money supply—we need every nickel of it. We're the first responders and you have to understand we're the ones who can make the best use of the money." If coordination is going to happen, it's going to have to happen by some means other than what currently happens with local governments. This implies a stronger role for the states and perhaps for the federal government as well.

There needs to be a different way of thinking about the federal aid system to solve these problems. Simply putting more money into the system would soon not produce any real improvement in homeland security until we solve the coordination problem. The only way to solve these issues is to use the funds as incentives to get local communities to do what otherwise they're not inclined to do. In short, what we have to do is try to encourage local governments to engage in unnatural acts: to engage in the kind of coordination that's required because, at its core, homeland security is an issue of coordination.

Elements of Successful Strategy for Homeland Security

If we wanted to solve these problems, what would we do? Let me try to outline what I think the elements of a successful strategy would be.

- *Create a Minimum Level of Protection*—The first thing we need to do is create a minimum floor for protection. Citizens should not be exposed to higher and unacceptable levels of risk because of the accident of where they happen to live, or because of the accident of where they might happen to be traveling in the event of an attack. . . .

  I think that it's clear that we need to establish some minimum national levels for local protection, so that there's at least a floor for the level of homeland security around the country. I think it's also clear that, for most of the country, this would be a higher level than is now in place. We will have to figure out how to get there.

  There are a lot of established practices for getting to this point. For example, there are some basic standards for fire protection that are used to set fire insurance rates. Insurance companies set these rates by a combination of response times, distance from fire hydrants, and other factors. We thus have some practice at setting standards for risky events, and for preparedness and response to levels of risk. One could imagine setting platinum, gold, and silver levels of protection, where a community could decide what level it sought. Local officials could then explain to their constituents why they were or were not up to the base level, how much more it would cost to go from silver to gold, or how much it would cost to have platinum-level protection. There is a variety of strategies that could be based on incentives that would help promote a minimum floor for protection.

- *Strengthen Local Coordination*—The second thing we need to do is strengthen local coordination. For homeland security to work, there has to be coordination; for coordination to work, there has to be a set of financial incentives associated with it. What this means is that we have to figure out two things: who is it that enforces the coordination; and how does the money flow?

  It is crucial that the states play an important role as the coordinating vehicles. As I've suggested, the kind of coordination that's required among local communities to create and enforce this local floor is, in essence, an unnatural act. It is not likely to happen spontaneously, for the same reasons that local communities often find it so difficult to work with each other in a wide variety of other things. That's especially true when you get to issues of police and fire protection. . . . Where homeland security systems have tended to work better, they've relied on either regional or statewide coordinating bodies. . . .

The logical level of government to do this is the states. The nature of the problems and the nature of the responses required vary substantially from state to state so that having the federal government do this is probably not a good idea. But allowing the decisions to slip too much below the state level is, in all likelihood, creating an increased likelihood that it's not going to occur at all. The key is to try to find the right level at which this could be done.

- *Modify Systems for Funding*—We need a different system of channeling intergovernmental aid from the federal government to the states, and then from the states to local governments. This means that the federal government needs to set minimum national standards and to identify best practices. The states could receive block grants with considerable discretion, and local governments would have primary responsibility for carrying this through. Those of you who are students of federalism will realize this is a familiar debate guaranteed to raise all the issues that so often have hamstrung intergovernmental systems for the last generation. In fact, this is like many other intergovernmental issues—except that the stakes are very high, and an effective intergovernmental response is essential.

At its core, this suggests two things. One is that allowing the money to flow as it has been flowing so far is, in all likelihood, not going to significantly improve the quality of the homeland defense system. And second, if we are serious about doing it, we're going to need to create a different system of intergovernmental aid to make sure that the problems that we have identified actually are solved.

- *Test Systems*—A fifth and final point is that it's not only important to write plans and create these new systems. It is also important to test them. . . . There are a lot of ways of testing these things in advance to make sure that the odds that they will work under pressure are improved.

Closing Remarks

In summary, homeland security is primarily an issue of coordination, but coordination is fundamentally a problem in intergovernmental relations and federalism. Left to its own devices, federalism is not likely to respond effectively. It's going to require some innovative strategies for coming at this problem. The consequences of failing to do so could very well prove to be dangerous—even catastrophic—so the urgency for attacking this problem is huge.

Let me step back just for a second. My concluding point emphasizes and underlines many of the same points that those of us who look at federalism have studied and poked around at for a long time. My guess is that there's little that I've said that is in many ways new at all. In fact, it's the fact that this debate occurs against the backdrop of September 11—and our realization of what the costs of a poorly performing system could be—that underlines just how important it is. The central issues of governance here are in many ways very familiar to students of federalism. Most of us who have studied this and have looked at this know that much of what I've suggested are problems that we need to confront in any event. And that if there's a ray of sunshine at all in this, it is that doing what we know we need to do for homeland security also will better equip our governmental system for solving a lot of other problems that we must also attack.

27

American Public Administration and Impacts of International Governance

Laurence J. O'Toole Jr. and Kenneth I. Hanf

Contrasts between global headlines and the day-to-day work of public managers seem, at first blush, immense. Yet, in an important sense, one is the obverse of the other. Federal and state environmental managers address issues of air quality in metropolitan regions, while world leaders voice open criticism of the laggard status of the United States in dealing with threats from global climate change. State and local public programs aimed at achieving economic development occupy the energies of thousands of officials, while the impact of such efforts is strongly influenced by provisions of the North American Free Trade Agreement (NAFTA). U.S. diplomats negotiate regimes to halt the flow of drugs from Latin America, while employees of several federal departments, state police agencies, and local law enforcement units sift through narcotics intelligence, search ships, and monitor suspected transport routes.

Far more vividly, managing threats from terrorism engages the efforts of many U.S. agencies—national and subnational—as aspects of the problem are negotiated at home and abroad. While New York City rescue crews sought to locate survivors in the wake of the September 11 attack, NATO convened in an unprecedented emergency session to invoke Article 5 of the Washington Treaty in assistance of American defense. While diplomats in the State Department tried to build a coalition for sustained antiterror efforts worldwide, FBI agents worked closely with police and investigatory units in numerous countries, the Centers for Disease Control and Prevention coordinated their bioterrorism efforts with foreign public health authorities, and bank regulators cooperated with colleagues abroad to tighten international financial systems.

From *Public Administration Review*, September 2002, Vol. 62, by Laurence J. O'Toole Jr. and Kenneth I. Hanf. Copyright © 2002 by Blackwell Publishing. Reprinted with the permission of Blackwell Publishing.

Daily, significant issues breach national borders in ways that confront administrative decision makers with new challenges to which no single actor can respond adequately. While "globalization" has become a much-abused cliché, researchers and practitioners of public administration, particularly in the United States, have yet to recognize the myriad ways that transnational developments frame and shape virtually the entire gamut of specialties and issues facing the field. U.S. administrative actors at all levels have already become insinuated into almost countless numbers of complicatedly networked arrays of governance (Frederickson 1999)—including components of social self-organizing and market arrangements as well as formal governing patterns.

These developments do not signify the collapse of nation-centered public administration, but they do reshape the sets of relations within which U.S. officials carry out their responsibilities. In today's administrative world, not to mention the future, these shifts call for a revision and critical reappraisal of our inherited notions of governance, management, and accountability. Even the contents and competencies of specialties in the practical details of administration are being refashioned in ways that scarcely have been noted, let alone examined in depth. . . .

Globalizing Governance: An Overview

The changed and changing context of public administration in the United States is best understood as one part of a shifting landscape of governance worldwide. Much is new about the forms and dynamics of present processes that link elements of political, social, and economic life ever more closely around the globe—particularly regarding the complexity of such arrangements today and the dramatically reduced time and varied transaction costs attending the expansion of global ties. One result is a set of significant limitations on the scope of unilateral action that is available to any given state (Held 1996, 20; Pierre and Peters 2000, 56–57). Although opinions differ regarding the degree to which economic forces have been internationalized, there is considerable consensus on the emergence of a disjuncture between the formal authority of any state and the spatial reach of contemporary systems of production, distribution, and exchange.

But those who would proclaim the death of the nation-state are premature. Key themes of this article, in fact, are that (1) the multiple forms of transnational cooperation that have emerged both limit national "autonomy" and also facilitate effective national action; and (2) public administration is a crucially important component of this dynamic.

The validity of the first point is seen in the creation of various forms of transnational cooperation. A vast array of regimes and organizations has been established to manage whole fields of activity and collective policy problems (Zacher 1993)—indeed, the United States has had to take explicit account of this complex matrix of ties in the aftermath of, and also long before, the catalyzing events of September 11. The spectrum of international agencies runs from those concerned primarily with technical, noncontroversial activities (Universal Postal Union, International Telecommunications Union, World Meteorological Organization) to those involved in more controversial questions about managing and allocating resources (United Nations, World Bank, International Monetary Fund, and the U.N. Educational, Scientific, and Cultural Organization). Also significant is a range of informal global networks, such as the G-8 grouping of economic powers.

This growing institutionalization consists of initiatives that are designed to facilitate the management of policy challenges beyond the control of any single state. International organizations have been recognized for decades as constituent parts of governance. Development of transnational networks, a recent trend, has had a crucial impact in this increasingly fluid era. The events of September 11 involved casualties from approximately 80 nations and were executed by operatives of an international terrorist network, al-Qaeda, with elements in perhaps 60 countries worldwide and a key coordinative node in the then-pariah state of Afghanistan. Responses, in turn, came not only from single countries and the European Union, NATO, and the 56-nation Organization of the Islamic Conference, but also from an array of more loosely networked actors spanning many nations—including extensive and intensive collaboration by numerous U.S. agencies working with counterpart units in many other countries on behalf of "homeland security." Counterterrorism suffers if it is conceived of only in terms of traditional organization-focused frames of reference (Wise 2002). Like global climate change and other international challenges, it too requires the involvement and effective collaboration of networked arrays of disparate actors within and without international organizations.

The development of problem-specific arrangements, each with a different spatial reach, is now a major fact of politico-administrative life, with consequences for the conduct of administration. These forms of multilateral decision making exhibit distinctive patterns involving governments, intergovernmental bodies, and a variety of international nongovernmental organizations. Nonstate actors or transnational bodies (multinational corporations, pressure groups, professional associations) participate actively, as do national, regional, and local government actors in different international arenas. The global expanse has become a highly complex, mixed-actor system. Furthermore, the problem-specific systems ramify into each other, often in unanticipated fashions. At the time NAFTA was developed, it was clear that trade agreements carry implications for environmental protection; few, on the other hand, had analyzed the implications of NAFTA for cross-border control of international terrorism.

Such complex arrays are most appropriately considered as evidence of strategies to reassert state control rather than of states' surrendering to competing models of governance (Pierre and Peters 2000, 16). To an increasing degree, a government's success in pursuing domestically defined national objectives depends on how effectively it can act within changing institutional contexts, including new transnational institutions. In this sense, the latter are not "outside" the state, imposing restrictions on its autonomy; rather, they function as new "opportunity structures" through which national actors can search for ways to pursue their domestic agendas—of course, under restrictions and implications flowing from forms of cooperative endeavor. Participants cannot do exactly what they may want—something, in any case, they cannot achieve on their own. Government actors find themselves necessarily engaged in forms of "collaborative management." The state is being reshaped, with qualitative changes evident in relationships among actors from different levels that cannot be adequately captured by the idea of "decline." The operative notion, rather, is that of "enmeshment."

The American Variant and an Environmental Slice

... The array of recent U.S. international commitments demonstrates the depth and breadth of current involvement. Formal international commitments consist of both treaties and executive agreements. The latter are far more numerous, even if often less visible. Both categories carry the force of law. A recent tabulation of *new* bi- and multilateral agreements entered into by the United States during 1981–96 totals 2,969, including numerous instances in virtually every policy field (Caruson 2001). Bilateral agreements are by far more numerous, more than 90 percent. Including the second Clinton term as well as earlier agreements that are still in force would further expand the total. Virtually all of these involve nontrivial contributions by and implications for American public administrators. Recent developments regarding terrorism and international efforts to address its challenges clearly fit into, and must take account of, this developing system. But it would be a mistake to view the implications as largely confined to the highly salient theme of security. In fact, the system now cuts across and carries implications for virtually every policy field and nearly every American priority.

Environmental challenges provide a vivid set of illustrations. Given that the state of the environment in any country is not merely the result of intranational forces, it is not sufficient to emphasize—as even the best recent scholarship on U.S. public management for the environment does—domestic matters to the exclusion of other international factors (O'Leary et al. 1999). Dealing with the salient environmental challenges requires finding ways to gain the cooperation of governments of other countries (Caldwell 1996).

Scenes of violent protestors in such cities as Seattle and Genoa create a casual impression that activists oppose the proliferation of international patterns of governance. But a central element of this opposition has been the rejection of efforts to globalize markets without corresponding multilateral initiatives on workforces and environmental safeguards. Many opponents of globalization have an agenda that, in effect, presses for *more* internationalization on certain key causes. And while Washington's rejection of the Kyoto Protocol understandably made headlines worldwide, the predominant trend has been toward the development of international commitments. Nor should it obscure the fact that the United States has played a leadership role in pushing for international cooperation on environmental problems. For environmental policy and management, more than 170 multilateral agreements have been adopted, most within the last 25 years (Victor, Raustiala, and Skolnikoff 1998; UNEP 1993). This count excludes bilateral agreements and includes only multilateral ones solely focused on environmental questions. Many of the agreements incorporate multiple legal instruments; more than 900 such instruments are currently in force (Jacobson and Weiss 1998, 1). Finally, many other agreements are under negotiation now, dealing with persistent organic pollutants, liability and compensation for transboundary movements of hazardous wastes, biosafety, and transboundary movements of heavy metals. Developments on such fronts, furthermore, can become insinuated into a range of other issues. In 2002, when U.S. political leaders tried to engage other nations in an international effort to disrupt terrorist networks, the issue was explicitly linked by European counterparts to American refusal to join the broad coalition on global climate change, among other nettlesome issues (such as defense). An antiterrorism agenda cannot be leveraged without multilateral enmeshment in several ostensibly far-flung policy fields.

For the United States and other nations, furthermore, each agreement responds to and stimulates domestic administrative activity. While this country has drawn scorn recently for environmental unilateralism, administrators in many agencies are busily at work implementing (and in some cases working toward the expansion of) such agreements as the Convention on International Trade in Endangered Species, the Montreal Protocol on ozone depletion, and others.

... That thousands of such agreements are in force is presumptive evidence that administrators are already heavily involved in policy and programs that extend beyond the borders—even if they may be unaware of it. But multilateral agreements constitute the significant core of the emerging governance pattern. These are visible signs of globalizing arrangements that involve administrators in the most consequential ways....

The Emerging Governance Framework: An Analytical View

... [T]he features of transnational governance do not suggest anything like a global government, designed more or less on the model of state-centered systems. Nor does an examination of the current system support a blanket characterization of globalized governance as, in effect, a mere facilitative vehicle for global capital—although, of course, the forces of global capitalism are important in the system. Rather, what one sees is the establishment of many functionally specific, multilateral regimes, often with some kind of (typically tiny) secretariat at the supranational level, but with the major portion of involved institutions and human talent retained in and by signatory states and their subnational elements. These are self-woven into and contribute to the shaping of the transnational order. Their administrative functions remain crucial, even if administration is being shaped by and through the globalizing developments. ...

Consider the massive set of international agreements to which the United States is a party. The total represents commitments in virtually every sphere of policy and carries implications for nearly every national agency. They form no unitary, coherent international regime but are embedded in a panoply of them. Note, too, how the U.S. response to the anthrax attacks in the fall of 2001 provoked the American government to execute nonstandard and vastly expanded production of an antibiotic whose patent was held by a German firm. This initiative could not be pressed in isolation because it carried implications for World Trade Organization negotiations in Qatar on the "right of developing countries to breach drug patents to combat public health crises such as AIDS" (Moynihan and Roberts 2002, 139).

The vast set of international regimes and understandings does not constitute a neomedieval chaos, any more than the hundreds of governments in a large U.S metropolitan area represent a descent onto a darkling urban plain. The web of international commitments has emerged in the presence and with the necessary participation of the nation and its institutions. The emergence of this new governance does not necessarily signal a recapitulation of national-level functions and designs at the transnational level. Instead, the embeddedness is considerably more complex, with many networks and many functionally specific regimes coexisting. Virtually all rely very heavily on national institutions, support, and administrative capacity for effective governance. . . .

Interdependent nations that are engaged in strategic decision making may find stable cooperative approaches that help each (all) to achieve objectives despite differing interests. Indeed, the fact of interdependence may make effective action more likely rather than less—depending on the circumstances. All or most nations may have an interest in establishing systems to monitor the epidemiology of certain diseases, for example, just as the vast majority share a collective interest in suppressing terrorist threats. In the case of the long-range transport of air pollution ("acid rain"), all signatory countries supported the creation of an effective scheme for monitoring emissions and identifying their countries of origin. Once such a system was created, the "mere" fact of a monitoring system gave impetus to serious national efforts to show their willingness to comply—so long as others did likewise. The result has been a surprisingly effective regime (Haas, Keohane, and Levy 1993; Underdal and Hanf 2000).

The details of this example support the notion of continued roles for state systems and public administration. The permanent staff of the regime numbers less than 10 for a set of multilateral agreements covering five pollutants and 34 countries. Virtually all of the action is handled through and mostly by the participating states through working groups within the overall framework of the U.N. Economic Commission for Europe (although the countries involved extend beyond Europe and include the United States). The international agreements have facilitated a set of understandings that could not have been achieved by any single nation, even a hegemonic one. Virtually all states gain from a collective agreement, even though none would have had an interest in going down that path alone. The resulting cooperation has increased the capacity of all participants to address issues beyond what they would have been able to achieve on their own. Yet the regime that has emerged is dwarfed by the scale and capacities of any of the members. . . .

One additional analogy is pertinent: intergovernmental relations within the United States. Here the comparison is imperfect, but the U.S. experiment, designed without unitary authority, has functioned over an extended period. Hundreds of functionally specific arrays link institutions and decision makers without causing subnational units to atrophy. While the system exhibits plenty of difficulties and is often criticized on equity grounds, it demonstrates that multilevel systems that lack a straightforward authority chain can deliver effective governance. Similarly, international governance is unlikely to siphon most talent and influence from national settings. . . .

Implications for American Public Administration

. . . Some administrative officials—thus far, almost exclusively national—participate directly in international activities. Virtually all federal cabinet-level departments have specialized units to deal with international aspects of their missions. Thousands of administrators exchange information with their counterparts in other countries or are involved in negotiations. The existence of so many such agreements and their periodic review and revision should make this point obvious. U.S. administrators, and not merely those in the State Department, are active in international meetings, interact regularly with administrative bodies or secretariats of international regimes, and evaluate and monitor the impact and effectiveness of international commitments.

Many more administrators and federal experts are implicated in international dimensions of policy and administration. Agreements carry domestic ramifications, particularly during their execution (Hanf and Underdal 1996). Up and down the chain, national administrators analyze the implications of options that are being considered in and through international regimes. To the extent that agencies' turf is involved, such units not only anticipate and react to events and decisions, but also advise other units of new commitments, discuss and disseminate the concrete details in a variety of directions, and prepare reports often required as part of commitments entered into by the United States. These duties may entail the development of routine contacts and exchanges with counterparts elsewhere and possibly joint implementation in more than one country.

These ramifications are not "merely" internal to administrative units. Many international commitments embrace objectives and carry implications that must be dealt with through a broader set of units domestically (Lambright 1997). . . . An agreement about banning the international transport of endangered species, for instance, connects the Customs Bureau with the Environmental Protection Agency (EPA) and the Bureau of Fish and Wildlife. Similarly, acid rain protocols tie the State Department, the EPA, and the Departments of Energy and Commerce (Weiss and Jacobson 1998). . . .

Basic managerial functions are influenced by such forces as well. One example is personnel. While international organizations are unlikely to experience a substantial "bulking" at the expense of national administration, internationalization shapes the perspectives of U.S. administrators. The professional orientations of those involved are molded by their interactions, especially collegial ties with others working on similar challenges. As a result, administrators are likely to develop a more transnational perspective, and the channels of influence are mutual. Personnel who were formally employed by international bodies or by other nations interact increasingly with their American counterparts. Results here include some "Americanization" of the perspectives in these settings as well.

Internationalization also shapes decision making in budgeting and finance. Connections can be quite direct, such as international agreements committing countries to lowering tariffs and other trade barriers—decisions that shape the macroeconomy, shifting fortunes of industries and employment in particular locales. All of these influence domestic politics and public finance.

Budgetary impacts also can be substantial. Just as "unfunded mandates" have exasperated subnational decision makers, international agreements can commit the United States to actions that enmesh national and subnational spending—as in the challenges being faced now to upgrade capacity to respond to public health and other aspects of bioterrorism. This is a relatively new experience for national decision makers. As subnational experience attests, such decisions do not necessarily vitiate authority or silence voice, even if international influences can bind uncomfortably at times.

Connections between globalizing dynamics and subnational public administration are also real, even if less direct. An environmental example again makes the point. Note the so-called "Local Agenda 21" process encouraged by the Rio Earth Summit in 1992, which calls for communities to embark on participatory processes of planning for a sustainable future. In some policy fields, subnational officials and managers have moved beyond their national counterparts in participating in internationally driven changes. There is growing interest, for example, in encouraging sustainable communities. "Many U.S. cities have joined the International Council for Local Environmental Initiatives' (ICLEI) Cities for Climate Protection programme [and] have put in place action plans to protect the global climate and reduce local air pollution. Several major cities have embraced the goal of a 20 per cent reduction in carbon-dioxide emissions, and a few have reduced emissions by as much as 15 per cent since 1995" (Bryner 2000, 283, 299). Although Washington has shunned the Kyoto Protocol, many state and local governments have taken steps to address the concerns. In August 2001, for instance, the six New England states joined five eastern Canadian provinces in a pact to reduce greenhouse gas emissions—thus illustrating both the transnational and subnational trends. The agreement includes quantitative and ambitious goals (*Los Angeles Times*, October 8, 2001, A1).

International links to subnational administration may be even more significant for regulation and associated questions of budgeting and finance. U.S. case law stipulates that, generally, an international commitment "trumps state law that adopts a contrary requirement" (O'Reilly 1997; see *Missouri v. Holland* [1920]), including voter-initiated state law. Such conflicts are not yet visible on the post–September 11 front, but they can be seen in other fields. Some have already emerged between trade obligations and subnational environmental requirements. Unlike domestic intergovernmental differences, however, this constraint on state action *limits* the kinds of regulation that a number of states have adopted in recent years.

There are two points here: International obligations may effectively direct and influence spending by states and localities. Second, the law commits subnational authorities to the international commitments of national authorities. The implication of both is likely to be increased involvement of subnational actors, including administrators, in monitoring the development of international agreements, as well as in lobbying national authorities and others. Such a process is already quite visible in Europe—for instance, through the European Council of Municipalities and Regions, which operates directly at the European level to influence decisions.

Such efforts are likely to be complex, just as intergovernmental relations are domestically. California may care deeply about strengthening its environmental constraints, while Texas desires more growth-oriented international commitments; they may operate at cross purposes. Still, more jurisdictions will look for points of leverage internationally. These developments necessitate a change in subnational administrators' understanding of the system in which they operate.

For many dimensions of U.S. public administration, then, and for multiple levels of domestic governance, there are implications for regulation and management, organizational structuring, human resources management, and budgeting and finance. Influences are mutual and multidirectional. The nation-state remains vigorous in the emerging pattern of governance, but America has clearly entered a system of broader and more complex influence. Further, U.S. administration is significant in the globalizing world, even if it is undeniably altered in crucial respects. . . .

The globalized future of public administration is already emerging, and the range extends far beyond international terrorism and national security. The context is not a worldwide government, and the U.S. content is not an increasingly irrelevant public administration. Developments are on their way into a more firmly institutionalized, polycentric system based largely on a multitude of functionally specific international regimes. Few of these are fully global, and none is busy performing basic state functions. Nor does the likely future offer an administrative apparatus passively enforcing norms set by some powerful, nongeographically rooted, nonstate head.

Territory will not disappear as a point of reference in determining administrative responsibilities. Increasingly, actors at all levels face the imperative of collaborating with others, public and private, from various jurisdictions and levels to deal with the problems that surpass the resources and problem-solving capacities of their territorially defined units. Accordingly, there are consequences for public management. The challenge is to reassess how to organize and how to do the public's business. Such internationalization extends the scope of governance while magnifying its complexity. These developments continue, even as the analytical and normative categories through which they are assessed and understood increasingly call out for redefinition. . . .

References

Bryner, Gary C. 2000. The United States: "Sorry—Not Our Problem." In *Implementing Sustainable Development: Strategies and Initiatives in High Consumption Societies,* edited by William M. Lafferty and James Meadowcroft, 273–302. Oxford, UK: Oxford University Press.

Caldwell, Lynton Keith. 1996. *International Environmental Policy: From the Twentieth to the Twenty-First Century.* 3rd ed. Durham, NC: Duke University Press.

Caruson, Kiki. 2001. Presidential Leadership Strategy in Foreign Affairs: An Analysis of Executive-Legislative Interaction. Ph.D. dissertation, University of Georgia.

Frederickson, H. George. 1999. The Repositioning of American Public Administration. *PS: Political Science and Politics* 32(4): 701–11.

Haas, Peter M., Robert O. Keohane, and Marc A. Levy, eds. 1993. *Institutions for the Earth: Sources of Effective International Environmental Protection.* Cambridge, MA: MIT Press.

Hanf, Kenneth I., and Arild Underdal. 1996. Domesticating International Commitments: Linking National and International Decision Making. In *The International Political Economy and International Institutions,* vol. II., edited by Oran Young, 1–20. Cheltenham, UK: Edward Elgar.

Held, David. 1996. *Democracy and the Global Order: From the Modern State to Cosmopolitan Governance.* Cambridge, UK: Polity Press.

Jacobson, Harold K., and Edith Brown Weiss. 1998. A Framework for Analysis. In *Engaging Countries,* edited by Edith Brown Weiss and Harold K. Jacobson, 1–18. Cambridge, MA: MIT Press.

Lambright, W. Henry. 1997. The Rise and Fall of Interagency Cooperation: The U.S. Global Change Research Program. *Public Administration Review* 57(1): 36–44.

Moynihan, Donald P., and Alasdair Roberts. 2002. Public Service Reform and the New Security Agenda. In *Governance and Public Security,* edited by Alasdair Roberts, 129–45. Syracuse, NY: Campbell Public Affairs Institute, Maxwell School, Syracuse University.

O'Leary, Rosemary, Robert F. Durant, Daniel J. Fiorino, and Paul S. Weiland. 1999. *Managing for the Environment: Understanding the Legal, Organizational, and Policy Challenges.* San Francisco, CA: Jossey-Bass.

O'Reilly, James T. 1997. Stop the World, We Want Our Own Labels: Treaties, State Voter Initiative Laws, and Federal Pre-Emption. *University of Pennsylvania Journal of International Economics and Law* 18(2): 617–53.

Pierre, Jon, and B. Guy Peters. 2000. *Governance, Politics, and the State*. London: Macmillan.

Underdal, Arild, and Kenneth Hanf. 2000. *International Environmental Agreements and Domestic Politics: The Case of Acid Rain*. Aldershot, UK: Ashgate Publishers.

United Nations Environmental Programme (UNEP). 1993. *Register of International Treaties and Other Agreements in the Field of the Environment*. Nairobi, Kenya: UNEP.

Victor, David G., Kal Raustiala, and Eugene B. Skolnikoff. 1998. *The Implementation and Effectiveness of International Environmental Commitments*. Cambridge, MA: MIT Press.

Weiss, Edith Brown, and Harold K. Jacobson, eds. 1998. *Engaging Countries: Strengthening Compliance with International Environmental Accords*. Cambridge, MA: MIT Press.

Wise, Charles R. 2002. Organizing for Homeland Security. *Public Administration Review* 62(2): 131–44.

Zacher, Mark W. 1993. *The International Political Economy of Natural Resources*. Aldershot, England: Edward Elgar.

28

Intergovernmental Relations and Federalism: Its Past, Present and Future, and Does Anyone Care?

Jonathan Walters, for the MacArthur Foundation

Intergovernmental Relations, a Study in Long-Standing Neglect

Odd as it may seem—given that we're a country based on the concept of tiered governance, local, state and federal—the actual study of intergovernmental relations as a separate and distinct discipline has, historically, been a fairly haphazard enterprise, and continues to be so today. With the exception of about 40 years in our history, there has been no single entity devoted to convening people, collecting and analyzing data or doing policy work related specifically to intergovernmental affairs, relationships and cooperation.

It's an especially surprising—some might say perplexing—fact, inasmuch as there is almost no policy area that the U.S. deals with that doesn't have some intergovernmental consequence or that doesn't demand some intergovernmental action or response. Even the war in Iraq, which some might argue is a completely national affair, is impacting states and localities from the standpoint of both drained personnel and strained fiscal resources. Vermont, for example, recently reported that criminal trials were being put on hold because of call-ups of state and local law enforcement officers who belong to the National Guard.

There are dozens of major policy areas, meanwhile, with obvious and direct intergovernmental connections and consequences, like environmental protection, education, health and social services, where the federal government sets policy and states and localities are primarily responsible for delivering results. In fact, from tax administration to immigration, energy to election reform, transportation to business regulation, there is really no policy area that doesn't in some way have some intergovernmental implications. In many cases they are very clear and significant. "It's marbled throughout everything we do," says [an expert in the field of federal budget analysis and intergovernmental relations]. And yet there is no single, collective, coherent effort to investigate how local, state and federal governments interact on an ongoing basis.

While it is perhaps surprising that there's been such sporadic and diffused interest in intergovernmental affairs as a distinct discipline, the reason for the lack of focus is pretty simple, if somewhat counterintuitive. The concept of intergovernmental relations and relationships is so deeply ingrained in the American way of governance—indeed, it's the foundation of our system of governance—that rising above the fray to analyze intergovernmental affairs as a specific area of study just doesn't seem to come very naturally. Whether the issue is tax reform, health care, or regulatory reform, policy these days tends to be debated on the merits and with a strong Washington spin. Will a federal tax cut boost the economy? Can Medicaid reform reduce the federal government's costs without angering too broad a constituency? Will federal banking deregulation be good for banks and how might it affect consumers? How such action will impact states or localities is frequently an afterthought—if policy makers think about it at all.

It's not that such policy questions go unanalyzed from an intergovernmental standpoint. But the job is more often than not left to a small army of scattered scholars and journalists, and frequently the analysis is done after the fact and not while policy is being debated and developed. Tax reform, prescription drug reform, education reform all have consequences to states and localities that aren't well vetted as legislation is fashioned in Washington. In fact, among the rarest of discussions these days at high levels in Washington is how to craft policies in a way that makes the most sense from an intergovernmental perspective. It should be noted that the phenomenon has its equivalent at the state level, where local government frequently feels ignored when it comes to governors and state legislatures shaping state-level policies and programs. "It's an issue that is just as critical out in states," says [an analyst well-versed in municipal fiscal affairs]. "There's very little conversation in the states about the intergovernmental consequences of programs and fiscal decisions between states and localities."

Clearly, though, such a lack of consistent attention to intergovernmental consequences of policy decisions is most powerfully manifested at the federal level. Take the recent battle over the creation of the Department of Homeland Security, notes Laurence J. O'Toole. . . . In an area of policy with sweeping and profound intergovernmental implications, congressional debate and discussion didn't revolve around figuring out how to create an agency that would be tuned in to the new roles that federal, state and local officials might have to play in delivering homeland security (not to mention who would be paying for it all). Rather, the fight was over whether or not the new employees of such a department would be covered by federal civil service rules. Amazing—even appalling—yes, agrees O'Toole, but not surprising. . . .

The fact of such a lack of debate and discussion specifically about the intergovernmental character of key issues has widespread consequences to states and localities, argue advocates of broader intergovernmental conversation. At the most overriding level, experts point to the issue of federal revenues versus spending. According to the Government Accountability Office, current federal revenues don't cover federal expenditures. If current federal revenue and spending trends were to continue unchanged, GAO reports that the federal government would *only be able to cover half of its fiscal commitments* by 2050, as spending on such things as Medicaid, Medicare, Social Security and interest on the federal debt explode[s]. The word "unsustainable" is cited frequently by GAO when it discusses the federal fiscal picture.

The trickle-down effects of the pending fiscal crunch could be severe, predict state and local government advocates. As the Bush administration promises to cut the budget, Medicaid and Medicare will be two of the largest potential targets, potentially shifting significant costs onto states and localities. Current discussion of a cap on federal Medicaid expenditures is one of the more acute examples of an issue that state and local officials believe requires an exceedingly thorough intergovernmental discussion, a discussion that state and local officials believe needs to take place outside the boundaries of the regular budget writing battleground. Citing the string of "difficult budgets" that have been hammered out in his state recently, [one former top-level state official] says that the proposed cap on Medicaid spending is a dangerously one-dimensional approach to dealing with the intertwined issues of money and health care policy. His summary of the current federal approach: "You have an already unmanageable problem and the feds are trying to make it worse."

The effects of the combination of federal fiscal strain—along with clearly deteriorated intergovernmental cooperative relationships—can be seen in policy areas ranging from environmental protection to mental health. The new book, *Redefining Federalism*, just published by the Environmental Law Institute (edited by Douglas T. Kendall), cites a number of examples of how reduced intergovernmental cooperation and action have led directly to environmental and public health problems. High rates of cancer in key areas of poor air quality and the contamination of aquifers in Midwestern states experiencing booming factory farms are just two examples of where a failure of intergovernmental cooperation and action are hurting not just the environment, but people. According to the Bazelon Center for Mental Health law, which monitors public policies affecting mental health services, threats to federal Medicaid funding (which provides the lion's share of federal money for mental health), proposed changes to the yet to be reauthorized Temporary Assistance to Needy Families bill, and also failure to enact key pieces of mental health–related legislation in the 108th Congress all could have potentially significant state and local trickle-down effects with regard to . . . the availability, quality and coherent delivery of mental health services nationwide. Yet none of these problems is being discussed from the standpoint of their intergovernmental impacts by policy makers and other experts in any sort of non-political, neutral forum.

Clearly how federal action impacts specific policy areas like the environment or mental health at the state and local level is worth studying. Also worth attention, the legal battles around which level of government ought to exert the most influence in what areas. But the overriding issue, the one that most clearly cuts across most policy and legal arenas—from health care to taxing authority—is the fiscal relationship of local, state and federal governments. It is that overriding issue that most of those who care about intergovernmental studies think deserves the most attention right now.

The Heyday of Intergovernmentalism

For those who care about intergovernmental relations and federalism, the value of studying the impacts of one level of government's actions on another, or analyzing how we might improve various governmental functions through a more cooperative intergovernmental approach, are self-evident. But with the exception of the years 1959 to 1996, there has been no fixed, recognized entity focused exclusively on looking at policy and programs from the standpoint of the fundamental interplay of local, state and federal governments, their programs, policies, personnel, revenue raising systems (and capacity) and budgets.

. . . [The author reviews the development and history of the Advisory Commission on Intergovernmental Relations and then recounts its downfall.—Ed.]

When asked about the forces that came together to produce an era of acute interest in dispassionate, participatory, intergovernmental study and discussion, scholars cite two intertwined forces: the increase in federal transfers to state and local government and the related migration of groups representing state and local government to Washington. It is a phenomenon, they add, that has really only been pulled together once, and it was more or less organic. For there to be a rekindling of a focus on intergovernmental studies and interest, "it will take folks focusing on this 52-weeks a year," says Larry O'Toole. The reason that it will take such an intensive, focused effort is straightforward and two-fold, O'Toole says. First, the whole area of public policy and intergovernmental cooperation has become incredibly complicated. "It's numbingly complex. You have tens of thousands governments and hundreds – or thousands, depending on how you want to count them—of programs. If you want serious, reliable information about such a system it has to come from a dedicated group of people working hard over the long term." Second, while he thinks rekindling some ACIR-like effort is a noble idea, the challenges involved in focusing interest on "a system that nobody in particular is responsible for" can't be overestimated.

In other words, advocates of a reinvigorated intergovernmental view of policy are going to have to push, because there is at the moment very little pull.

The Current State of Intergovernmental Studies

"We are now living in an era when the federal government has stopped sending you money and is instead sending you problems." That's the blunt, contemporary assessment of intergovernmental relations offered by [one prominent analyst]. [This expert] made those comments [in] October [2004] at *Governing* magazine's annual Management Conference in Austin, Texas.

[His] comments reflect three important things: First, there has been a profound shift in the relationship of federal, state and local governments in the past quarter century. Second, there are plenty of scholars and analysts, like [this expert], who understand this and who are studying the effects of such a shift. Third, it reflects just how far the country has drifted from the days when all three levels of government actually could—and would—sit down to hash out policy and budget issues in a way that if not always ending up to every party's satisfaction, at least evinced a clear mutual appreciation for the intertwined, interdependent nature of government and governance in America.

. . . [S]cores of individuals and institutions have continued to analyze local, state and national issues from an intergovernmental standpoint, however. Recently, the National Academy of Public Administration put together a position paper investigating the possibility of creating a Forum for Intergovernmental Cooperation, a standing institution that would convene interested individuals from all levels of government to discuss and debate the intergovernmental angle of important issues, and also conduct, commission and/or coordinate ongoing research on intergovernmental affairs (much more on the NAPA effort in a moment).

In that paper, NAPA observes that *"many organizations are working on issues within the intergovernmental system, but no organization is looking at federalism systemically. There are universities, usually in schools of public administration and public policy, that bring small numbers of governmental leaders together for the purpose of sharing experiences and learning better ways of doing the public's business. There are think-tanks that analyze aspects of the federal system—the Urban Institute, for example, has a project entitled Assessing the New Federalism, which is looking particularly at health and welfare issues. There [are] non-profit research organizations looking at many programs that involve the federal system—homeland security, health care, education and transportation—often as contractors to specific federal or state agencies. . . . But no organization, at least at first glance, appears to be collecting data or analyzing the performance of the federal system as a whole; and no one appears to be working continuously with political leaders or officials with the aim of improving the performance of the federal system as a system."* . . .

. . . [W]hile there may be no shortage of individuals and organizations looking at myriad pieces of the intergovernmental puzzle, in the final analysis there is nobody doing what ACIR used to do, which is look at the issues and the data consistently, uniformly and over time; regularly convene key actors; and work to communicate the importance of an intergovernmental viewpoint to key policy makers.

The fact that nobody has really replaced ACIR begs three questions: What effect does that have on governance in America? Does anybody really care? And who might pick up the standard?

The Prospects for a "New ACIR"

Virtually everyone interviewed for this paper (more than two dozen experts in intergovernmental relations) agreed that the current state of intergovernmental awareness and cooperation is in critical condition. As [one] states it, "Our leadership has for the last several years recognized a widespread unraveling of intergovernmental systems, and a real lack of understanding of the implications of actions taken at one level of government and the consequences that those actions have at another level." Such consequences range from the state and local costs of the No Child Left Behind Act, to revenue costs to states and localities of the moratorium on Internet taxes, to the trickle-down costs of federal tax cuts, notes [this expert].

Virtually everybody interviewed for this paper agreed that the loss of ACIR has left a gaping hole in terms of encouraging better intergovernmental relations, generally, and smarter intergovernmental policy making, specifically. The loss is clear in terms of tracking trends in federalism, in terms of convening experts (policy makers and analysts alike) to consider issues from the standpoint of marble-cake federalism, and in terms of providing policy makers and analysts with regular, topical reports on key issues of the day, analyzed with a federalist spin. (In particular, those who attended the GAO intergovernmental affairs forum cited the issues of out-of-balance revenues and spending demand across governments; health care finance, particularly long-term health care for the elderly and disabled; current tax structures at all levels of government and the interrelationships between them; and the need to consider reassigning responsibilities among governments as four of the top issues worth tackling.)

Virtually everybody interviewed for this paper agreed there would be value in rekindling some center or forum for the study of intergovernmental issues, although the extent to which such an entity might actually influence law making and regulation coming out of Washington—or state capitals, for that matter—was a matter of some debate. ([One scholar's] assessment of a possible rekindling of an ACIR-like effort was the most concise: "My first inclination is to say that would be terrific, my second is to say, good luck.") Even some Capitol Hill staff interviewed for the paper express dismay at the widespread indifference they see from members of Congress and their staffs when it comes to the effects of federal law and regulation on local and state governments. As a number of those interviewed pointed out, the number of congresspeople actually willing to step up and expend some political capital fighting for policies that reflect intergovernmental concerns can be counted, literally, on the fingers of one hand.

Not everybody was pessimistic about the potential for rekindling a passion for—or at least sincere interest in—intergovernmental affairs among federal officials, however. [An analyst] cited the recent resurrection of the Administrative Conference of the United States as evidence of an awakening on the part of Congress to the importance of a more intergovernmental view. The ACUS entered its formative years along with ACIR as a body set up to consider and help hash out intergovernmental issues associated with administrative law and procedures (and, as mentioned earlier, was defunded around the same time as ACIR). Congress's decision to resurrect the conference is a hopeful indicator, thinks [this expert]. "I'm much less cynical than many people about Washington. My impression is that there are lots of people in Washington who want to make the place work and are receptive to discussions about intergovernmental issues."

Others noted that while Capitol Hill may not appear to care much about intergovernmentalism, key agencies like the U.S. Environmental Protection Agency and the Department of Health and Human Services, which both depend heavily on state and local officials for their own success, are keenly aware of the need for state and federal cooperation in getting big jobs done. Even the Department of Homeland Security has an office of state and local cooperation (even if it has no method for gauging the cost to states and localities every time the country kicks its security alert to a higher level).

[One former state official] says he senses a real hunger among state officials for good information on finance and economic policy, including historical information. "I've testified twice recently before [my state's] legislative committees asking about tax policy in previous decades, what was proposed, what was adopted and what happened, and I sensed a real interest and appreciation among legislators in knowing some of the history of tax policy in [that state]." [He] thinks that same appetite for information and history exists at the federal level among a new generation of policy makers around intergovernmental relations and cooperation. "It's easy to be skeptical, but my experience suggests that there's a real hunger for good information, especially information that's not coming from lobbyists." [He] notes that ACIR offered both good, neutral information to policy makers and also good historical data ("institutional memory," he says) with regard to policies with significant intergovernmental implications. Indeed, both Senate staffers interviewed for this paper expressed an interest in more reliable information on intergovernmental affairs along with a fresh look at how responsibilities might be sorted among the three levels of government.

Still others pointed out the chicken and egg nature of the problem. The longer Washington goes without some forum on intergovernmental relations, the less likely new generations of policy makers and analysts will get it or care. The less they care, the less likely that such an institution will be relevant or have any chance of being influential.

At any rate, the next set of intertwined questions that sift out are clearly: Should it be deemed worth trying, who might lead or house an institution dedicated to intergovernmental debate, discussion and study? If such an effort is rekindled, could it actually make a difference? In particular, what steps might such an institution take to rebuild interest in federalism among Washington officials, especially in Congress?

. . . [The author reviews some of the options and concludes that an intergovernmental forum organized by a Washington think tank, the National Academy of Public Administration, is the best option.—Ed.]

What ought to be avoided, though, argue many of those interviewed for this paper, is any heavy-handed push to centralize intergovernmental studies and analysis. "The issue is how do we look at the thousand flowers that are blooming," says [a researcher at a major think tank]. "In a lot of ways what ACIR argued for is being enshrined in how the federal government is investing in long-term technology and data gathering," [this expert] adds. "There are a lot of civil servants in the federal bureaucracy doing the right thing in that regard, it's just not at a high amplitude." One question for a rekindled intergovernmental studies effort, she says, "How do you recognize all the good things that are happening inside the federal government?"

Indeed, some "virtual" or networked group of experts, publications, schools of public affairs, foundations and other interested institutions would seem to make sense from the standpoint of ensuring broad-based support, while also ensuring that "the thousand flowers" are recognized and nurtured. Such an approach not only helps support a widespread and deep pool of expertise, but it also has the potential to tap into the absolutely vital marketing and communication expertise that it's going to take to launch and sustain any effort to refocus the nation on the issue of intergovernmental issues and cooperation. . . .

Part V

Review Questions

1. The mayor of a city with a population of three million hires you as special assistant for intergovernmental relations. You are asked for a status report on the current system. What are some of the major intergovernmental problems cities currently face and are likely to face? What opportunities and complications should be noted?

2. Assess the nation's intergovernmental pattern in terms of its ability to respond to major natural disasters. What options should be considered for improving performance? What cautions should be considered?

3. Actors in the intergovernmental system favor "coordination" as much as anyone. As the readings by Walters and Kettl and by Kettl indicate, coordination is more easily endorsed than accomplished. What features of the intergovernmental system make it difficult to generate coordination? Are there benefits to maintaining some degree of uncoordinated action? Consider the essay by Morton Grodzins (no. 3) in the first part of this book. Has the U.S. approach to intergovernmental relations become outmoded in an era demanding quick response and high performance?

4. You have been appointed special assistant for intergovernmental relations in the U.S. Department of Homeland Security. What would you tell the secretary in your effort to apprise him or her about the most pressing intergovernmental challenges of the department's job? What would you say to state and local officials when you meet with them?

5. O'Toole and Hanf assert that "the features of transnational governance do not suggest anything like a global government, designed more or less on the model of state-centered systems." How, then, would you characterize the overall system, or set of systems, including the international "level"? What kind of intergovernmental relations model, from those sketched by Deil Wright in Part I of this book, is implied in the sketch offered by O'Toole and Hanf? Would a model other than those covered by Wright be needed?

6. In the intergovernmental webs of global governance, who is in charge, if anyone? In a pattern such as this one, is it old fashioned to even consider democratic governance as a feasible objective? How *should* one assess the design and performance of the entire array?

7. Given the sketch of the globalized pattern in reading no. 27, is the U.S. intergovernmental system becoming stronger and more effective or weaker and more dependent? Or both? Support your conclusion with examples.

8. Why is it difficult to get most major policymakers to develop and act upon consistent principles of intergovernmental relations? What is the result of the relative inattention to the overall shape of the system when policymakers negotiate the details of individual programs? Consider the essay by Jonathan Walters in your response. What recommendations do you have for improving system coherence? Is coherence even a sensible goal? Why or why not?

9. Assess the U.S. intergovernmental pattern from the perspective of a constitutional Founder like James Madison. Given the trajectory through which the system has traveled during its development, and given the major developments and challenges sketched in several readings in this part, what would Madison think? Would he favor systemic reform or be surprised but pleased at what has happened?

AMERICAN INTERGOVERNMENTAL
RELATIONS: CONCLUDING THOUGHTS

Today, a formidable set of intergovernmental issues and problems stretches before us, yet it is important to realize that both the achievements and dilemmas of the contemporary scene are bound up with the choices made at the nation's founding, as well as with the pressing issues of the twenty-first century. The framers of the American federal system made conscious decisions about the structure and relationships within and among American governments. To protect freedom, to stimulate diversity, and to foster such civic virtues as active citizen involvement in the affairs of state, the Founders established a basic framework that would facilitate, indeed stimulate, dynamic, vigorous intergovernmental relations. These early Americans were under few illusions about the character of the emerging nation. They realized that structuring the basic powers and relationships of the governments would not eliminate disputes or establish some neat, orderly, static pattern. Nor, however, would an absence of central authority serve legitimate interests. Instead, the Founders crafted a system designed to provide a forum for the inevitable conflict and bargaining in the large and diverse new nation.

Although the intergovernmental system has changed tremendously from the earliest decades, the basic framework continues to play a part in the perpetuation of dynamic intergovernmental relations. Historical and contemporary imperatives toward cooperation across governmental—even national—lines notwithstanding, the framework has allowed and even encouraged the rise of today's pattern, one of conflict and bargaining in a system characterized by complexity and interdependence.

The enormous complexity of a system composed of more than 87,000 governments suggests that it is impossible to have enough information to operate within it in a consistently rational fashion. There are too many other parties and sets of relationships, many of them highly dynamic. And in recent decades this complexity has been further increased by the addition of new elements in the makeup of the intergovernmental "mix": intergovernmental coordinating bodies, PIGs, an active court system, lobbying groups representing myriad interests, the emergence of pressing policy issues at multiple levels in the system, more complicated fiscal instruments, a growing array of regulatory mechanisms, manifold bargaining processes undertaken without the luxury of much budgetary flexibility to inspire cooperation, and a range of international influences and institutions. Some actors, including the U.S. Advisory Commission on Intergovernmental Relations, have disappeared in the fray, but others, like those operating at a global level, have expanded the pattern. A result of this complexity is that efforts to orchestrate dramatic change by any party, no matter how important in the pattern, are bound to fall short of expectations and may well complicate matters still further. We have seen how the efforts by one level of government to exercise control at another, the redesign of the federal government's grant structure, the trimming of federal aid, and the attempt to enforce an end to unfunded mandates may produce unintended consequences.

A second important characteristic of the system—interdependence—fuels the complexity. This point is clearly demonstrated by the intergovernmental sharing of power, even within functions. Action by one unit requires support or at least acquiescence on the part of others, and participants can often halt or delay action they oppose. Thus, intergovernmental patterns do not fit a hierarchical command-and-control pattern. Instead, different governments need each other, and bargaining of various types—even if not among or between equals—is the norm.

High levels of both interdependence and complexity in the system help explain one of the most persistent dilemmas in the American network: the tension between generalists (whose responsibility is to a geographic area or general government) and specialists (who focus on and advocate for specific functions that are parts of modern governments, perhaps at multiple levels). Efforts to modify the intergovernmental system often are aimed at shifting the balance between these two groups or emphases. The frequent recurrence of serious proposals to replace categoricals with block grants, for instance, is motivated in part by a desire to take power from the specialists and to give general-purpose executives more clout. Indeed, the relative influence of these two groups *can* be altered at the margin, and quite significantly in selected policy fields. However, the perseverance of the tension is no accident, because the conflict derives from the original design of the system: its complexity generates a continuing need for specialists at all levels and its interdependence drives an imperative for coordination that generalists can facilitate. The interweaving of these dynamics has now even reached across borders and connected local governments with international patterns of governance.

The fiscal aspects of the intergovernmental system also reflect the characteristics of interdependence and complexity. Grants emerge from as well as create bargaining contests across levels of government and between specialists and generalists. Although the politics and administration of the various fiscal instruments can differ greatly, the grant system in general exhibits resistance to change, as can be seen in efforts—from the Reagan era to the time of Republican majorities in Congress—to shrink the federal role or to reassign program responsibilities. This apparent intransigence to explicit redesign—as with the many other difficulties with the system—does not stem exclusively or primarily from intrusion, domination, or ill will on the part of one level of government in dealing with the others. Rather, the interdependence and complexity of the system mitigate against disentangling the several knots that hold the parts of the system together.

This observation is particularly timely today. In the more distant past (for instance, in the 1950s), efforts to induce "reform" to control specific programs, modify general characteristics of the intergovernmental system, or significantly alter the balance of roles among governments had been singularly unsuccessful. The fact of interdependence, along with the persistent sense among the American people that government should continue to be active in many fields to solve pressing and complex problems, had insulated the system itself from major reform. Two factors made, and continue to make, the task of consolidating majority coalitions in favor of systemic change of almost any sort nearly impossible: the multiple interconnections of participants built into the system and the prospect of the significant dislocations—for agencies and their functions, program recipients and other interested parties—often generated by reform.

Yet it would be equally mistaken to conclude from these cautionary comments that significant change in the system is not to be expected. Indeed, the historical development of the intergovernmental system in the United States documents repeated adaptations in the face of political, social, and economic events. The same holds true as the new century begins. In spite of the desire of citizens and officials to retain existing programs and the structural status quo, many observers lately have developed an acute sense of the problems of a perhaps overly complex and strained system. Considerable policy initiative has moved from Washington to the states and localities at a time when forces beyond the national borders have increased the sense that more centralization may be impelled by events—for instance, the emergence of multiple, persistent threats like terrorism or flu pandemics, and the serious harm such events may inflict. The popularity of tax cuts and the high costs of major entitlement programs limit the number and size of new nationally created programs, and patterns of decision making in the courts indicate continuing efforts on the part of the nation's judiciary to treat the fundamentals of the original federal bargain with renewed attention. Meanwhile, forms of influence like intergovernmental mandating have become costly, controversial, and resistant to wholesale reduction. The American intergovernmental network seems caught in the midst of a myriad of forces, and the contemporary system offers few signs of balance or resolution.

Some of these tensions are not unique to the United States. Recent decades have seen efforts within the European Union, among the new nations of the former Soviet Union, in various parts of the old Yugoslav federation, across the Indian subcontinent, as well as in nations closer to home, including Canada and Mexico, to wrestle with the themes of partial sovereignty in the current world. Issues like the globalization of the economy and the systemic nature of environmental problems vie with regional and ethnic pride, tradition, and competitiveness in many lands, not merely this one. As the new century dawns, then, the themes of governance so prominent during more than two centuries of American experience are high on the global agenda.

Yet, as has been seen in this volume, the system of American intergovernmental relations is under increasing challenge. Can the basic framework continue to fulfill its essential function? Can the pragmatic bargaining often viewed as so much a part of the arrangement be sustained in an era of resource constraints and global patterns of influence? Can the contrasting trends of politics and governance under way now be brought into some reconciliation or creative dialogue? Can the American experience offer some guidance to those who face similar issues elsewhere in the world? Or, in turn, can some of the struggles over interdependence and complexity occurring abroad provide enlightenment and encourage creative action in the United States? The answer to these practical questions will go far toward determining whether we can resolve the difficult policy problems thrust on today's intergovernmental relationships.

Index

About the Editor

Laurence J. O'Toole Jr. is the Robert T. and Margaret Hughes Golembiewski Professor of Public Administration and head of the Department of Public Administration and Policy, School of Public and International Affairs, at the University of Georgia. He received a PhD from the Maxwell School of Citizenship and Public Affairs, Syracuse University. The recipient of many teaching and research awards, he is coeditor of *Public Services Performance: Perspectives on Measurement and Management* (2006), as well as coauthor of *Bureaucracy in a Democratic State: A Governance Perspective* (2006). He is currently president of the Public Management Research Association, and coeditor for public management of the *Journal of Policy Analysis and Management.*